ULTRAMAN 10

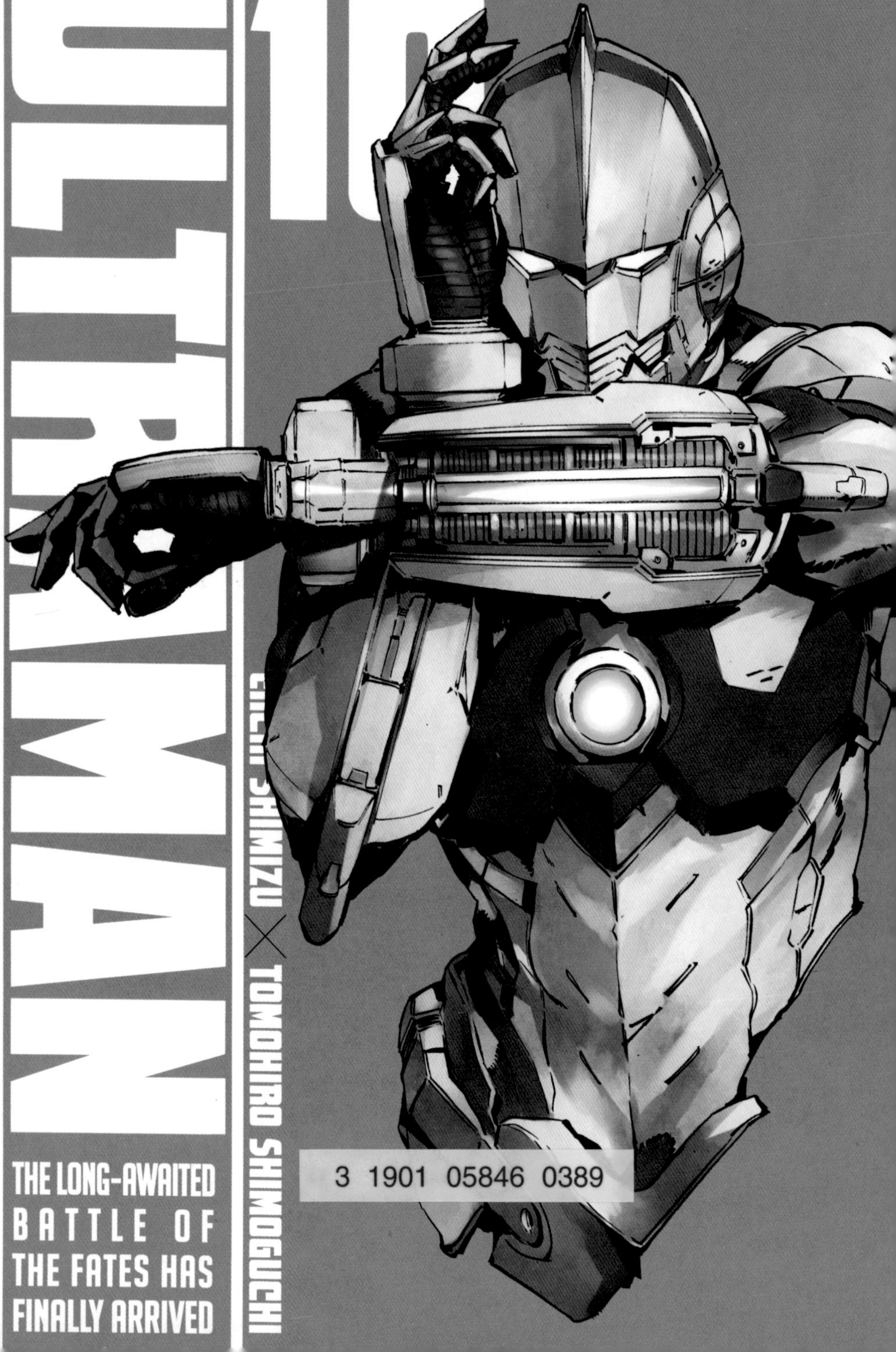

EIICHI SHIMIZU × TOMOHIRO SHIMOGUCHI

THE LONG-AWAITED BATTLE OF THE FATES HAS FINALLY ARRIVED

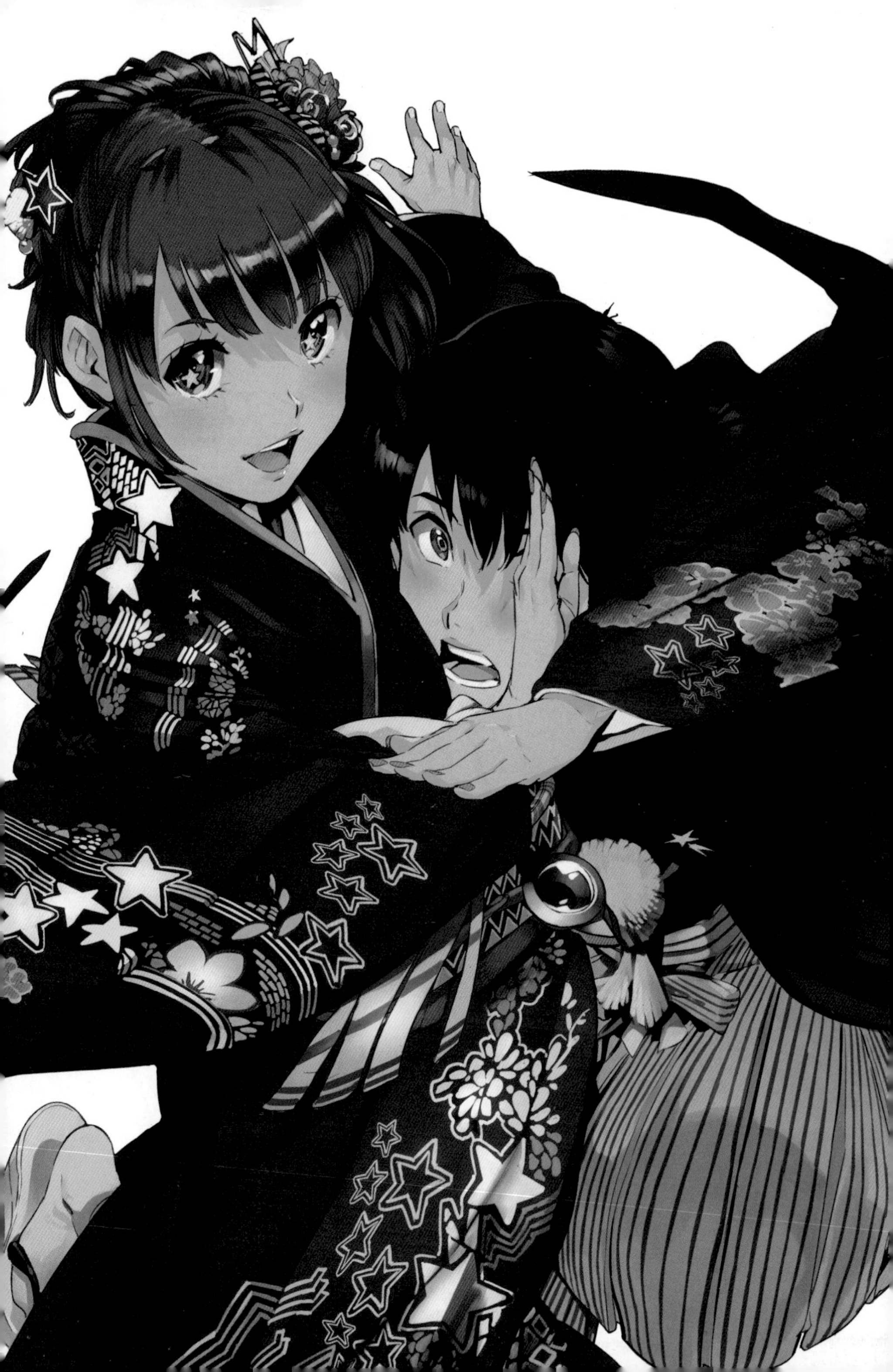

THIS IS THE BEGINNING OF A NEW AGE.

10

CONTENTS

CHAPTER 60   TO THE WEST...   005
CHAPTER 61   MIXED POWER   025
CHAPTER 62   PROJECT JACK   055
CHAPTER 63   PLANET EXPOSED   085
CHAPTER 64   FORTRESS DESCENDING FROM THE HEAVENS   115
CHAPTER 65   SIX HEROES   151

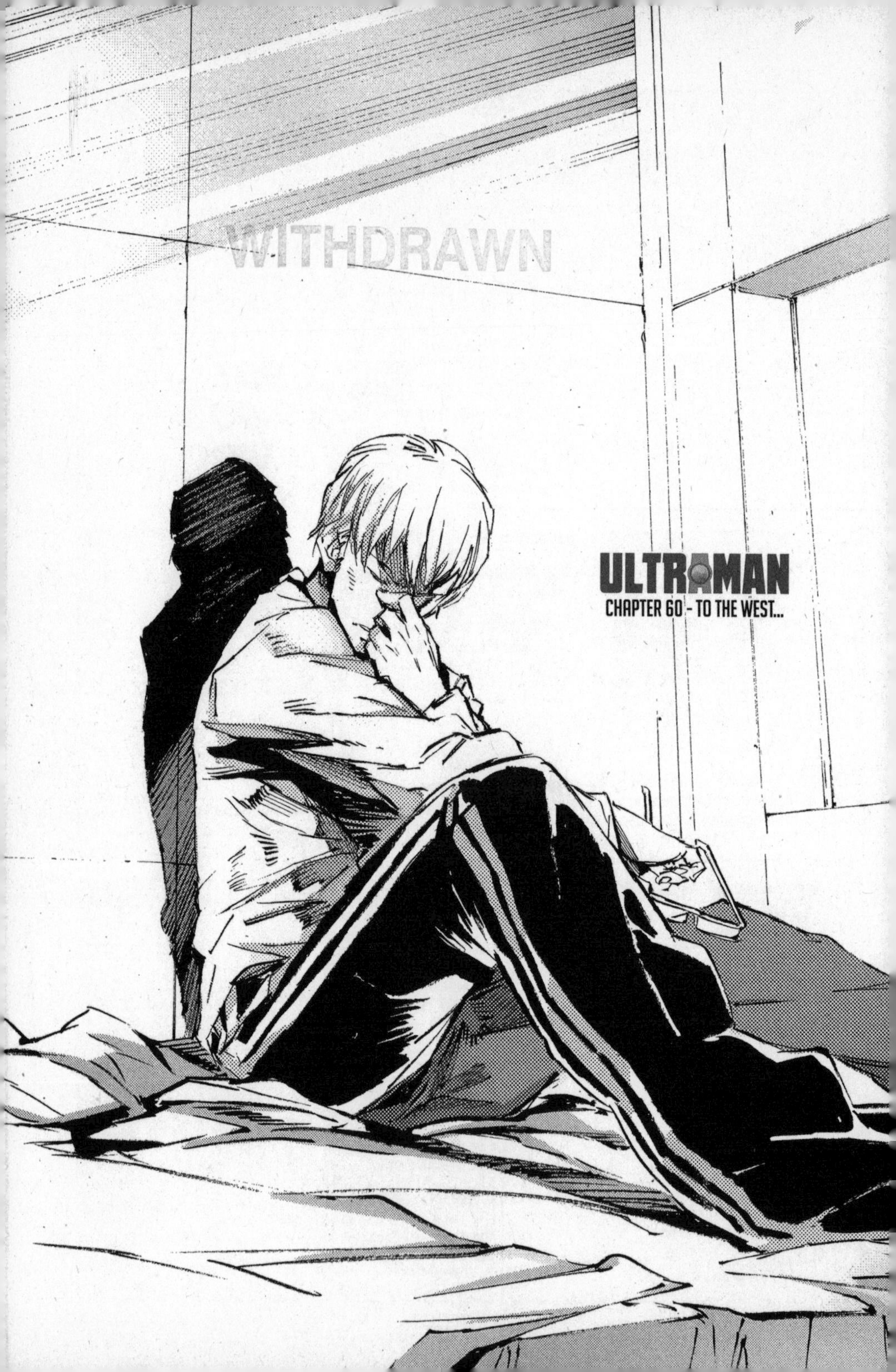
ULTRAMAN
CHAPTER 60 - TO THE WEST...

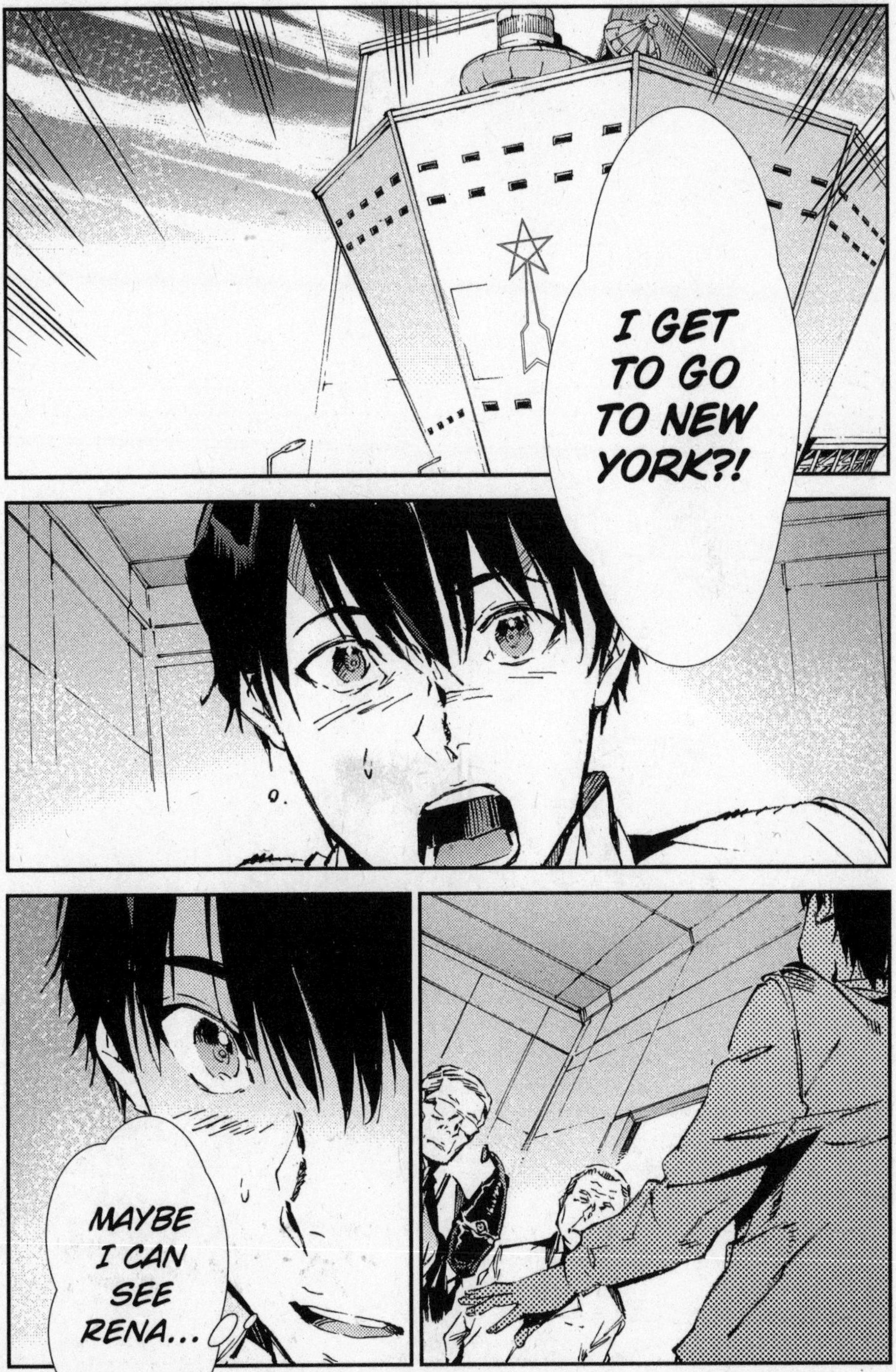
I GET TO GO TO NEW YORK?!
MAYBE I CAN SEE RENA...

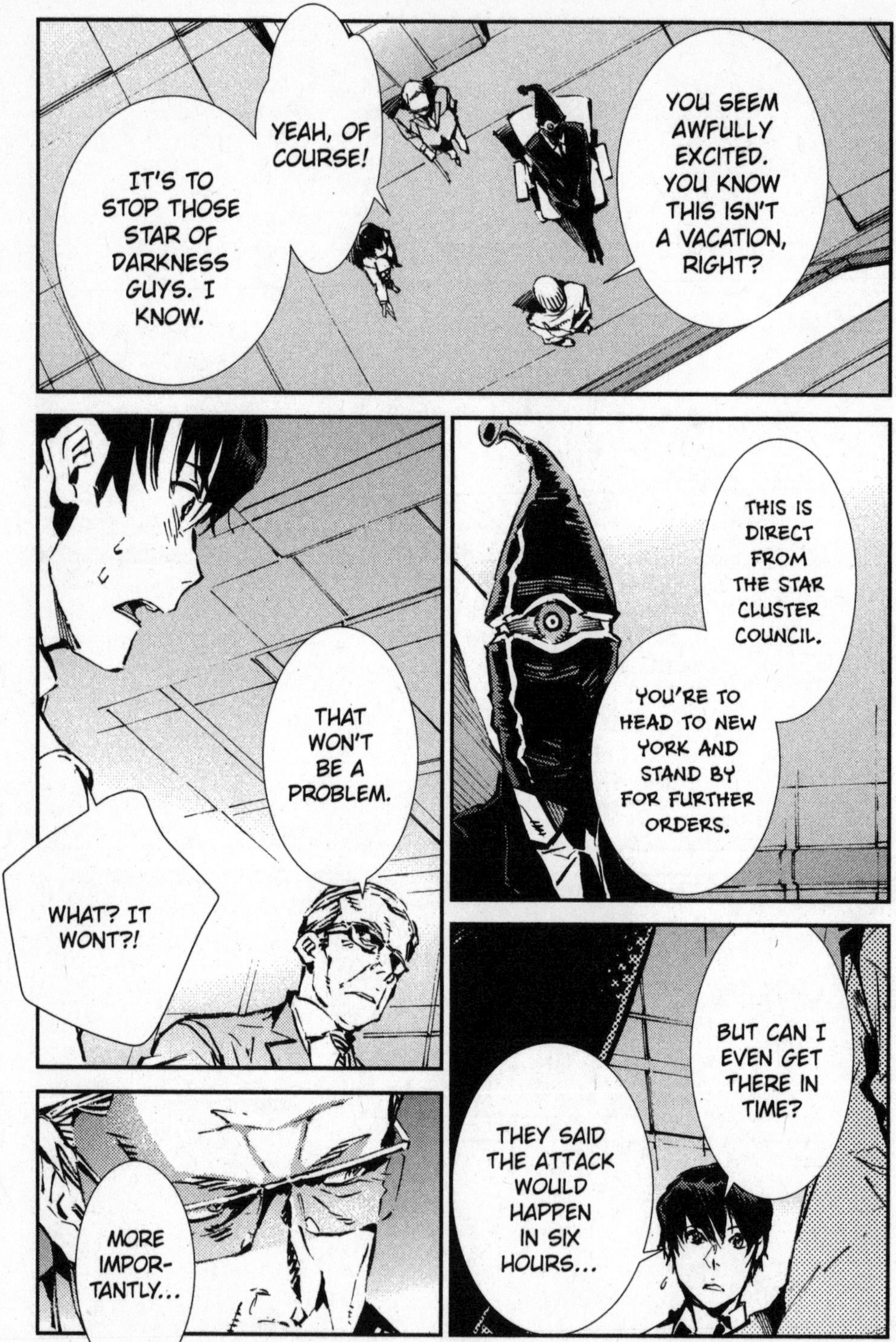
YOU SEEM AWFULLY EXCITED. YOU KNOW THIS ISN'T A VACATION, RIGHT?
YEAH, OF COURSE!
IT'S TO STOP THOSE STAR OF DARKNESS GUYS. I KNOW.
THIS IS DIRECT FROM THE STAR CLUSTER COUNCIL.
YOU'RE TO HEAD TO NEW YORK AND STAND BY FOR FURTHER ORDERS.
BUT CAN I EVEN GET THERE IN TIME?
THEY SAID THE ATTACK WOULD HAPPEN IN SIX HOURS...
THAT WON'T BE A PROBLEM.
WHAT? IT WONT?!
MORE IMPOR-TANTLY...

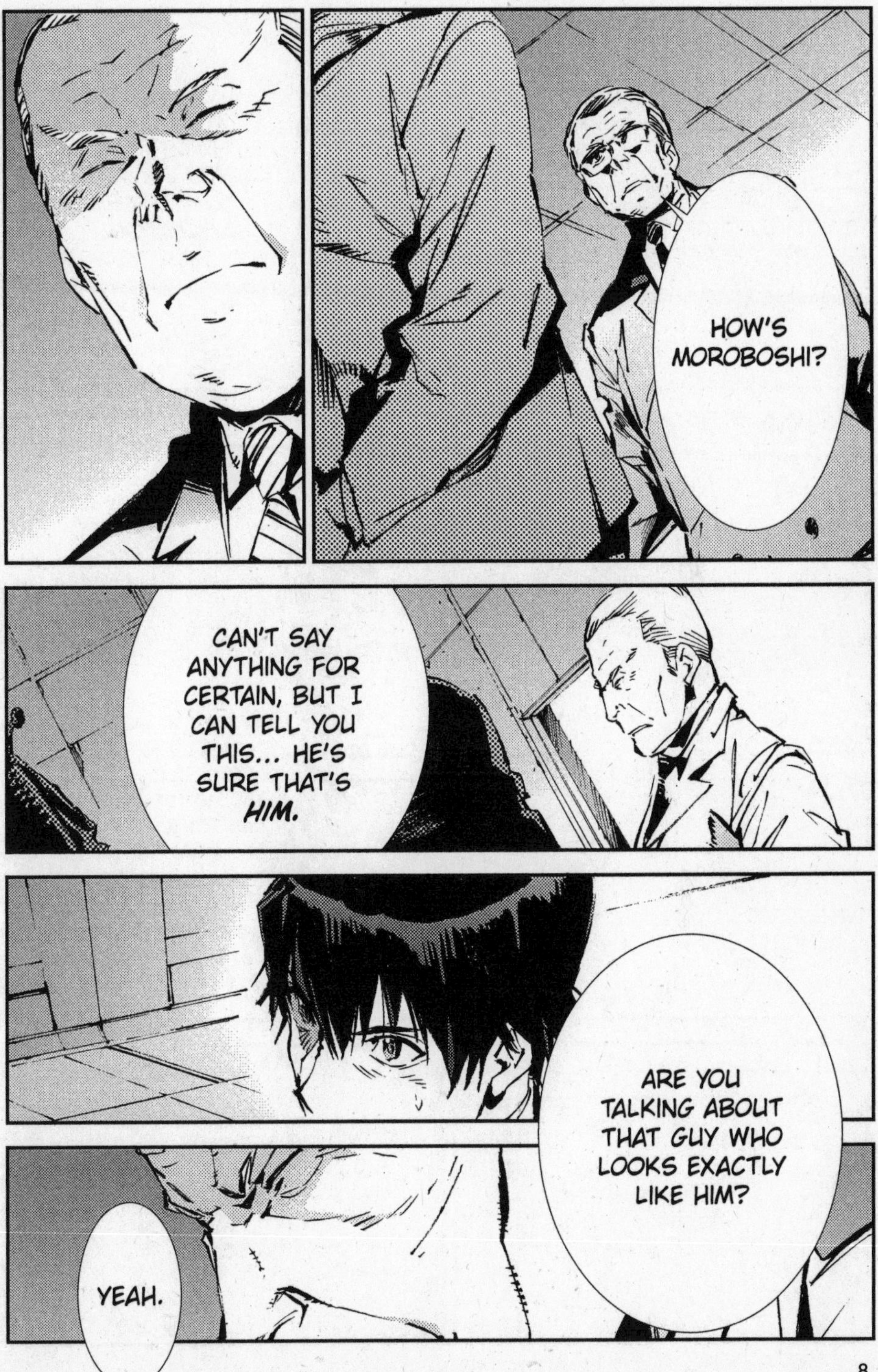
HOW'S MOROBOSHI?
CAN'T SAY ANYTHING FOR CERTAIN, BUT I CAN TELL YOU THIS... HE'S SURE THAT'S *HIM.*
ARE YOU TALKING ABOUT THAT GUY WHO LOOKS EXACTLY LIKE HIM?
YEAH.

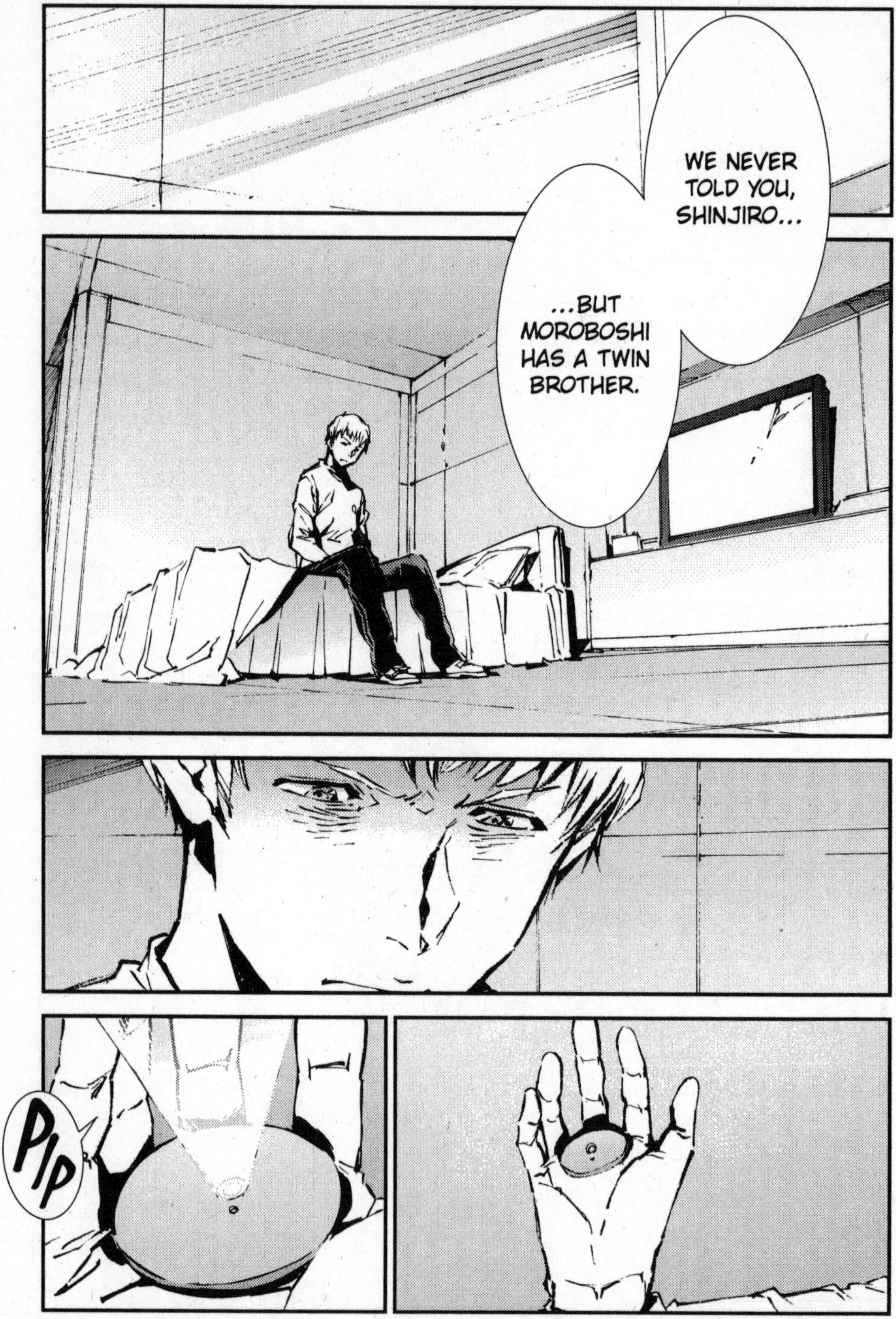
WE NEVER TOLD YOU, SHINJIRO...
...BUT MOROBOSHI HAS A TWIN BROTHER.
PIP

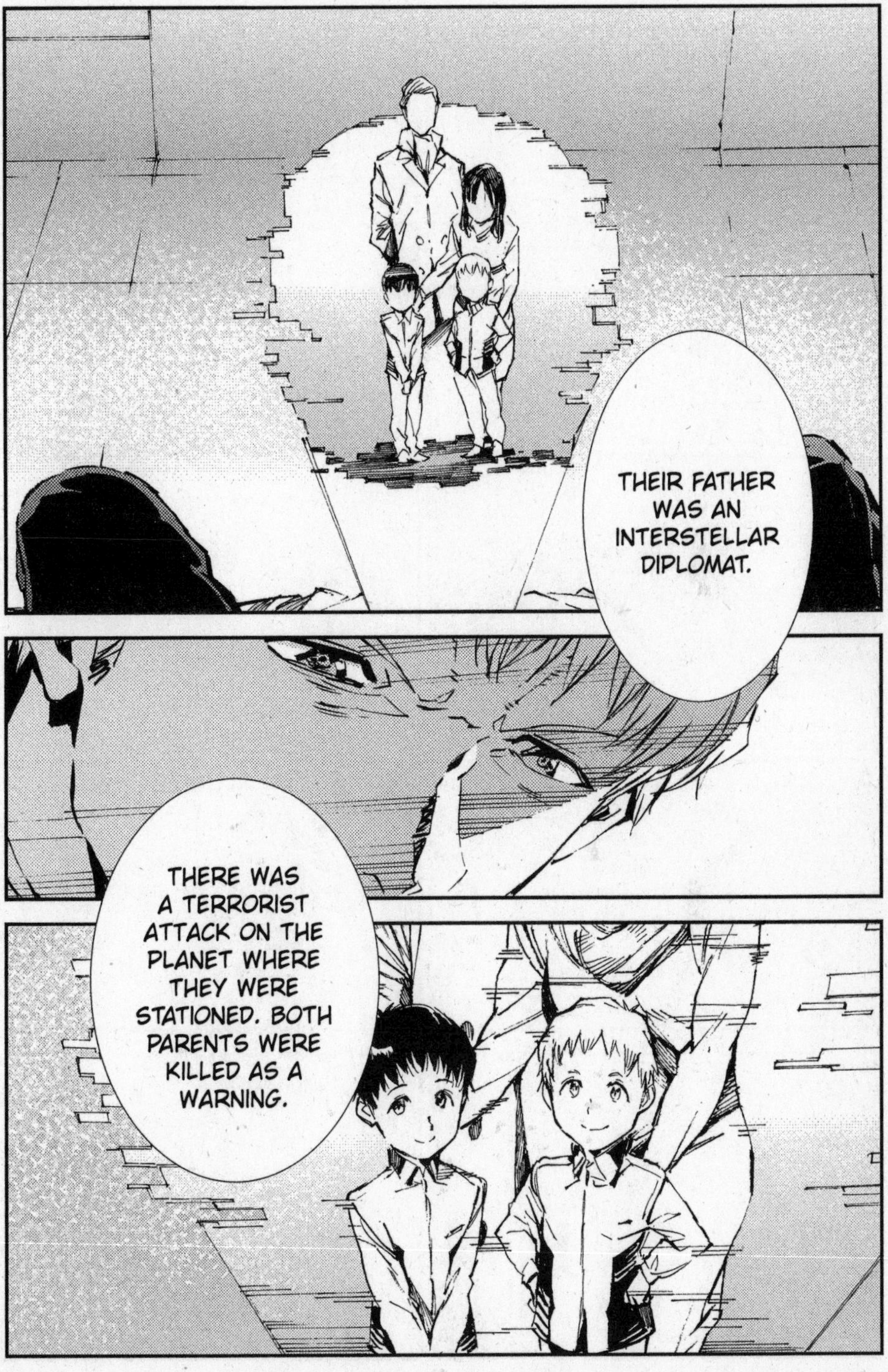
THEIR FATHER WAS AN INTERSTELLAR DIPLOMAT.
THERE WAS A TERRORIST ATTACK ON THE PLANET WHERE THEY WERE STATIONED. BOTH PARENTS WERE KILLED AS A WARNING.

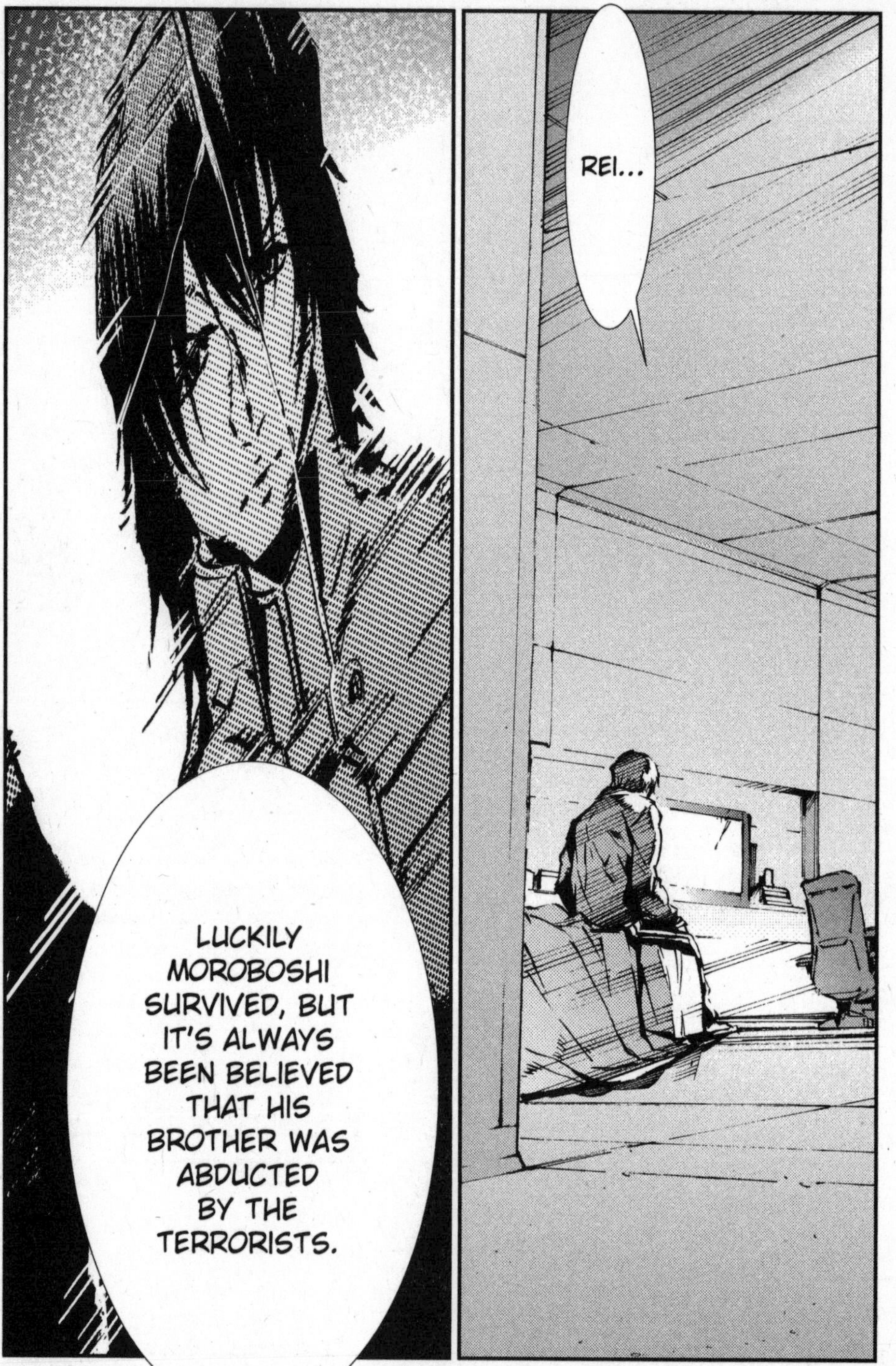

REI...

LUCKILY
MOROBOSHI
SURVIVED, BUT
IT'S ALWAYS
BEEN BELIEVED
THAT HIS
BROTHER WAS
ABDUCTED
BY THE
TERRORISTS.

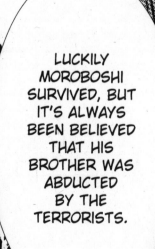

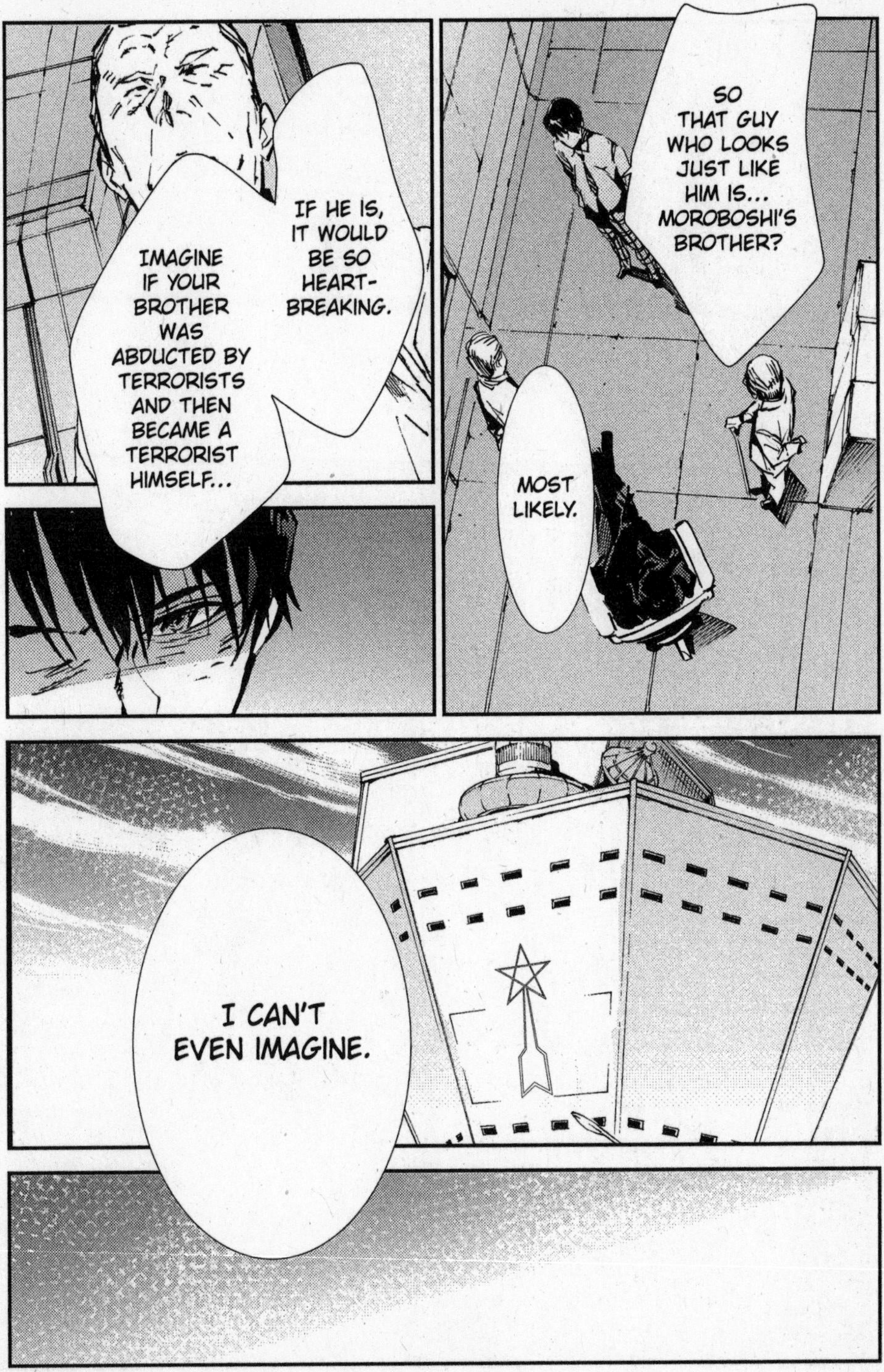
SO THAT GUY WHO LOOKS JUST LIKE HIM IS... MOROBOSHI'S BROTHER?
MOST LIKELY.
IF HE IS, IT WOULD BE SO HEART-BREAKING.
IMAGINE IF YOUR BROTHER WAS ABDUCTED BY TERRORISTS AND THEN BECAME A TERRORIST HIMSELF...
I CAN'T EVEN IMAGINE.

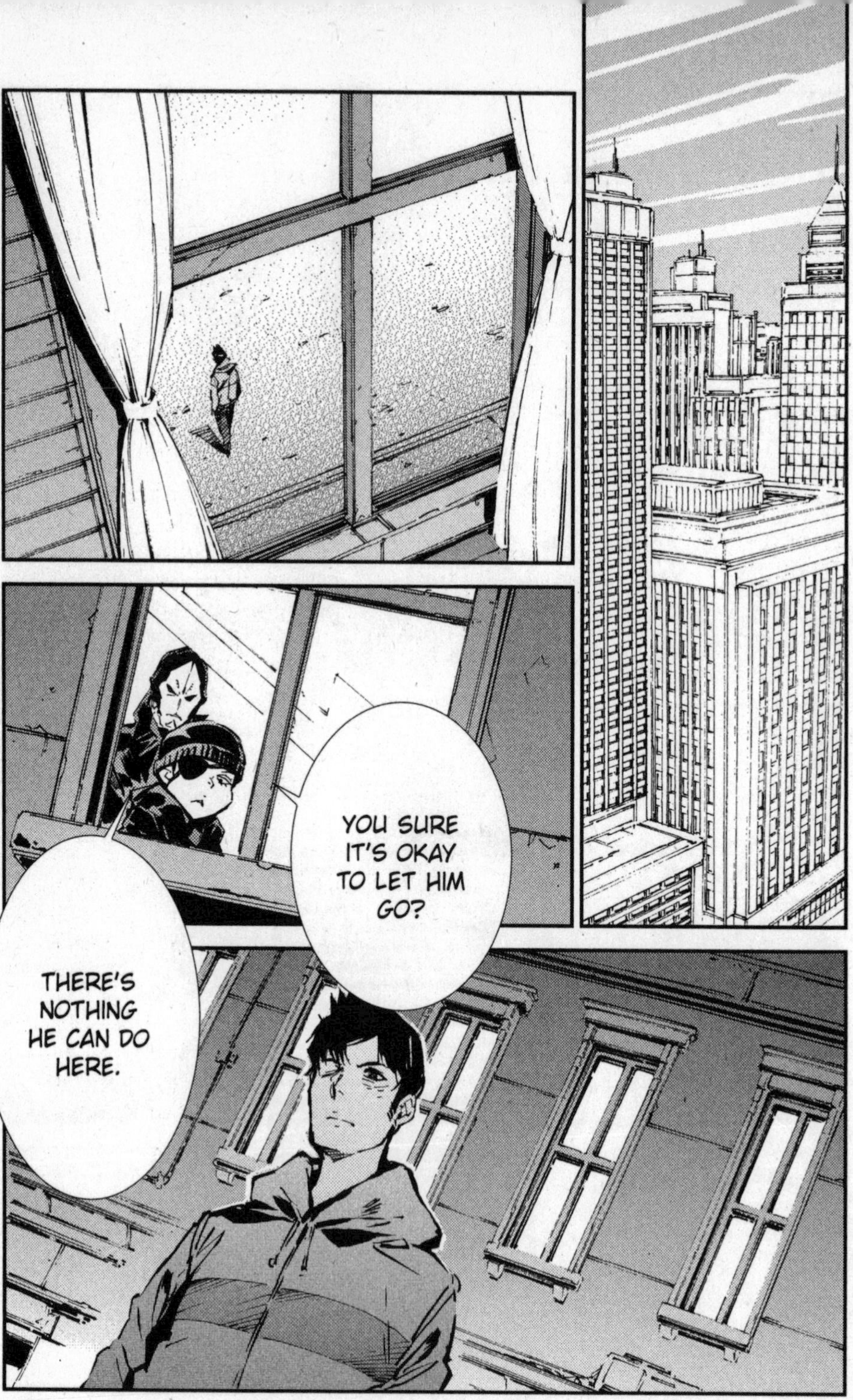
YOU SURE IT'S OKAY TO LET HIM GO?
THERE'S NOTHING HE CAN DO HERE.

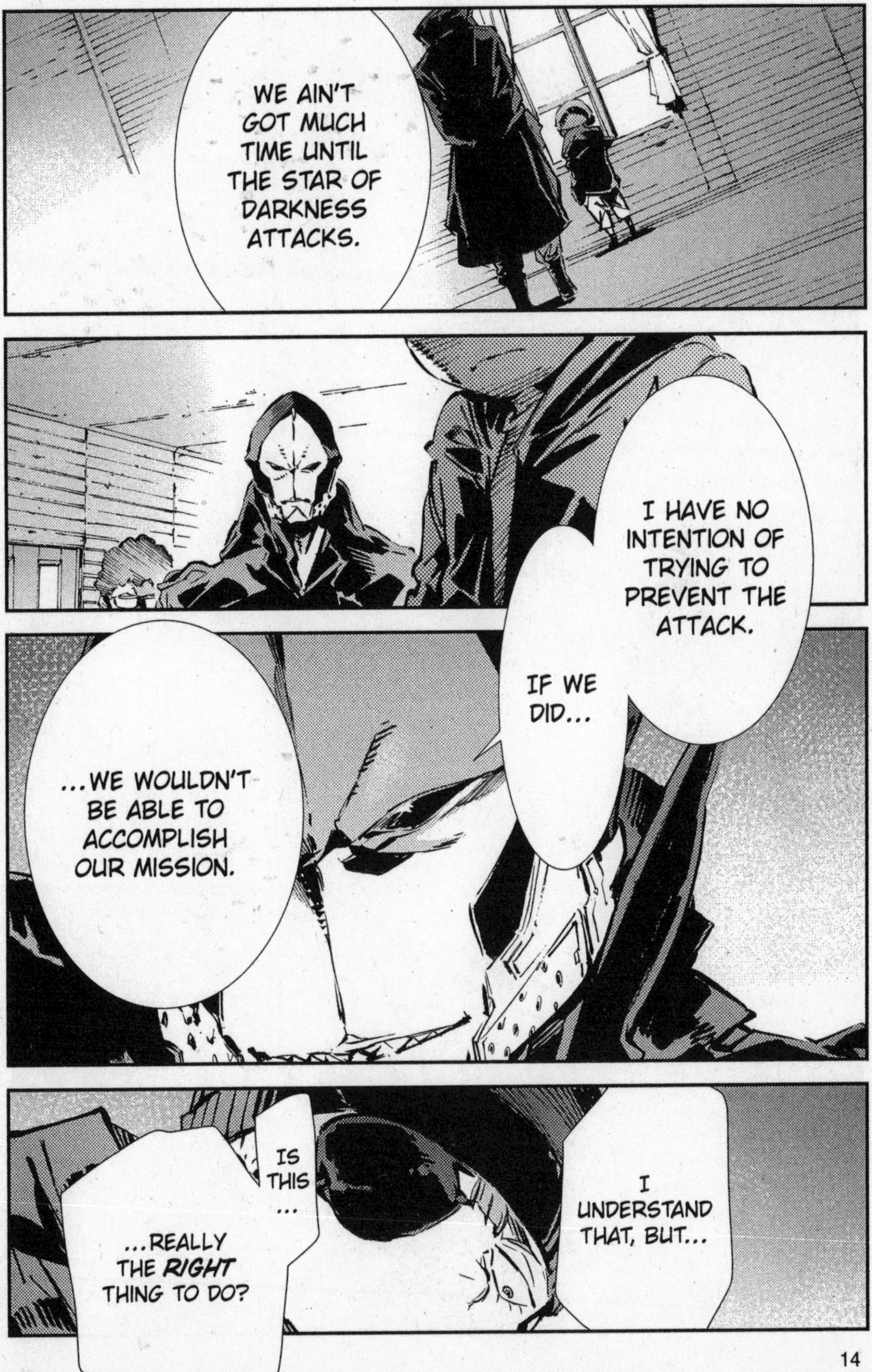
WE AIN'T GOT MUCH TIME UNTIL THE STAR OF DARKNESS ATTACKS.
I HAVE NO INTENTION OF TRYING TO PREVENT THE ATTACK.
IF WE DID...
...WE WOULDN'T BE ABLE TO ACCOMPLISH OUR MISSION.
I UNDERSTAND THAT, BUT...
IS THIS...
...REALLY THE *RIGHT* THING TO DO?

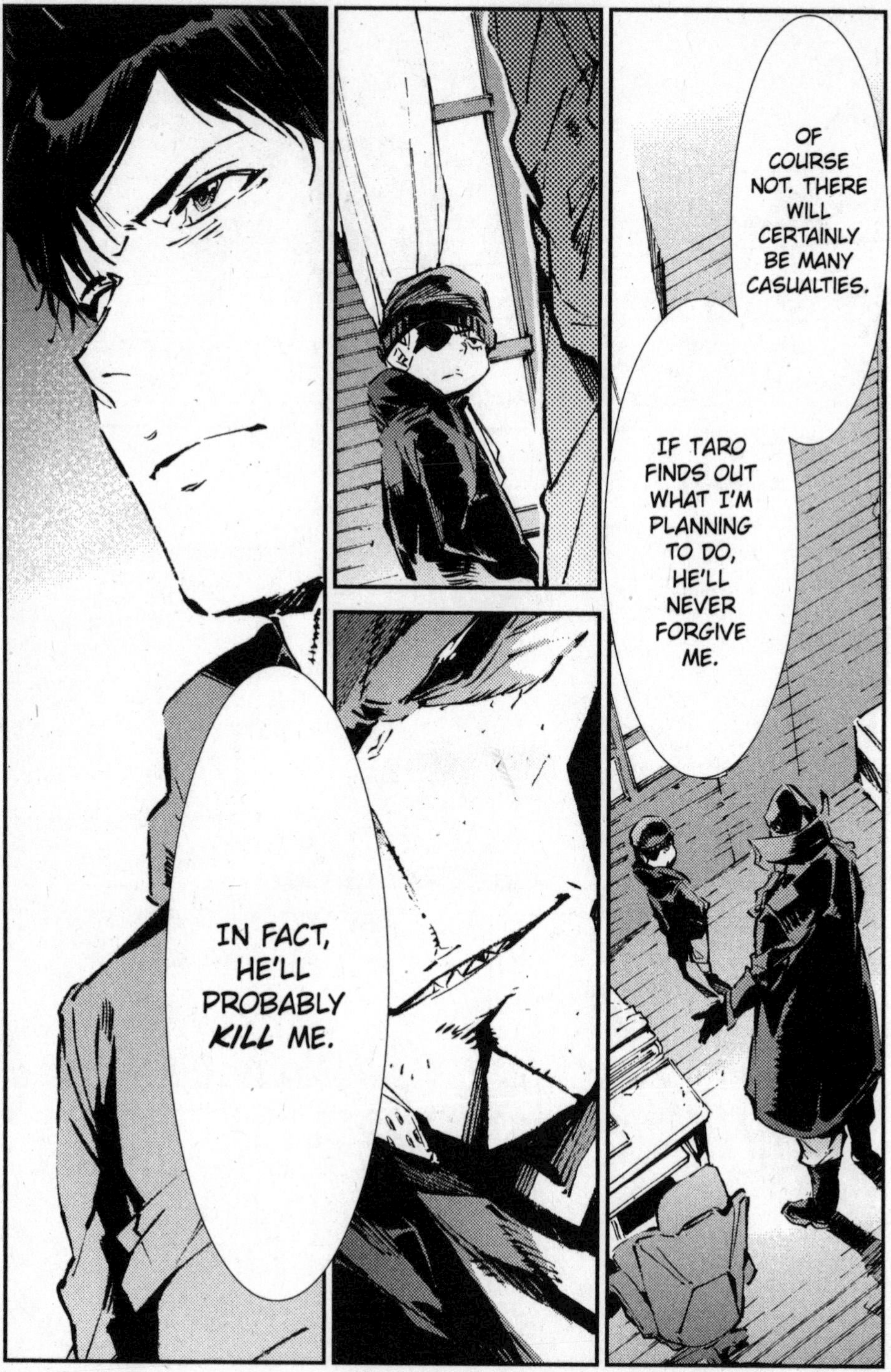
OF COURSE NOT. THERE WILL CERTAINLY BE MANY CASUALTIES.
IF TARO FINDS OUT WHAT I'M PLANNING TO DO, HE'LL NEVER FORGIVE ME.
IN FACT, HE'LL PROBABLY *KILL* ME.

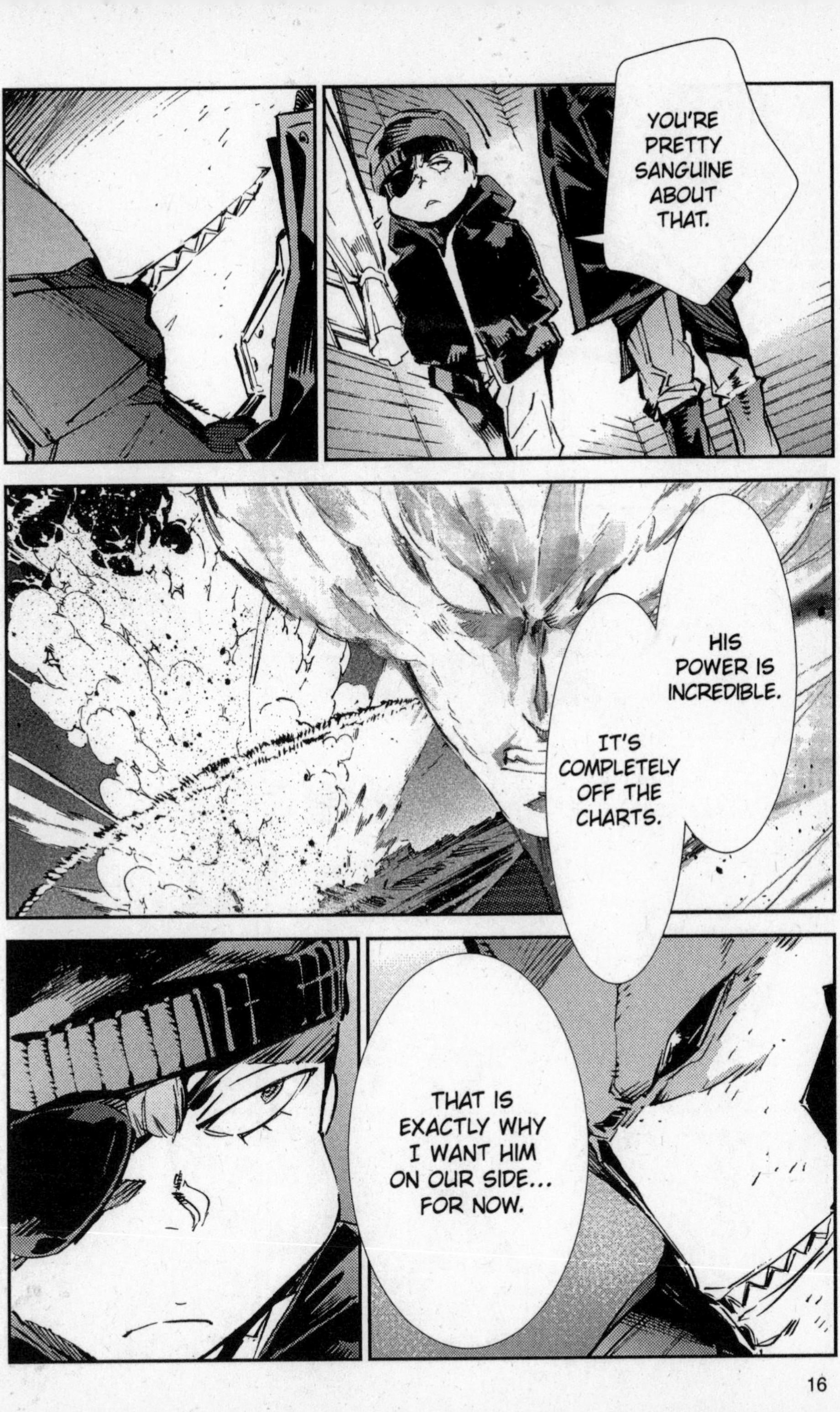
YOU'RE PRETTY SANGUINE ABOUT THAT.
HIS POWER IS INCREDIBLE.
IT'S COMPLETELY OFF THE CHARTS.
THAT IS EXACTLY WHY I WANT HIM ON OUR SIDE... FOR NOW.

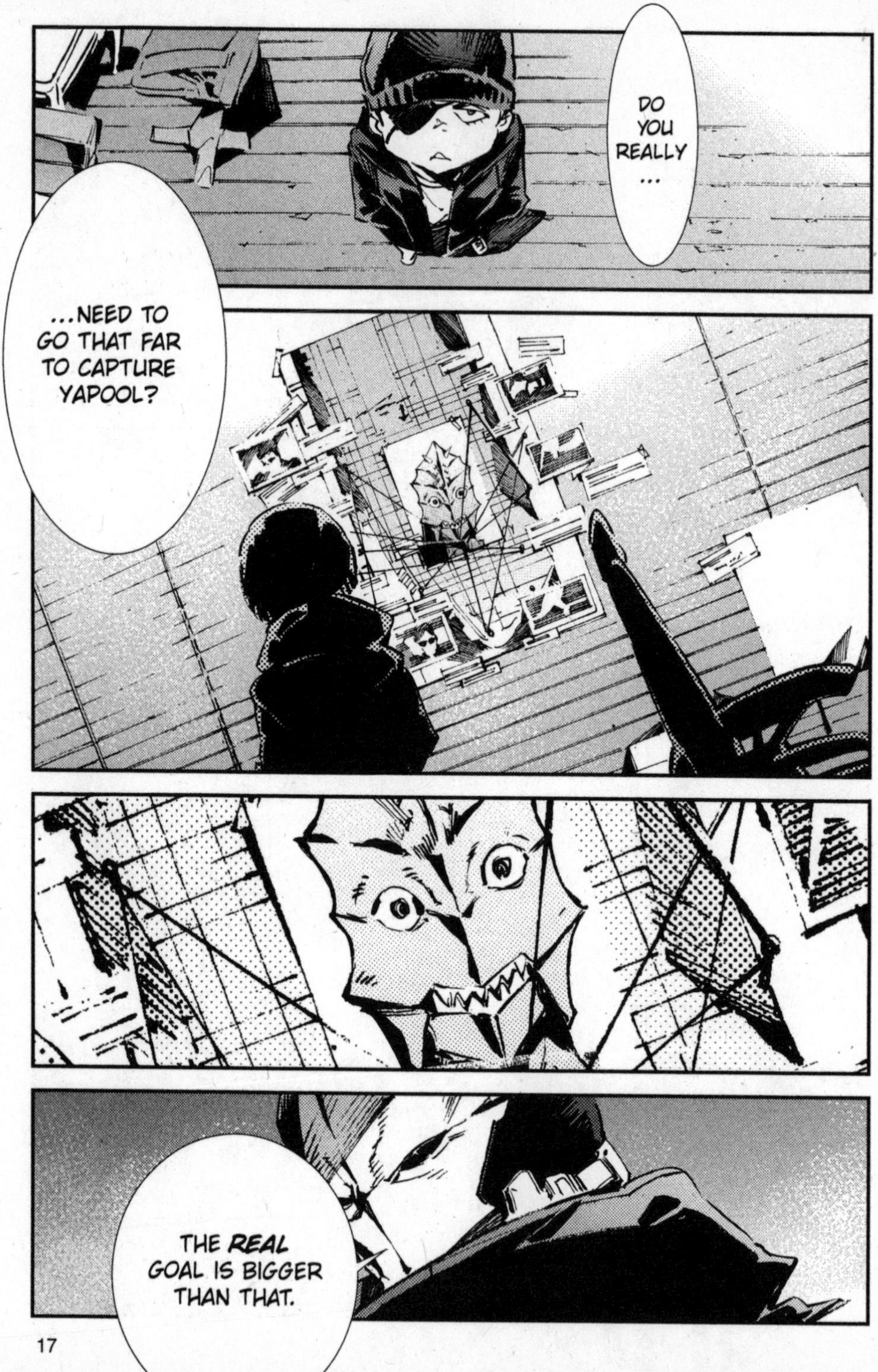
DO YOU REALLY ...
...NEED TO GO THAT FAR TO CAPTURE YAPOOL?
THE REAL GOAL IS BIGGER THAN THAT.

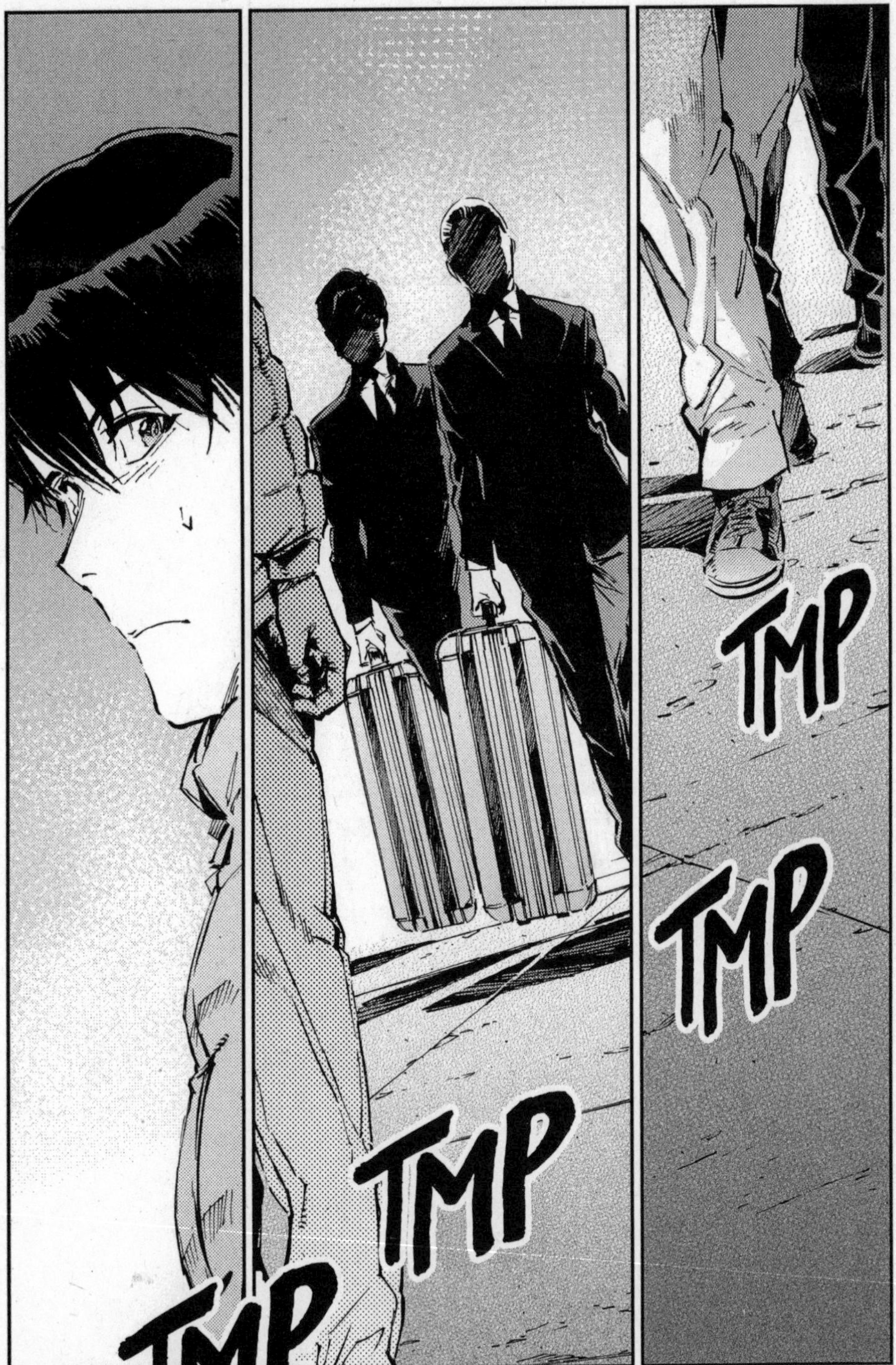
TMP
TMP
TMP
TMP

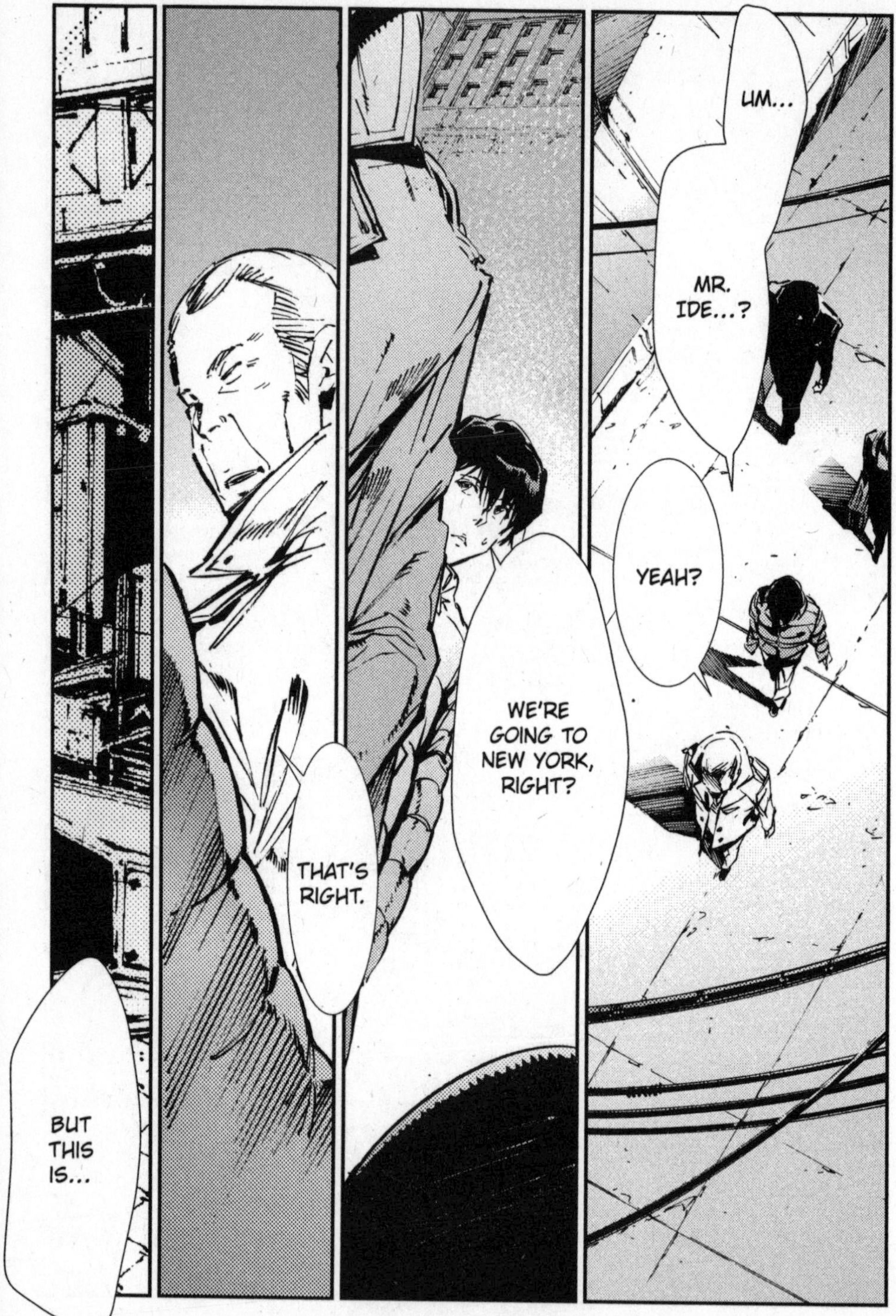
UM...
MR. IDE...?
YEAH?
WE'RE GOING TO NEW YORK, RIGHT?
THAT'S RIGHT.
BUT THIS IS...

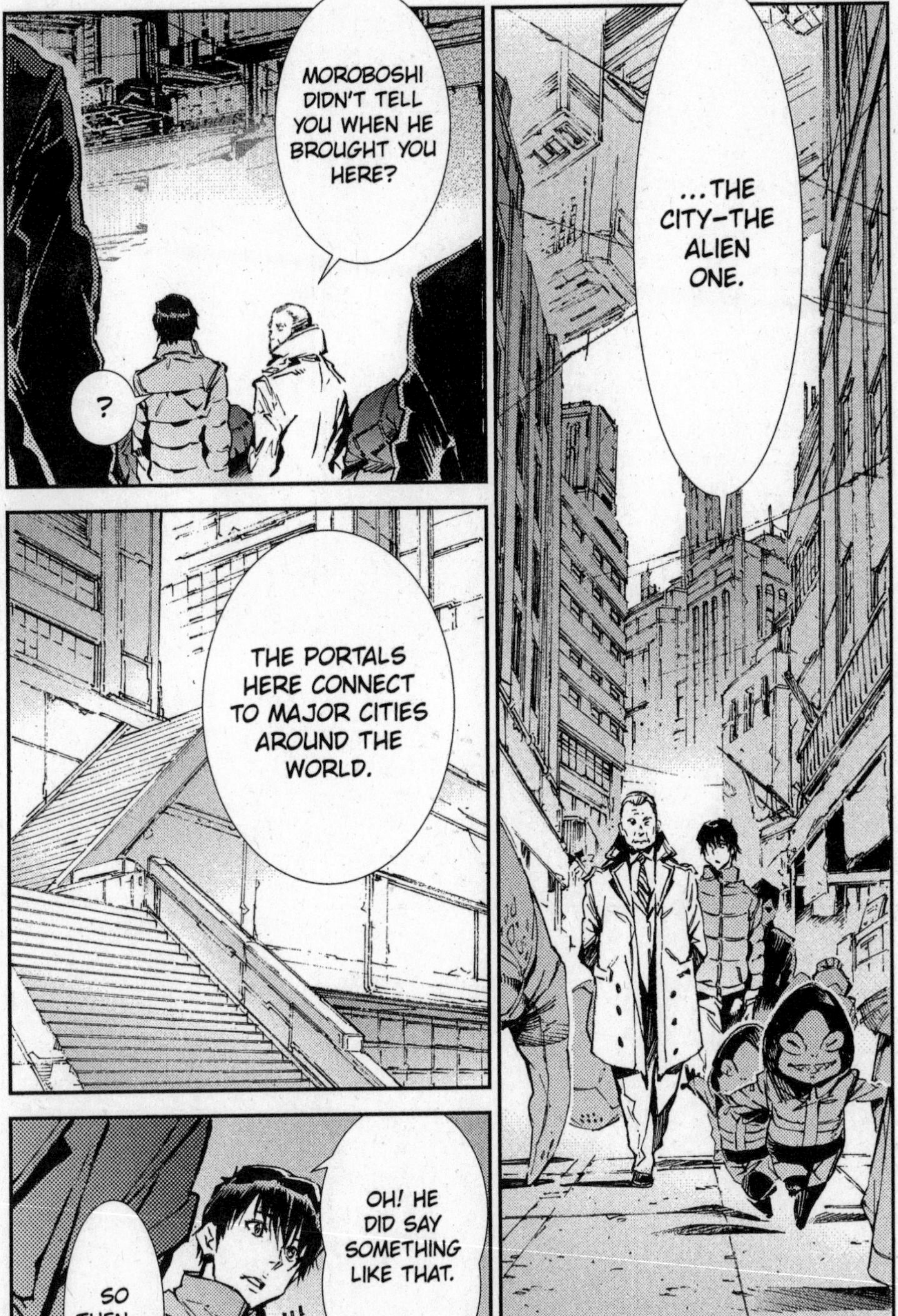
MOROBOSHI DIDN'T TELL YOU WHEN HE BROUGHT YOU HERE?
?
THE PORTALS HERE CONNECT TO MAJOR CITIES AROUND THE WORLD.
OH! HE DID SAY SOMETHING LIKE THAT.
SO THEN...
...THE CITY—THE ALIEN ONE.

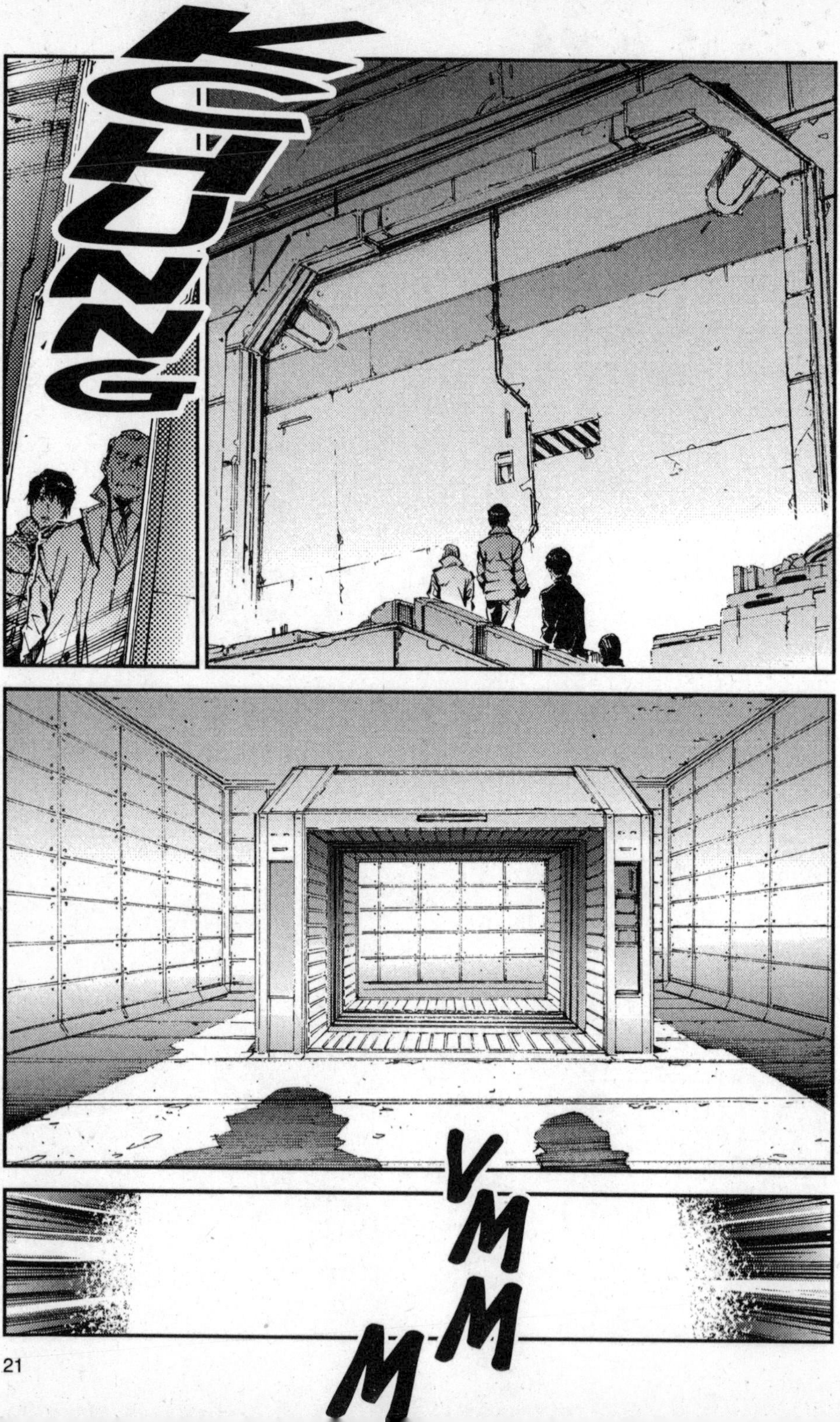
KCHUNNG
VMMMM

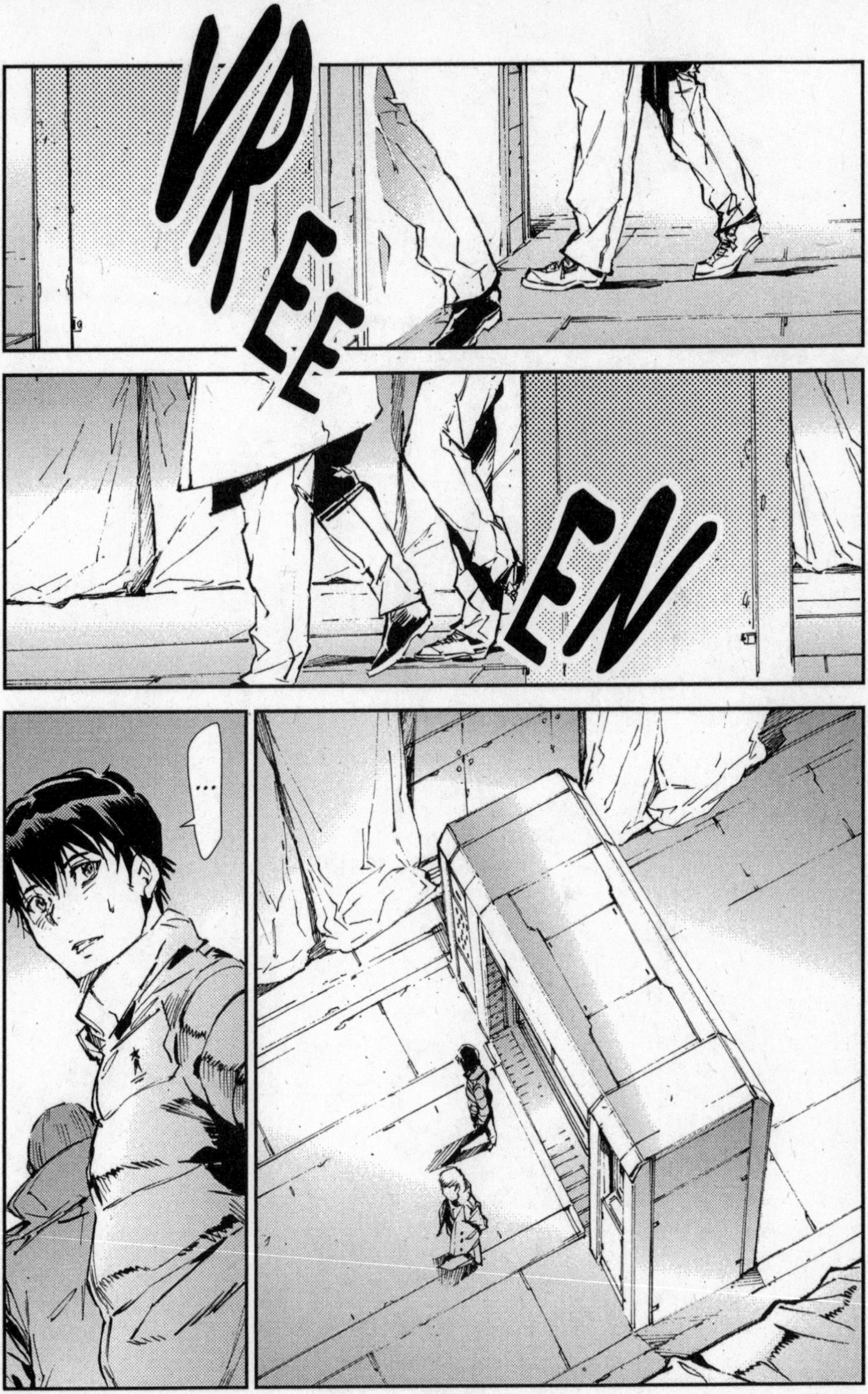
VREE
EN
...

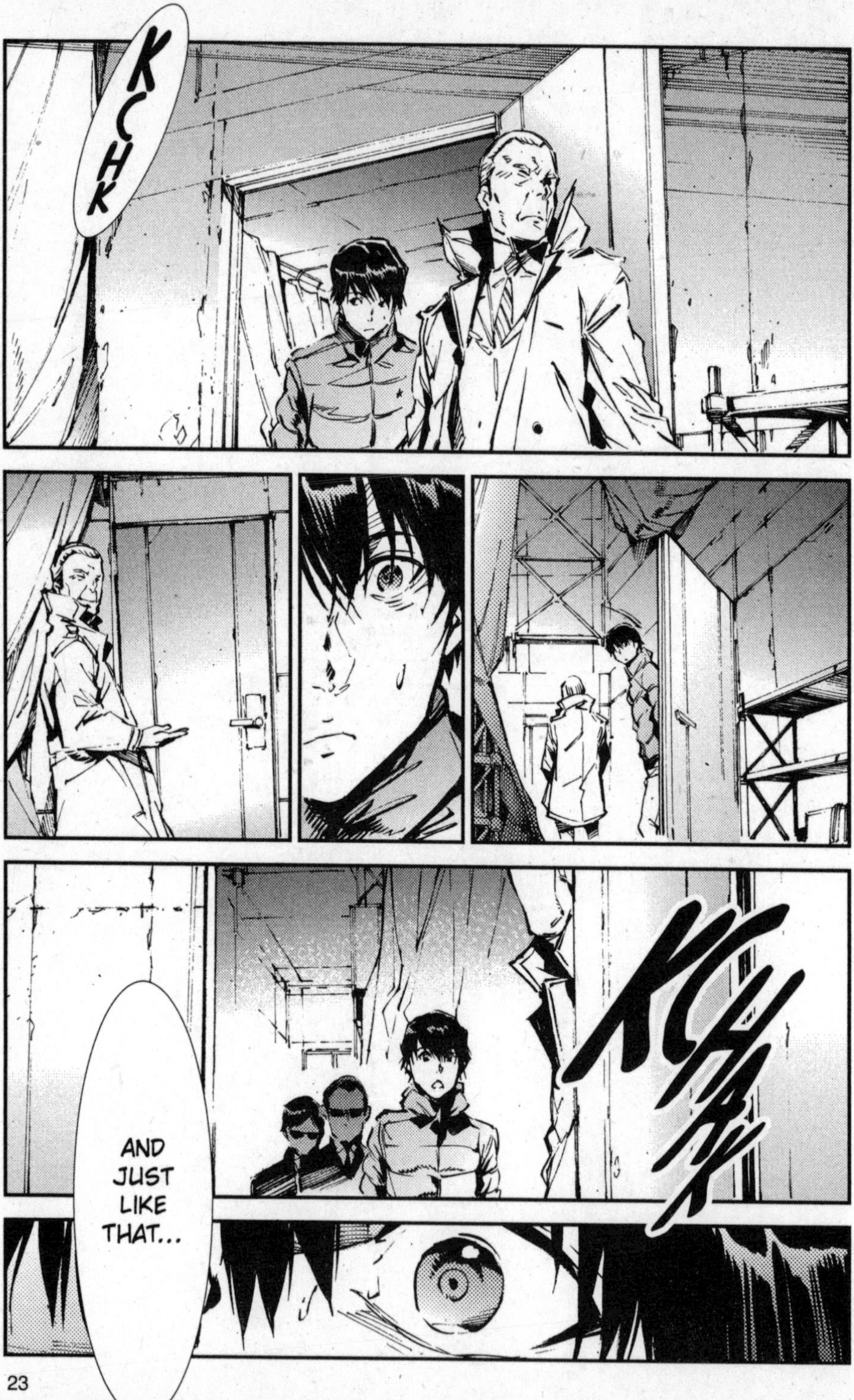
KCHK
KCHAK
AND JUST LIKE THAT...

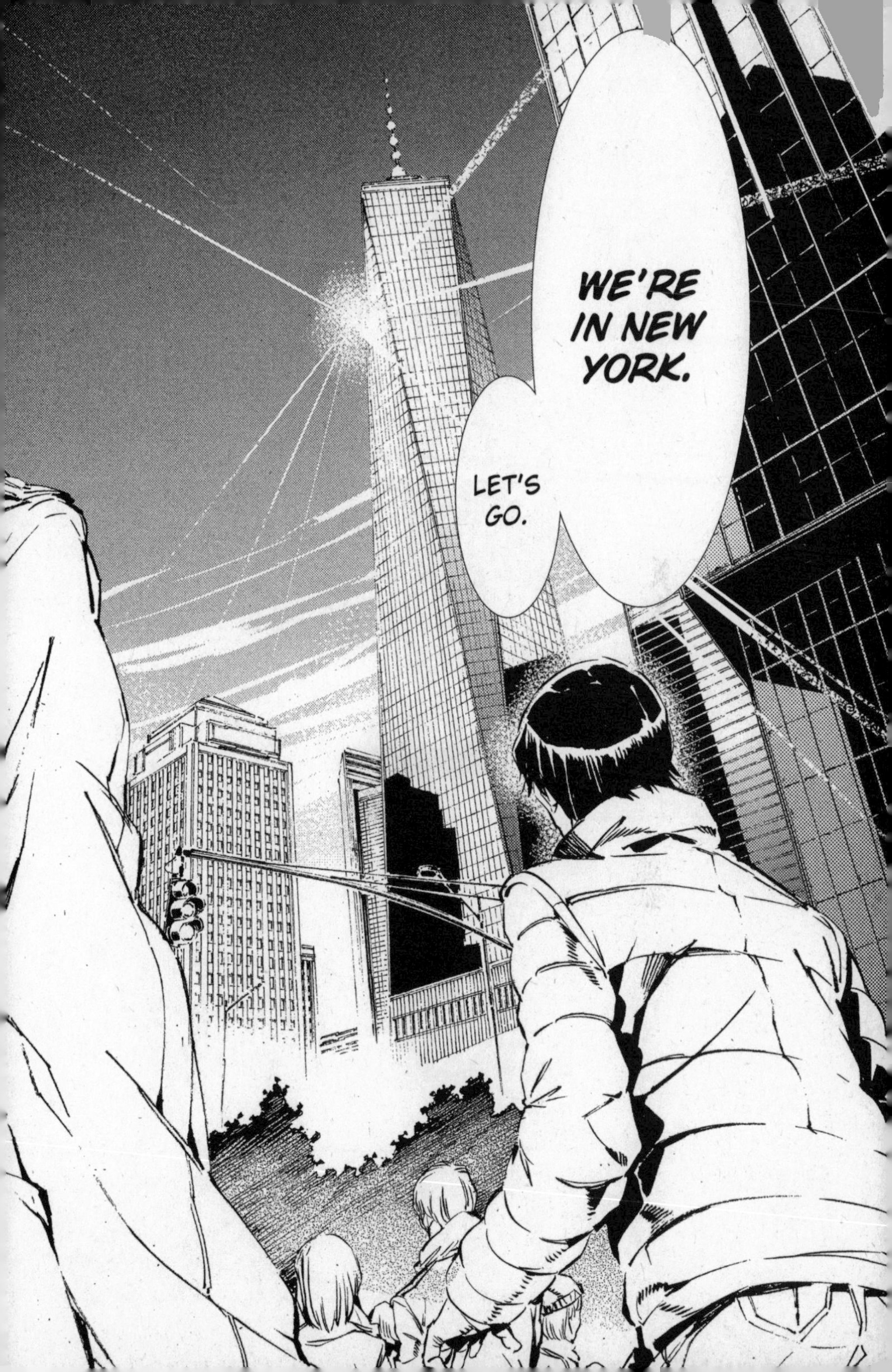
WE'RE IN NEW YORK.
LET'S GO.

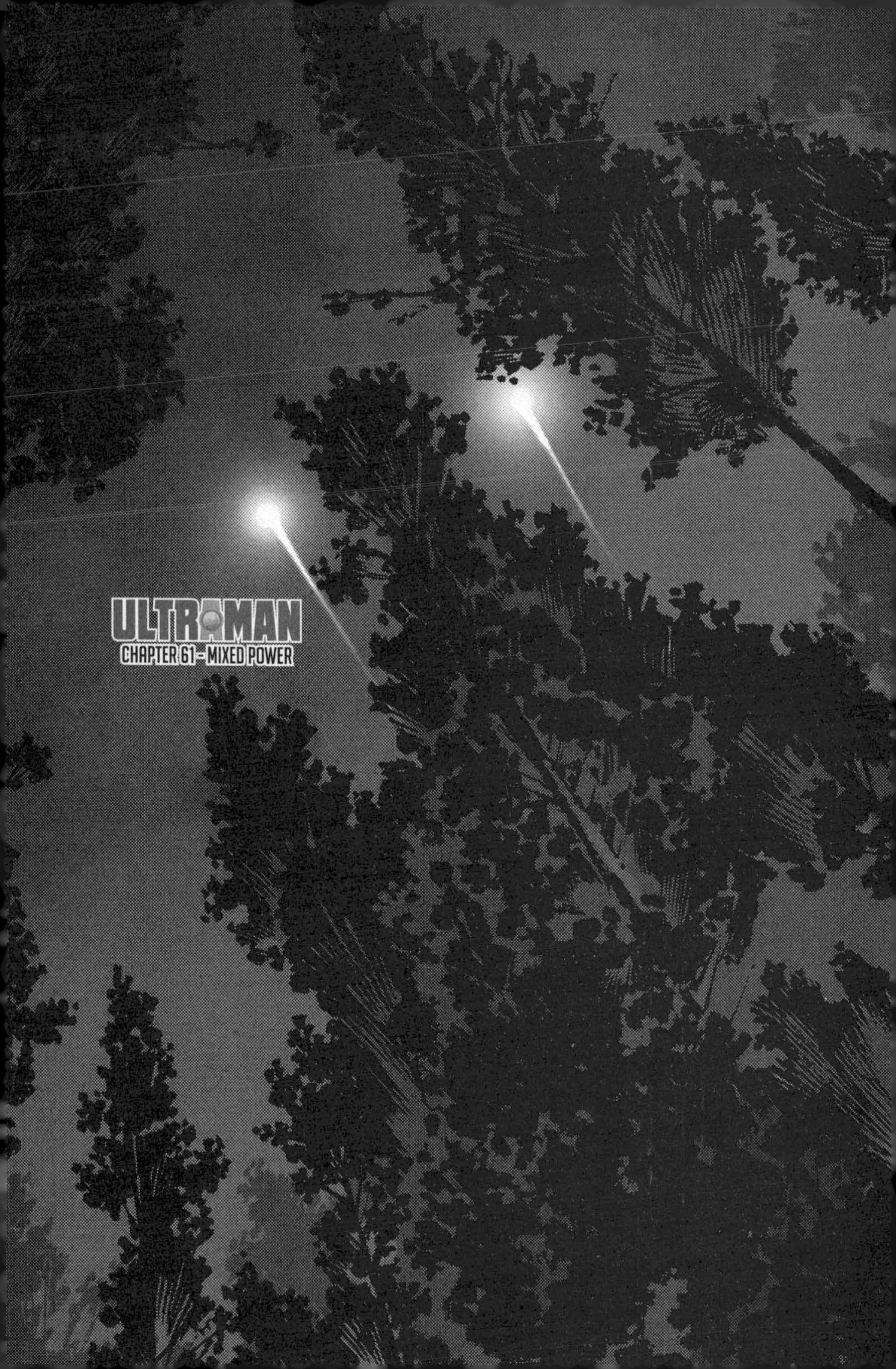
ULTRAMAN
CHAPTER 61 - MIXED POWER

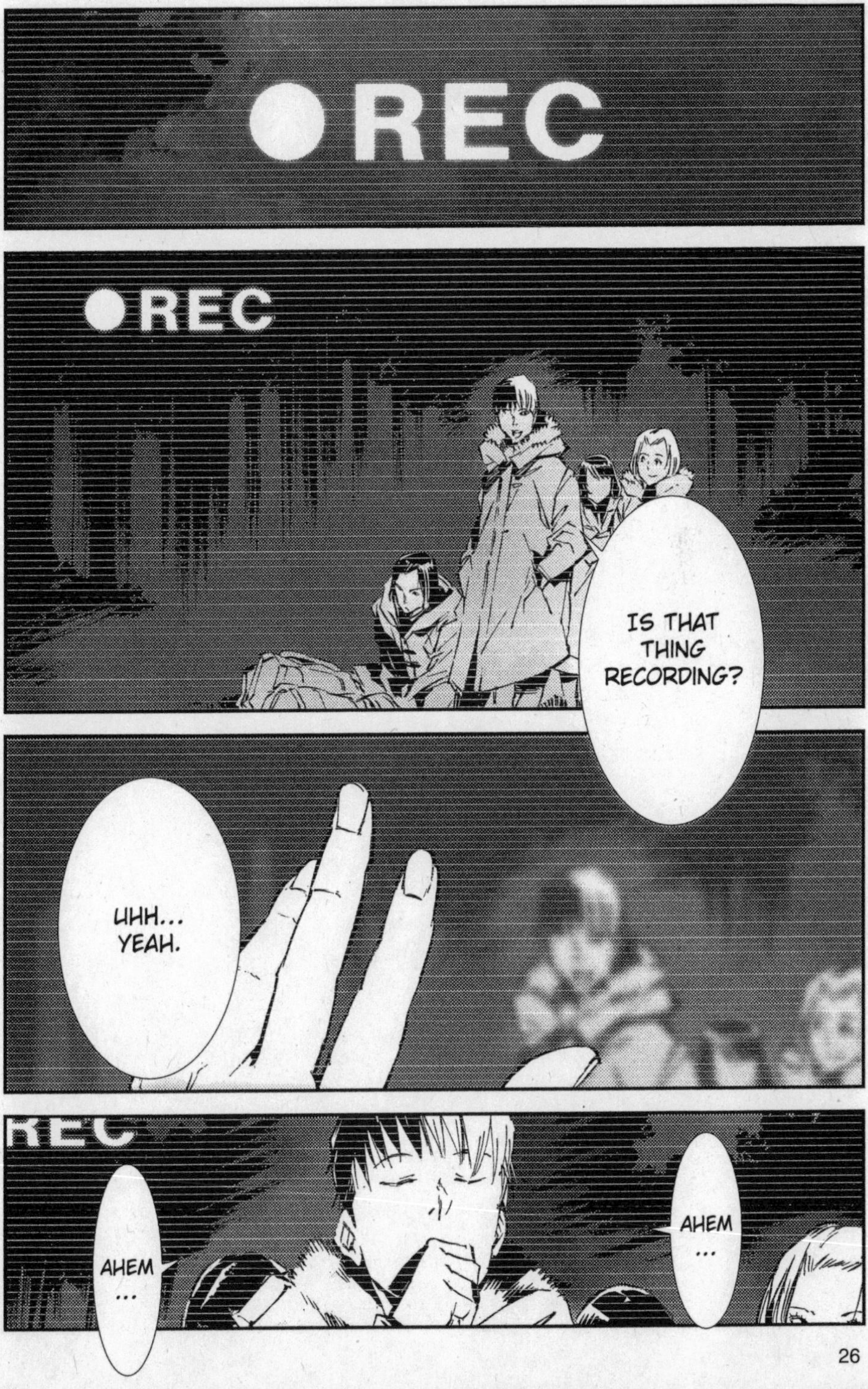

●REC
●REC
IS THAT THING RECORDING?
UHH... YEAH.
REC
AHEM ...
AHEM ...

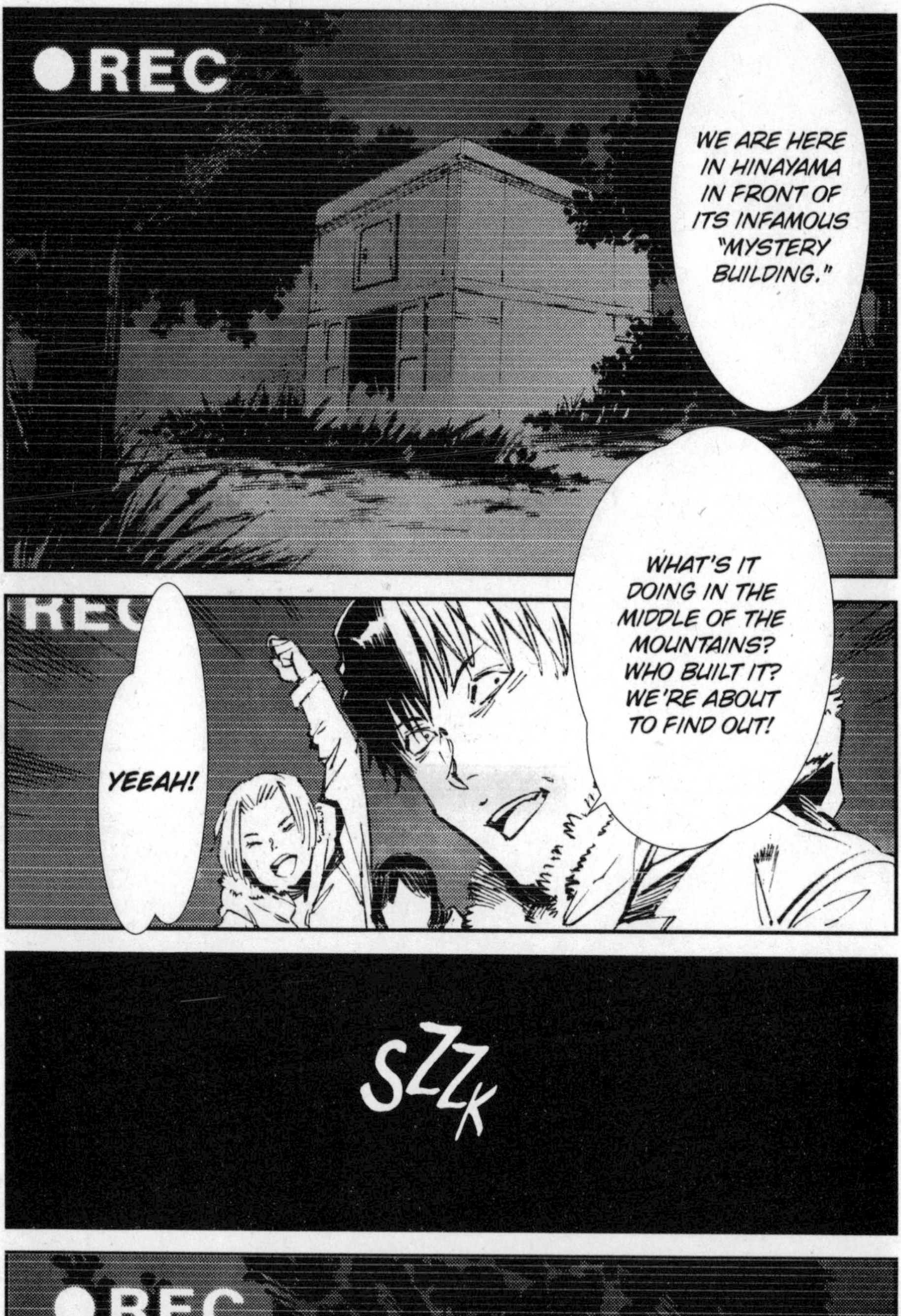
REC
WE ARE HERE IN HINAYAMA IN FRONT OF ITS INFAMOUS "MYSTERY BUILDING."
WHAT'S IT DOING IN THE MIDDLE OF THE MOUNTAINS? WHO BUILT IT? WE'RE ABOUT TO FIND OUT!
YEEAH!
SZZK
REC

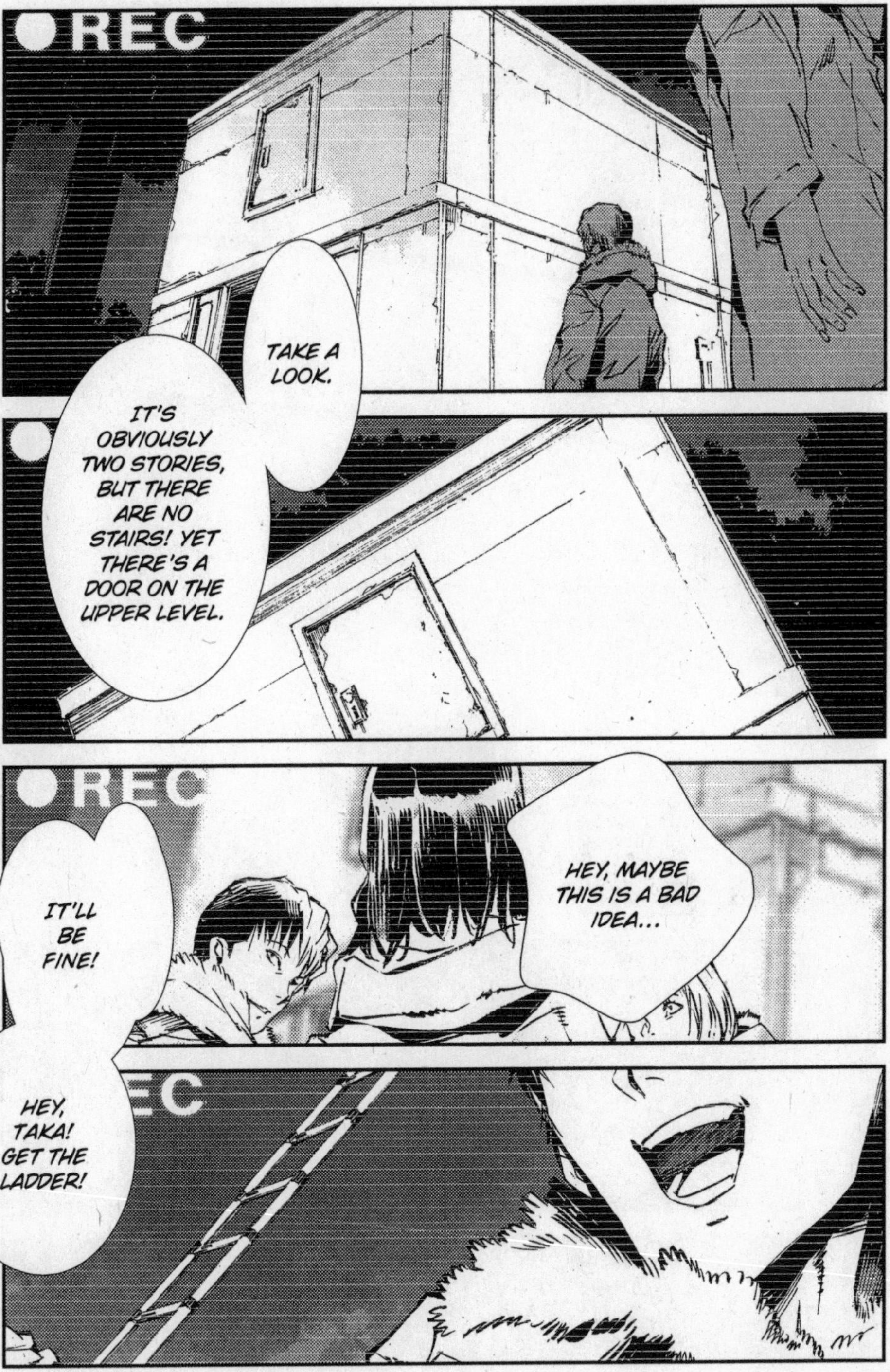
REC
TAKE A LOOK.
IT'S OBVIOUSLY TWO STORIES, BUT THERE ARE NO STAIRS! YET THERE'S A DOOR ON THE UPPER LEVEL.
REC
HEY, MAYBE THIS IS A BAD IDEA...
IT'LL BE FINE!
HEY, TAKA! GET THE LADDER!

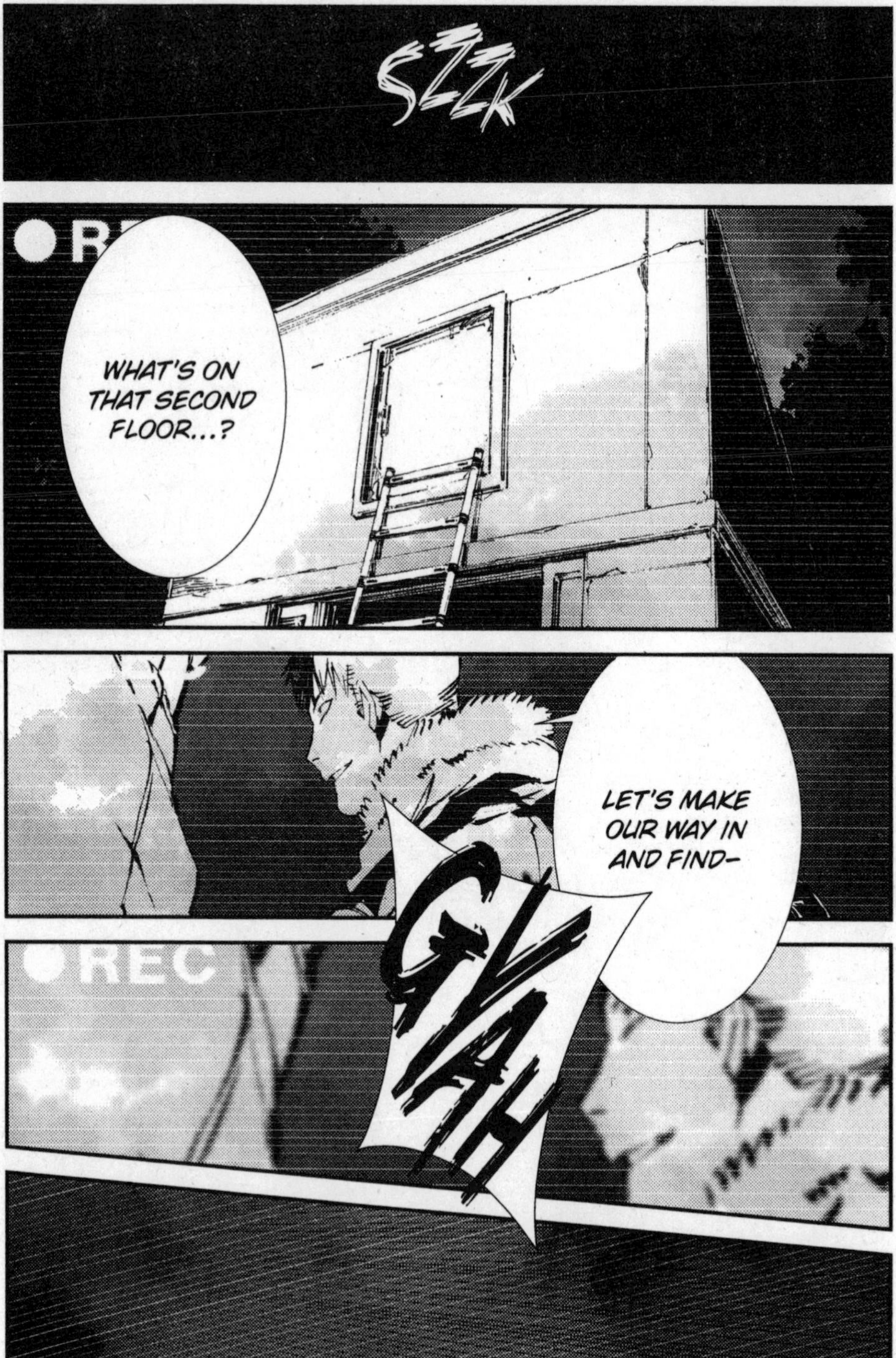
SZZK
WHAT'S ON THAT SECOND FLOOR...?
LET'S MAKE OUR WAY IN AND FIND-
GYAAH
REC

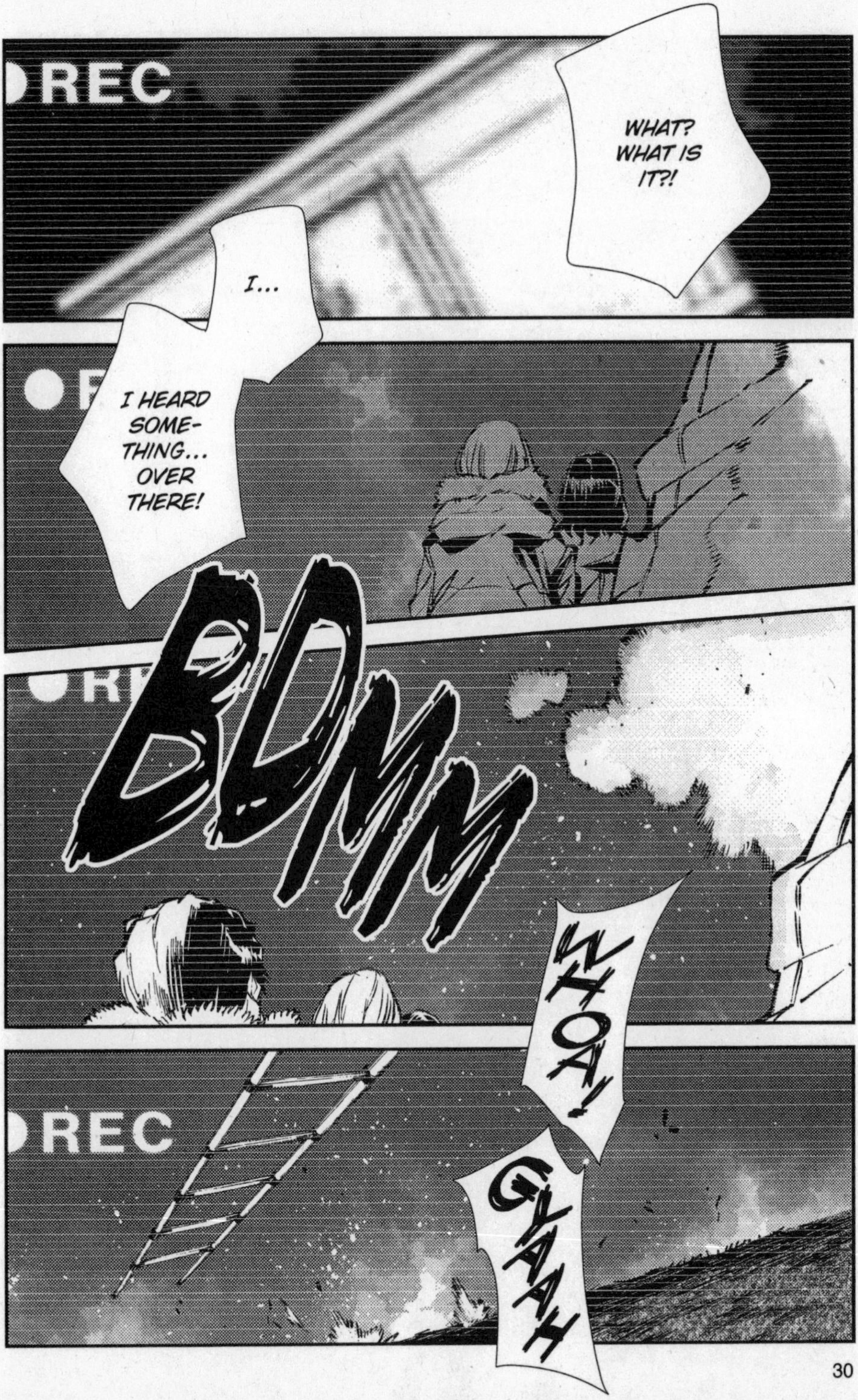
REC
WHAT? WHAT IS IT?!
I...
I HEARD SOME- THING... OVER THERE!
BDMM
WHOA!
GYAAH
REC

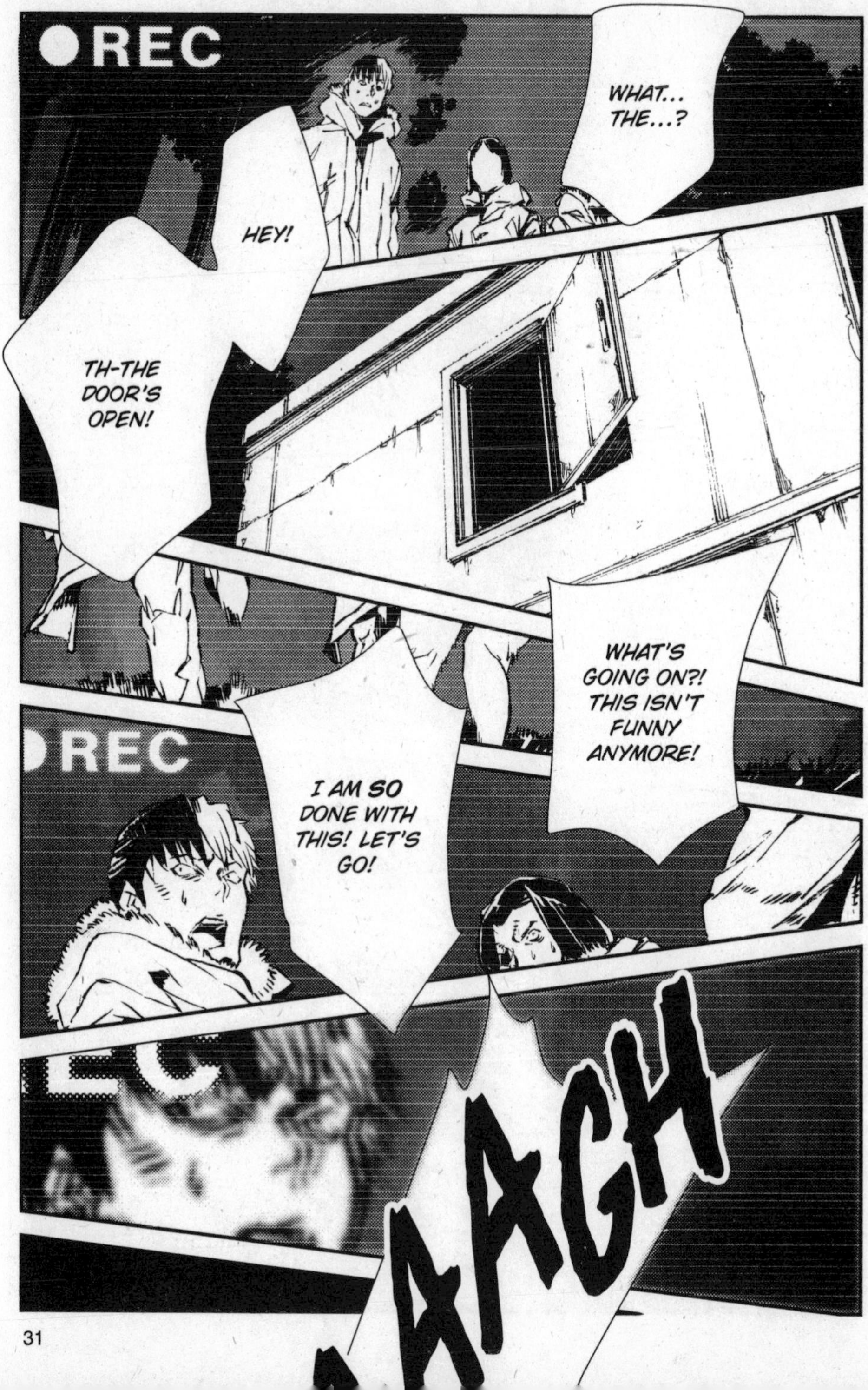
REC
WHAT... THE...?
HEY!
TH-THE DOOR'S OPEN!
WHAT'S GOING ON?! THIS ISN'T FUNNY ANYMORE!
REC
I AM SO DONE WITH THIS! LET'S GO!
AACH

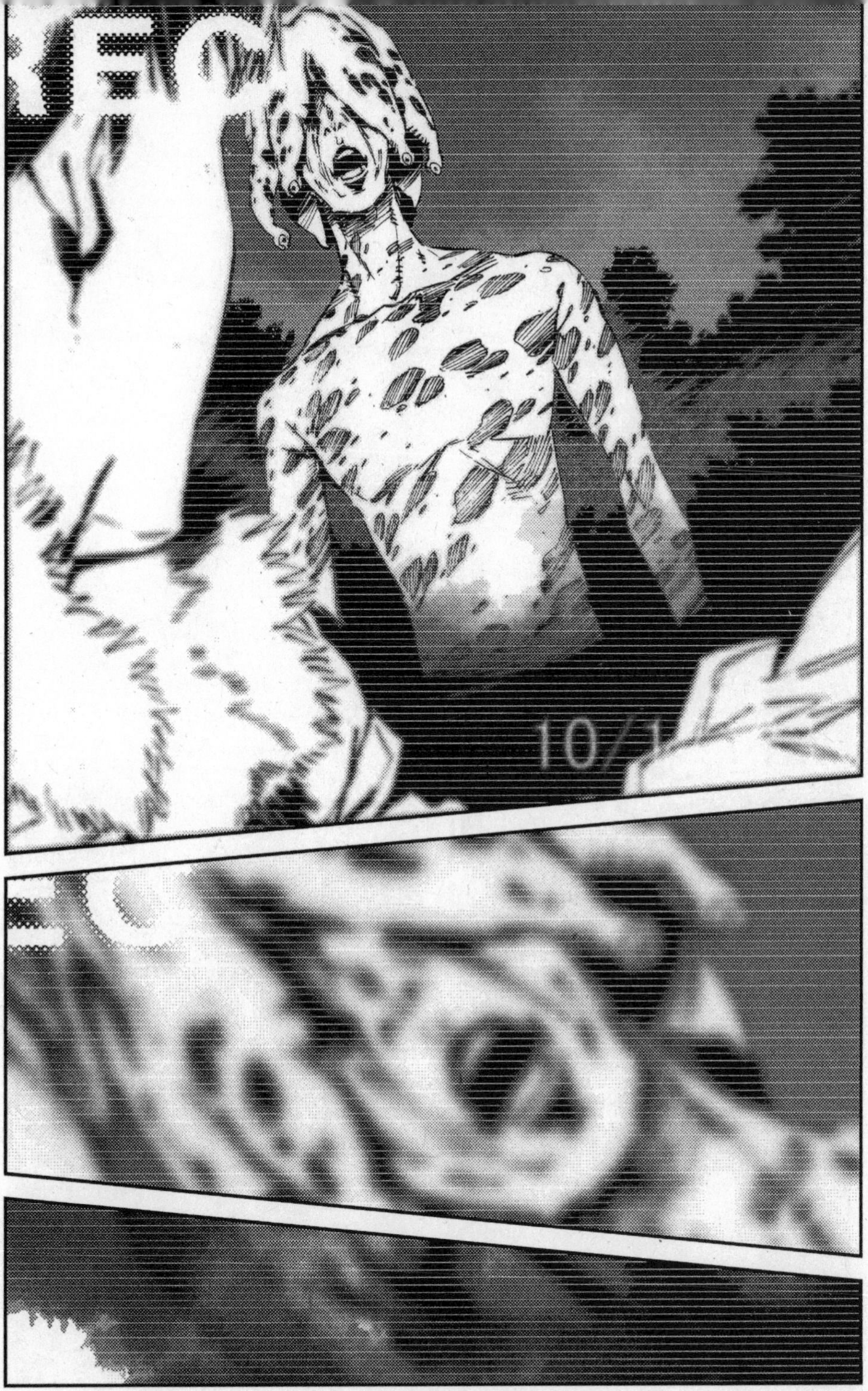

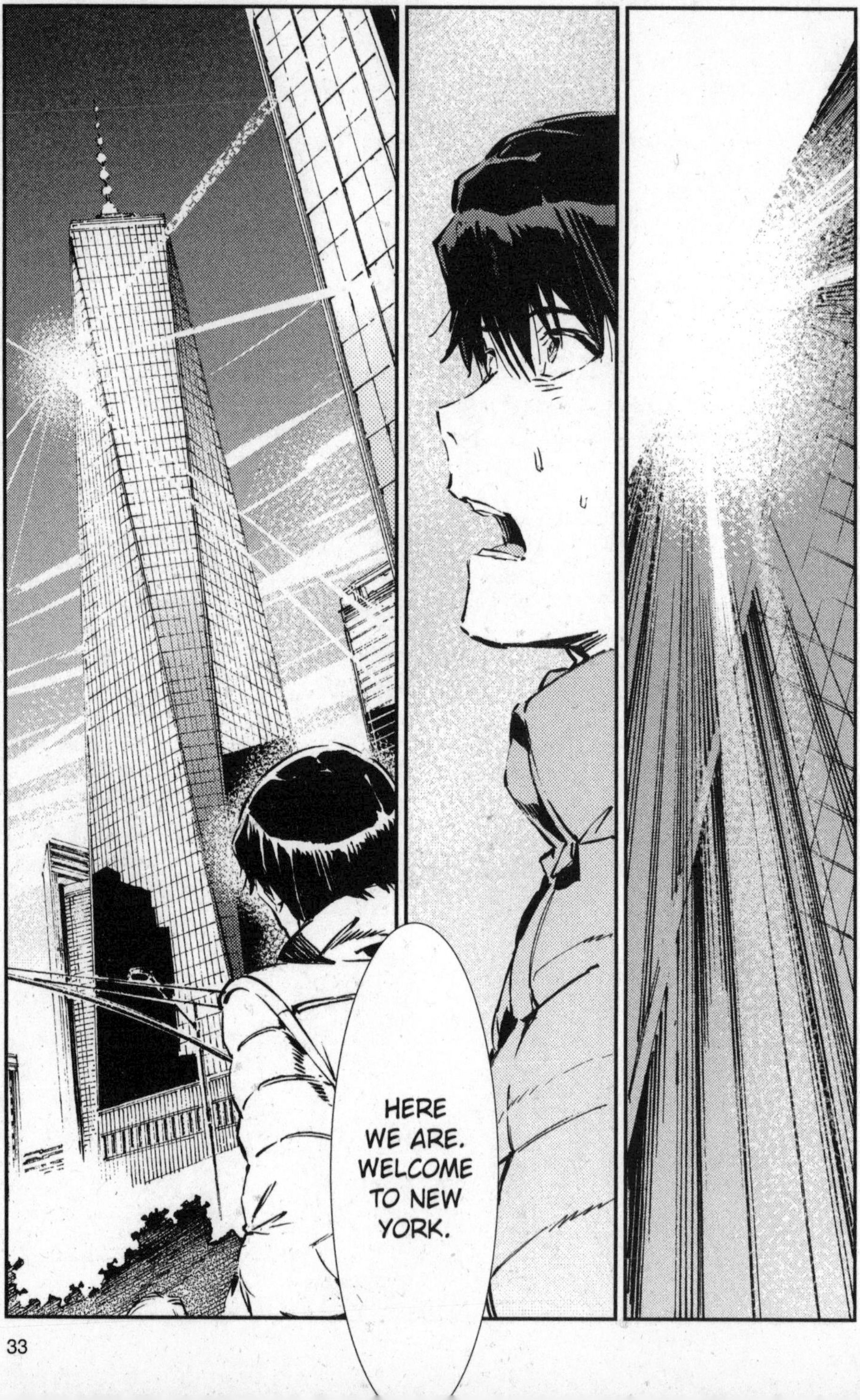
HERE WE ARE. WELCOME TO NEW YORK.

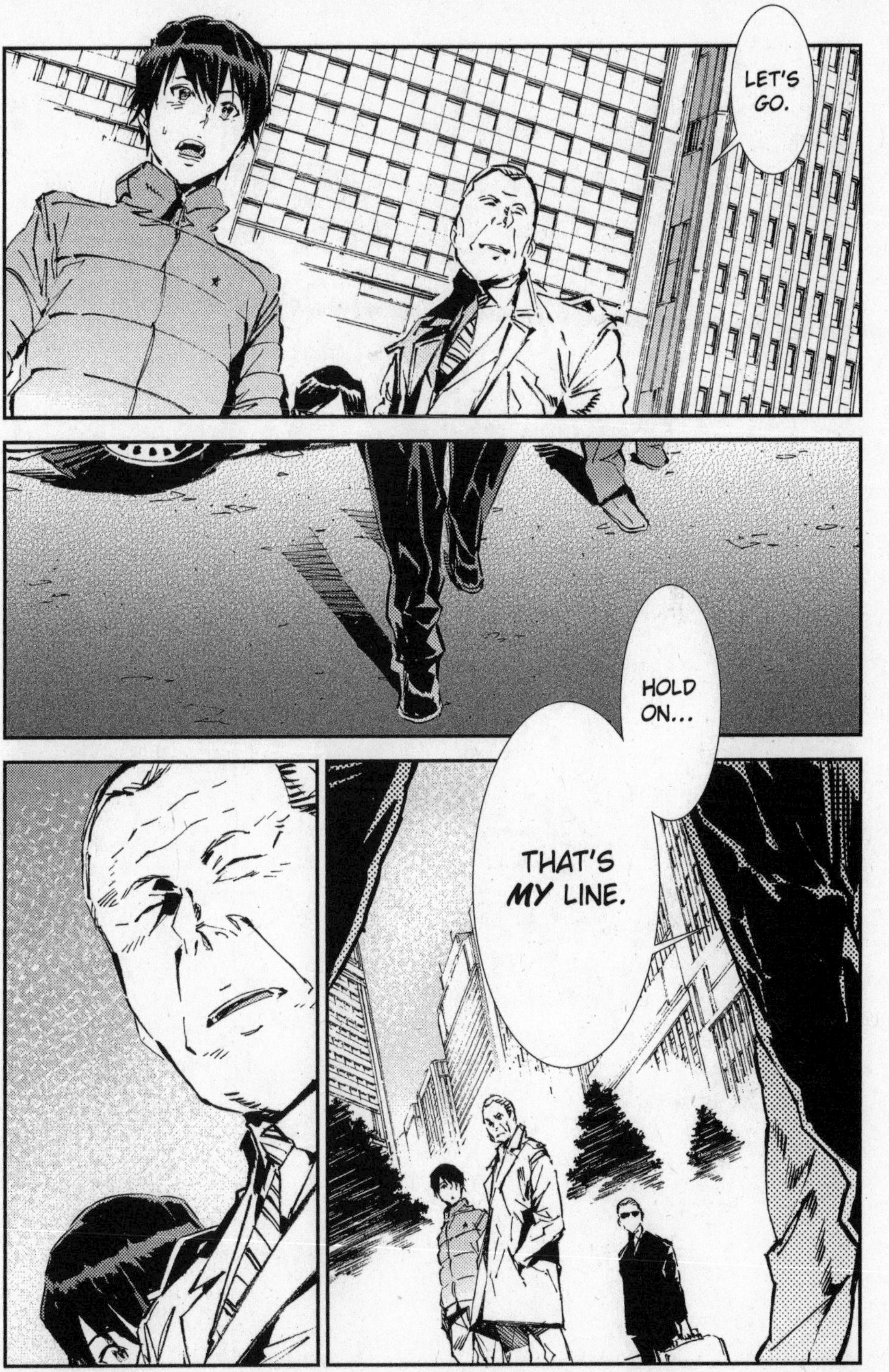
LET'S GO.
HOLD ON...
THAT'S MY LINE.

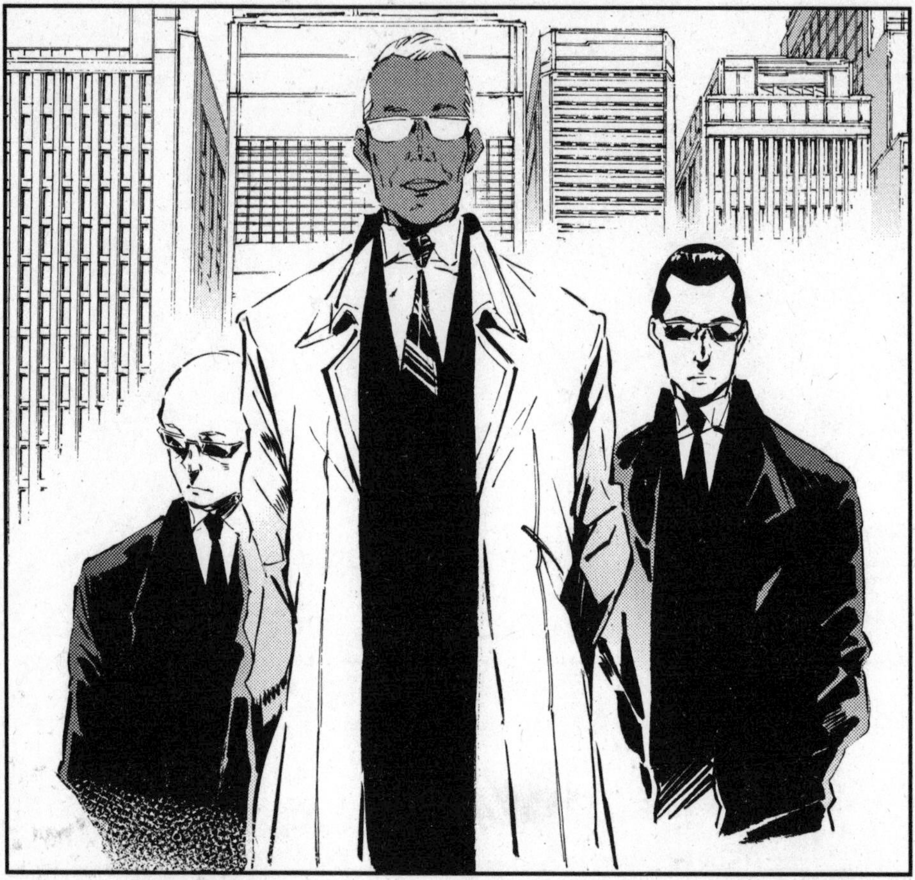

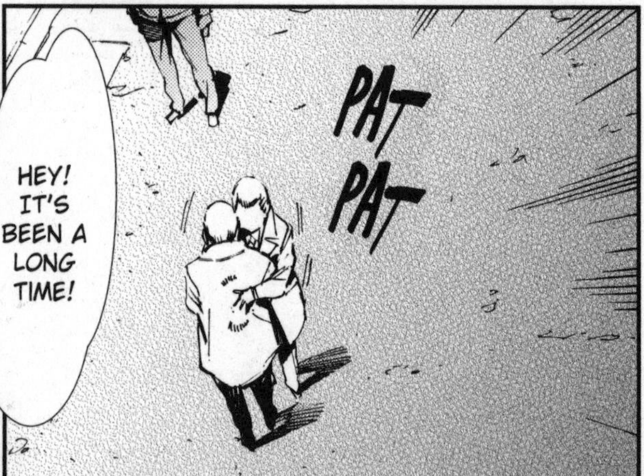
HEY! IT'S BEEN A LONG TIME!
PAT PAT

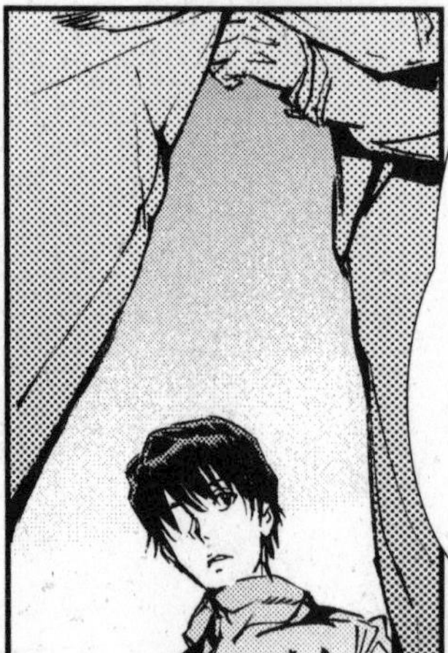

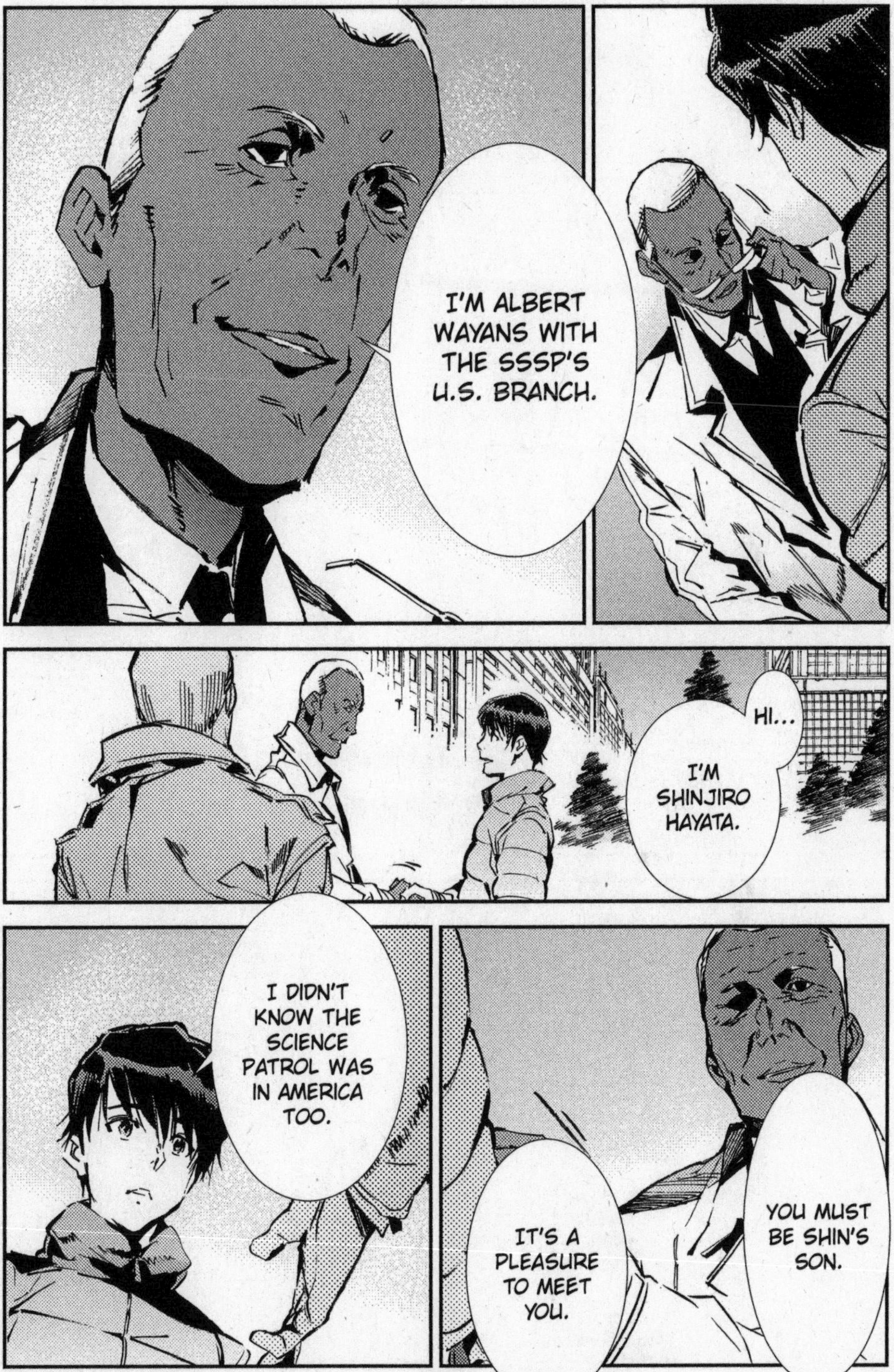
I'M ALBERT WAYANS WITH THE SSSP'S U.S. BRANCH.
HI...
I'M SHINJIRO HAYATA.
YOU MUST BE SHIN'S SON.
IT'S A PLEASURE TO MEET YOU.
I DIDN'T KNOW THE SCIENCE PATROL WAS IN AMERICA TOO.

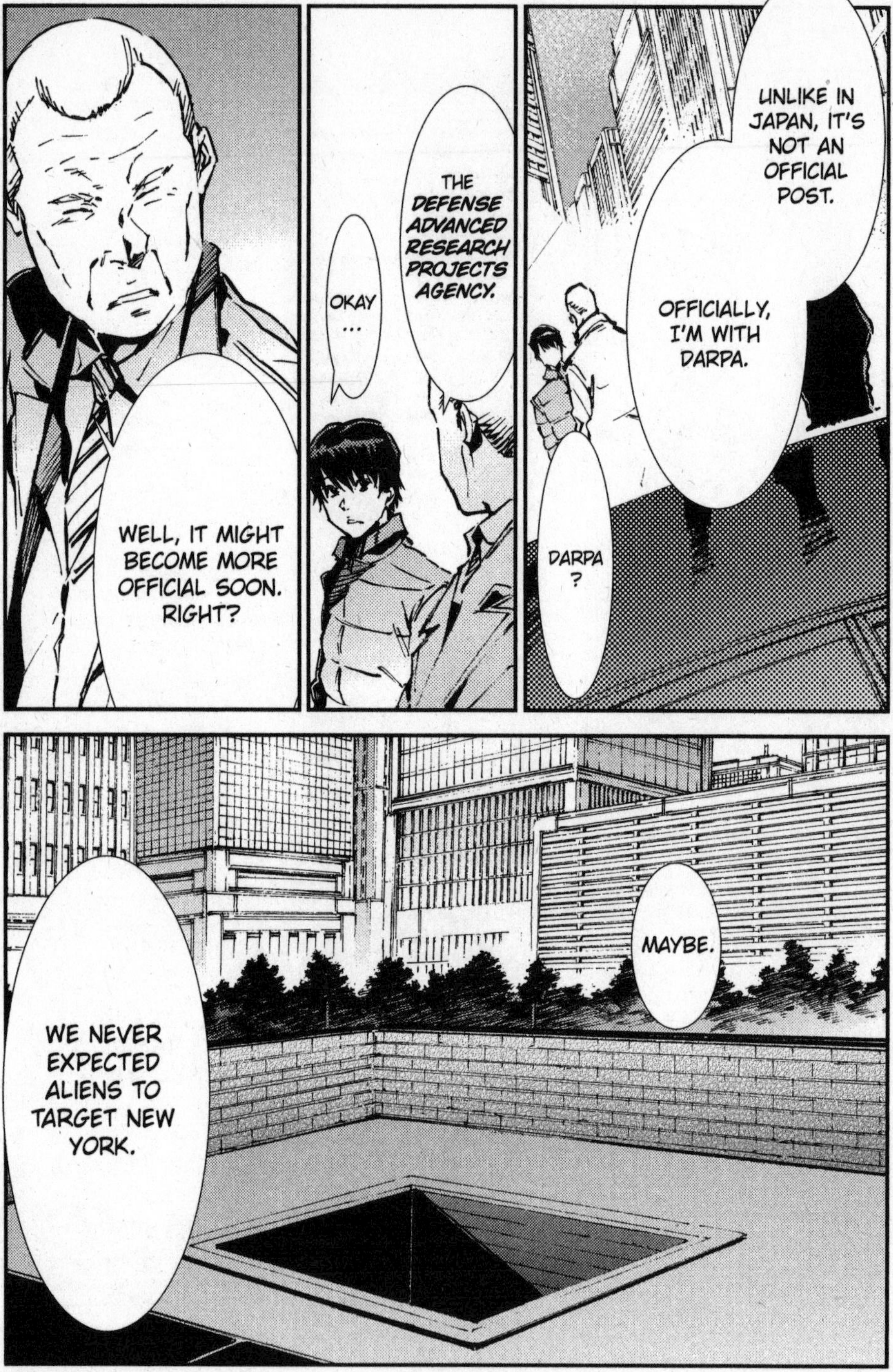
UNLIKE IN JAPAN, IT'S NOT AN OFFICIAL POST.
OFFICIALLY, I'M WITH DARPA.
DARPA?
THE *DEFENSE ADVANCED RESEARCH PROJECTS AGENCY.*
OKAY ...
WELL, IT MIGHT BECOME MORE OFFICIAL SOON. RIGHT?
MAYBE.
WE NEVER EXPECTED ALIENS TO TARGET NEW YORK.

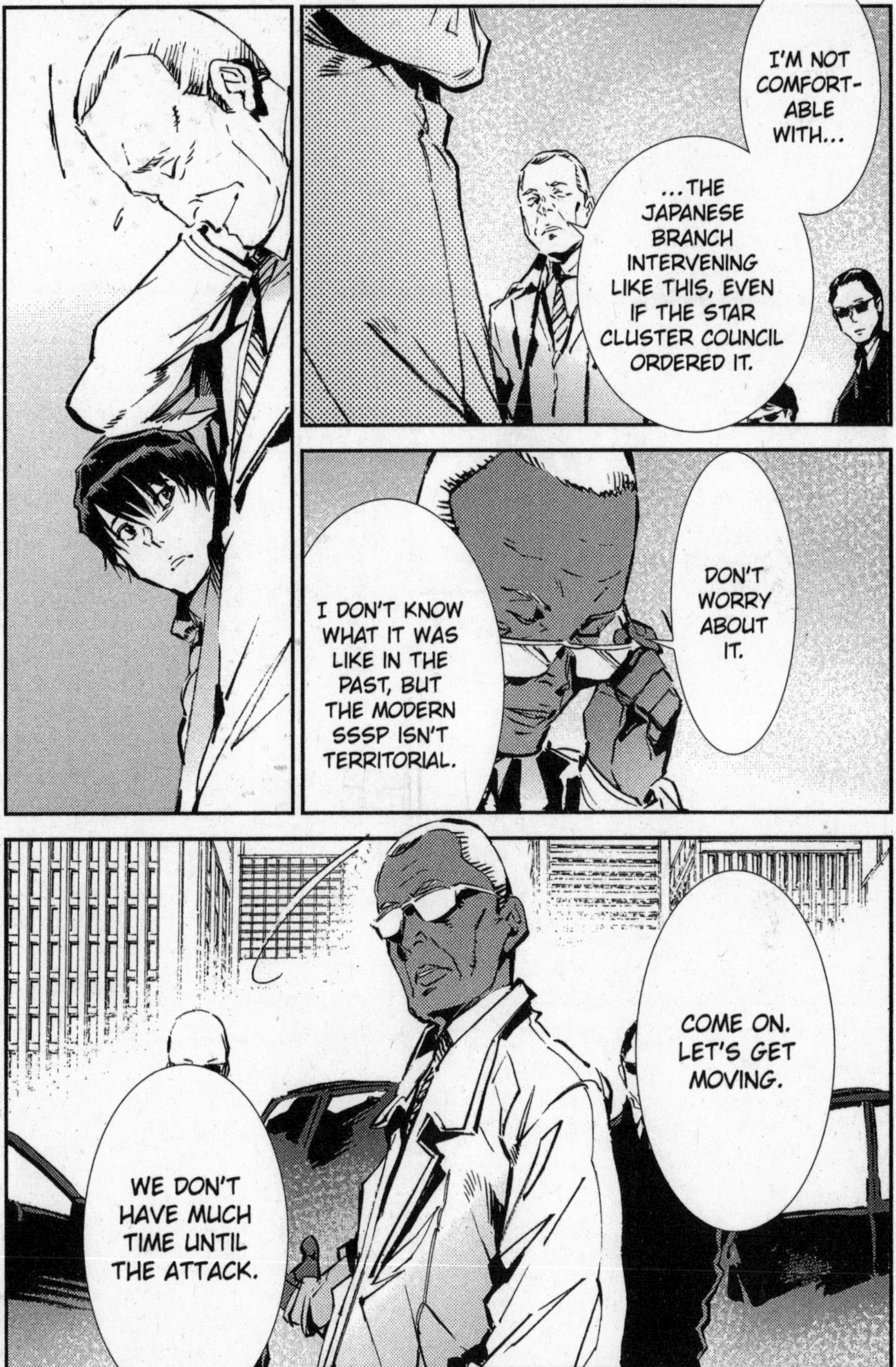
I'M NOT COMFORT-ABLE WITH...
...THE JAPANESE BRANCH INTERVENING LIKE THIS, EVEN IF THE STAR CLUSTER COUNCIL ORDERED IT.
DON'T WORRY ABOUT IT.
I DON'T KNOW WHAT IT WAS LIKE IN THE PAST, BUT THE MODERN SSSP ISN'T TERRITORIAL.
COME ON. LET'S GET MOVING.
WE DON'T HAVE MUCH TIME UNTIL THE ATTACK.

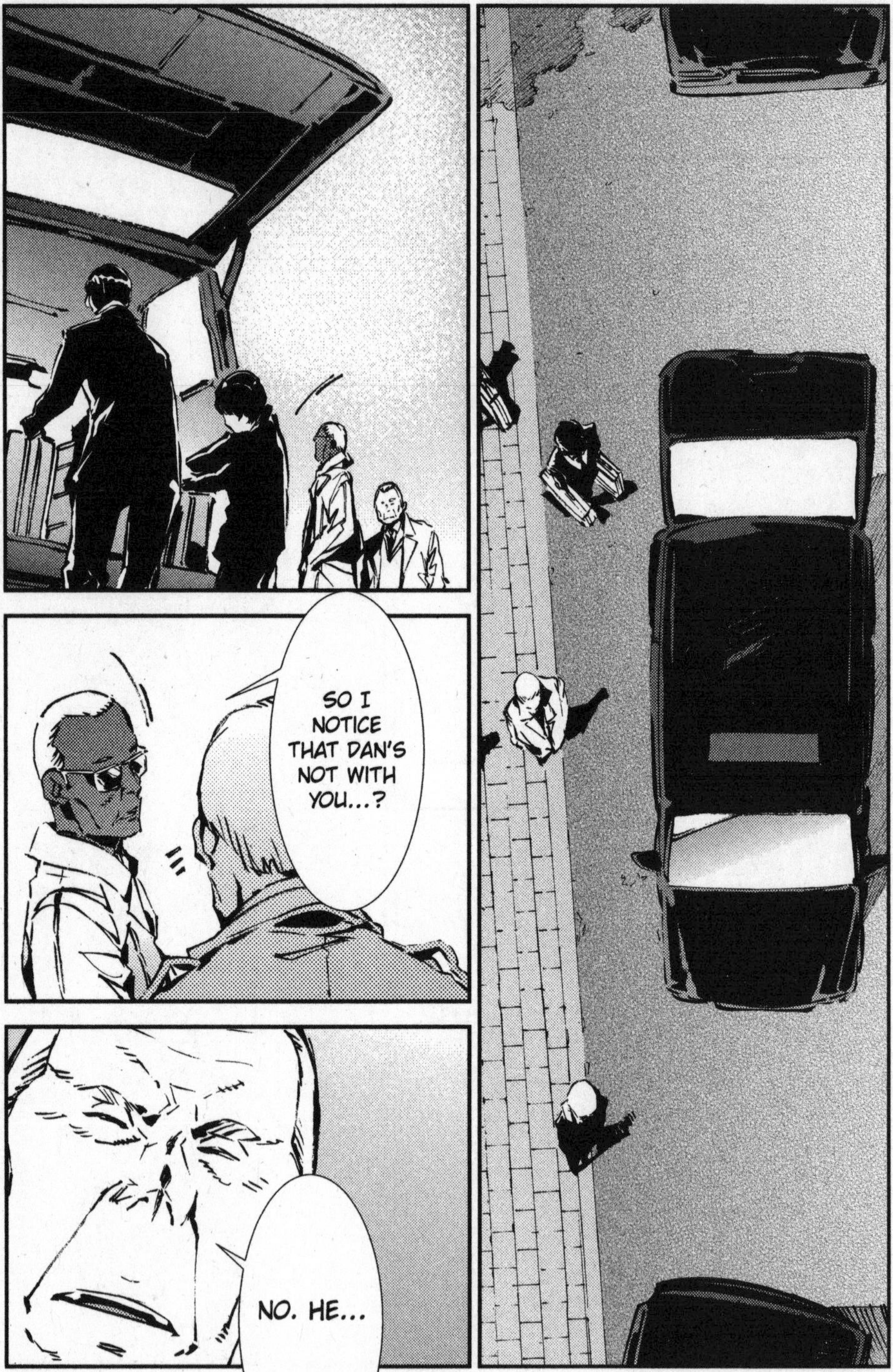
SO I NOTICE THAT DAN'S NOT WITH YOU...?
NO. HE...

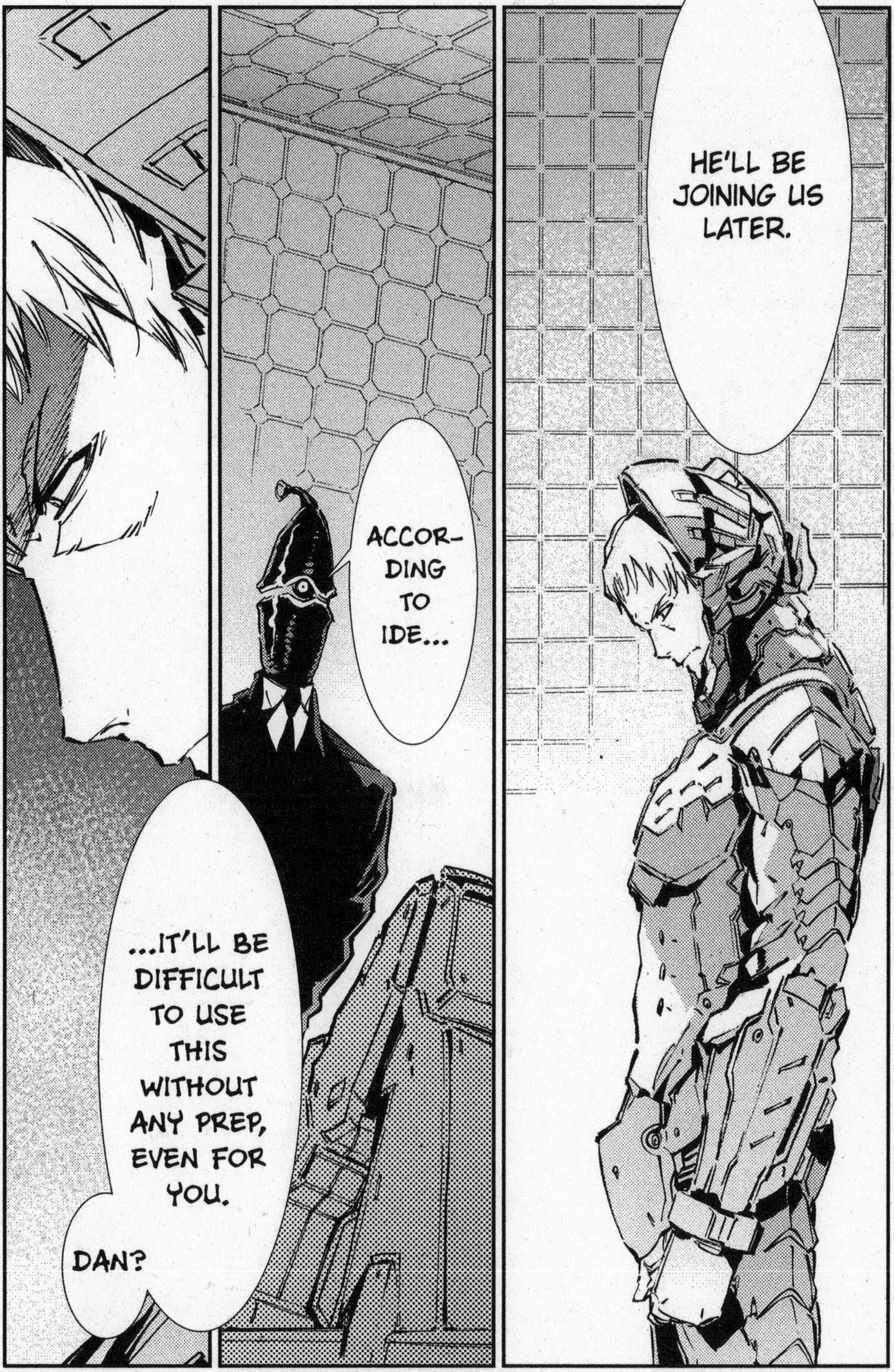
HE'LL BE JOINING US LATER.
ACCORDING TO IDE...
...IT'LL BE DIFFICULT TO USE THIS WITHOUT ANY PREP, EVEN FOR YOU.
DAN?

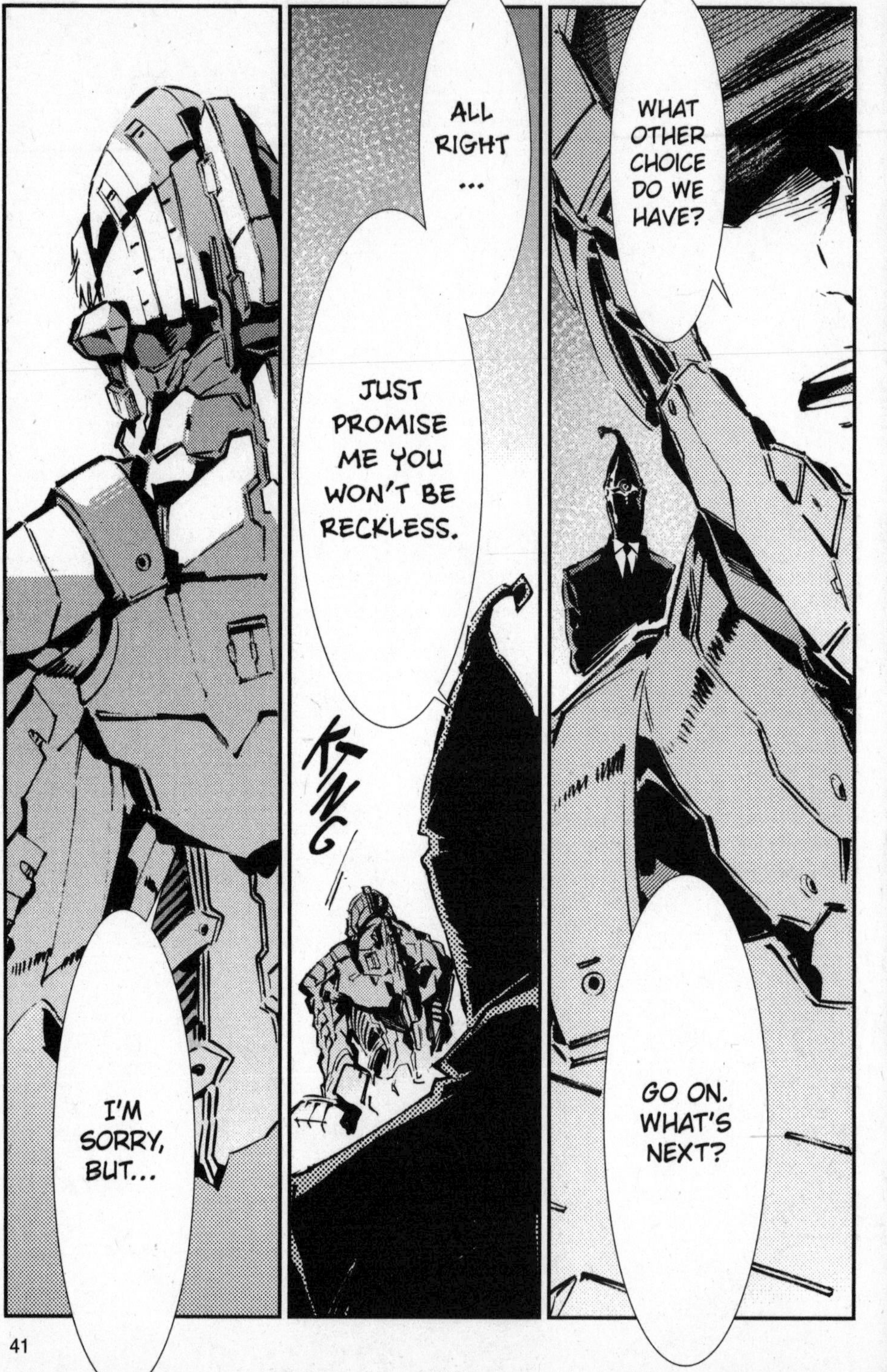
WHAT OTHER CHOICE DO WE HAVE?
GO ON. WHAT'S NEXT?
ALL RIGHT ...
JUST PROMISE ME YOU WON'T BE RECKLESS.
KTING
I'M SORRY, BUT...

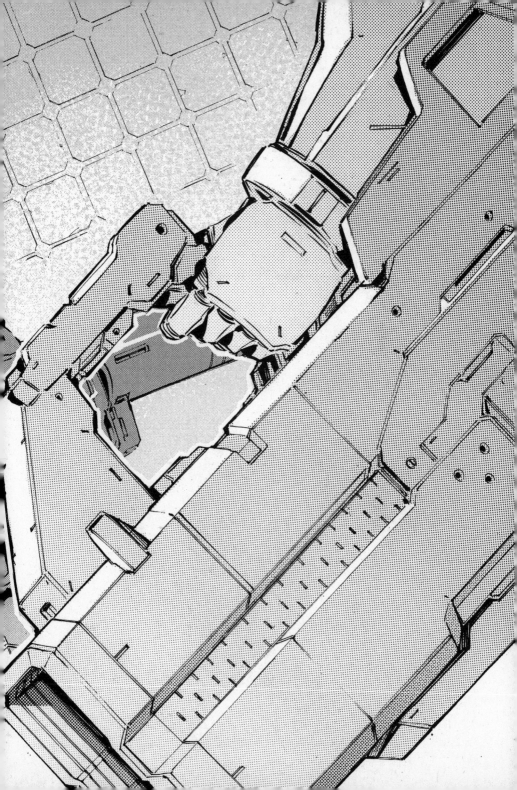

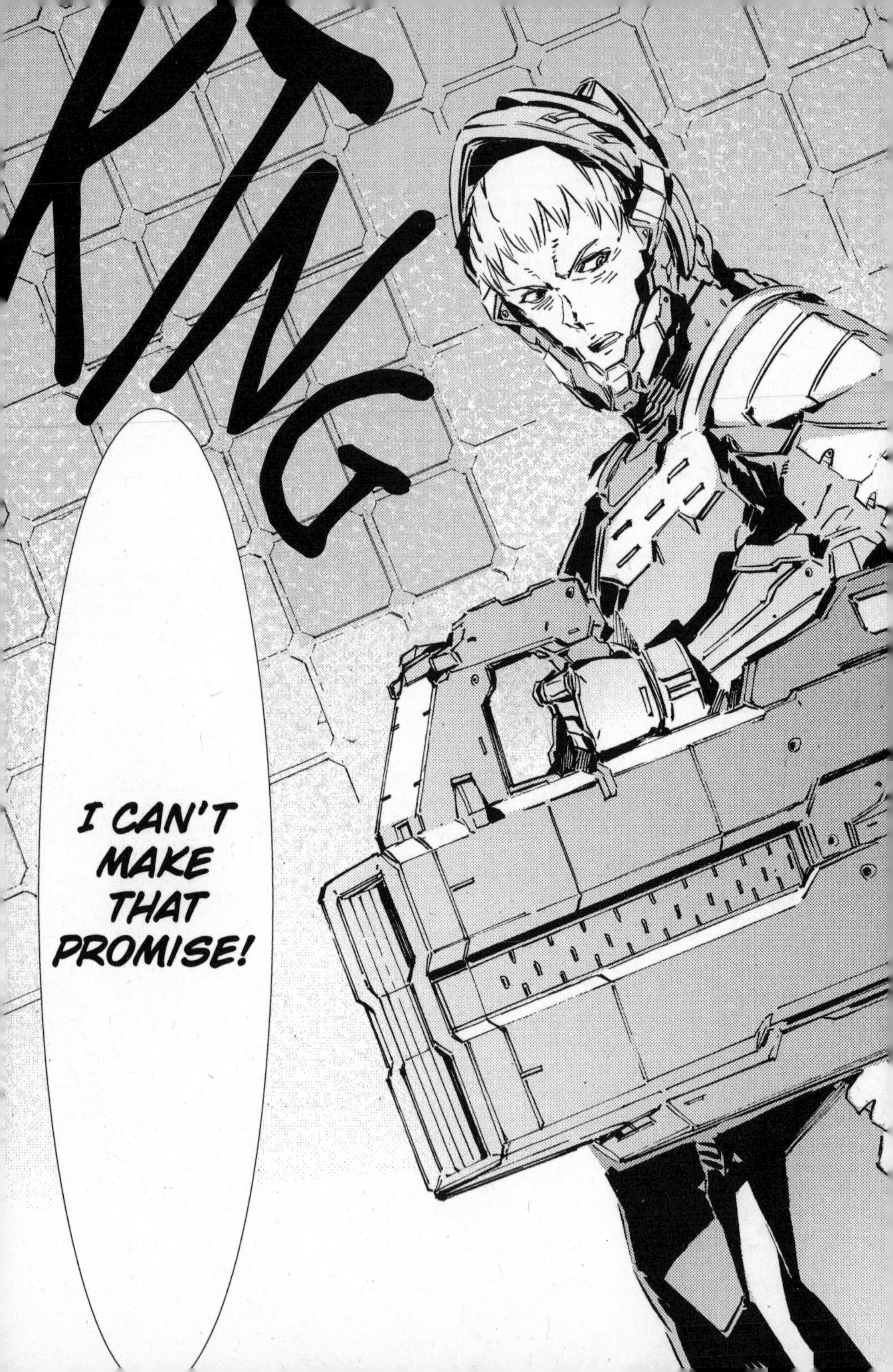
KING
I CAN'T MAKE THAT PROMISE!

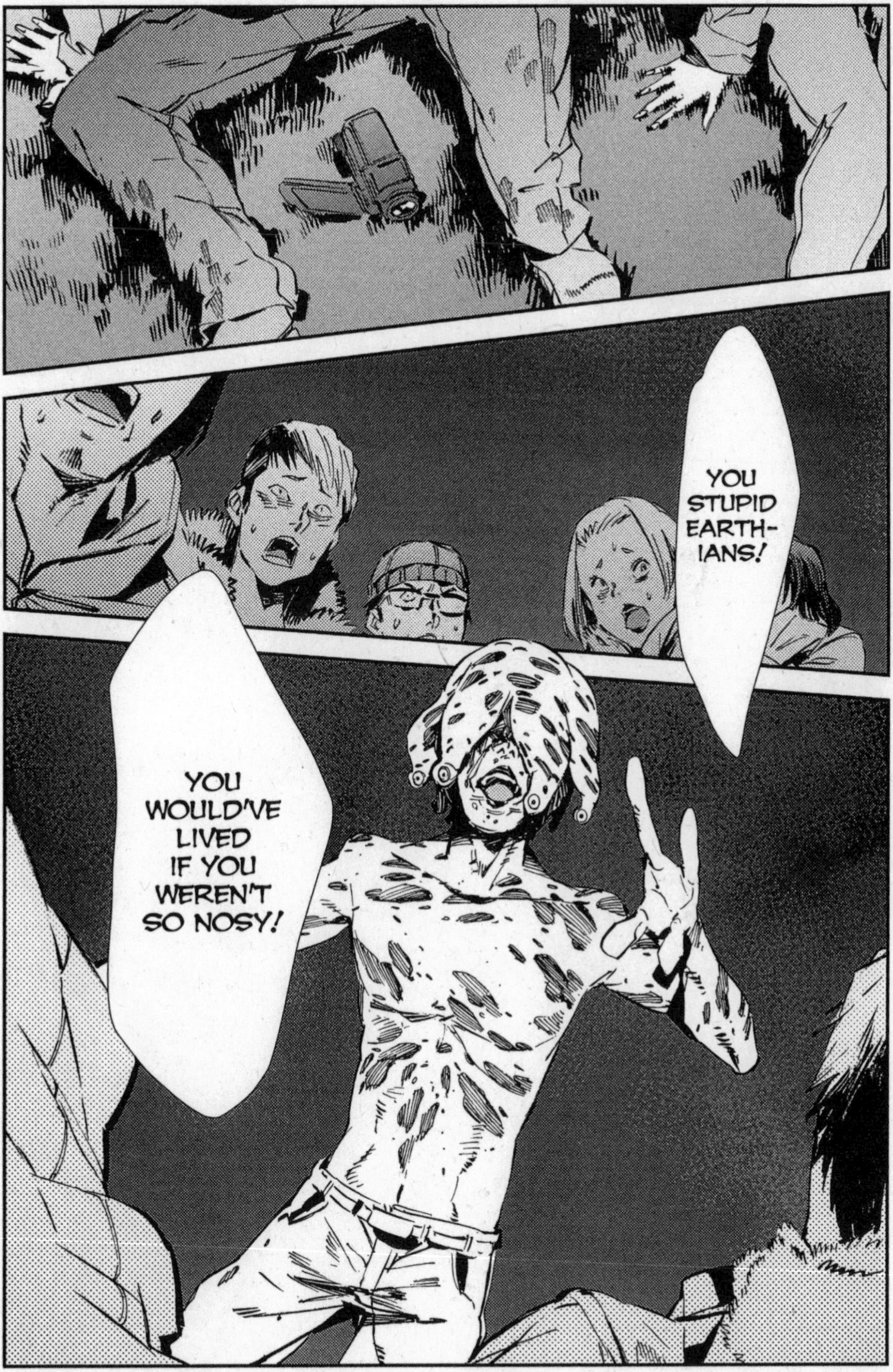
YOU STUPID EARTH-IANS!
YOU WOULD'VE LIVED IF YOU WEREN'T SO NOSY!

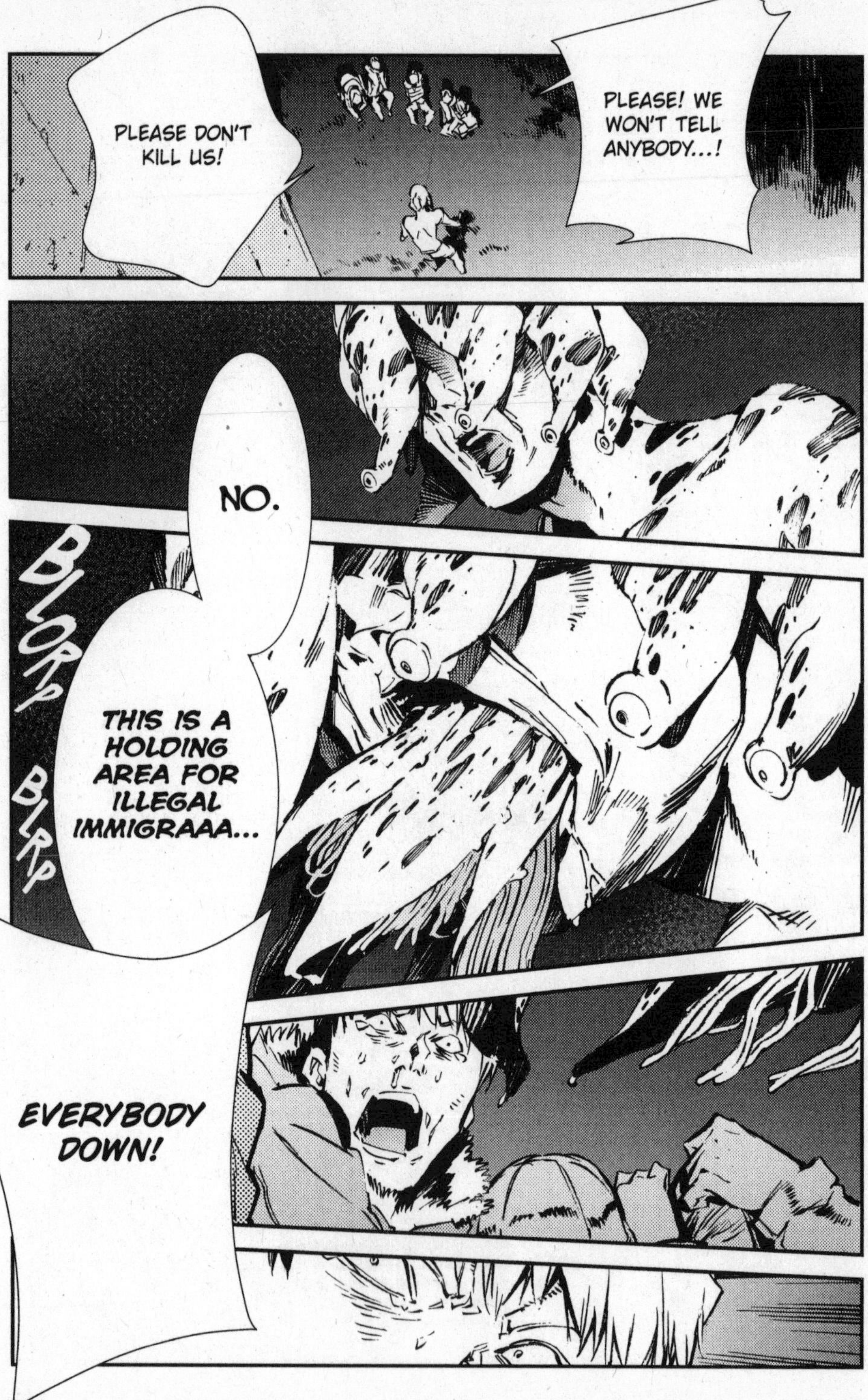
PLEASE! WE WON'T TELL ANYBODY...!
PLEASE DON'T KILL US!
NO.
BLORP BLRP
THIS IS A HOLDING AREA FOR ILLEGAL IMMIGRAAA...
EVERYBODY DOWN!

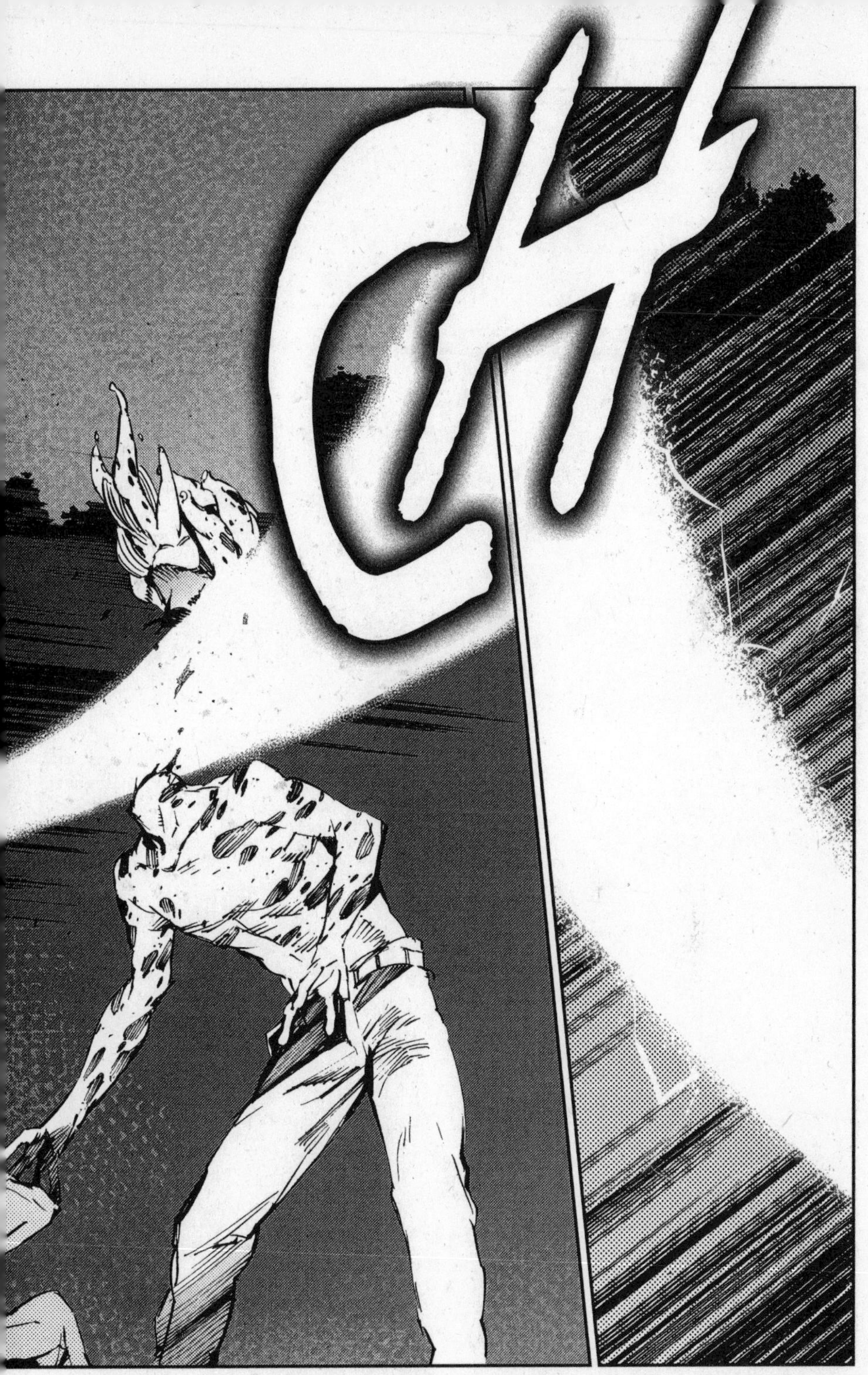
CH

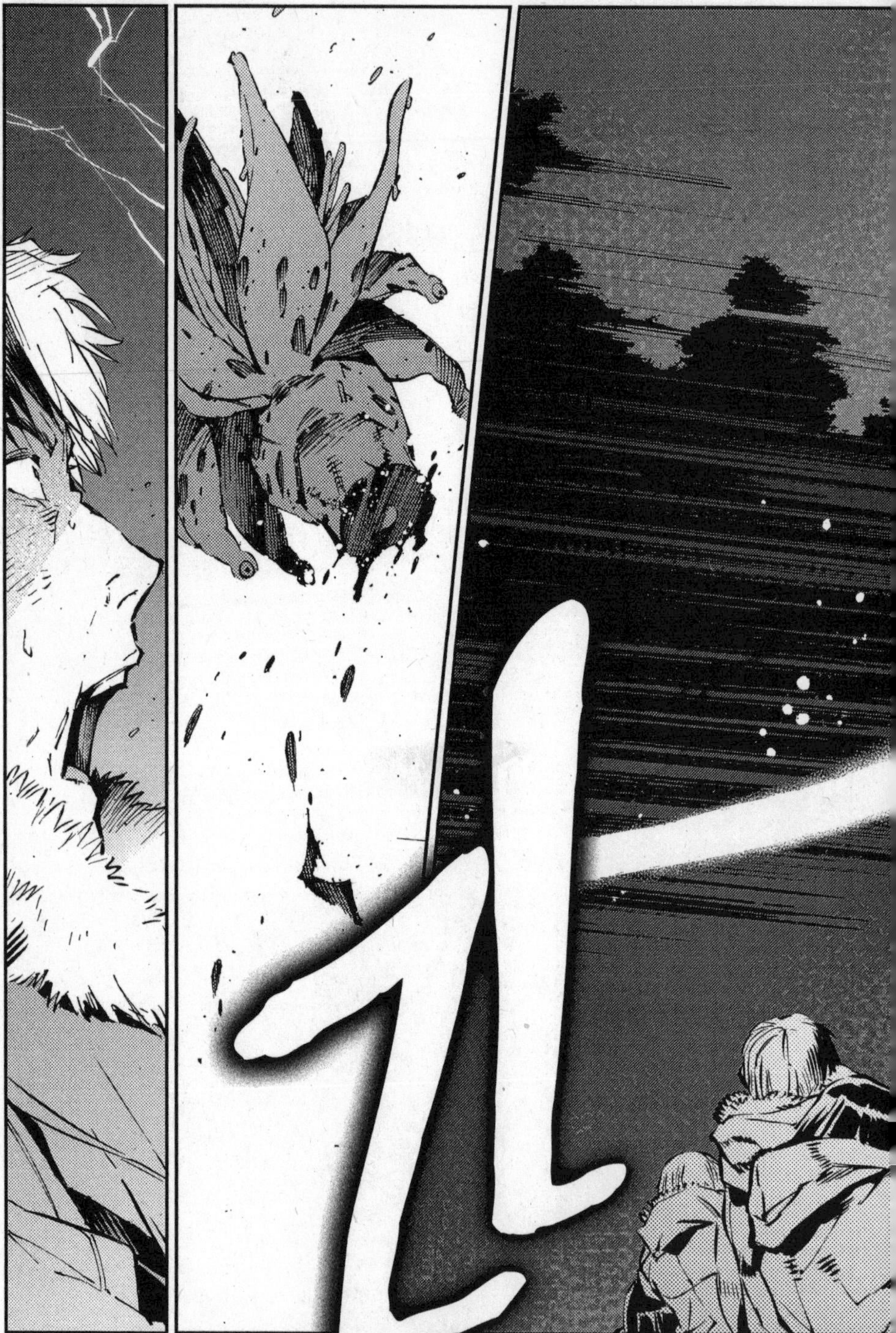

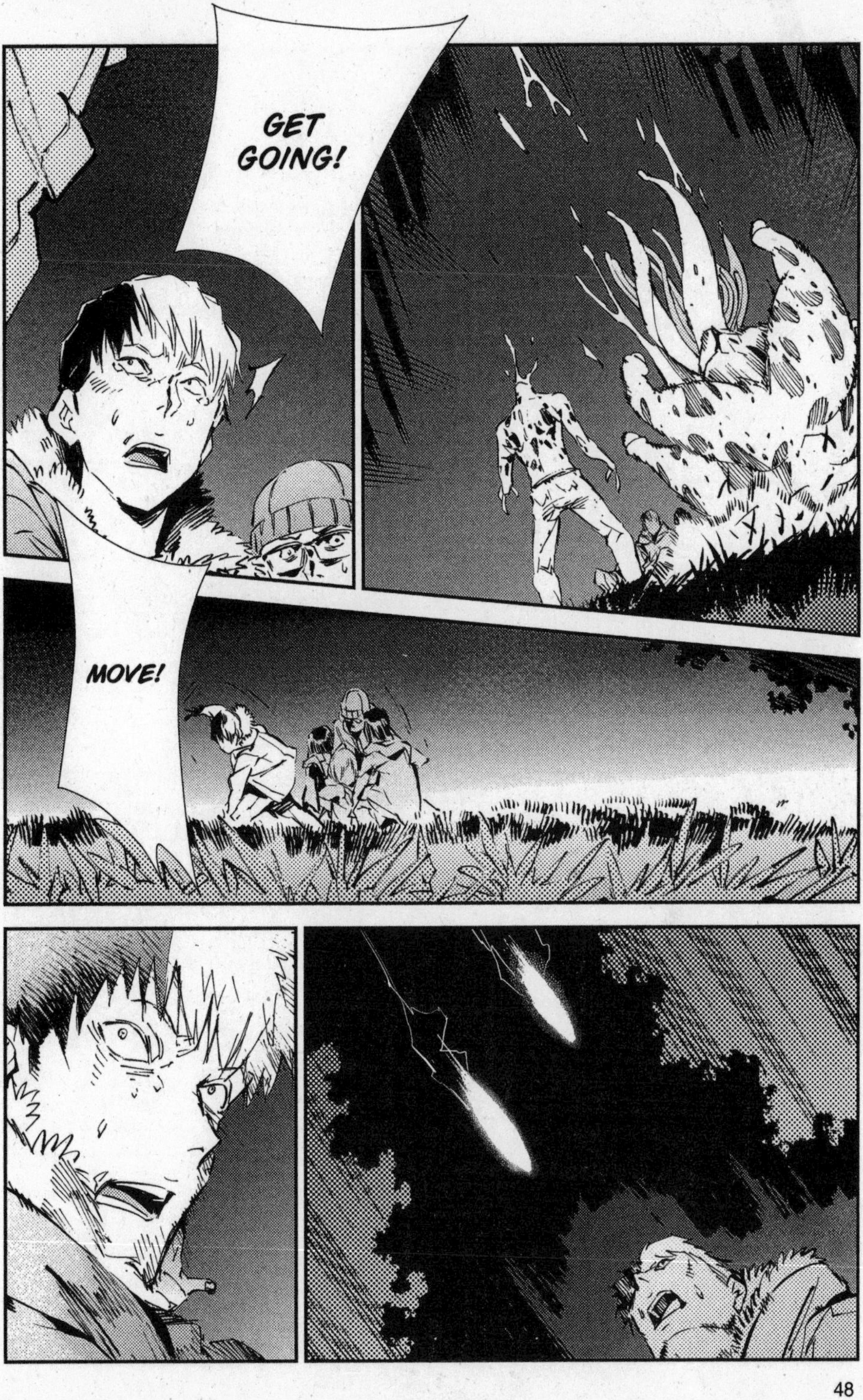
GET GOING!
MOVE!

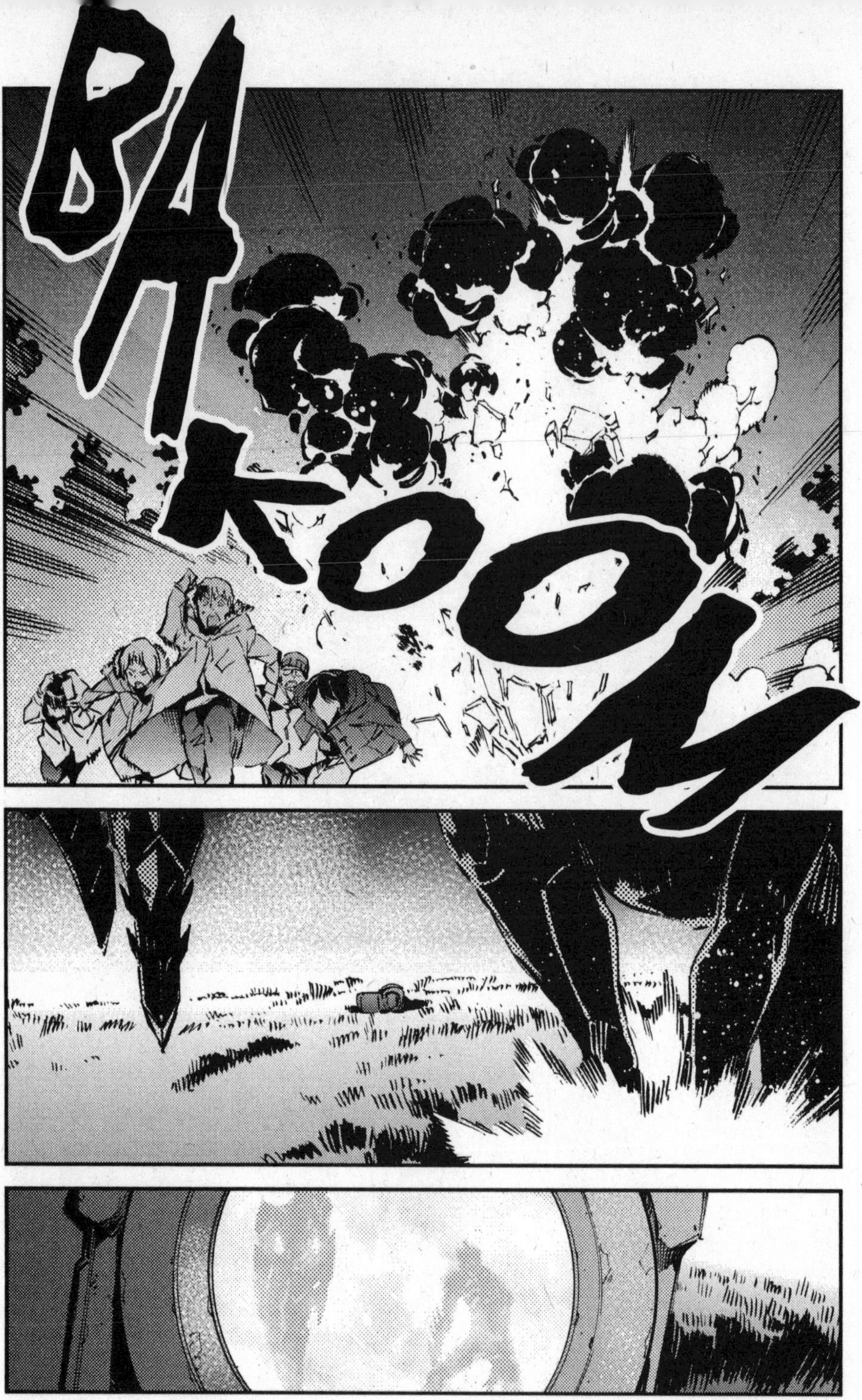
BA-KOOOM

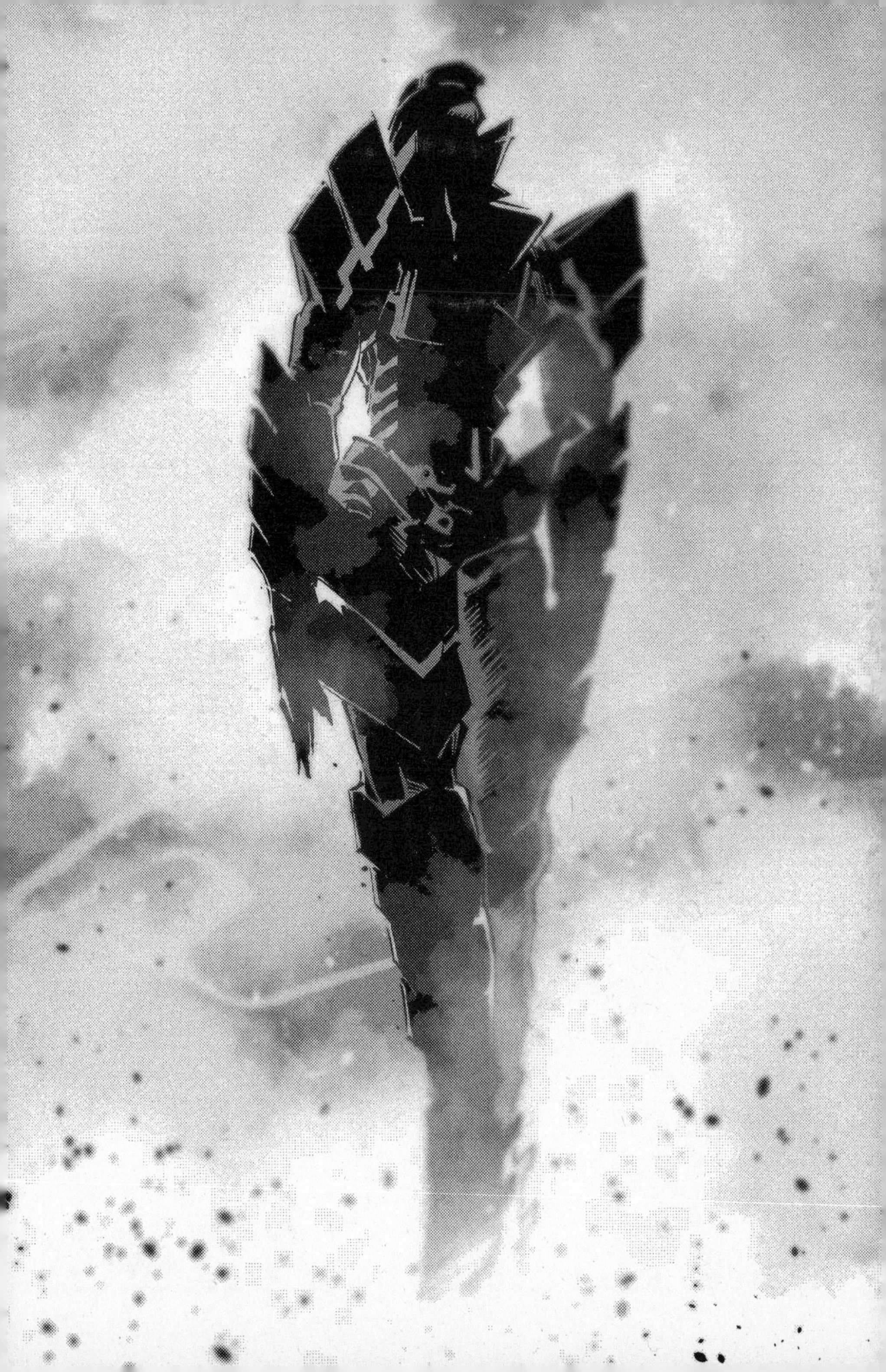

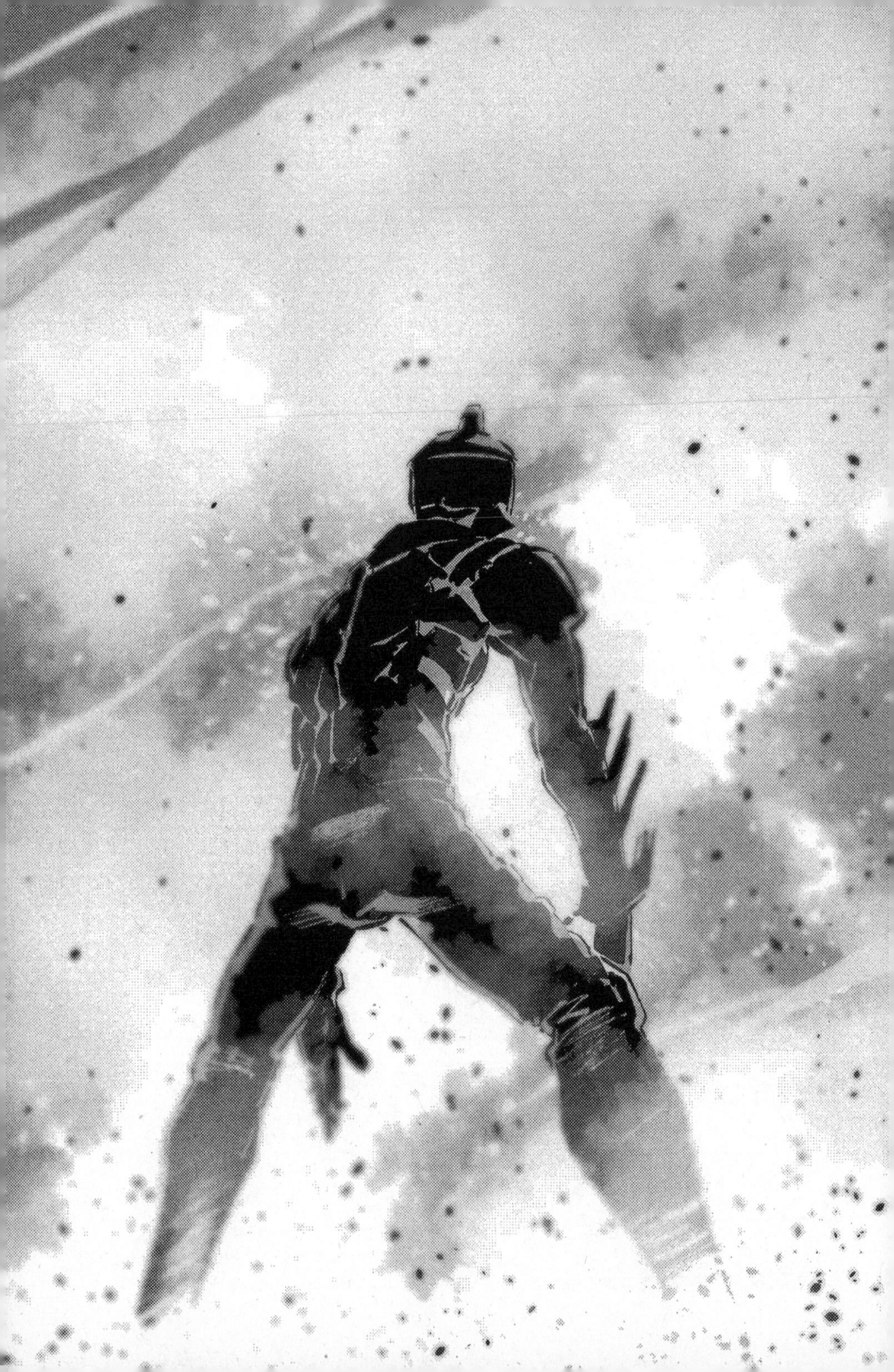

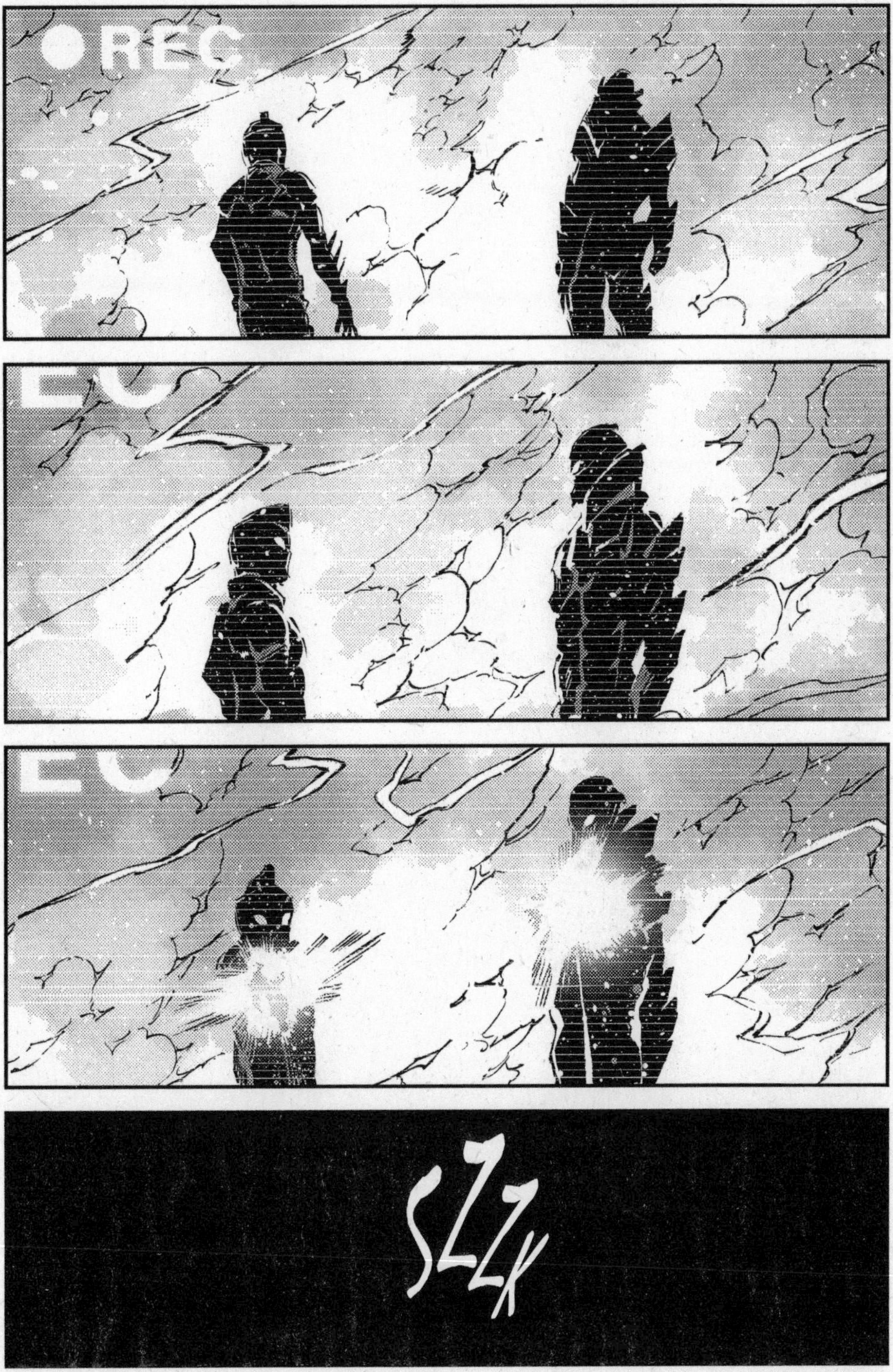
REC
EC
EC
SZZK

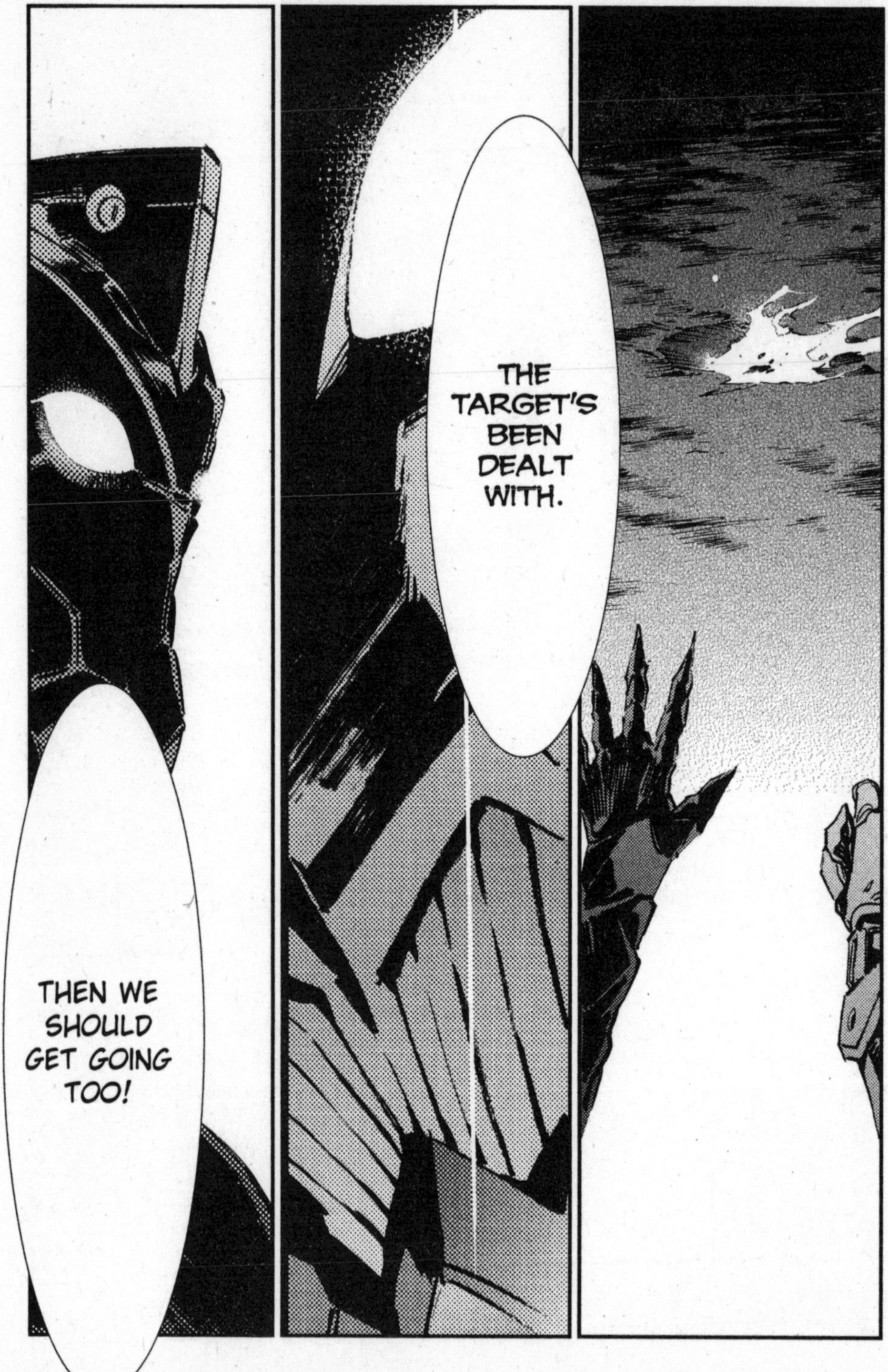
THE TARGET'S BEEN DEALT WITH.
THEN WE SHOULD GET GOING TOO!

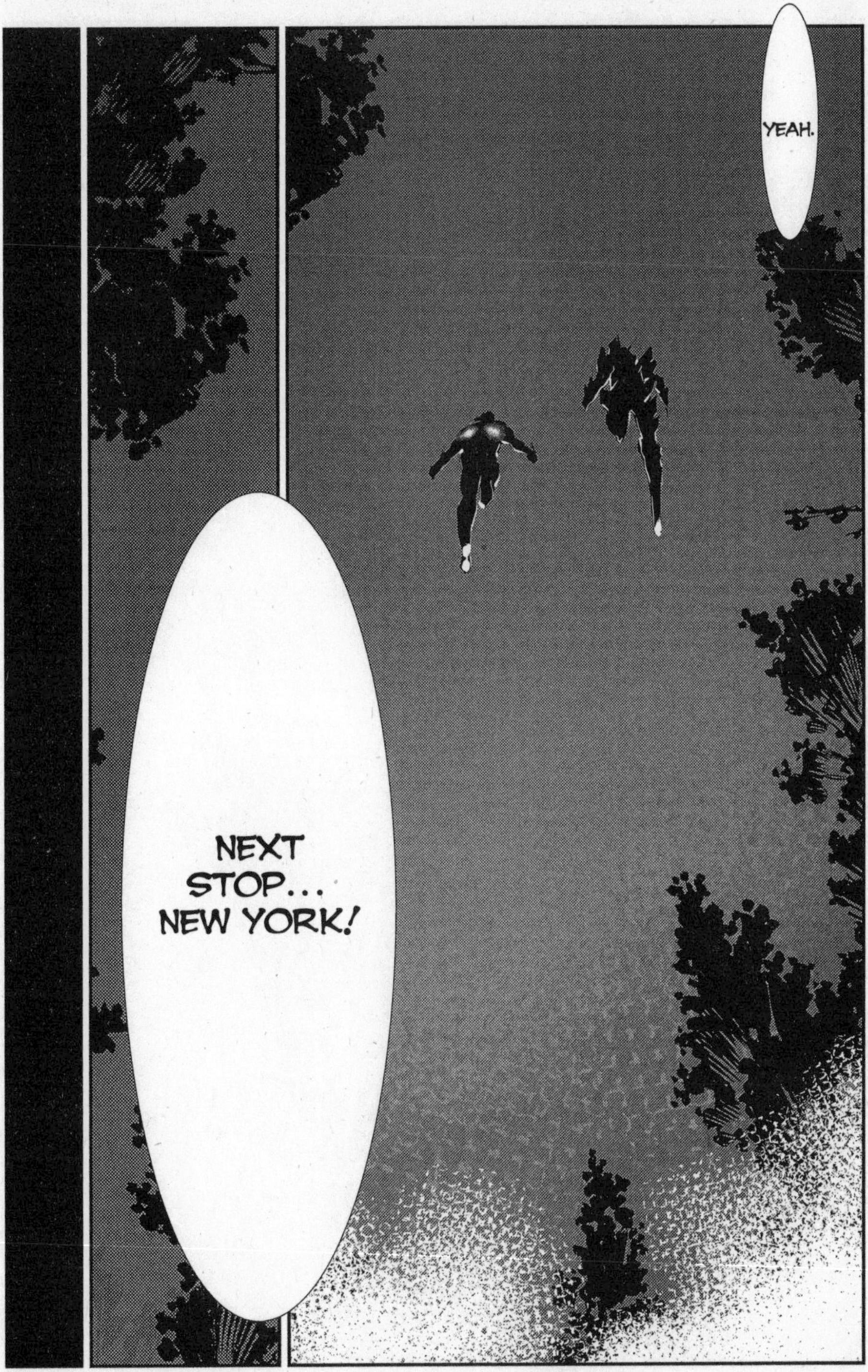
YEAH.
NEXT STOP... NEW YORK!

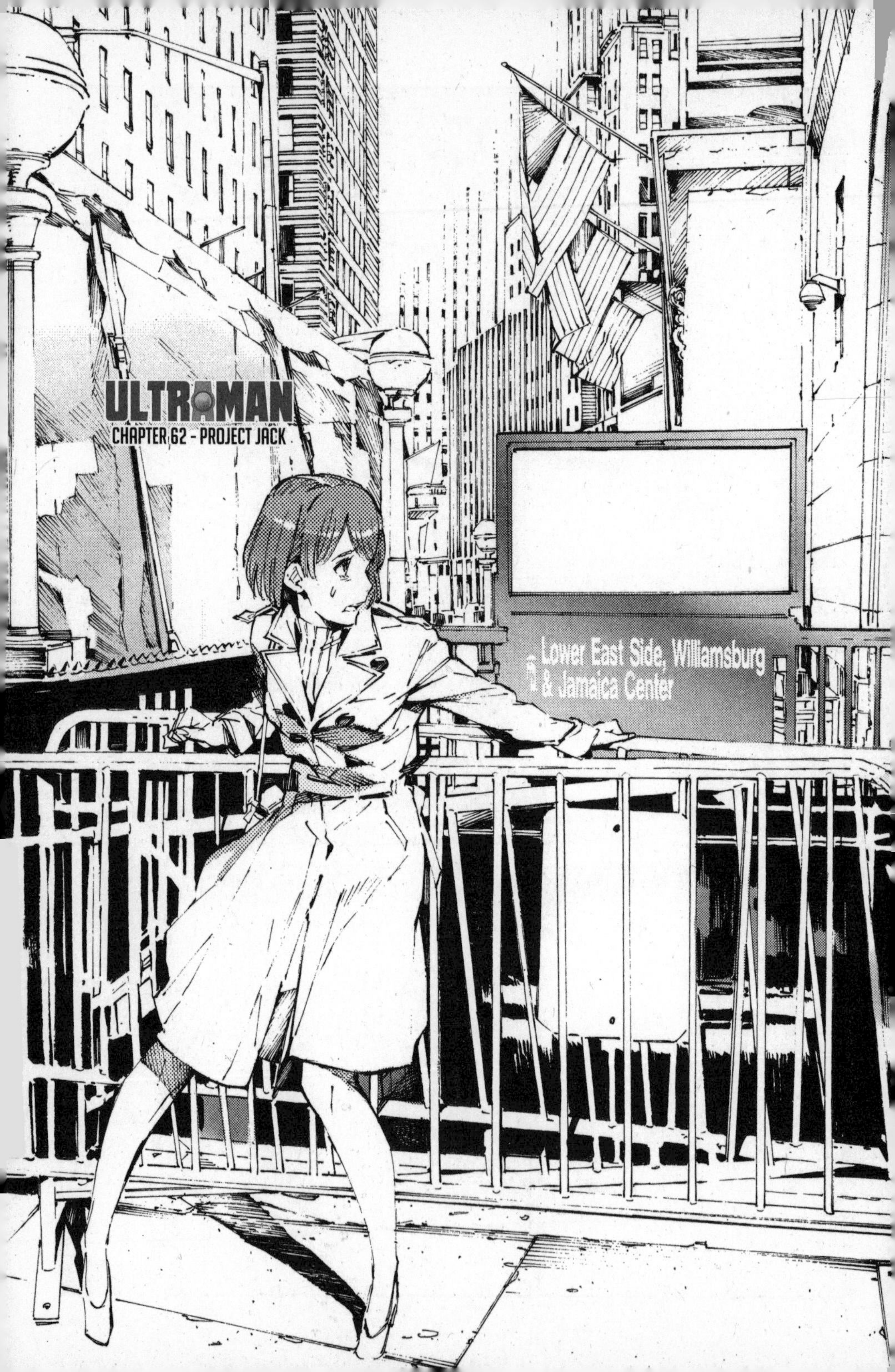
ULTRAMAN
CHAPTER 62 - PROJECT JACK
Lower East Side, Williamsburg
& Jamaica Center

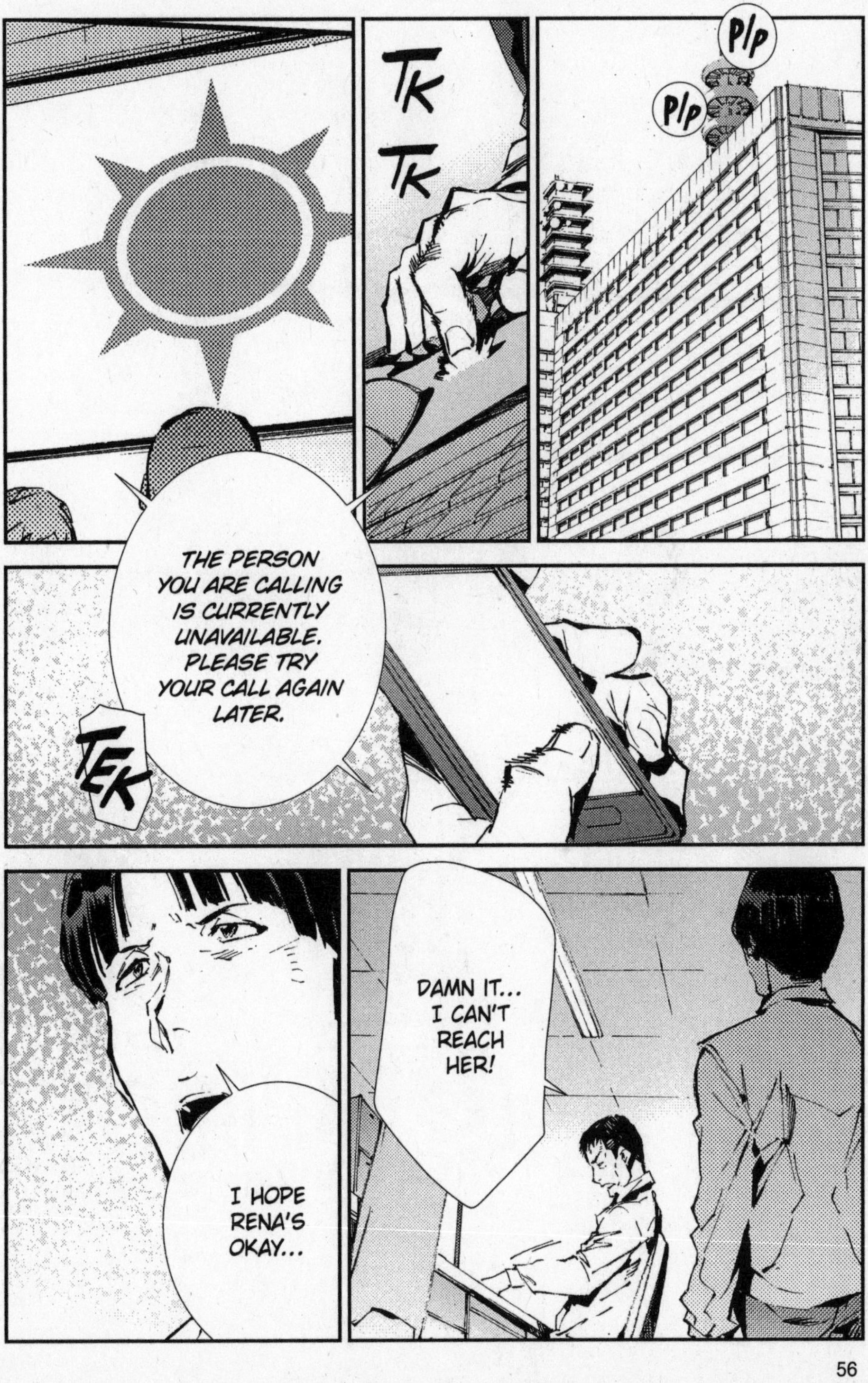
P/P
P/P
TK
TK
THE PERSON YOU ARE CALLING IS CURRENTLY UNAVAILABLE. PLEASE TRY YOUR CALL AGAIN LATER.
TEK
DAMN IT... I CAN'T REACH HER!
I HOPE RENA'S OKAY...

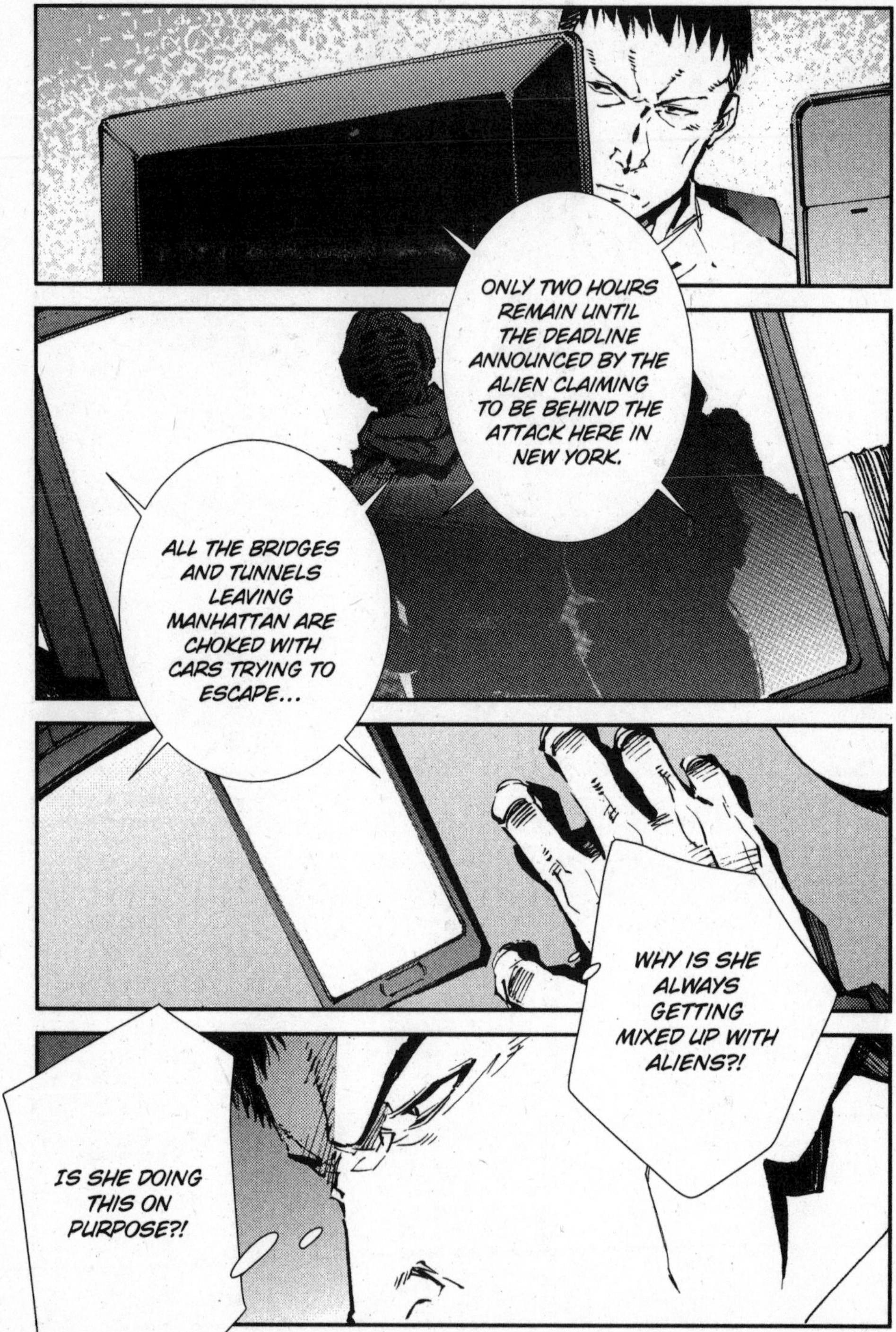
ONLY TWO HOURS REMAIN UNTIL THE DEADLINE ANNOUNCED BY THE ALIEN CLAIMING TO BE BEHIND THE ATTACK HERE IN NEW YORK.
ALL THE BRIDGES AND TUNNELS LEAVING MANHATTAN ARE CHOKED WITH CARS TRYING TO ESCAPE...
WHY IS SHE ALWAYS GETTING MIXED UP WITH ALIENS?!
IS SHE DOING THIS ON PURPOSE?!

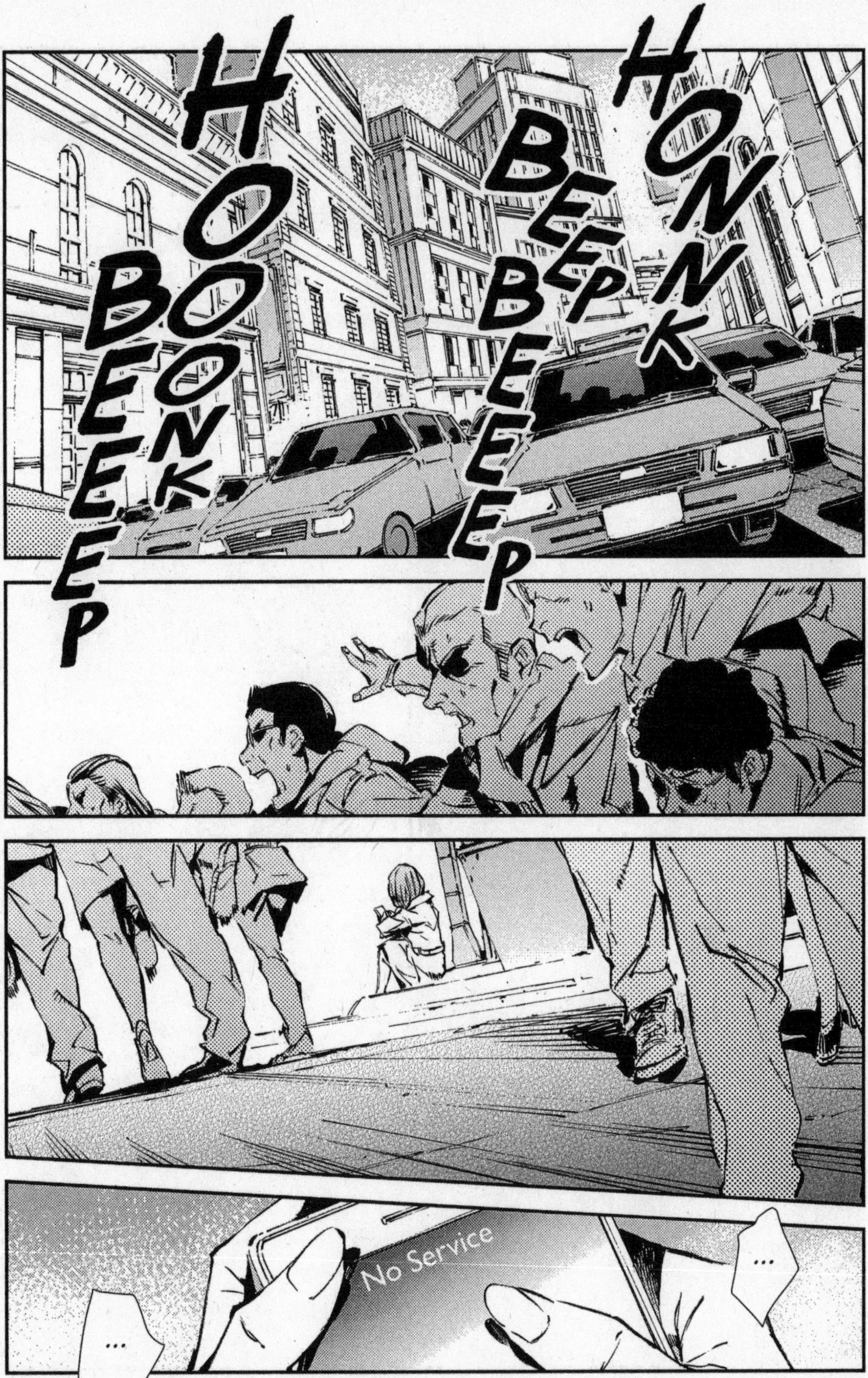
HONNK
BEEP
BEEEEEP
HOONK
BEEEEEP
No Service
...
...

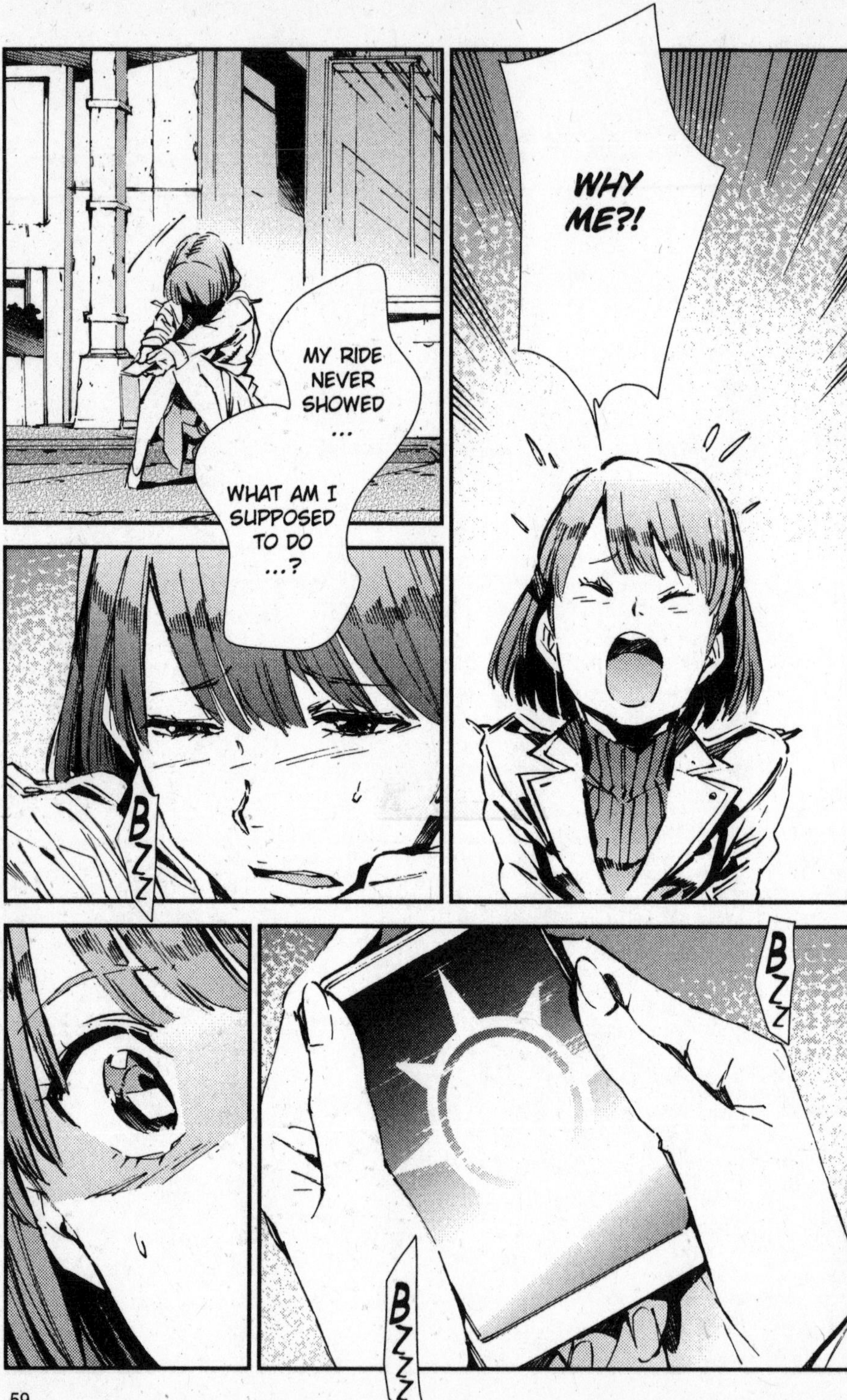
WHY ME?!
MY RIDE NEVER SHOWED ...
WHAT AM I SUPPOSED TO DO ...?
BZZZ
BZZ
BZZZ

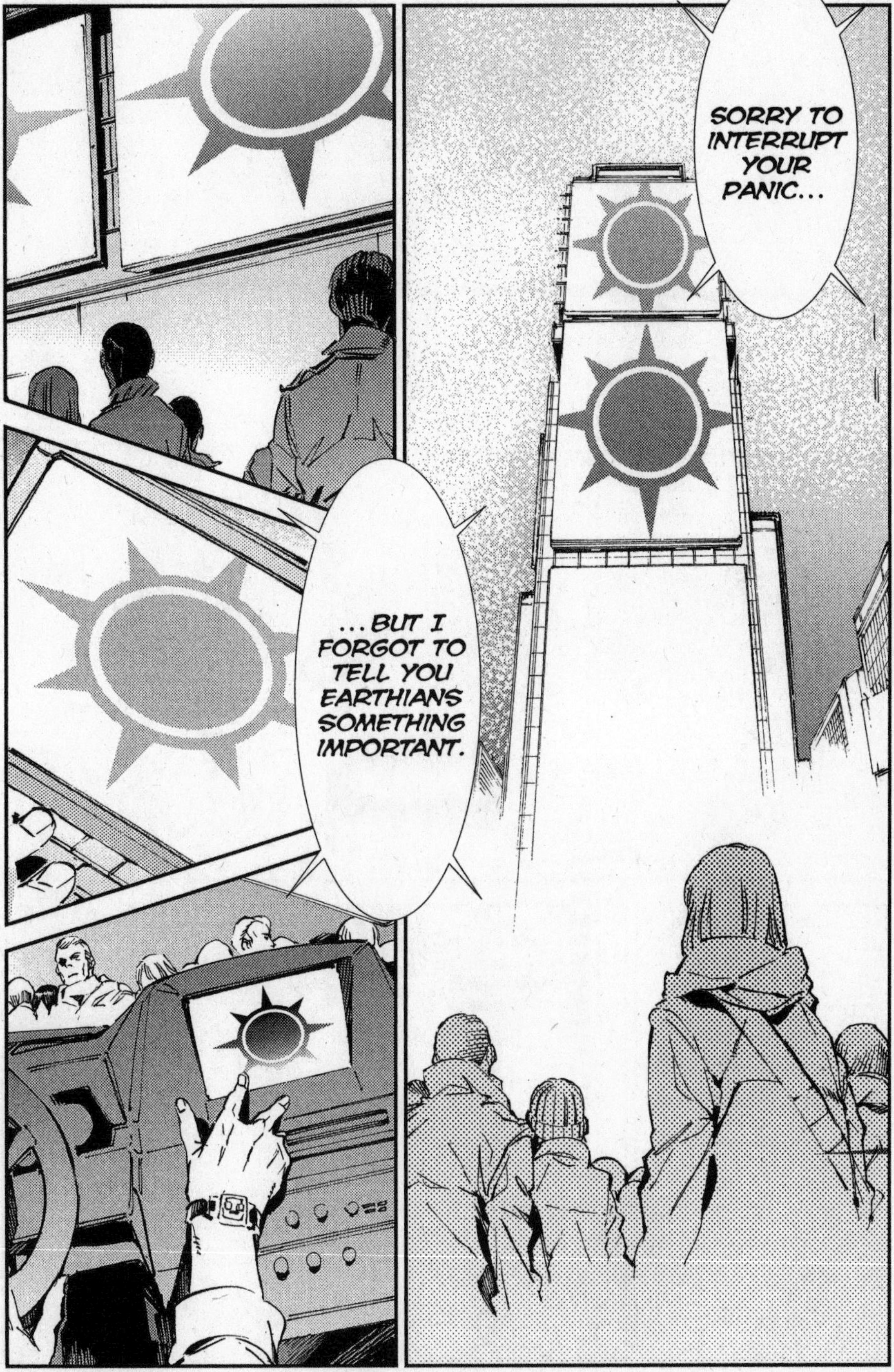
SORRY TO INTERRUPT YOUR PANIC...
...BUT I FORGOT TO TELL YOU EARTHIANS SOMETHING IMPORTANT.

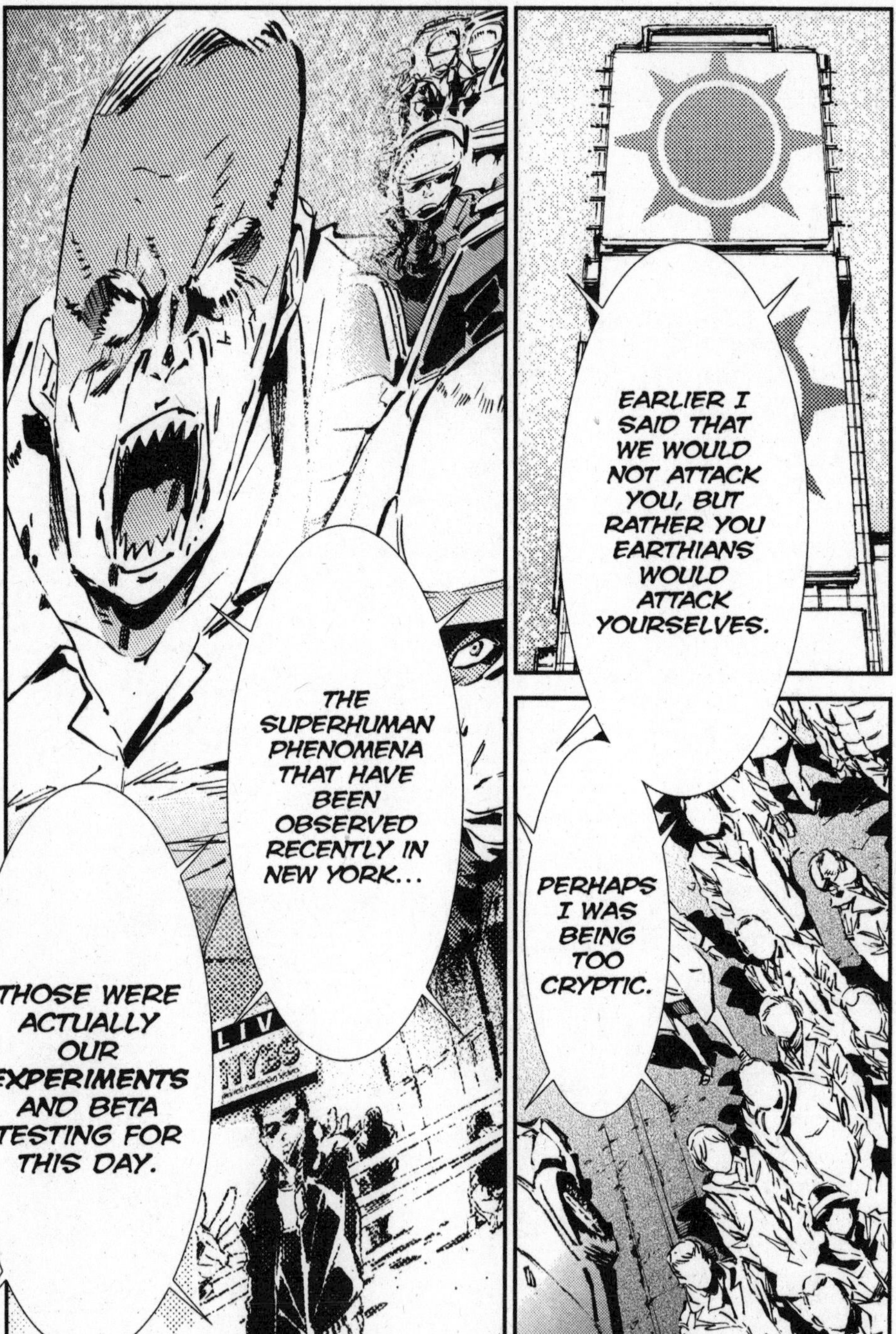
EARLIER I SAID THAT WE WOULD NOT ATTACK YOU, BUT RATHER YOU EARTHIANS WOULD ATTACK YOURSELVES.
PERHAPS I WAS BEING TOO CRYPTIC.
THE SUPERHUMAN PHENOMENA THAT HAVE BEEN OBSERVED RECENTLY IN NEW YORK...
THOSE WERE ACTUALLY OUR EXPERIMENTS AND BETA TESTING FOR THIS DAY.

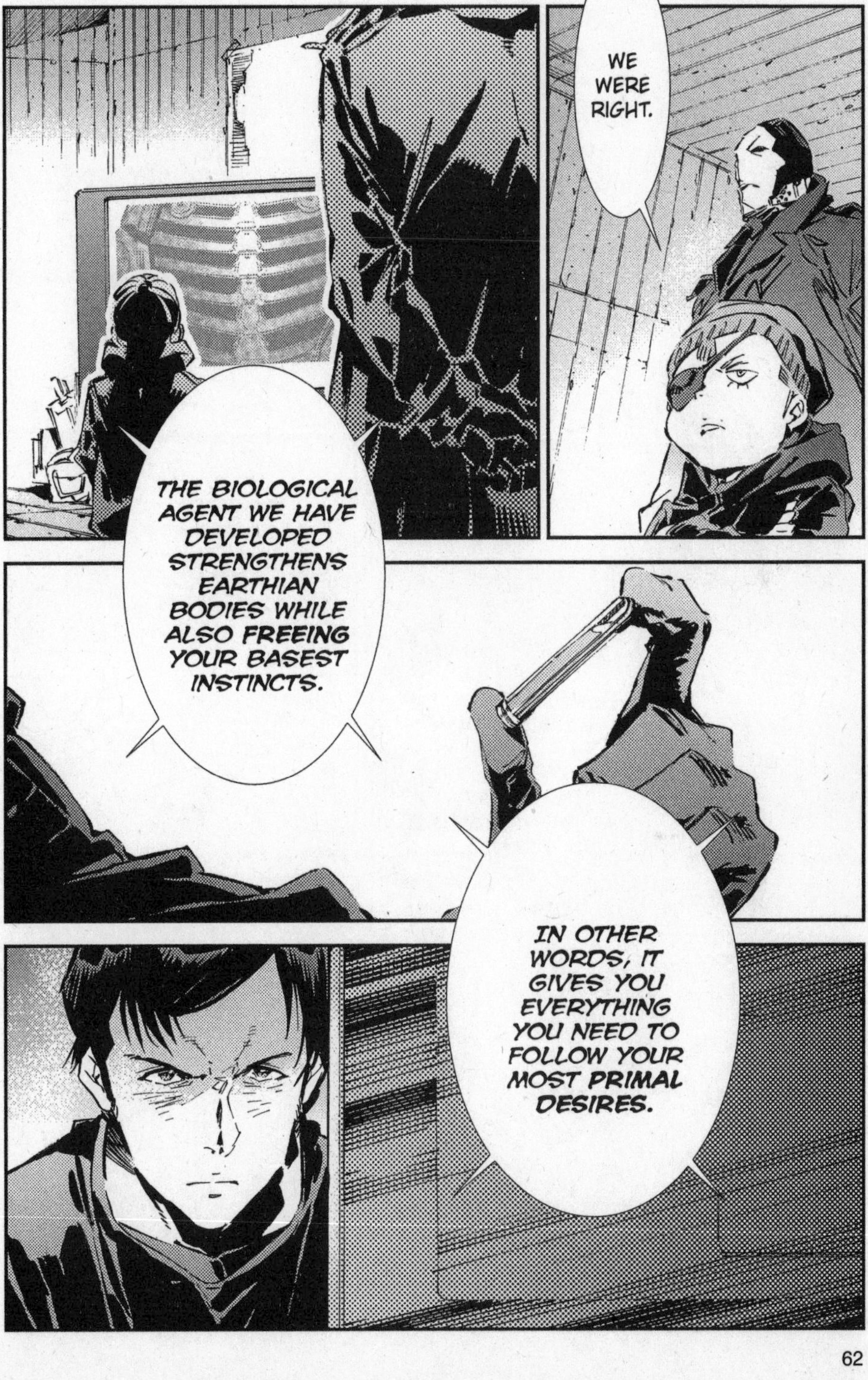
WE WERE RIGHT.
THE BIOLOGICAL AGENT WE HAVE DEVELOPED STRENGTHENS EARTHIAN BODIES WHILE ALSO FREEING YOUR BASEST INSTINCTS.
IN OTHER WORDS, IT GIVES YOU EVERYTHING YOU NEED TO FOLLOW YOUR MOST PRIMAL DESIRES.

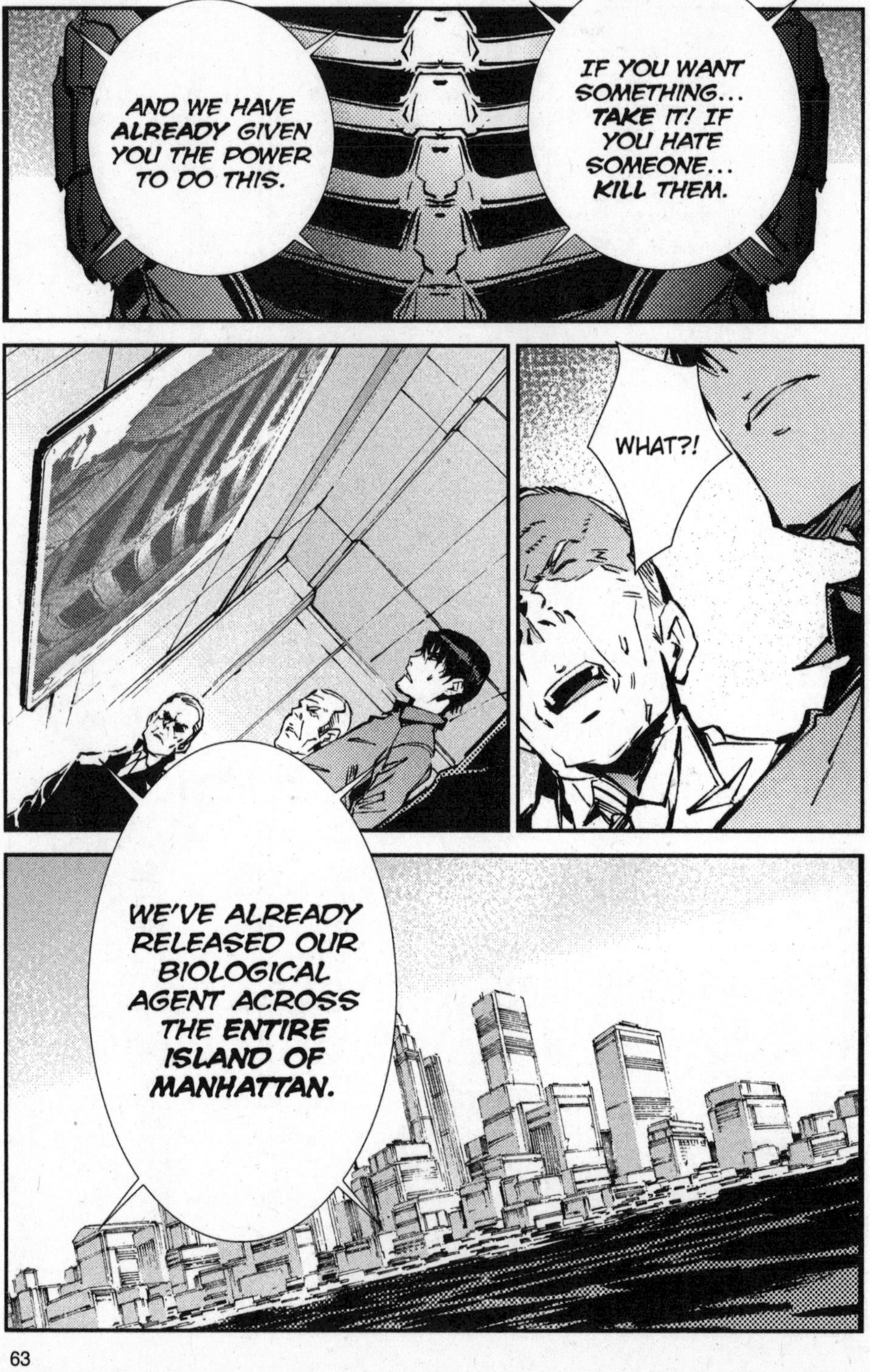
IF YOU WANT SOMETHING... TAKE IT! IF YOU HATE SOMEONE... KILL THEM.
AND WE HAVE ALREADY GIVEN YOU THE POWER TO DO THIS.
WHAT?!
WE'VE ALREADY RELEASED OUR BIOLOGICAL AGENT ACROSS THE ENTIRE ISLAND OF MANHATTAN.

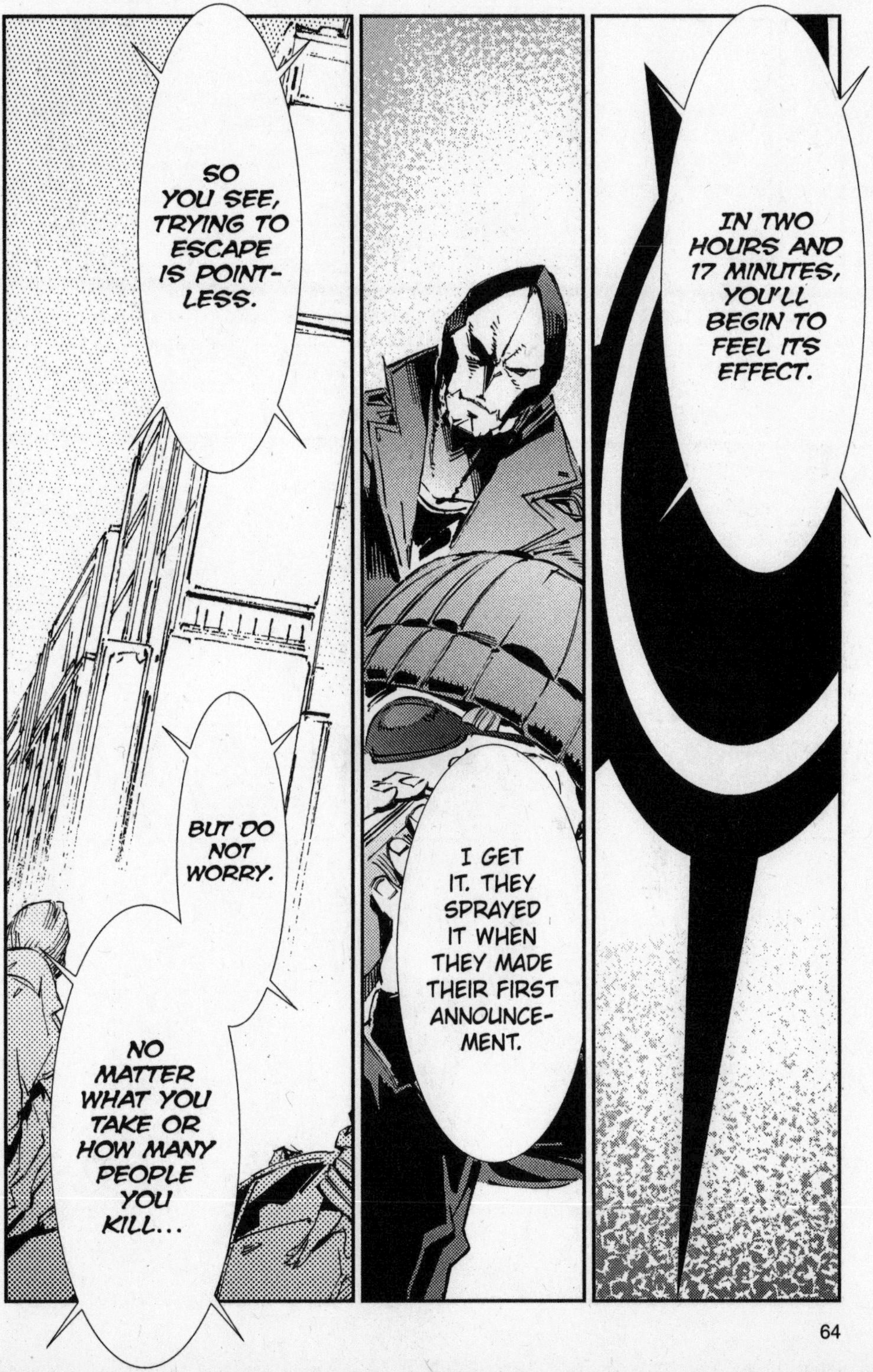
IN TWO HOURS AND 17 MINUTES, YOU'LL BEGIN TO FEEL ITS EFFECT.
I GET IT. THEY SPRAYED IT WHEN THEY MADE THEIR FIRST ANNOUNCE-MENT.
SO YOU SEE, TRYING TO ESCAPE IS POINT-LESS.
BUT DO NOT WORRY.
NO MATTER WHAT YOU TAKE OR HOW MANY PEOPLE YOU KILL...

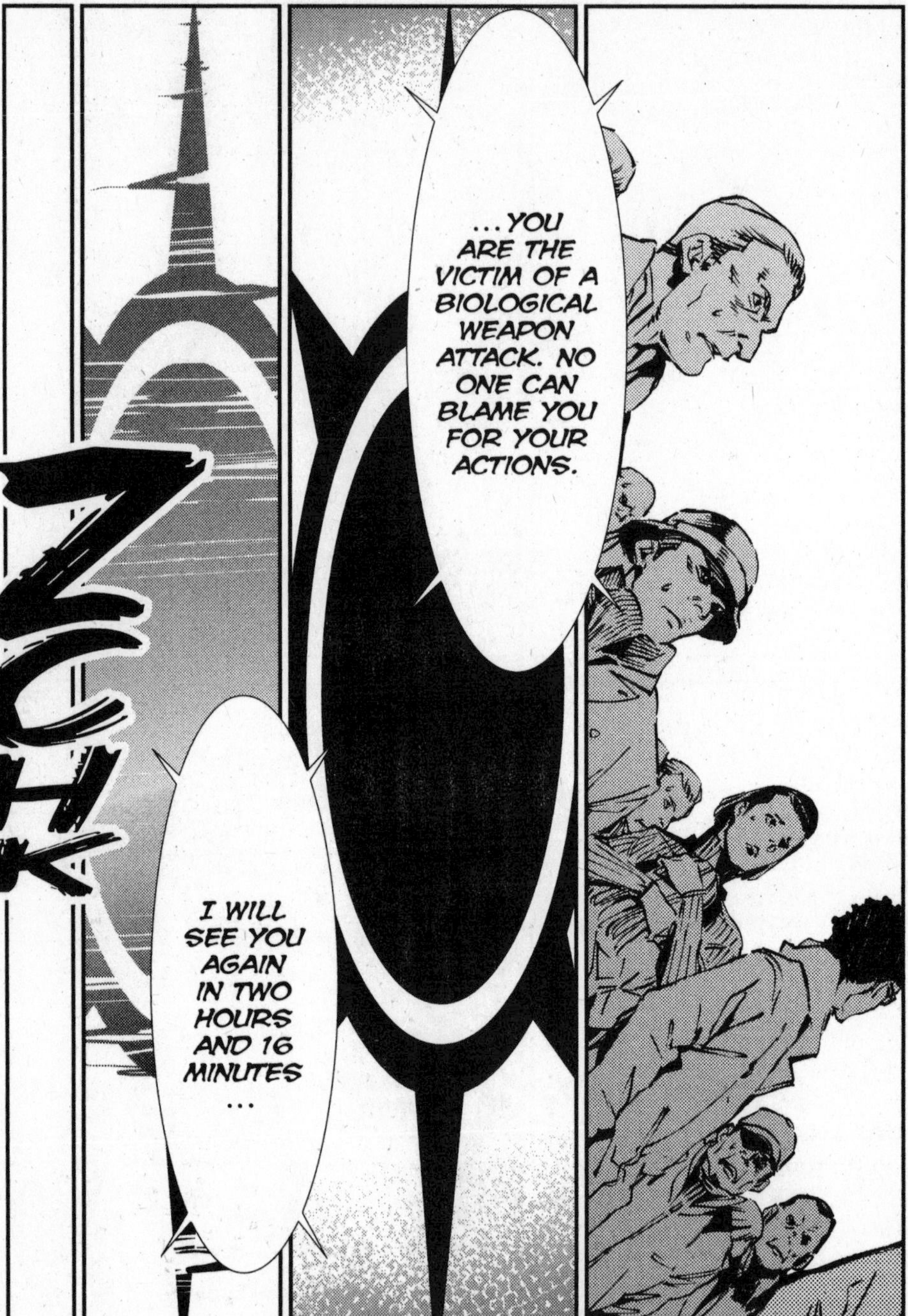
...YOU ARE THE VICTIM OF A BIOLOGICAL WEAPON ATTACK. NO ONE CAN BLAME YOU FOR YOUR ACTIONS.
I WILL SEE YOU AGAIN IN TWO HOURS AND 16 MINUTES ...

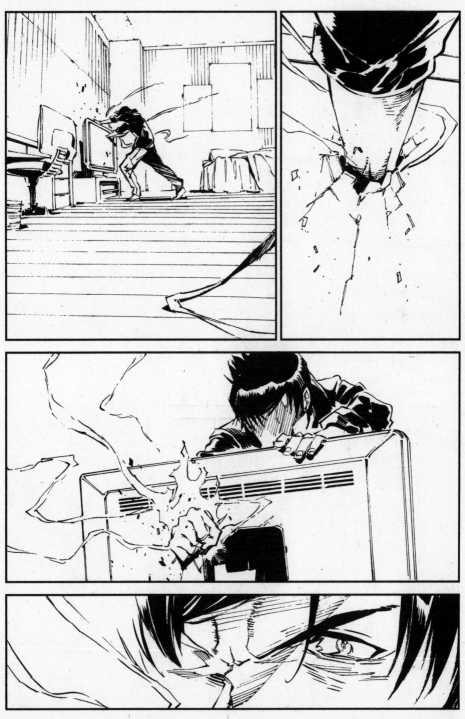

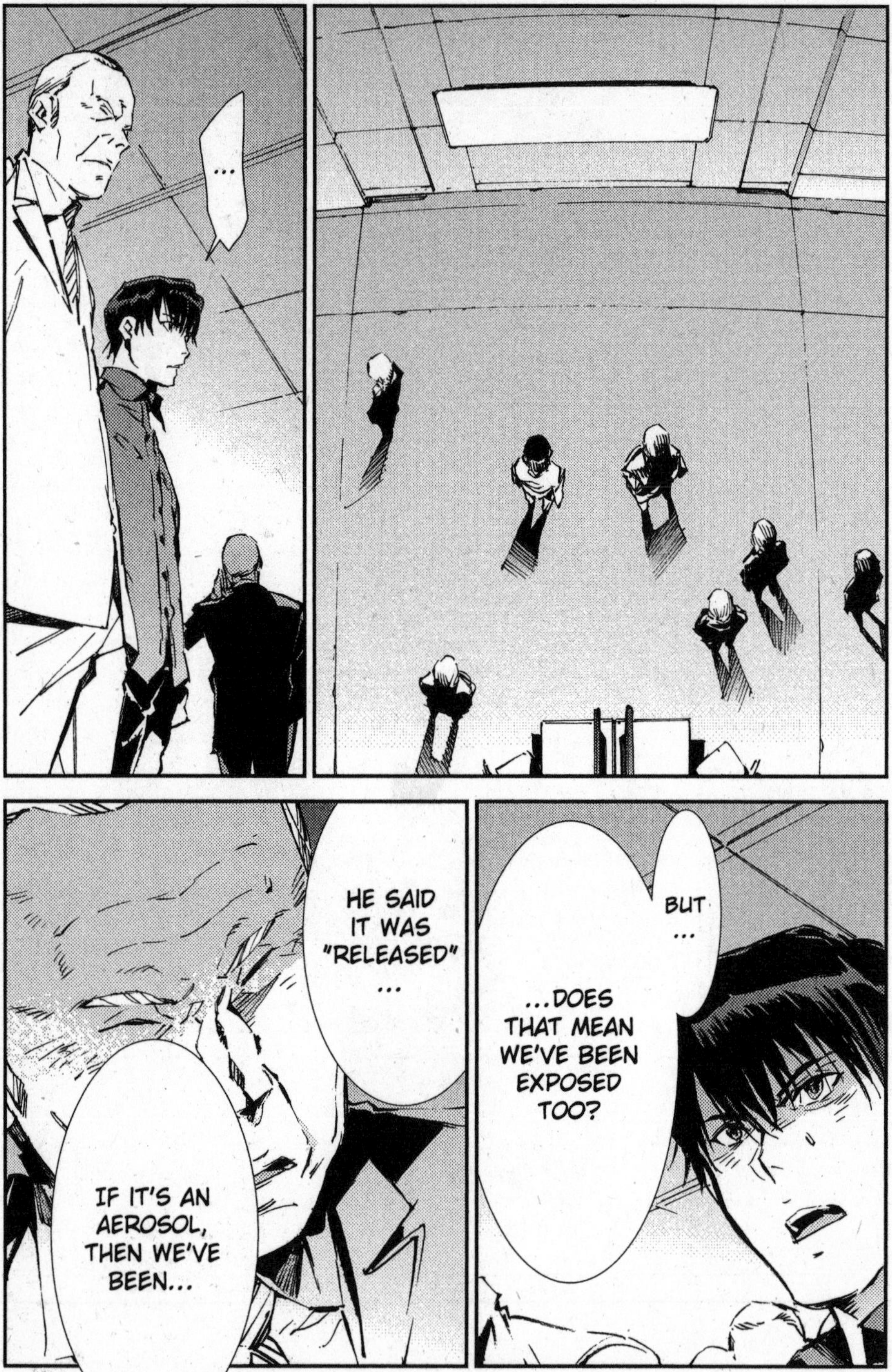
...
BUT...
...DOES THAT MEAN WE'VE BEEN EXPOSED TOO?
HE SAID IT WAS "RELEASED"...
IF IT'S AN AEROSOL, THEN WE'VE BEEN...

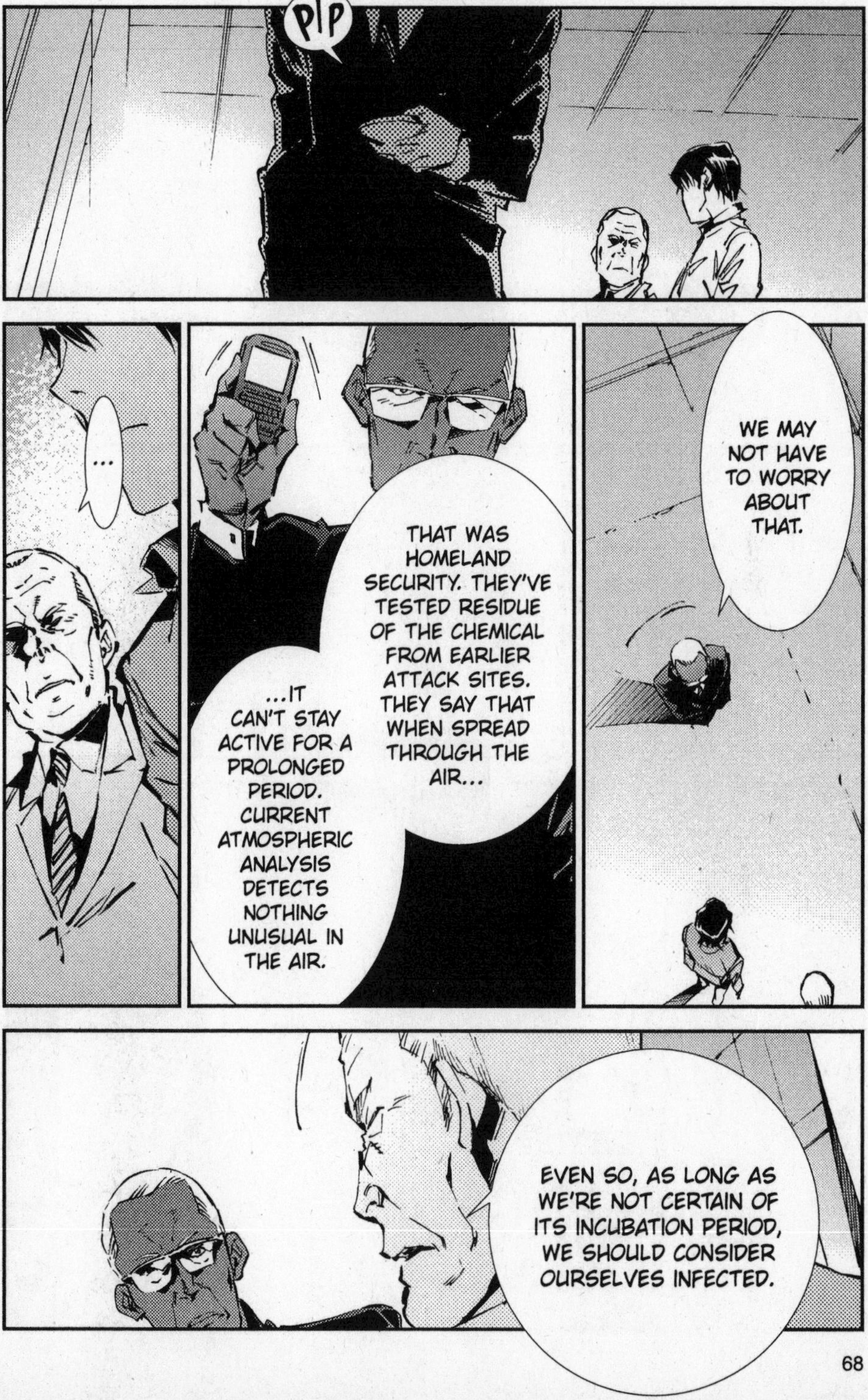
PIP
WE MAY NOT HAVE TO WORRY ABOUT THAT.
THAT WAS HOMELAND SECURITY. THEY'VE TESTED RESIDUE OF THE CHEMICAL FROM EARLIER ATTACK SITES. THEY SAY THAT WHEN SPREAD THROUGH THE AIR...
...IT CAN'T STAY ACTIVE FOR A PROLONGED PERIOD. CURRENT ATMOSPHERIC ANALYSIS DETECTS NOTHING UNUSUAL IN THE AIR.
...
EVEN SO, AS LONG AS WE'RE NOT CERTAIN OF ITS INCUBATION PERIOD, WE SHOULD CONSIDER OURSELVES INFECTED.

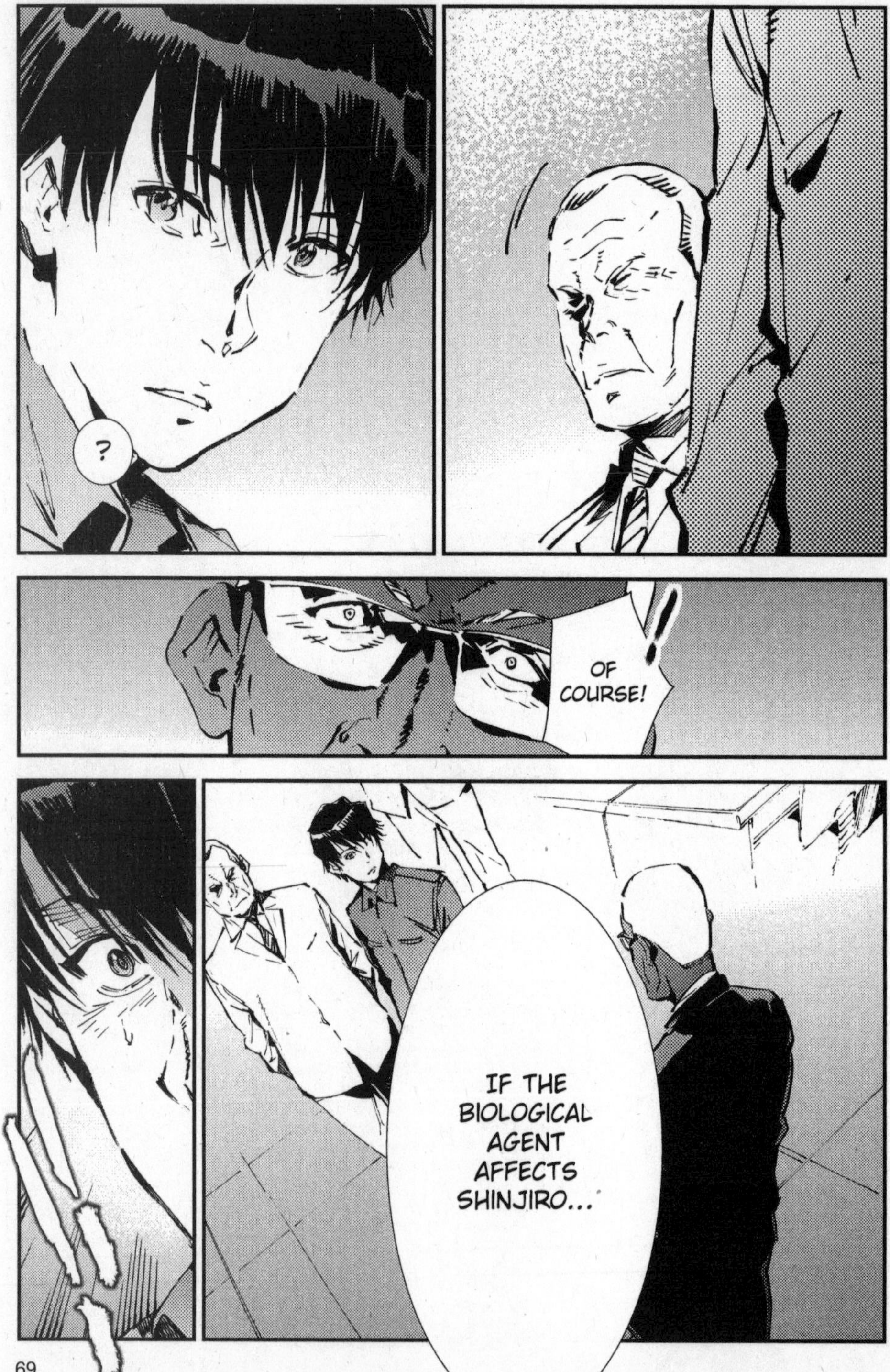
?
OF COURSE!
IF THE BIOLOGICAL AGENT AFFECTS SHINJIRO...

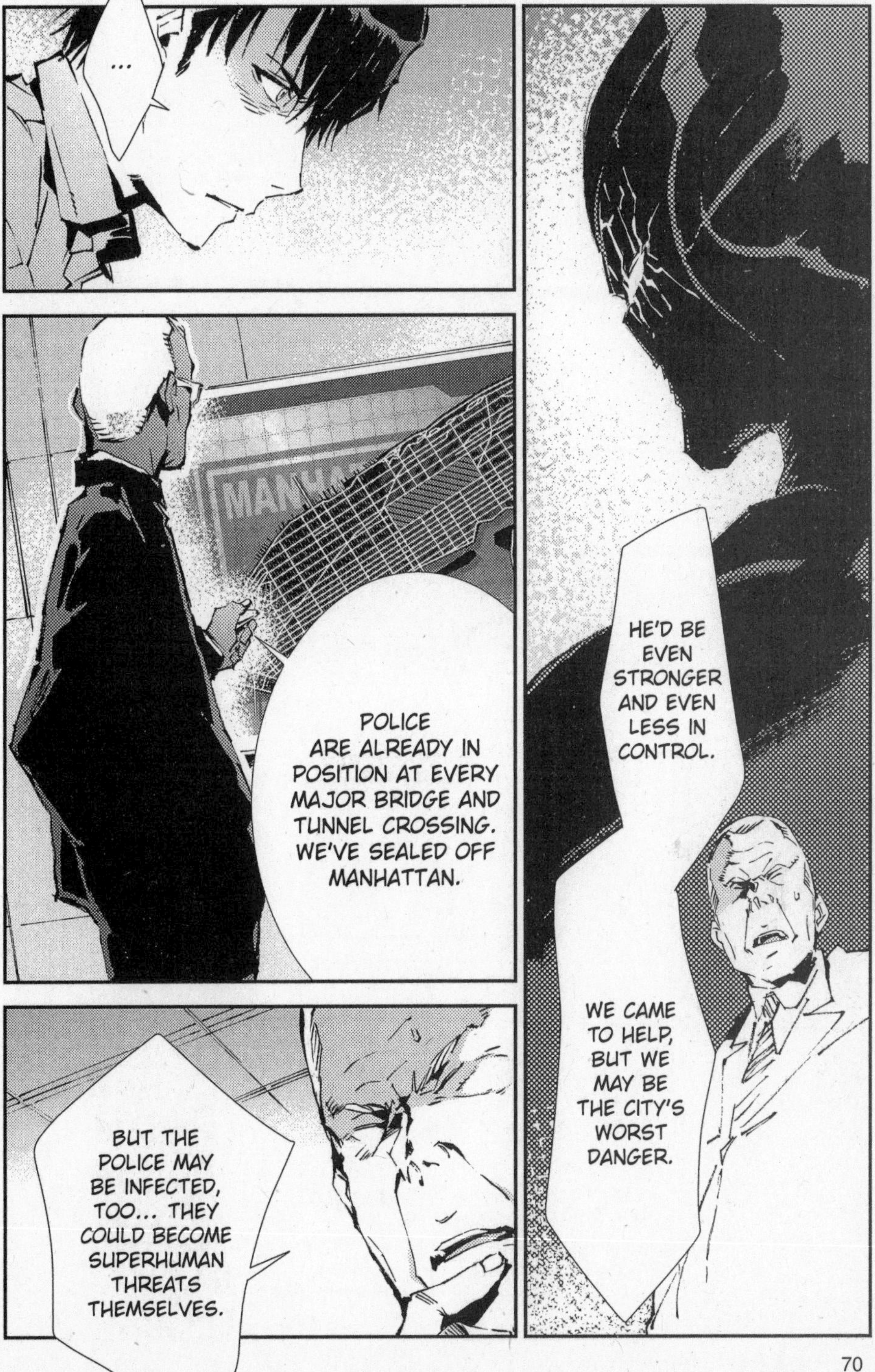
...
POLICE ARE ALREADY IN POSITION AT EVERY MAJOR BRIDGE AND TUNNEL CROSSING. WE'VE SEALED OFF MANHATTAN.
BUT THE POLICE MAY BE INFECTED, TOO... THEY COULD BECOME SUPERHUMAN THREATS THEMSELVES.
HE'D BE EVEN STRONGER AND EVEN LESS IN CONTROL.
WE CAME TO HELP, BUT WE MAY BE THE CITY'S WORST DANGER.

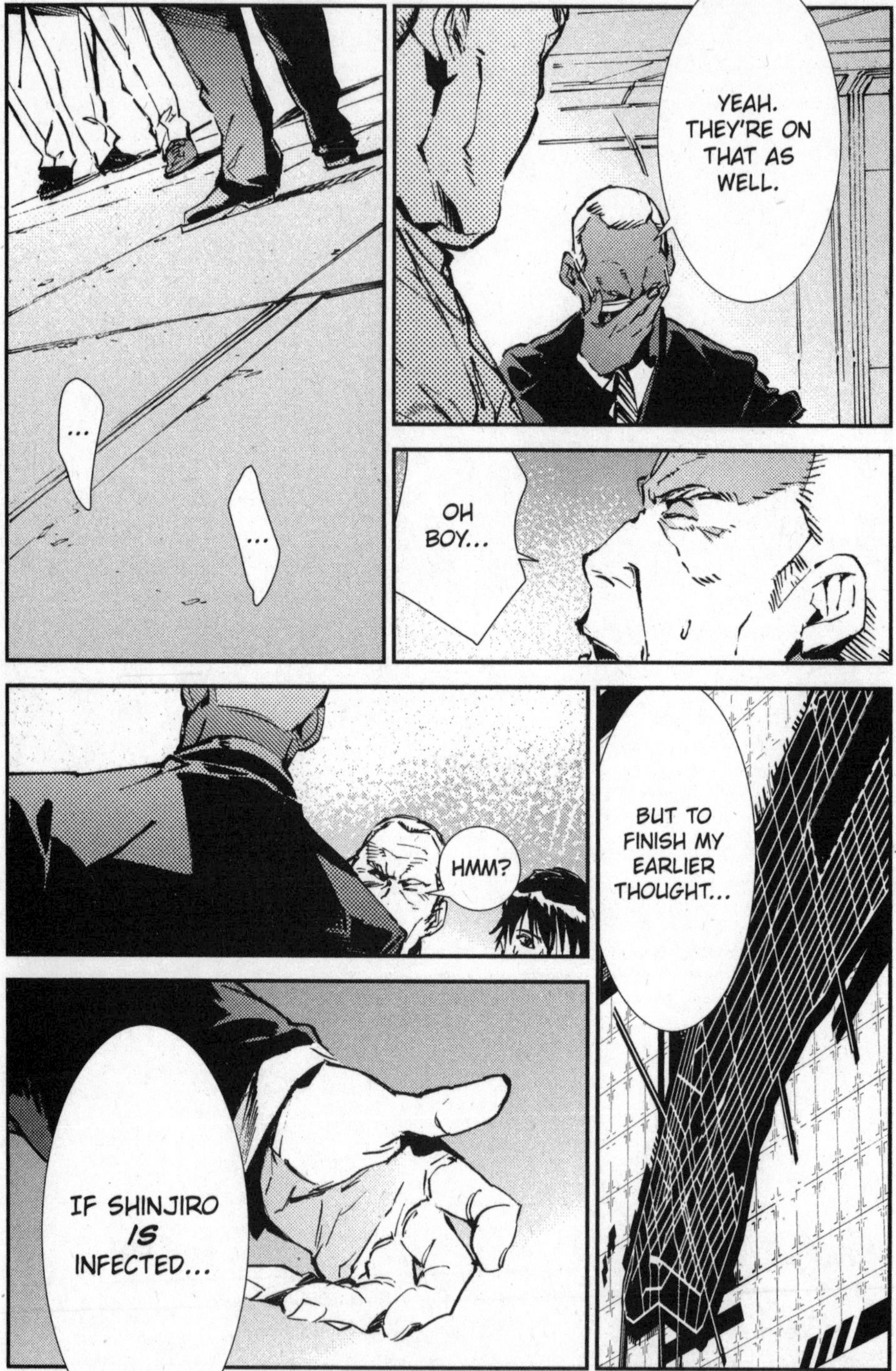
YEAH. THEY'RE ON THAT AS WELL.
OH BOY...
...
...
BUT TO FINISH MY EARLIER THOUGHT...
HMM?
IF SHINJIRO *IS* INFECTED...

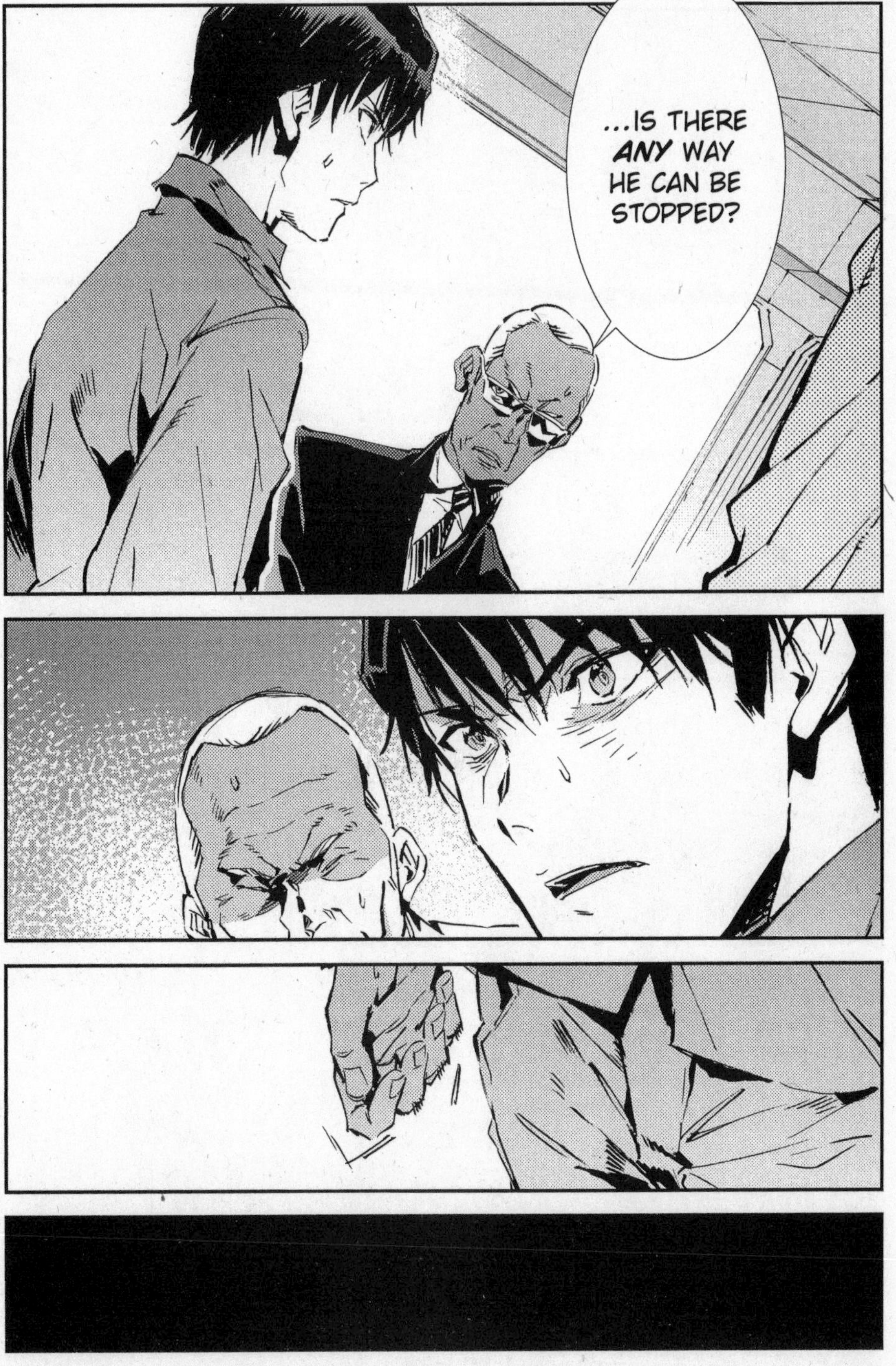
...IS THERE ANY WAY HE CAN BE STOPPED?

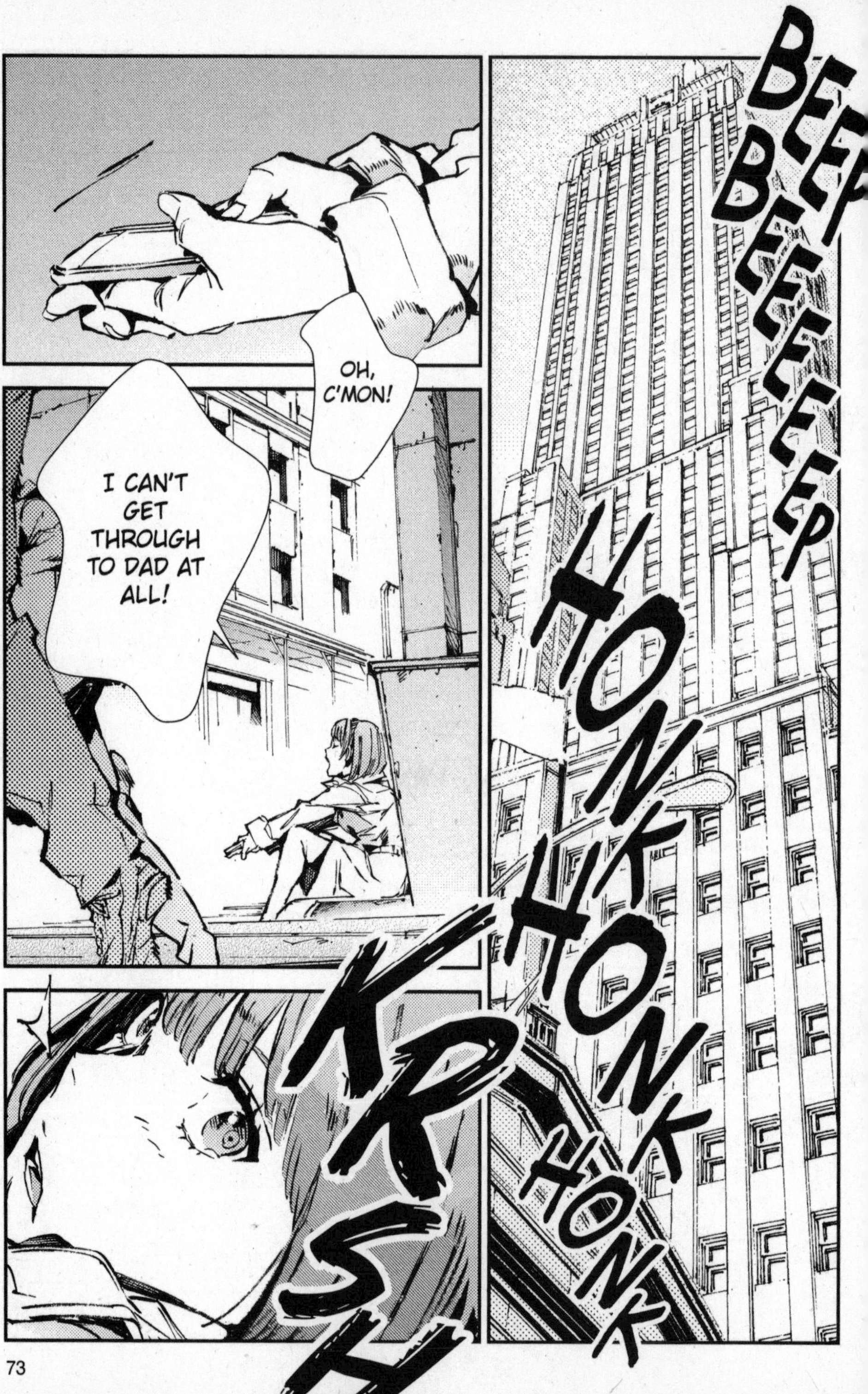
BEEP
BEEEEEP
HONK
HONK
HONK
HONK
OH, C'MON!
I CAN'T GET THROUGH TO DAD AT ALL!
KRSH

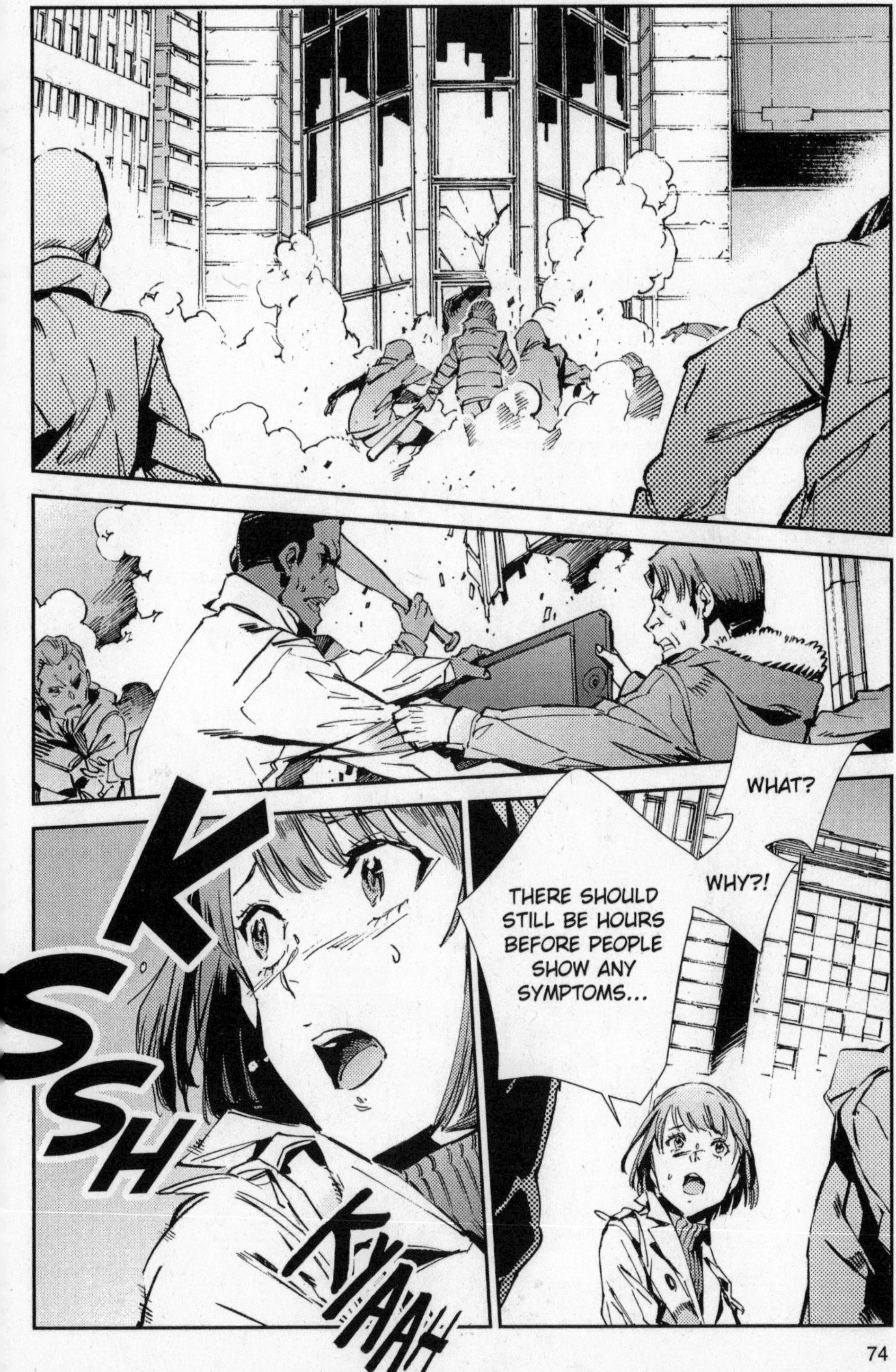

WHAT?
WHY?!
THERE SHOULD STILL BE HOURS BEFORE PEOPLE SHOW ANY SYMPTOMS...
KSSH
KYAAAH

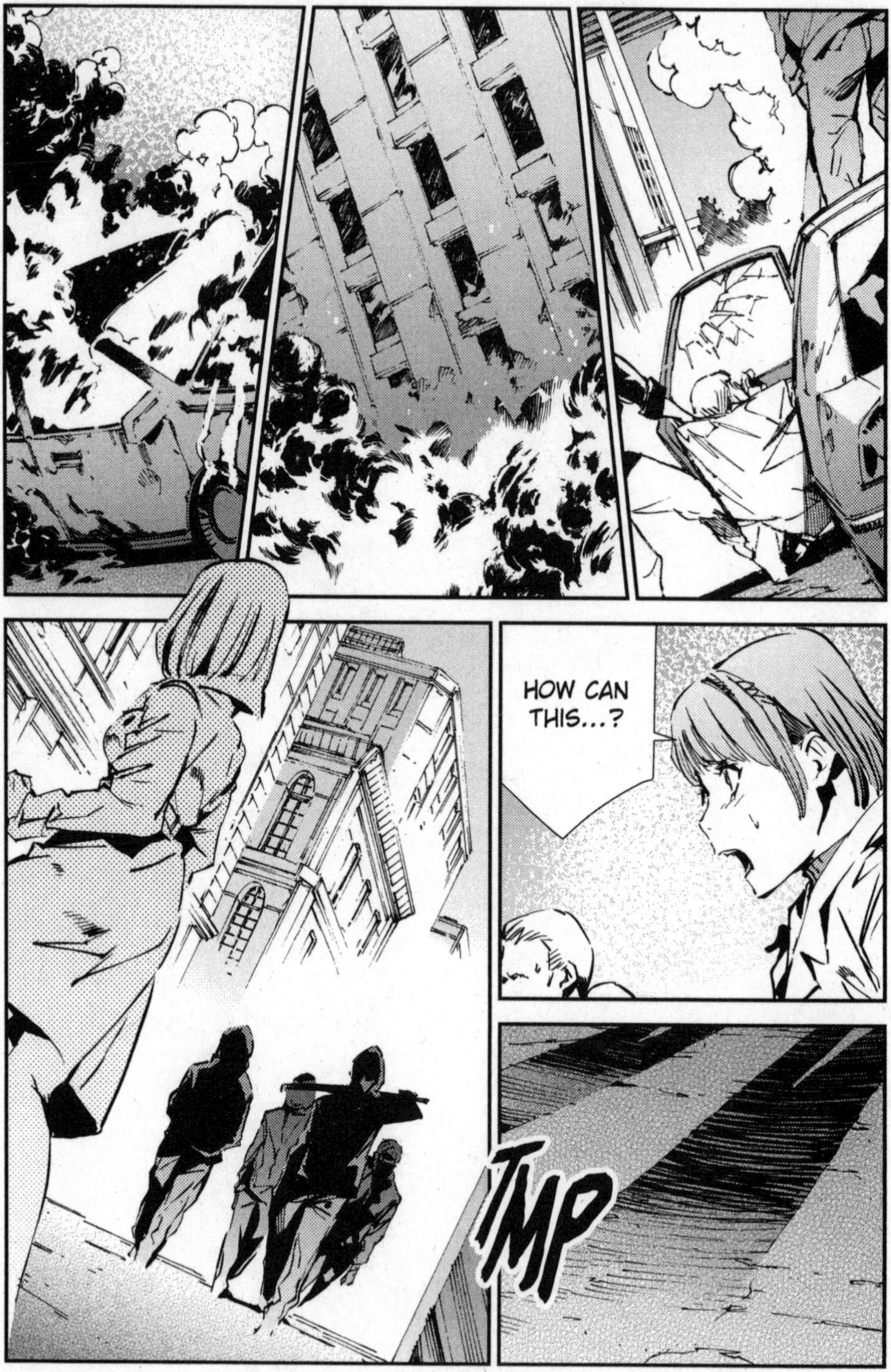
HOW CAN THIS...?
TMP

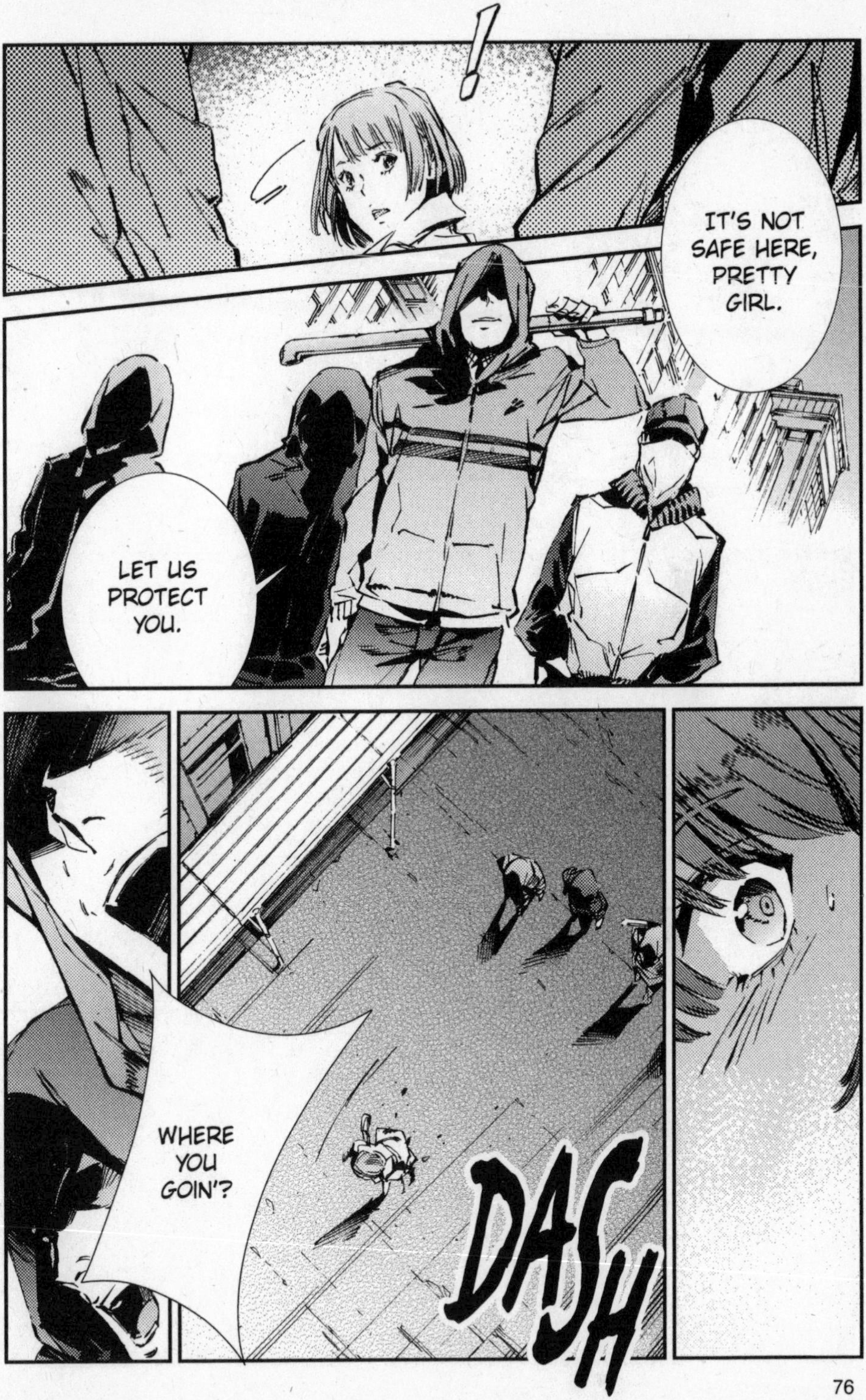
!
IT'S NOT SAFE HERE, PRETTY GIRL.
LET US PROTECT YOU.
WHERE YOU GOIN'?
DASH

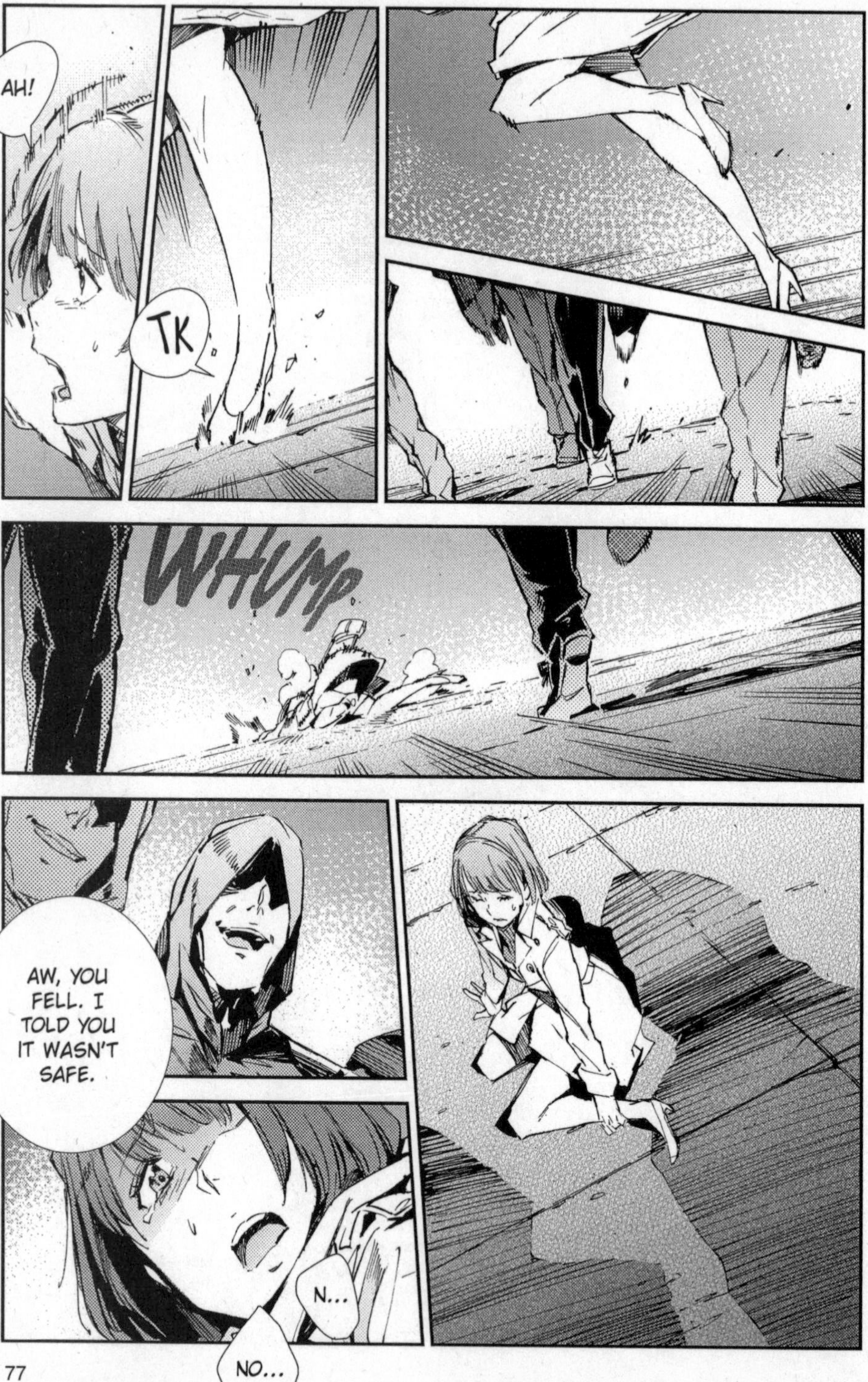
TK
AH!
WHUMP
AW, YOU FELL. I TOLD YOU IT WASN'T SAFE.
N...
NO...

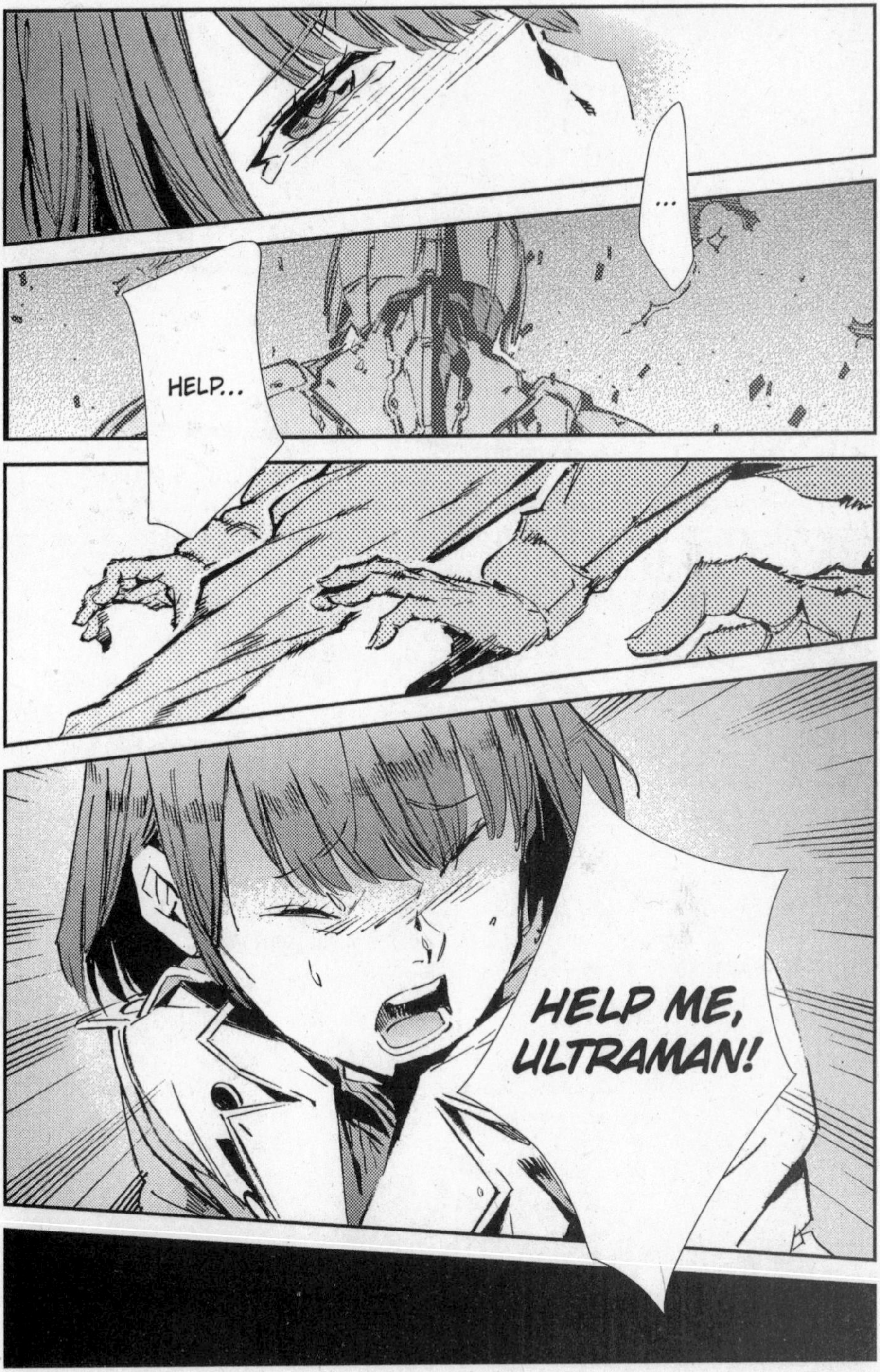
...
HELP...
HELP ME, ULTRAMAN!

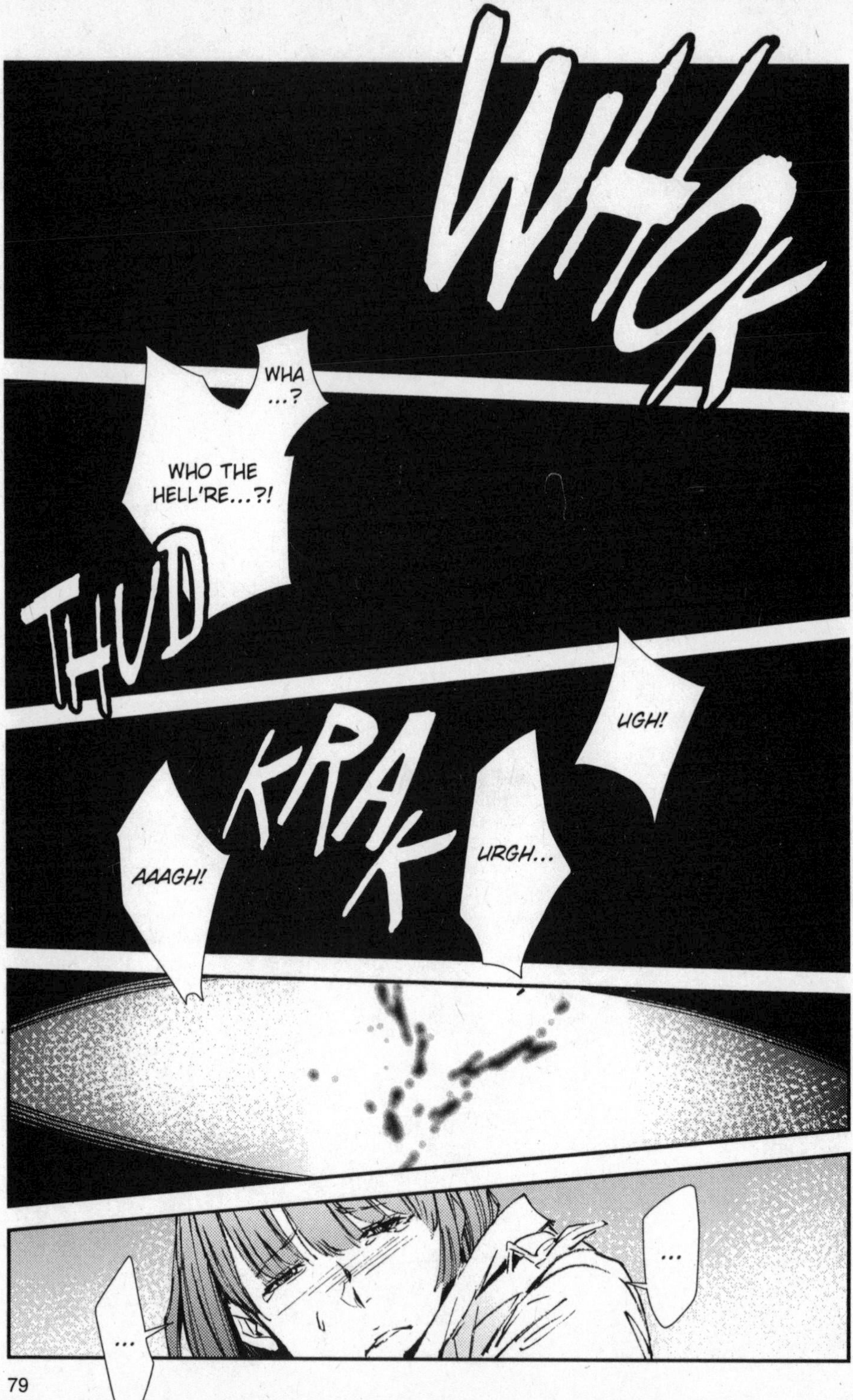
WHOK
WHA ...?
WHO THE HELL'RE...?!
THUD
UGH!
URGH...
KRAK
AAAGH!
...
...

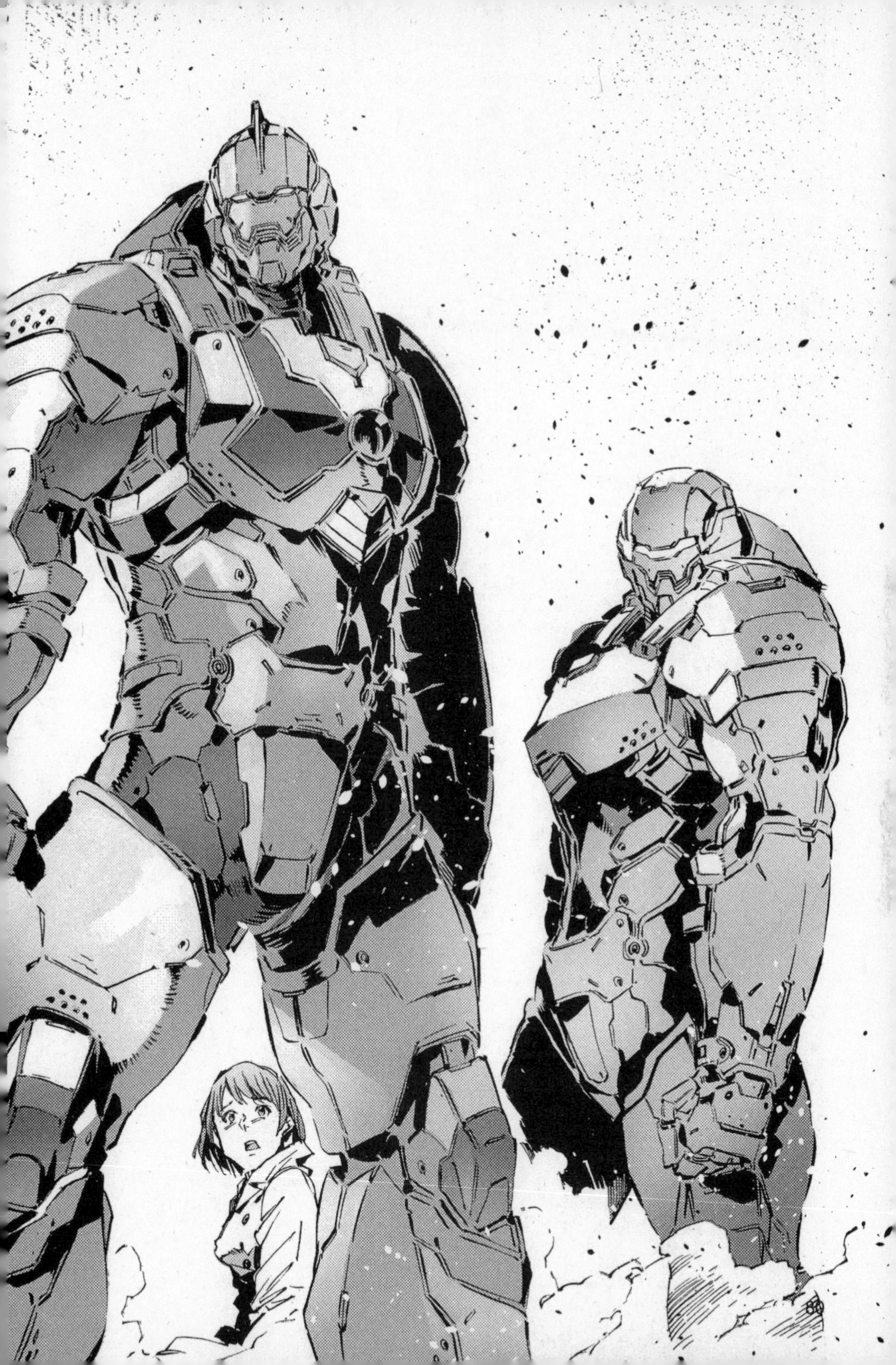
80

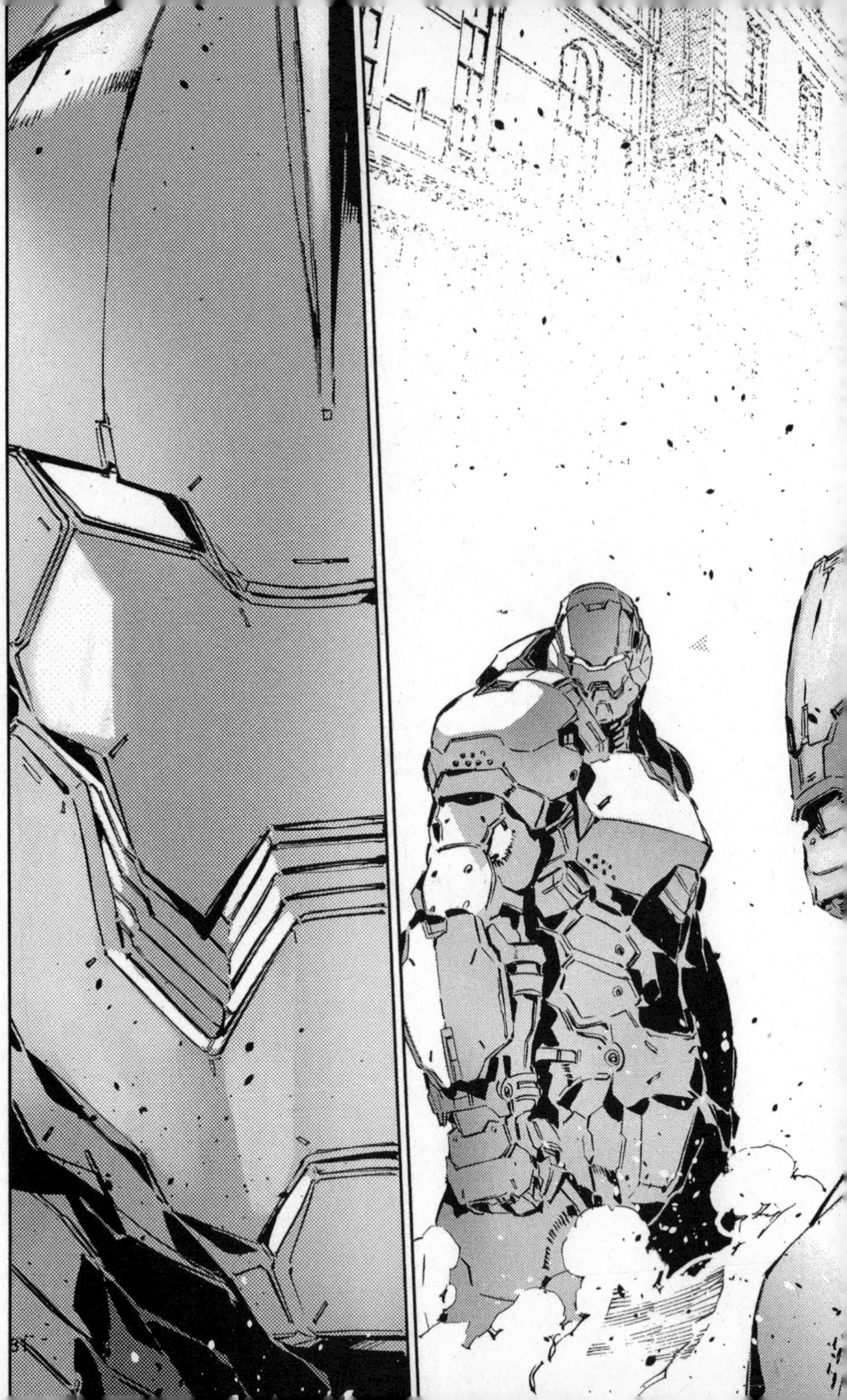

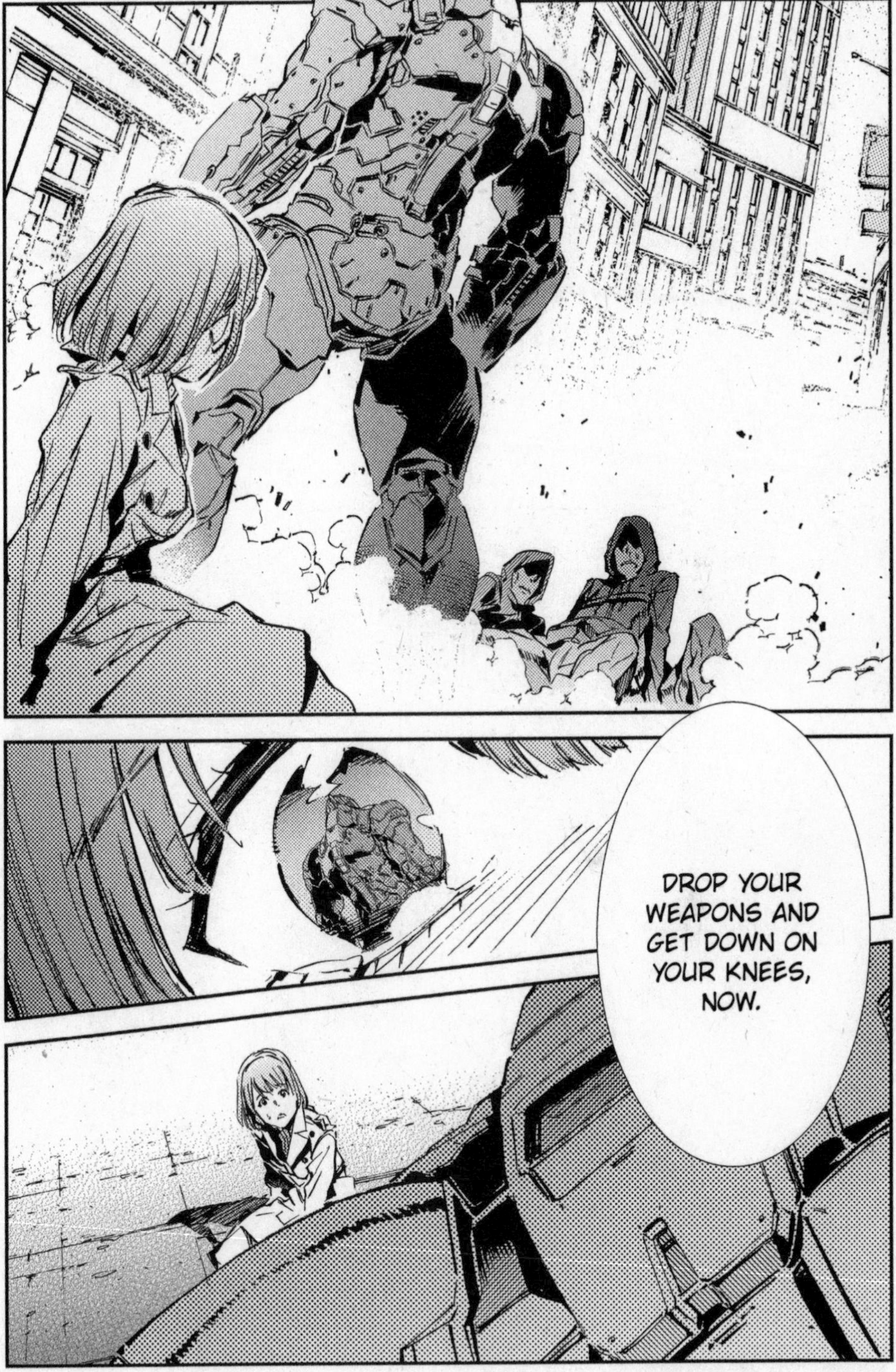
DROP YOUR WEAPONS AND GET DOWN ON YOUR KNEES, NOW.

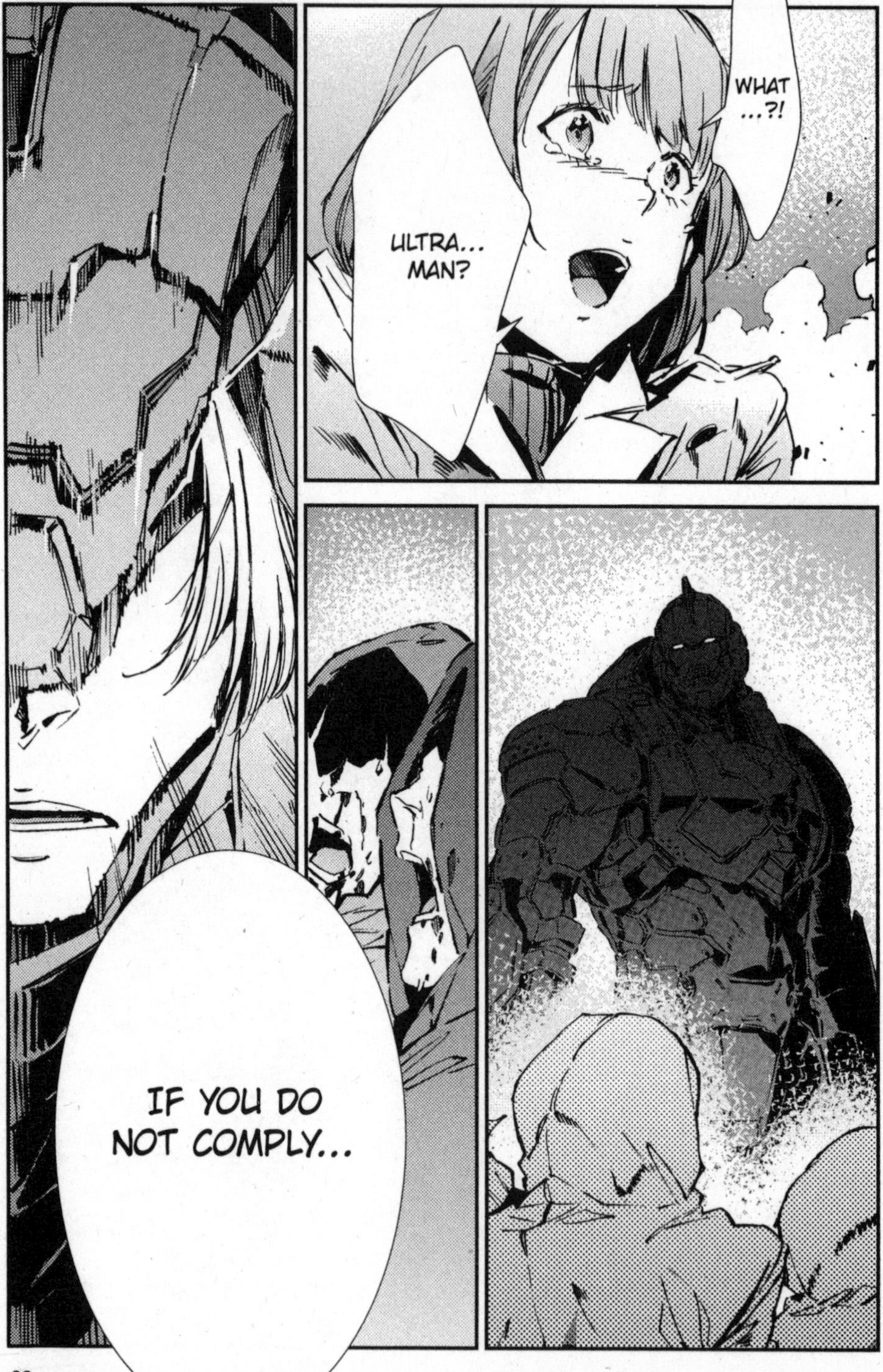
WHAT ...?!
ULTRA... MAN?
IF YOU DO NOT COMPLY...

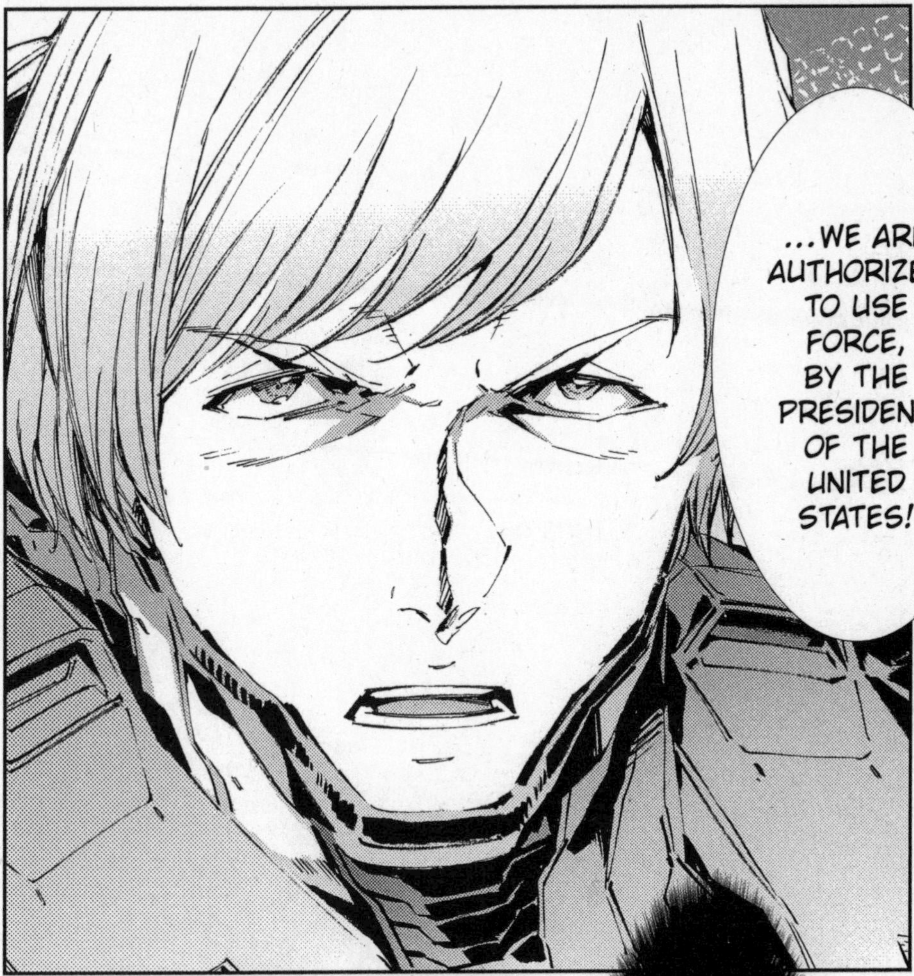
...WE ARE AUTHORIZED TO USE FORCE, BY THE PRESIDENT OF THE UNITED STATES!

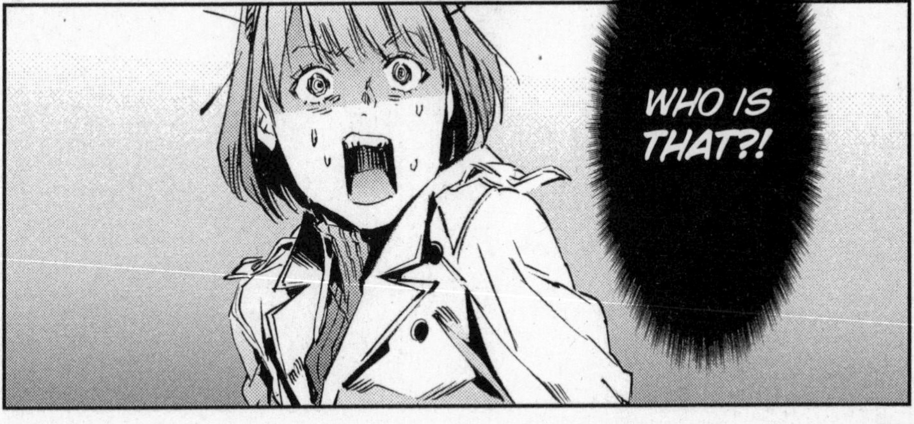
WHO IS THAT?!

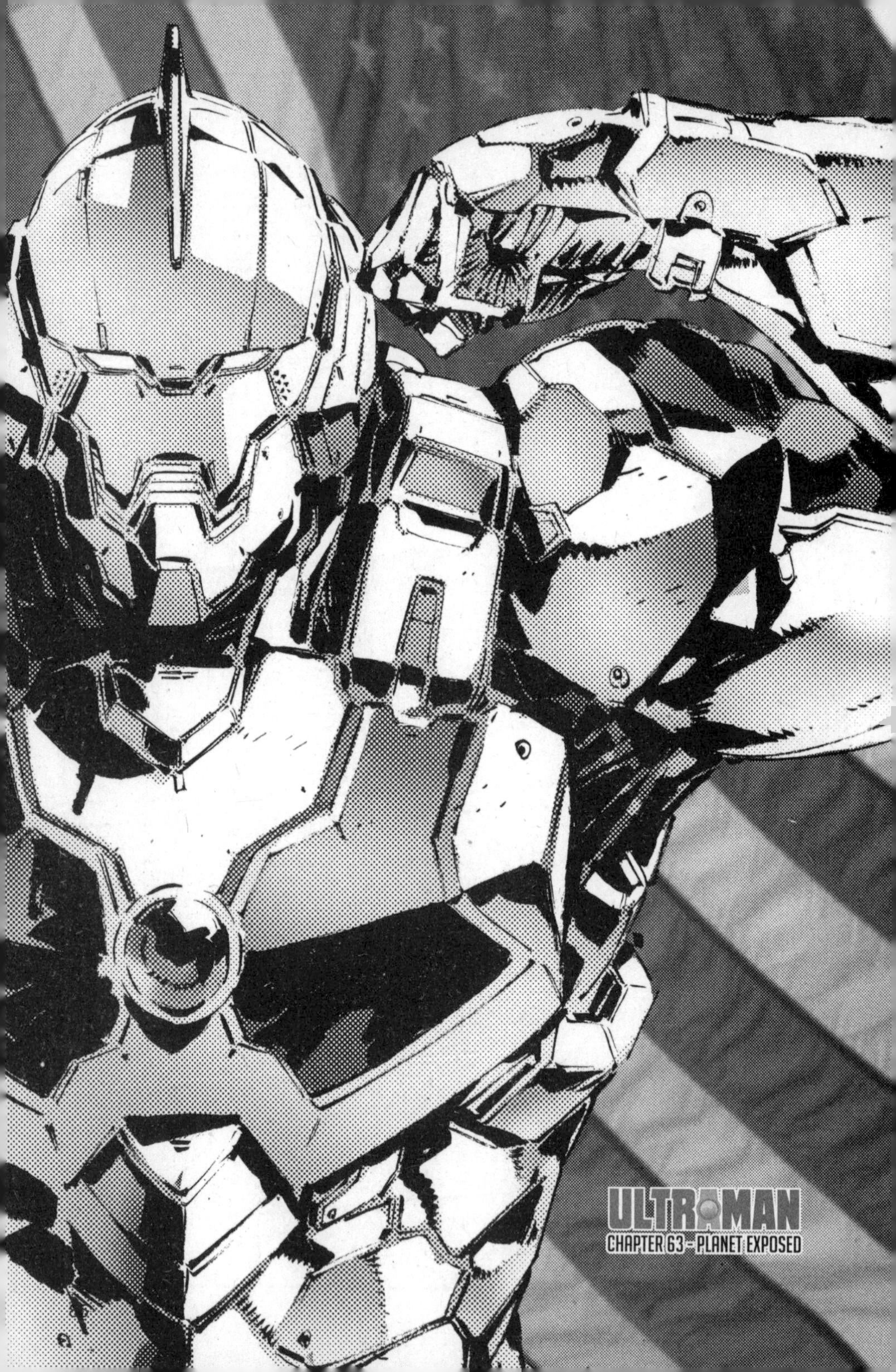
ULTRAMAN
CHAPTER 63 - PLANET EXPOSED

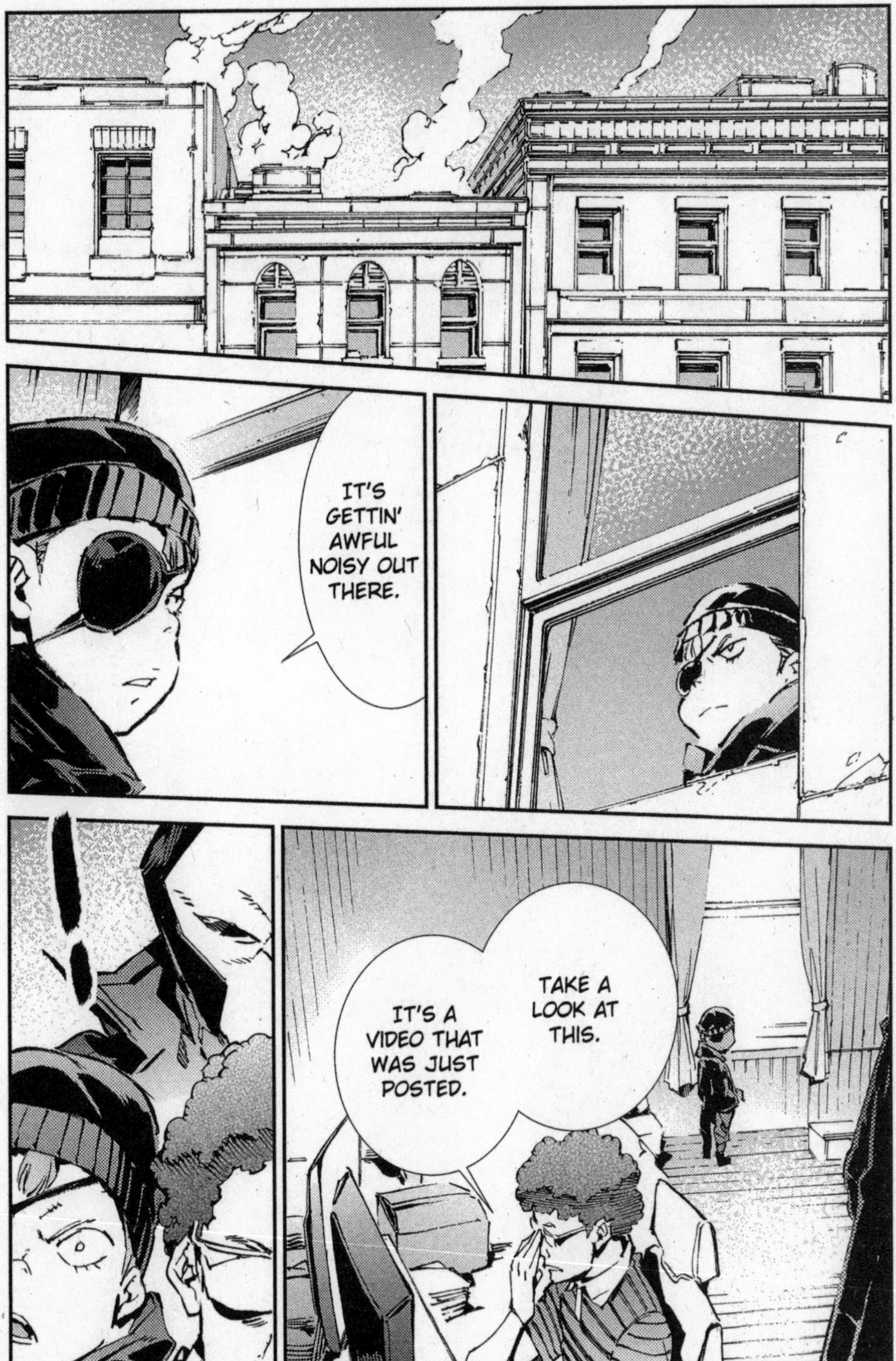
IT'S GETTIN' AWFUL NOISY OUT THERE.
TAKE A LOOK AT THIS.
IT'S A VIDEO THAT WAS JUST POSTED.

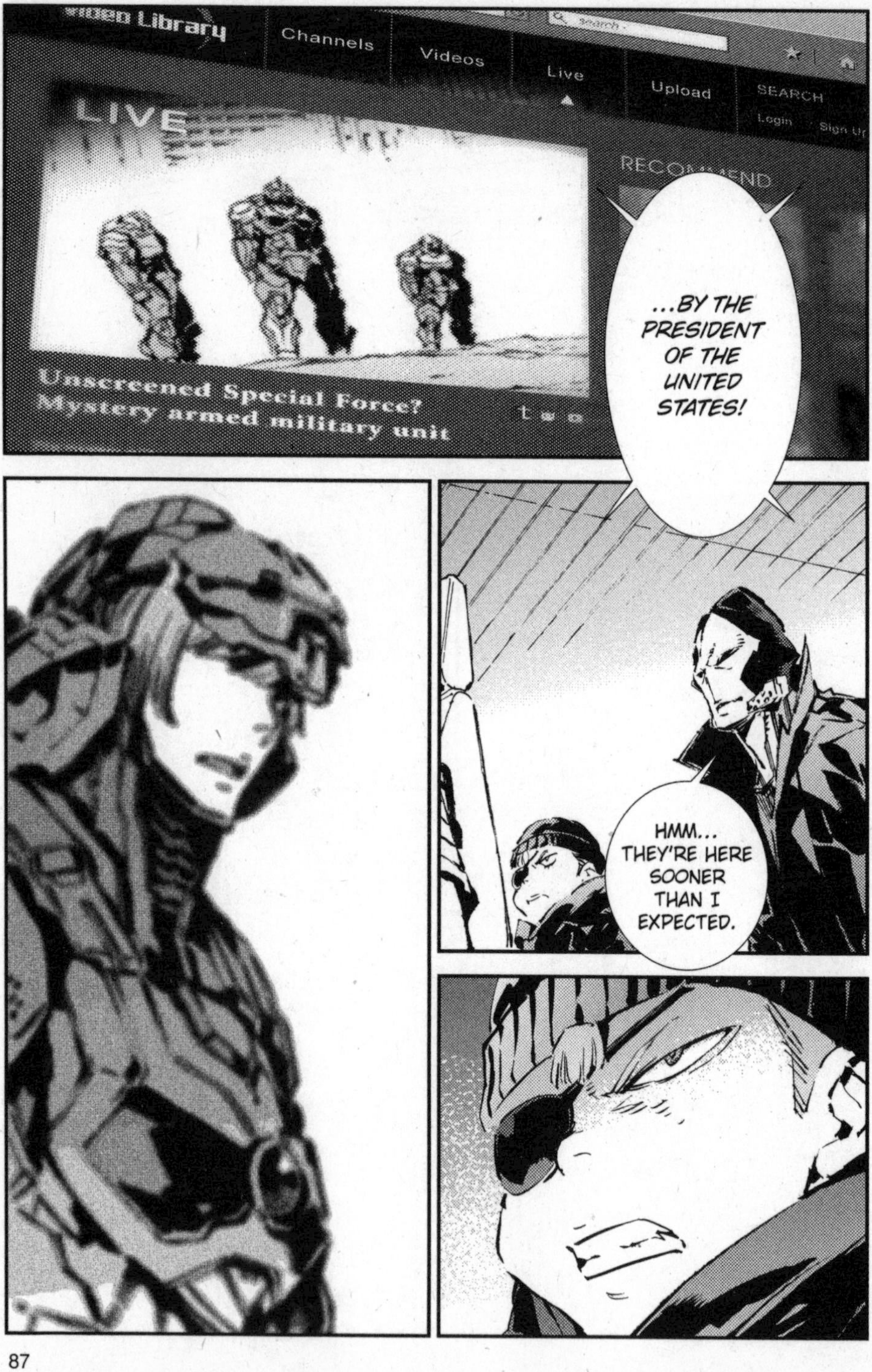
Channels
Videos
Live
Upload
SEARCH
Login
LIVE
Unscreened Special Force?
Mystery armed military unit
...BY THE PRESIDENT OF THE UNITED STATES!
HMM... THEY'RE HERE SOONER THAN I EXPECTED.

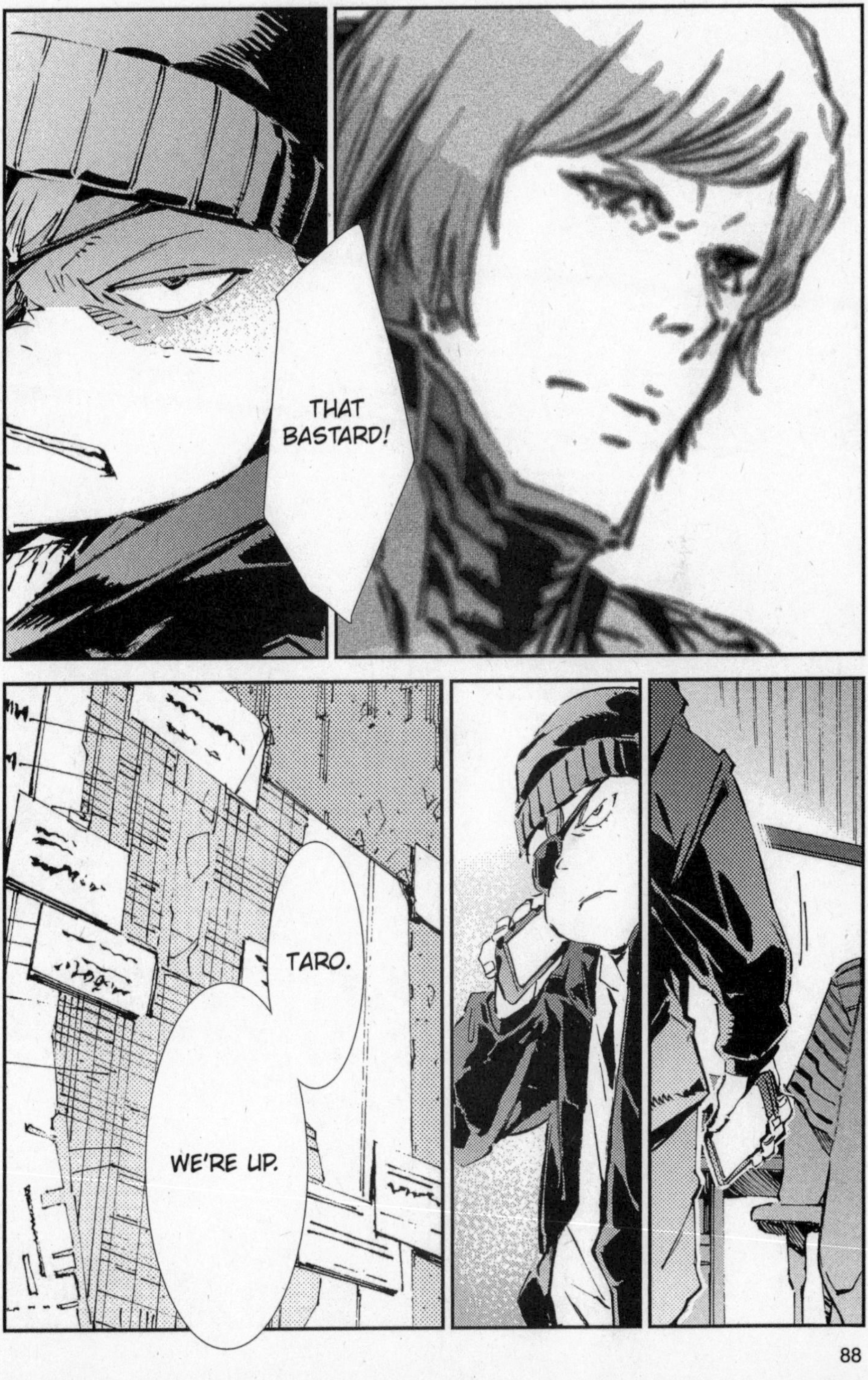
THAT BASTARD!
TARO.
WE'RE UP.

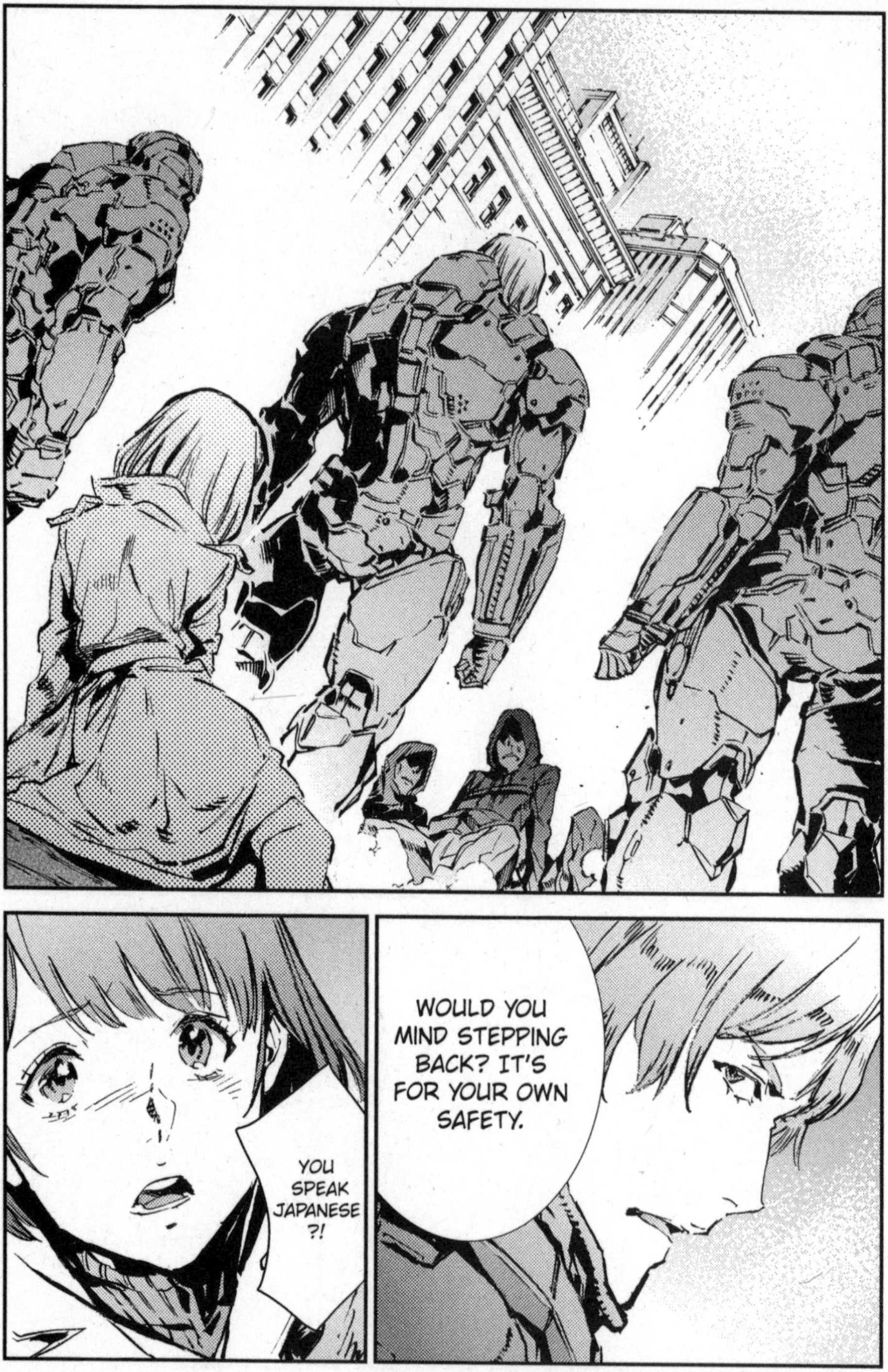
WOULD YOU MIND STEPPING BACK? IT'S FOR YOUR OWN SAFETY.
YOU SPEAK JAPANESE ?!

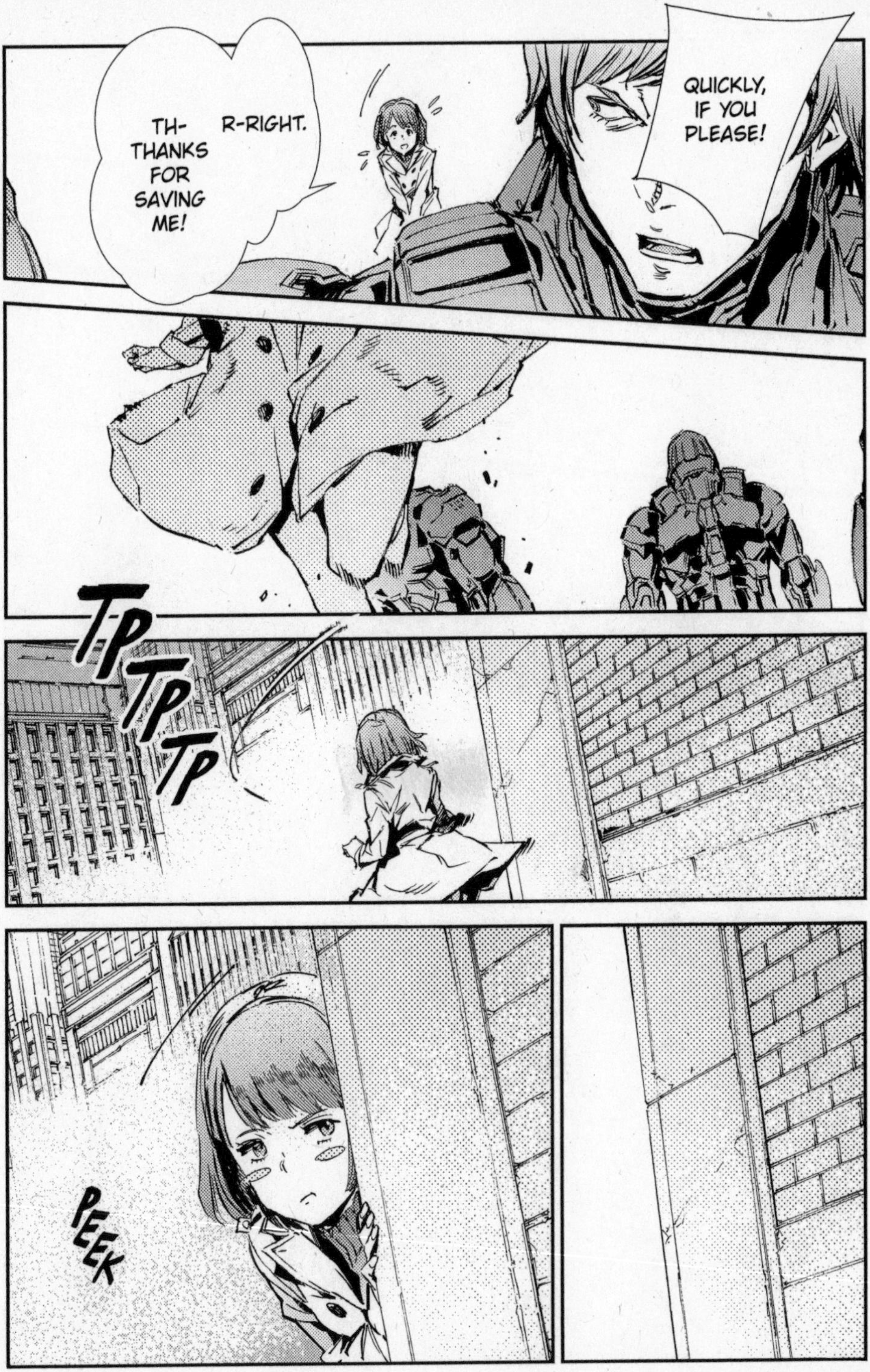
QUICKLY, IF YOU PLEASE!
R-RIGHT.
TH- THANKS FOR SAVING ME!
T-P TP TP
PEEK

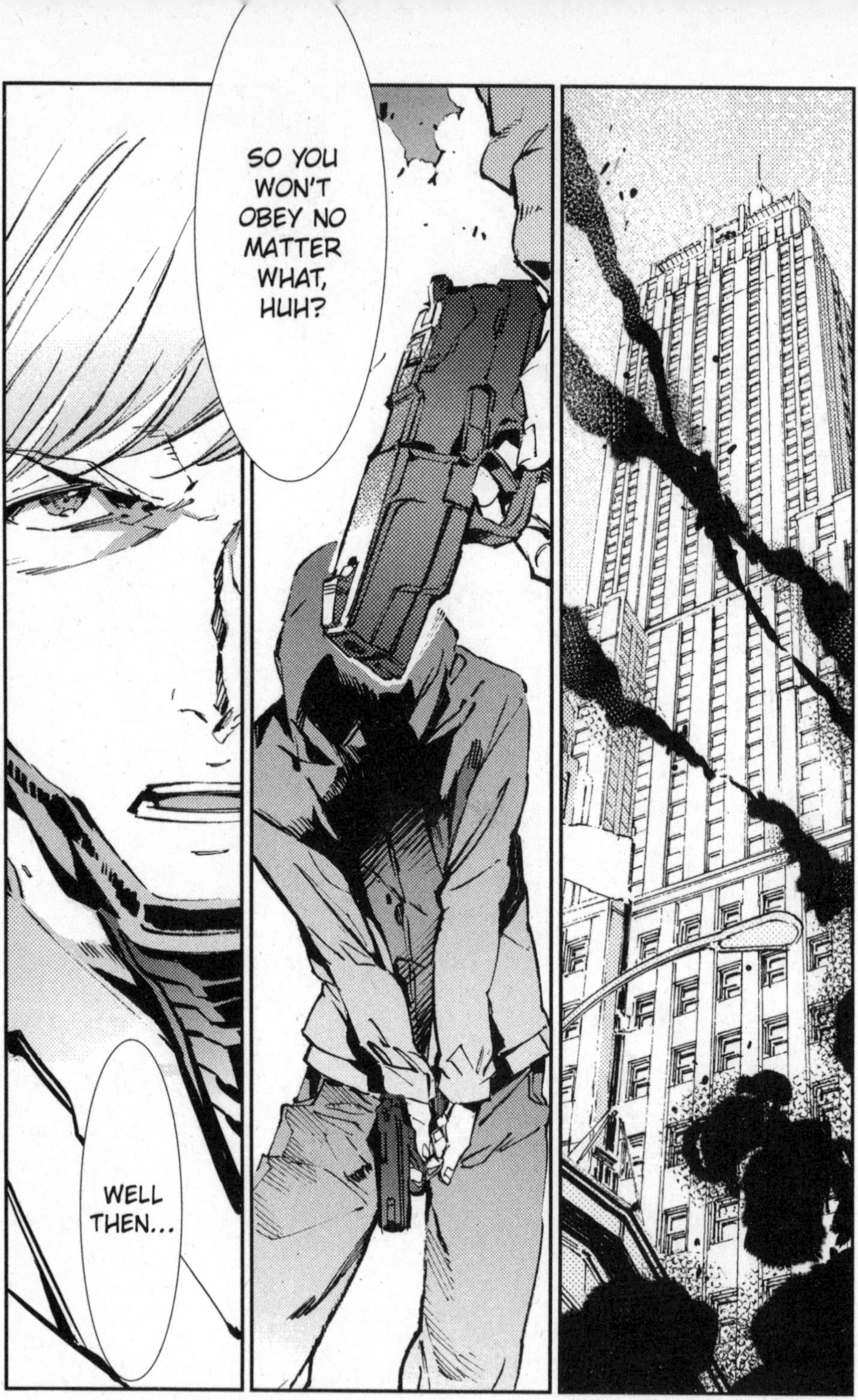
SO YOU WON'T OBEY NO MATTER WHAT, HUH?
WELL THEN...

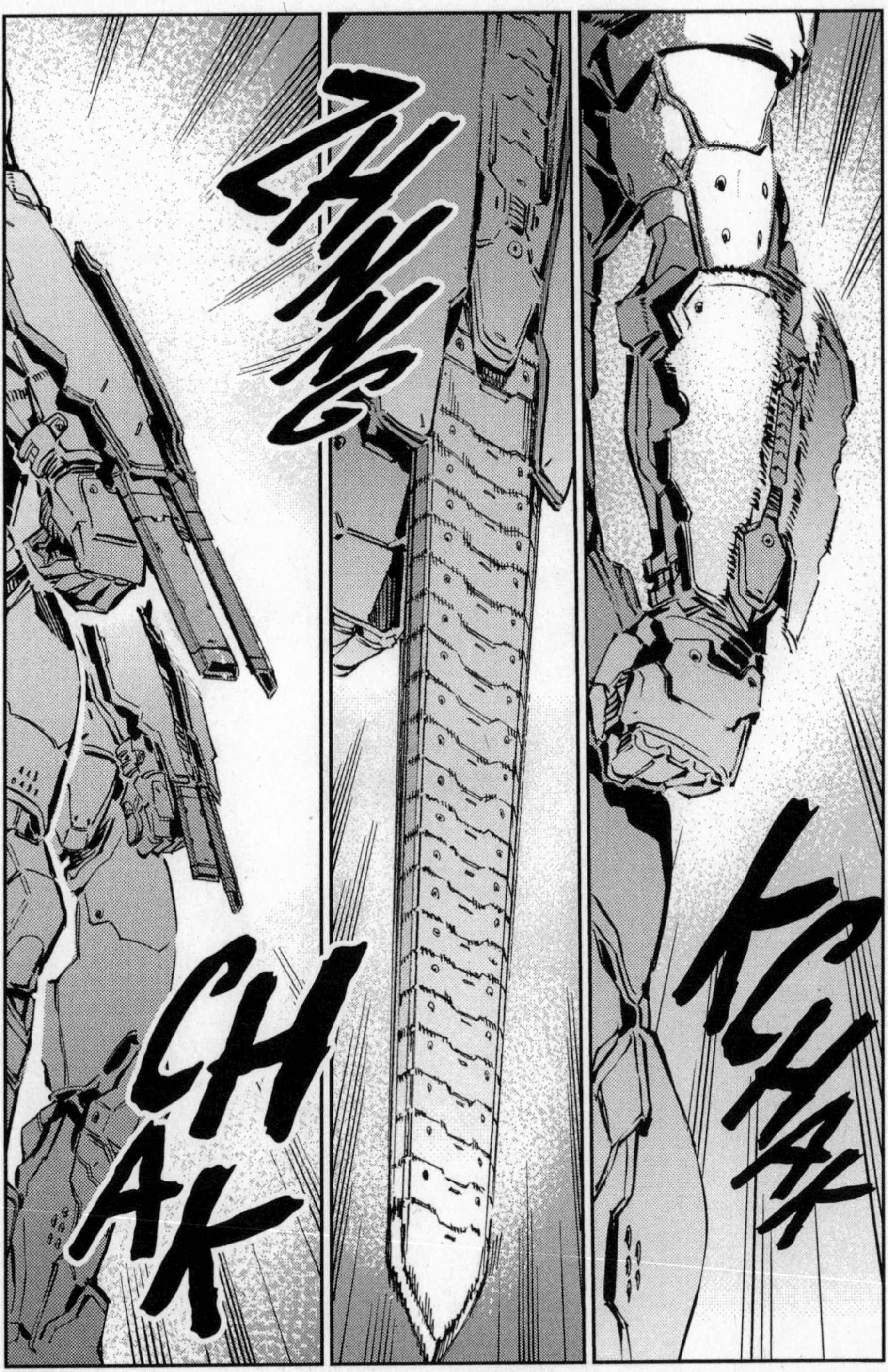
KCHAK
ZHNNG
CHAK

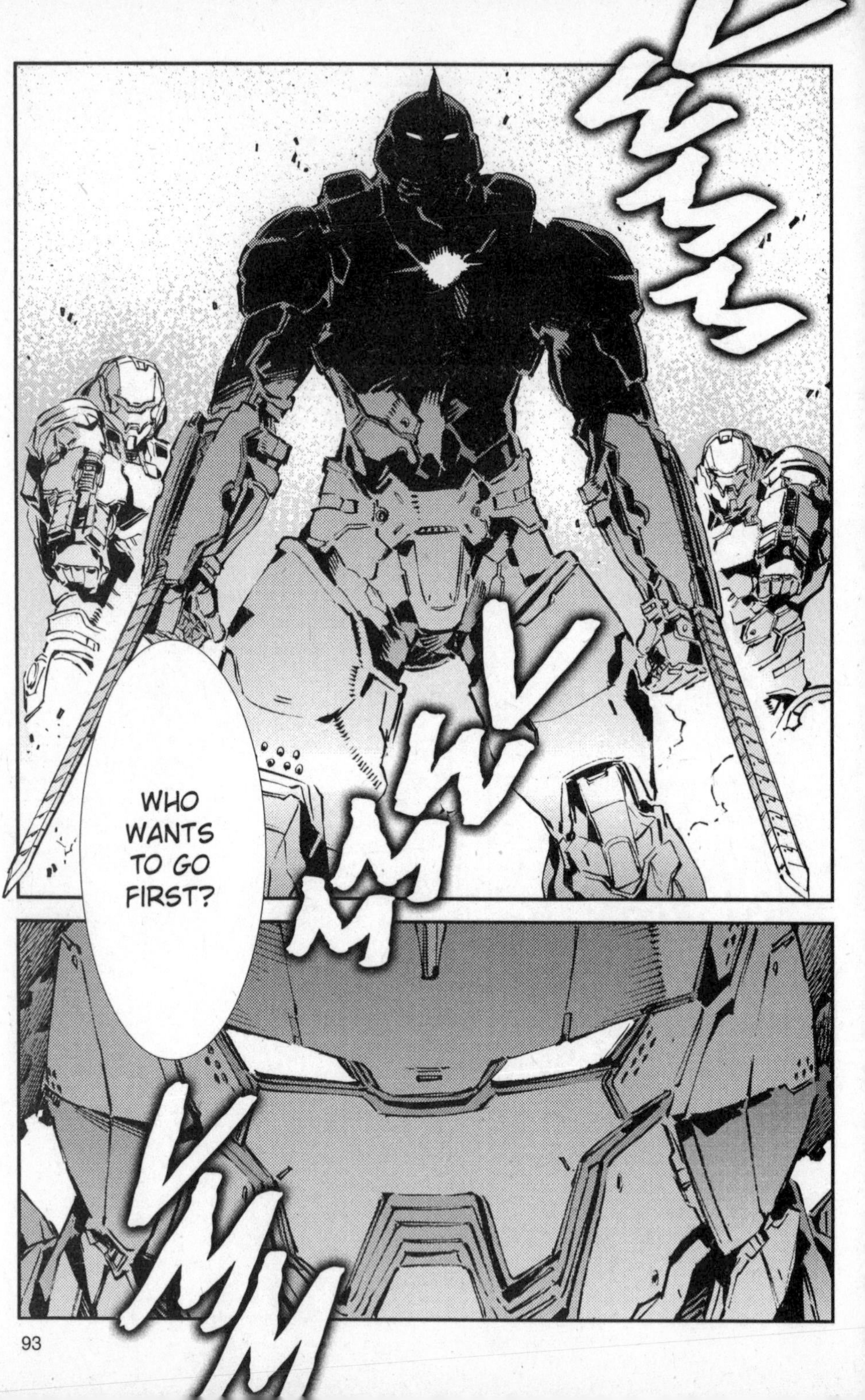
VWMM
VWMM
WHO WANTS TO GO FIRST?
VMM

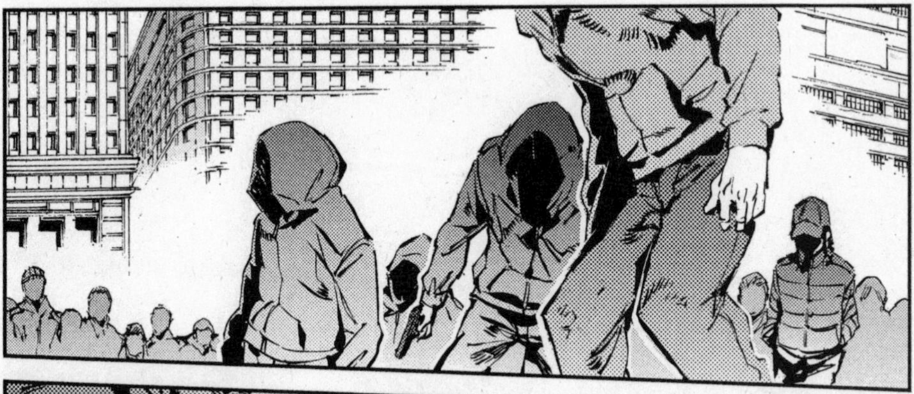

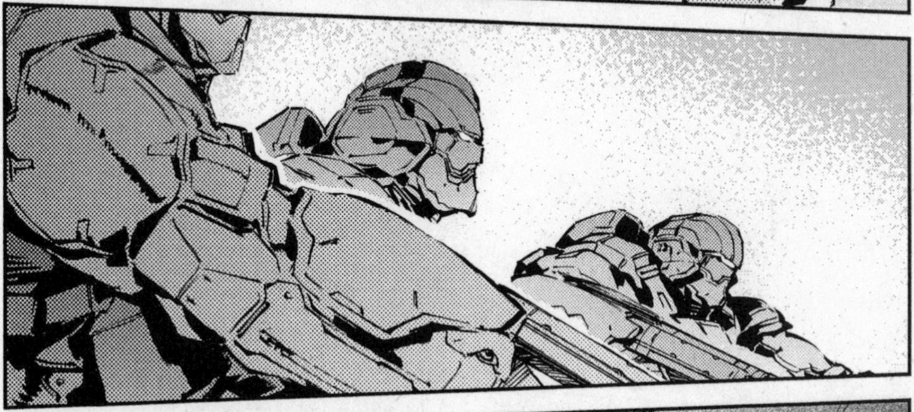

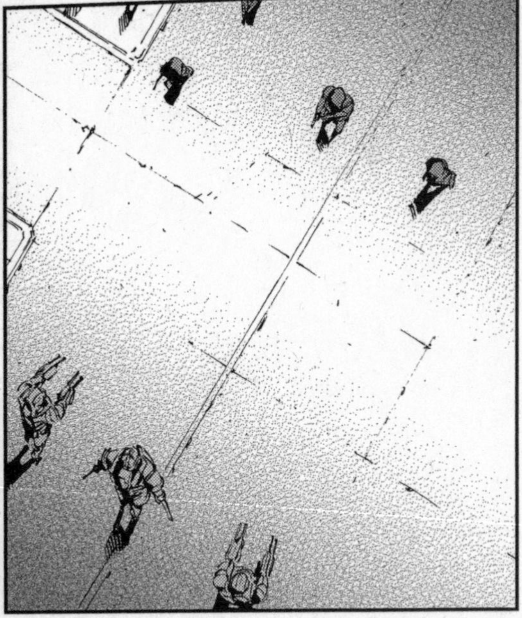

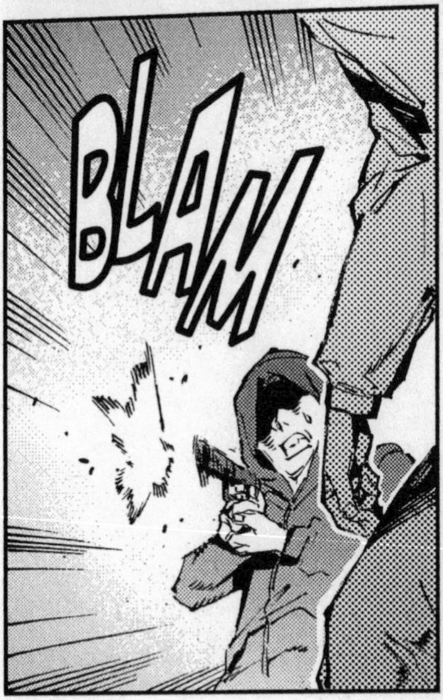
BLAM

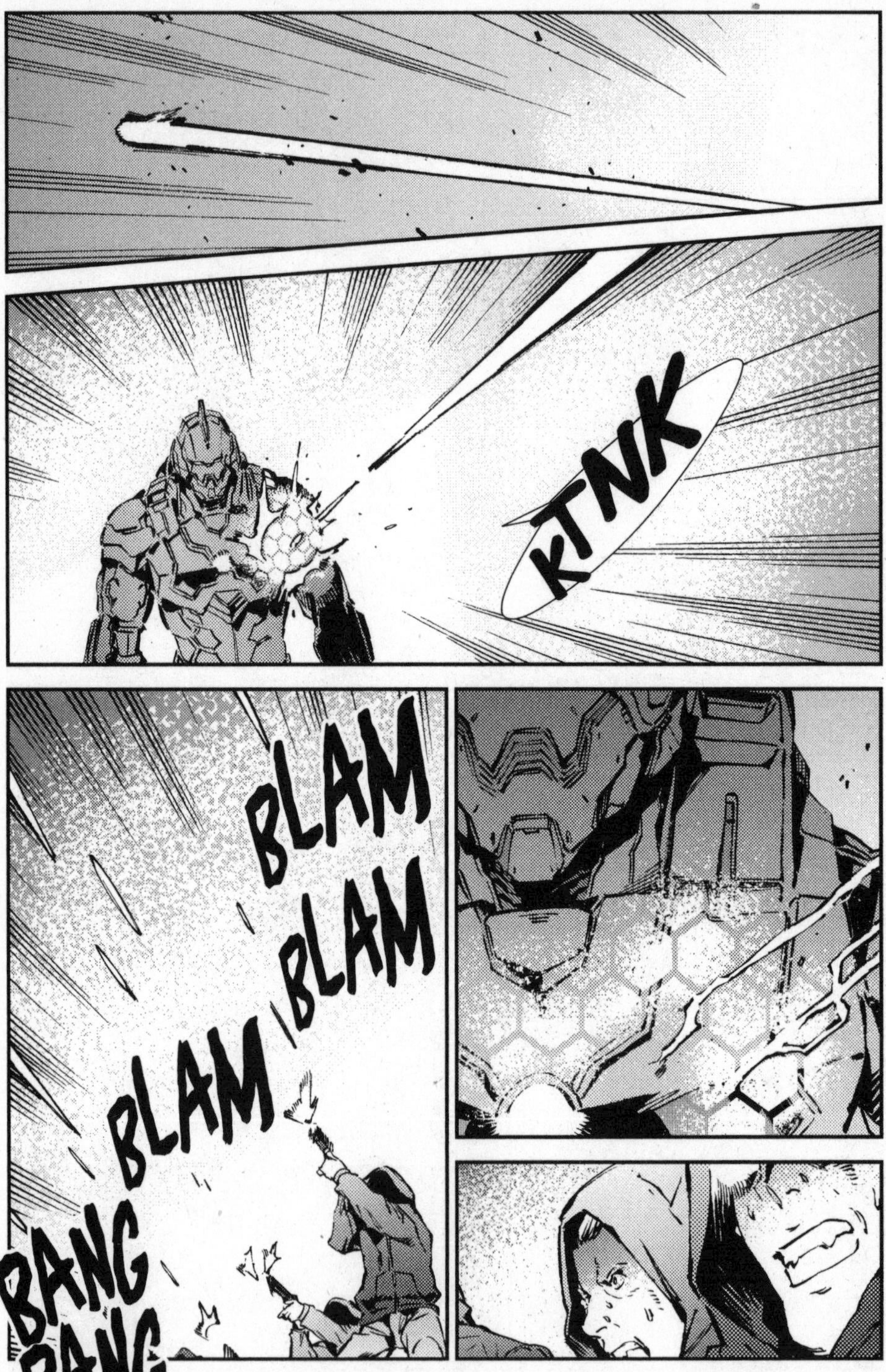
KTNK
BLAM
BLAM
BLAM
BANG
BANG

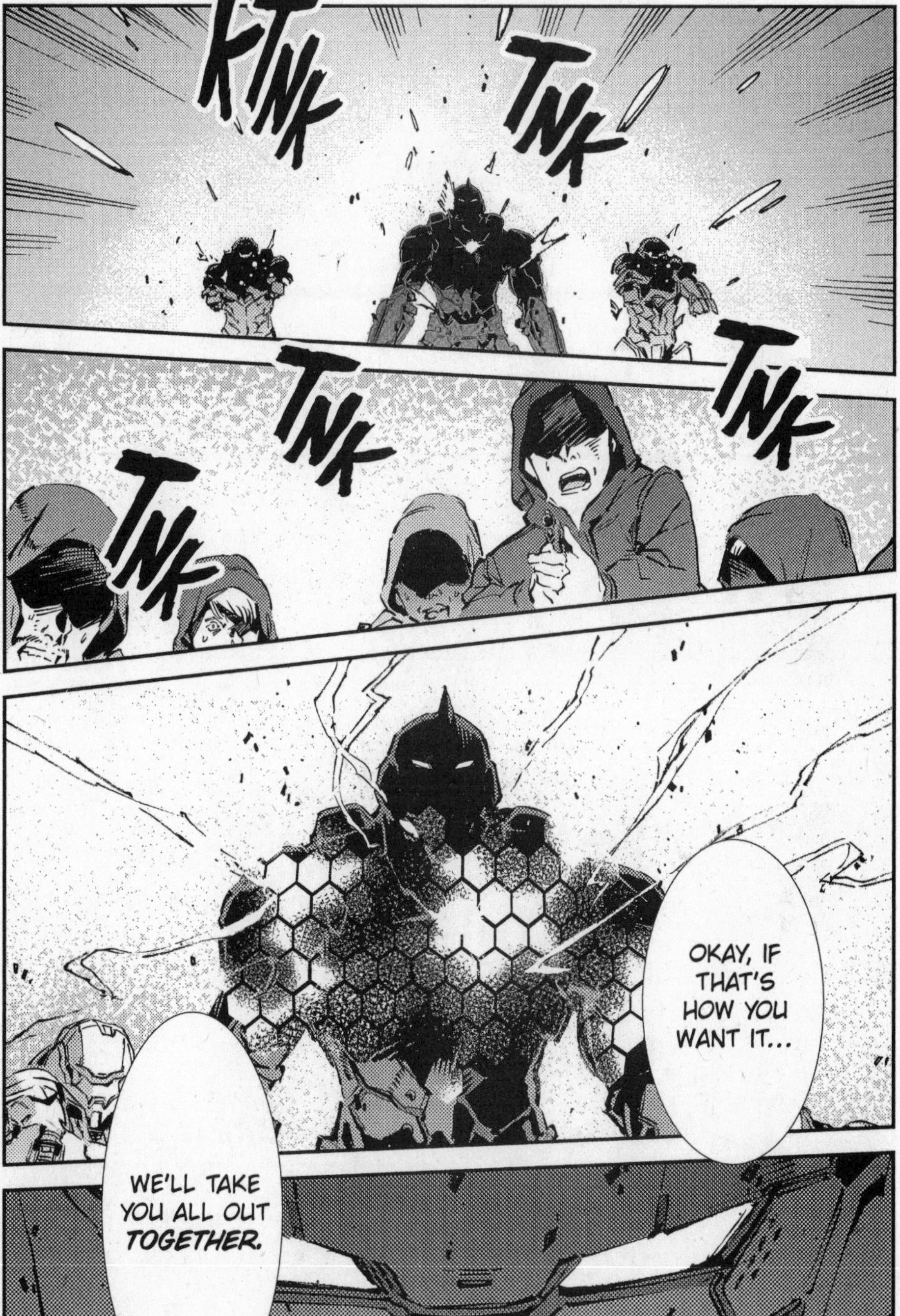
TNK
KTNK
TNK
TNK
TNK
OKAY, IF THAT'S HOW YOU WANT IT...
WE'LL TAKE YOU ALL OUT *TOGETHER.*

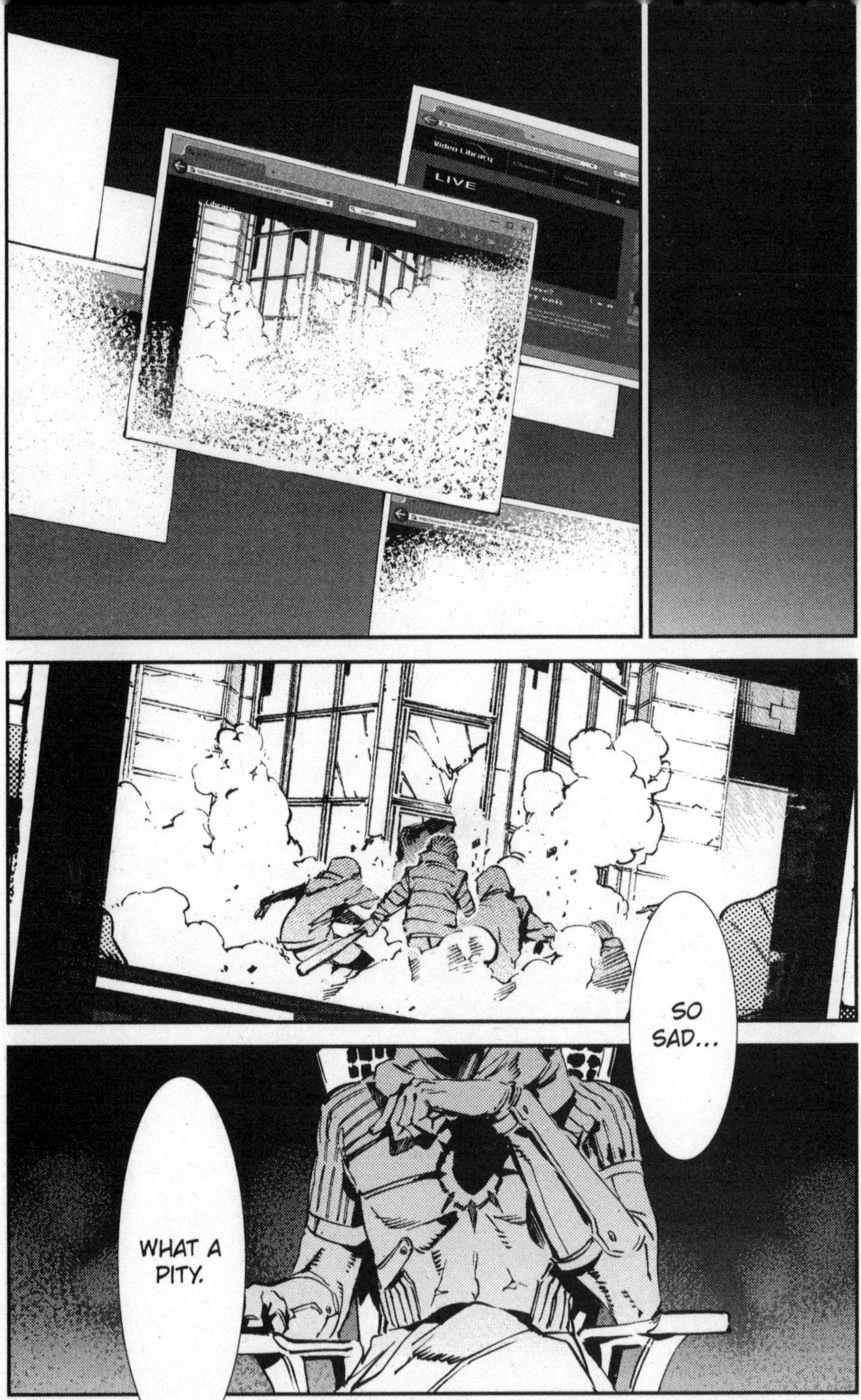
Video Library
Channels
Videos
LIVE
SO SAD...
WHAT A PITY.

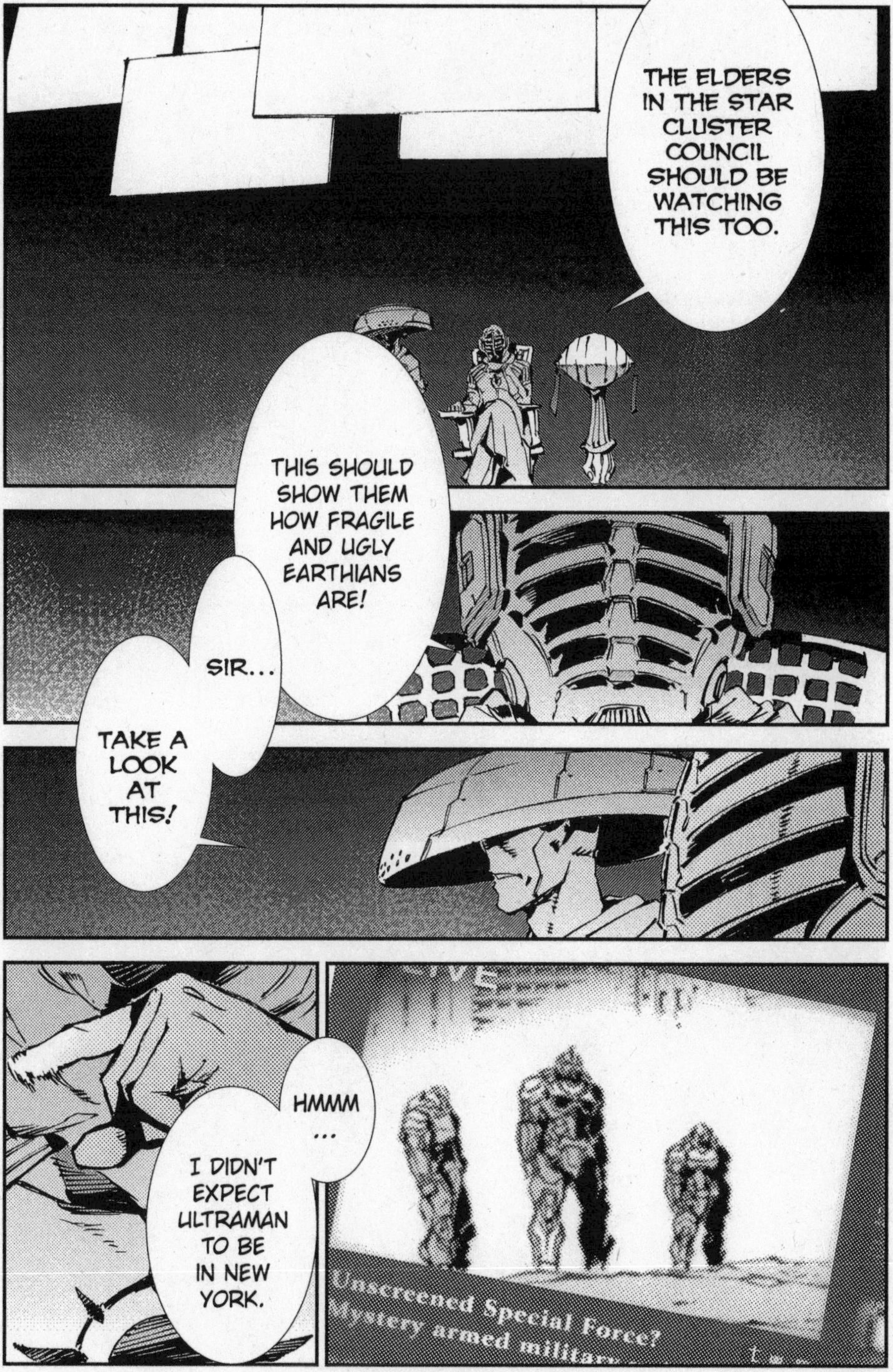
THE ELDERS IN THE STAR CLUSTER COUNCIL SHOULD BE WATCHING THIS TOO.
THIS SHOULD SHOW THEM HOW FRAGILE AND UGLY EARTHIANS ARE!
SIR...
TAKE A LOOK AT THIS!
Unscreened Special Force?
Mystery armed militar
HMMM...
I DIDN'T EXPECT ULTRAMAN TO BE IN NEW YORK.

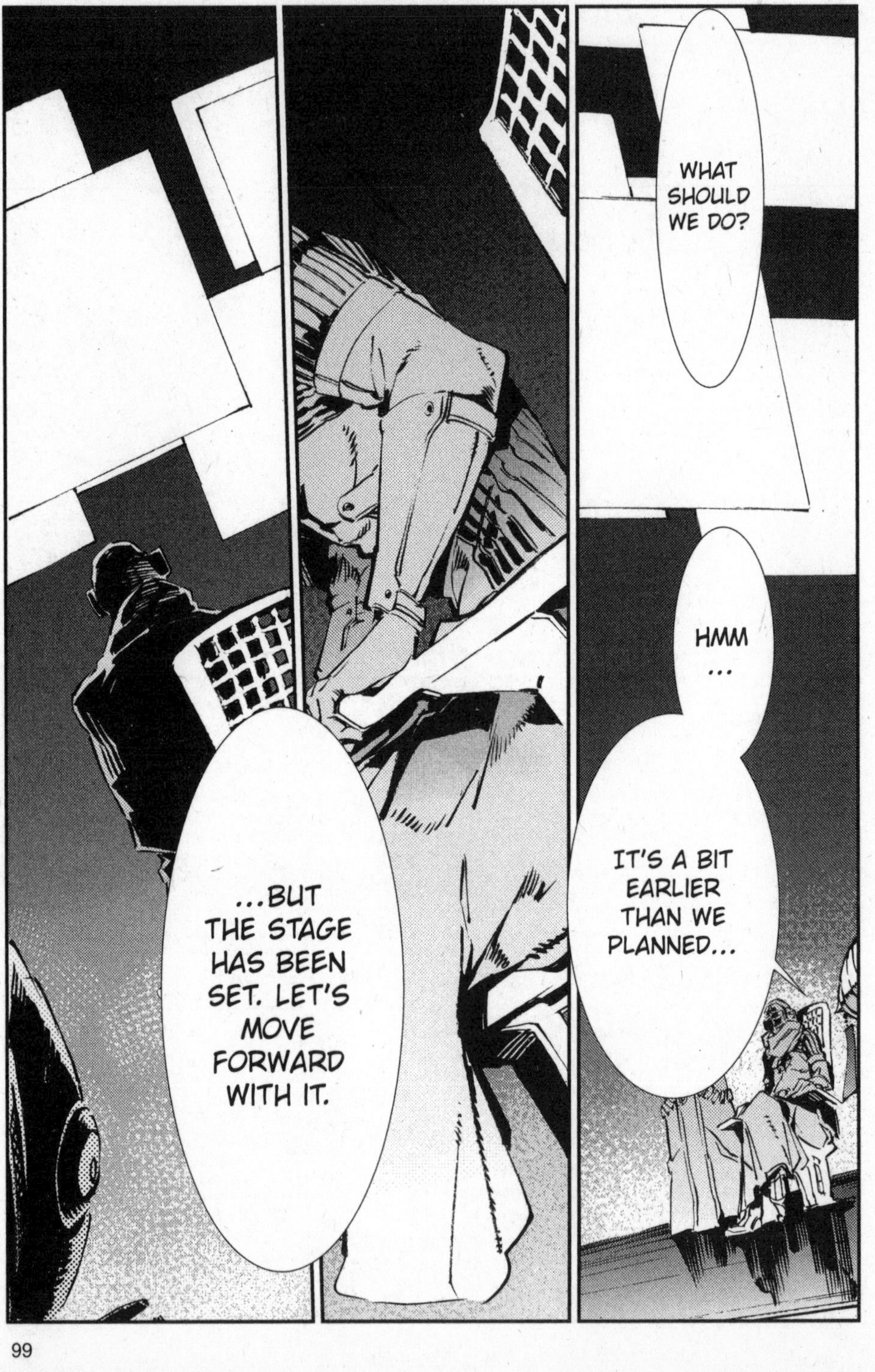
WHAT SHOULD WE DO?
HMM...
IT'S A BIT EARLIER THAN WE PLANNED...
...BUT THE STAGE HAS BEEN SET. LET'S MOVE FORWARD WITH IT.

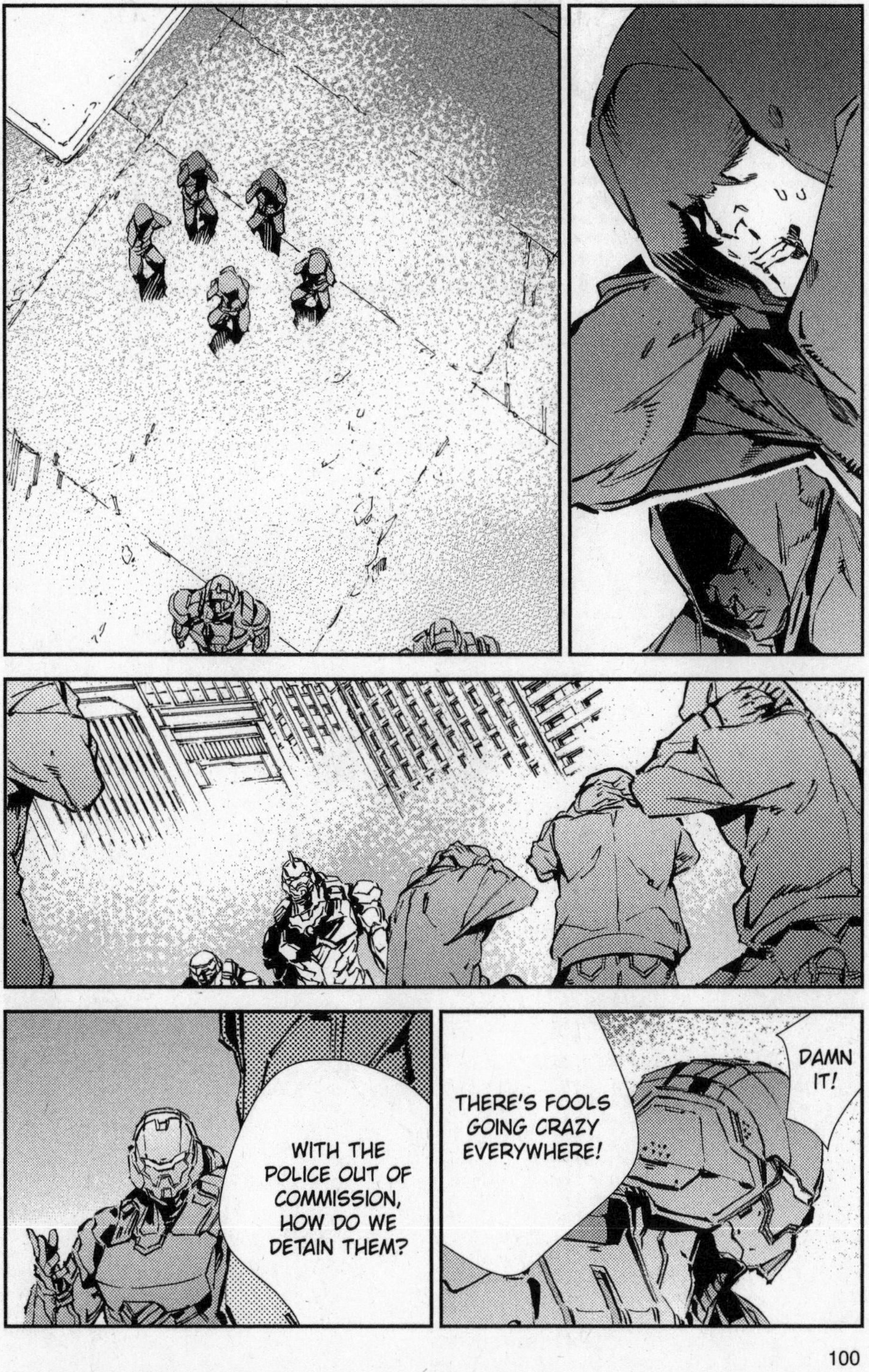
DAMN IT!
THERE'S FOOLS GOING CRAZY EVERYWHERE!
WITH THE POLICE OUT OF COMMISSION, HOW DO WE DETAIN THEM?

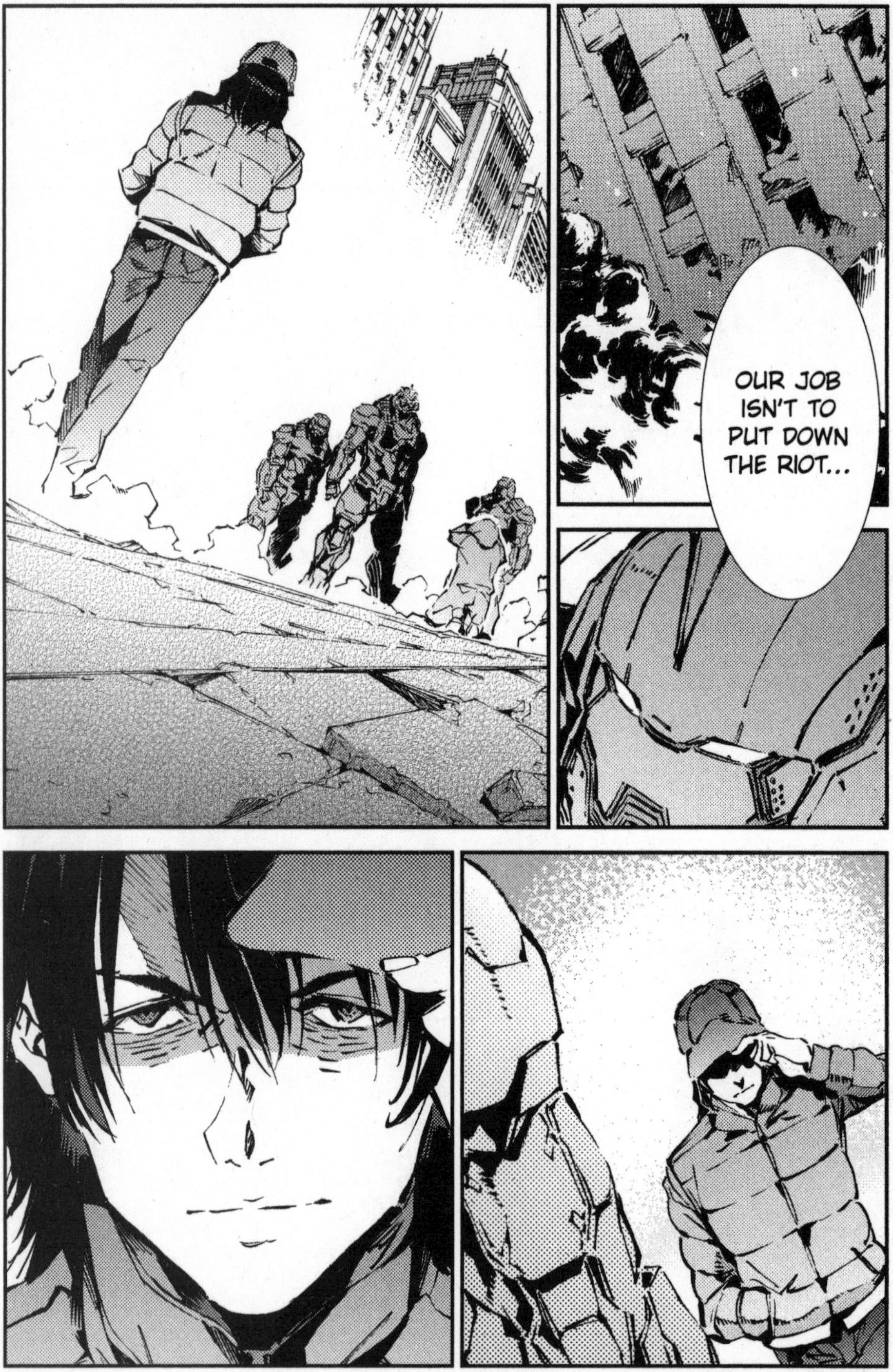
OUR JOB ISN'T TO PUT DOWN THE RIOT...

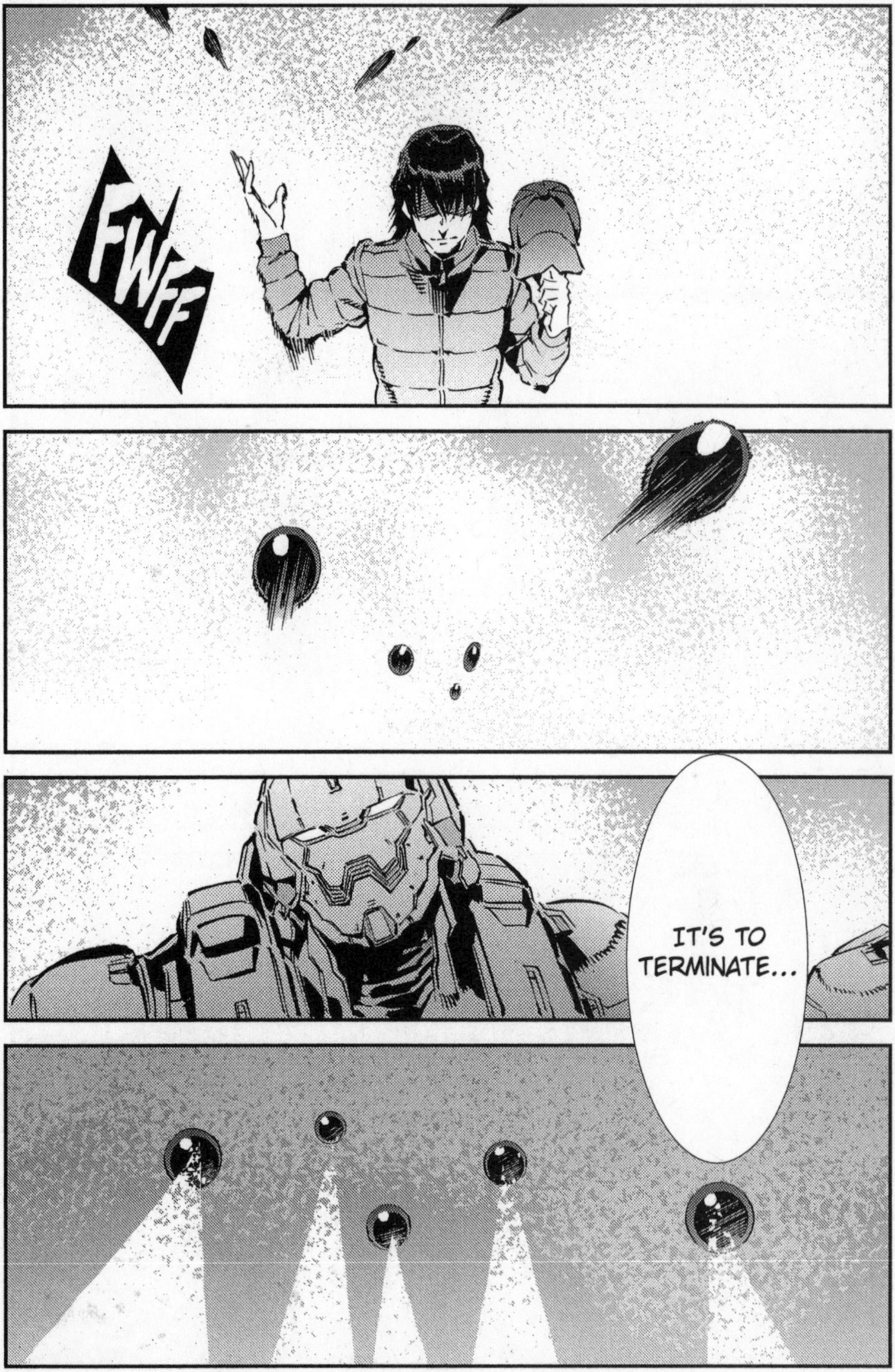
FWFF
IT'S TO TERMINATE...

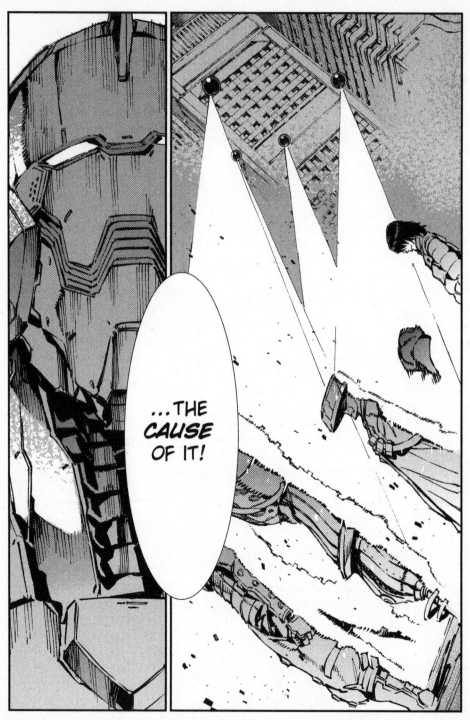

...THE **CAUSE** OF IT!

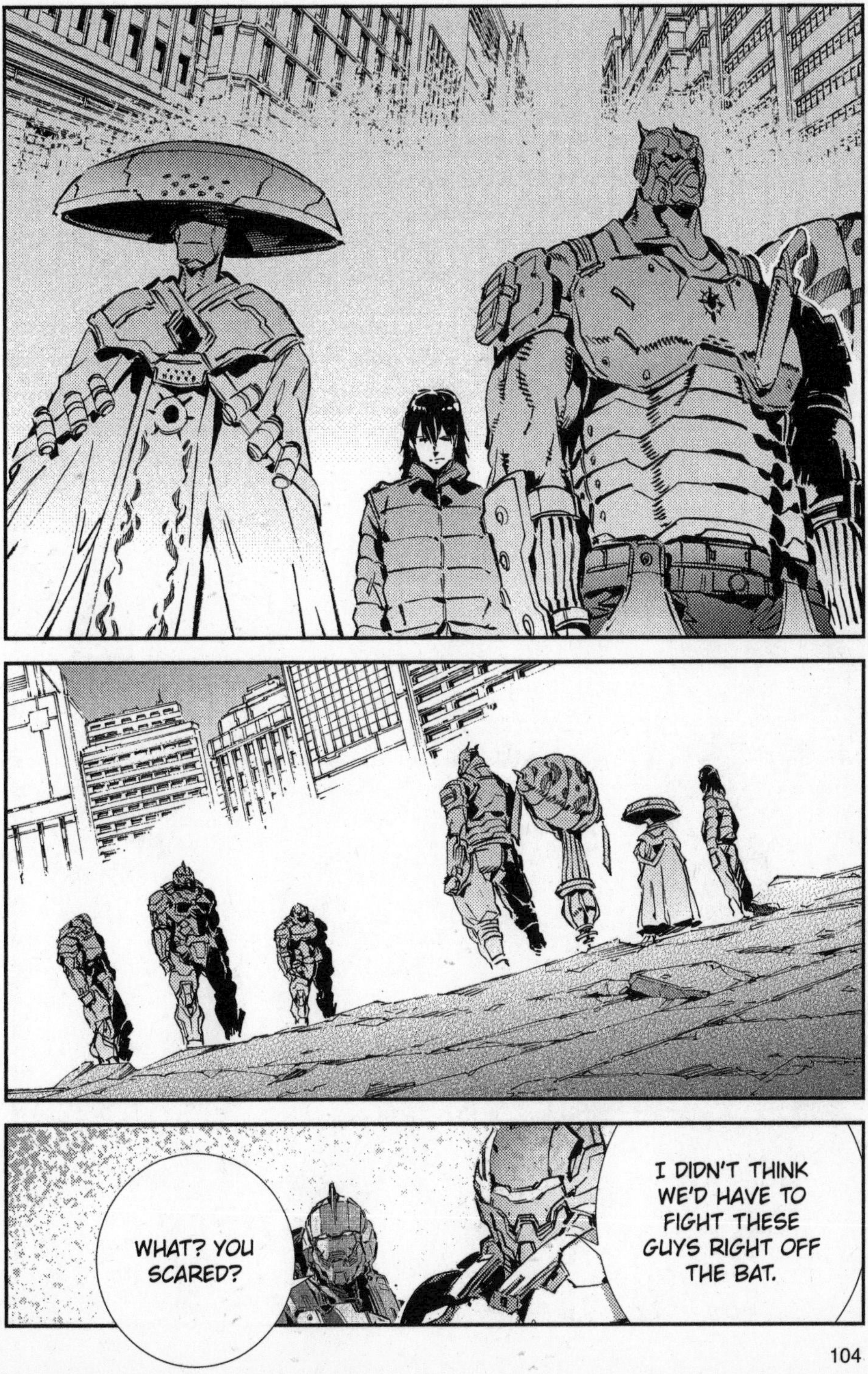
I DIDN'T THINK WE'D HAVE TO FIGHT THESE GUYS RIGHT OFF THE BAT.
WHAT? YOU SCARED?

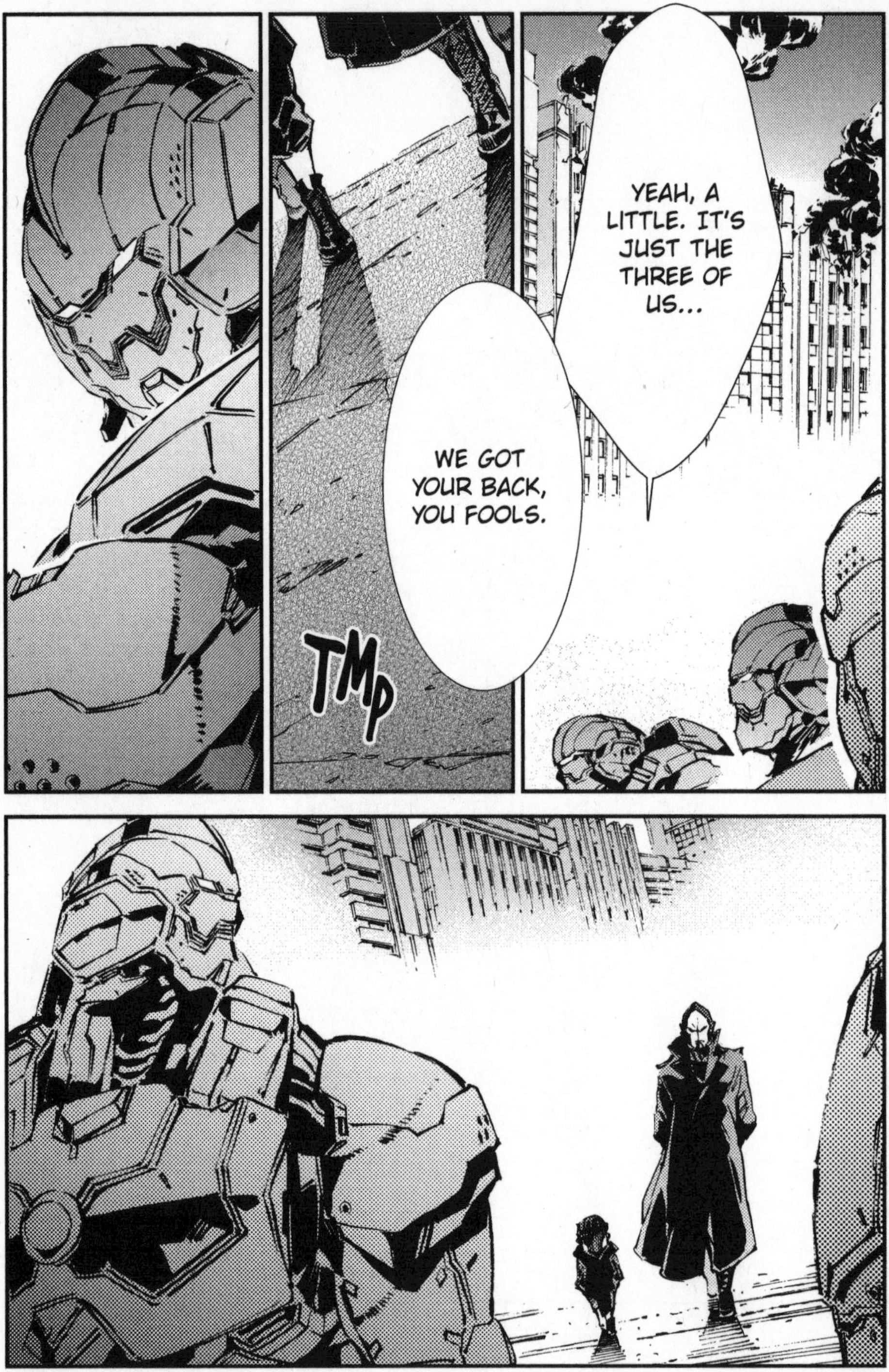
YEAH, A LITTLE. IT'S JUST THE THREE OF US...
WE GOT YOUR BACK, YOU FOOLS.
TMP

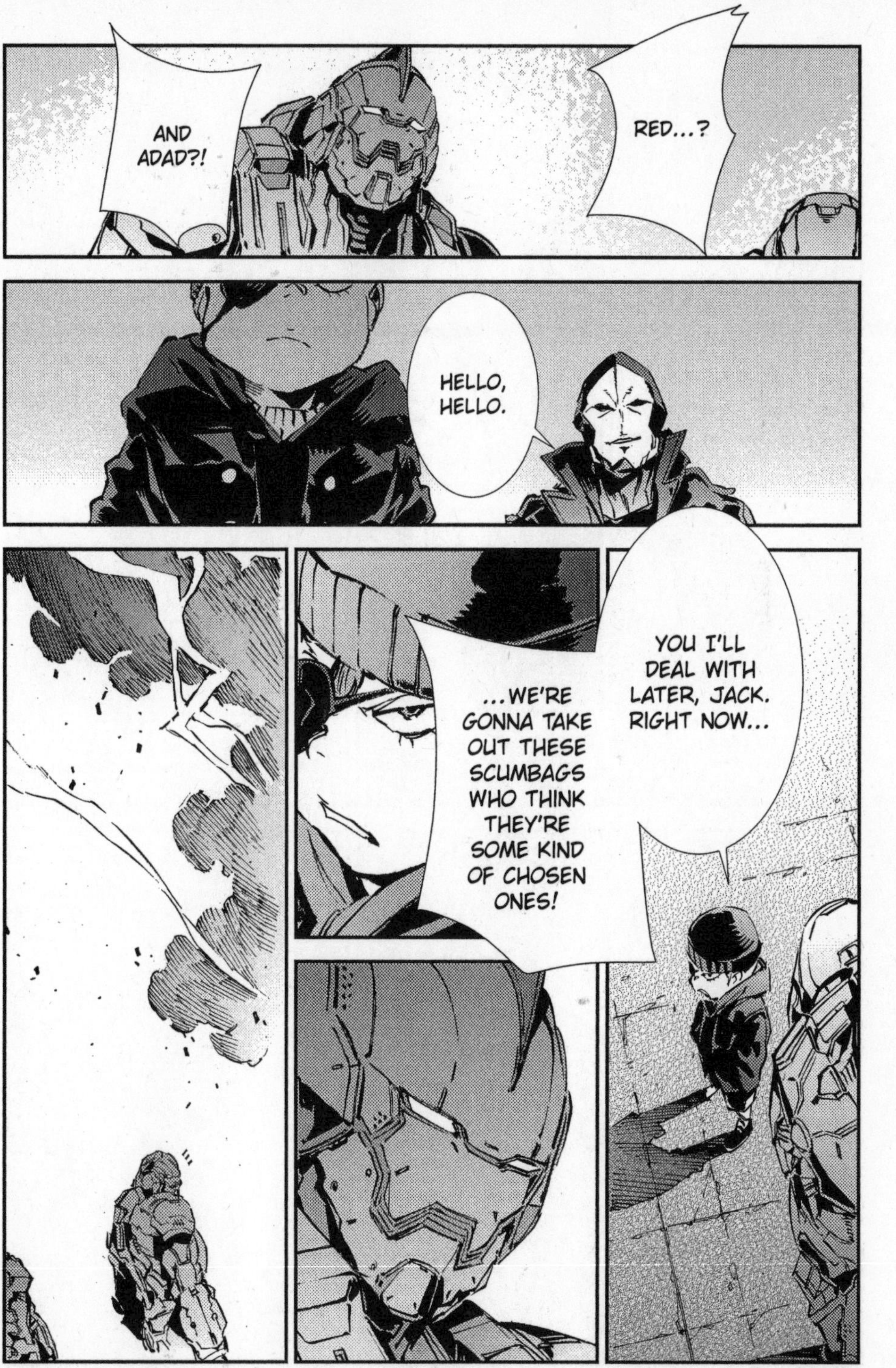
RED...?
AND ADAD?!
HELLO, HELLO.
YOU I'LL DEAL WITH LATER, JACK. RIGHT NOW...
...WE'RE GONNA TAKE OUT THESE SCUMBAGS WHO THINK THEY'RE SOME KIND OF CHOSEN ONES!

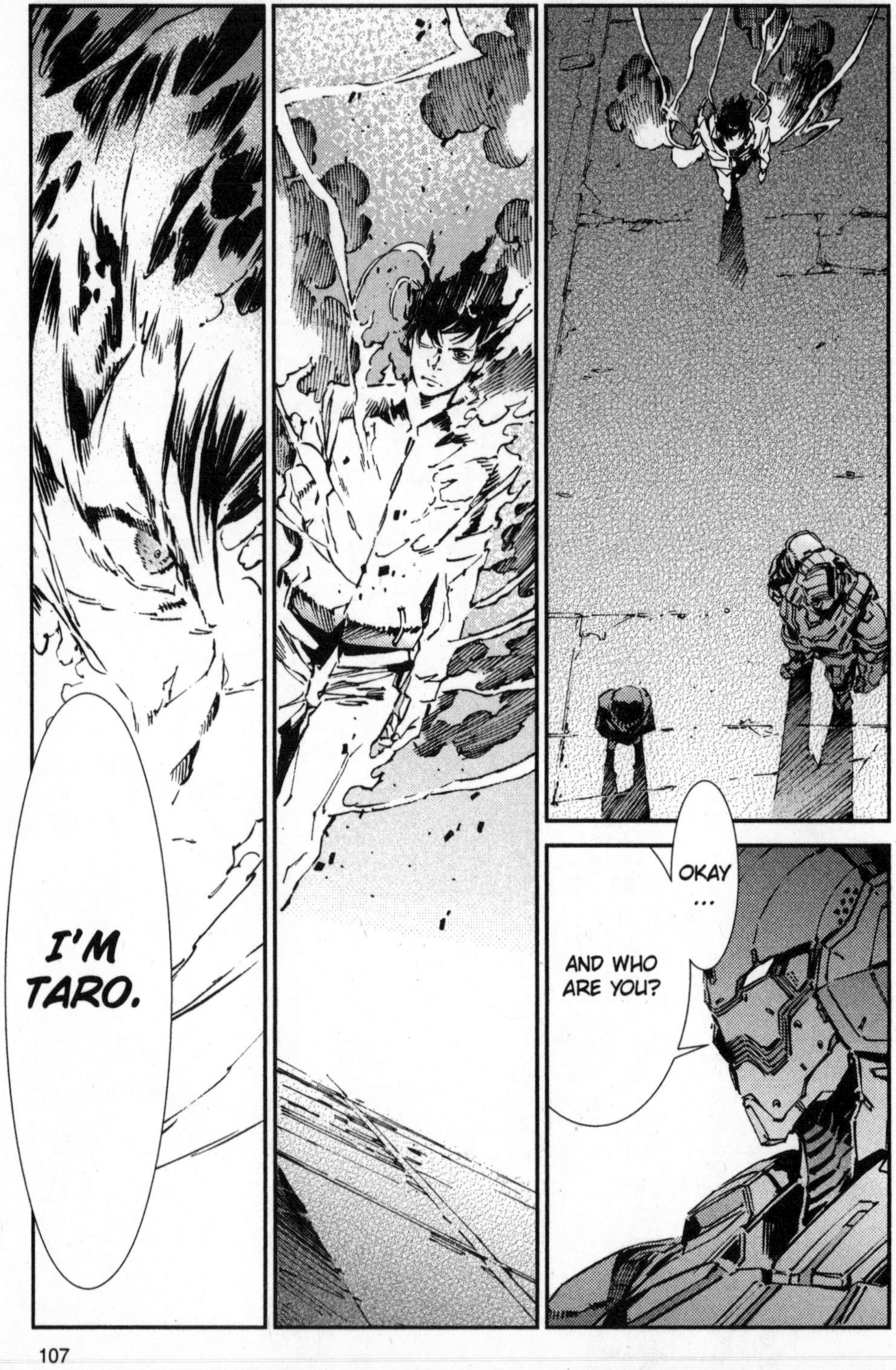
OKAY ...
AND WHO ARE YOU?
I'M TARO.

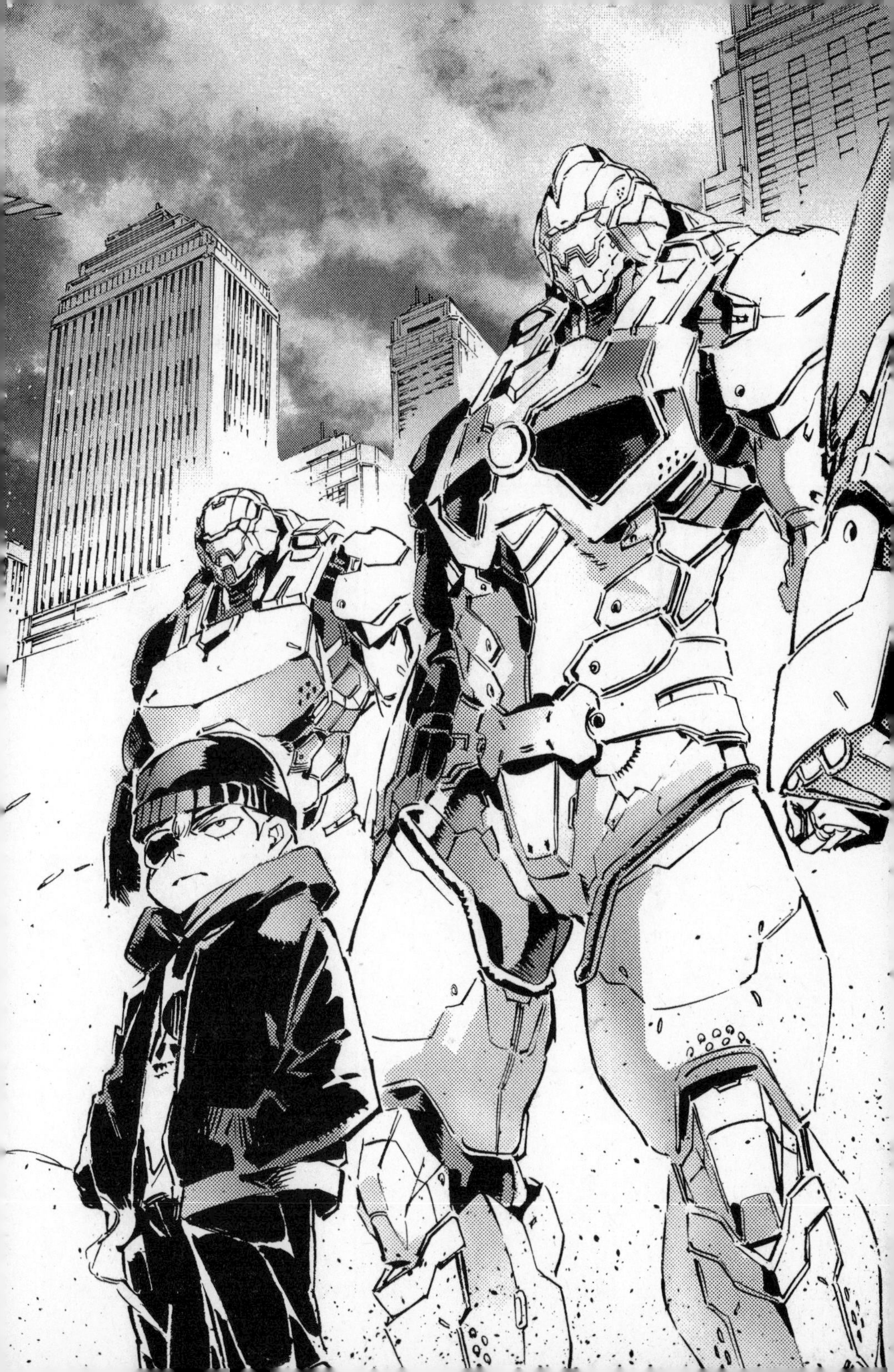

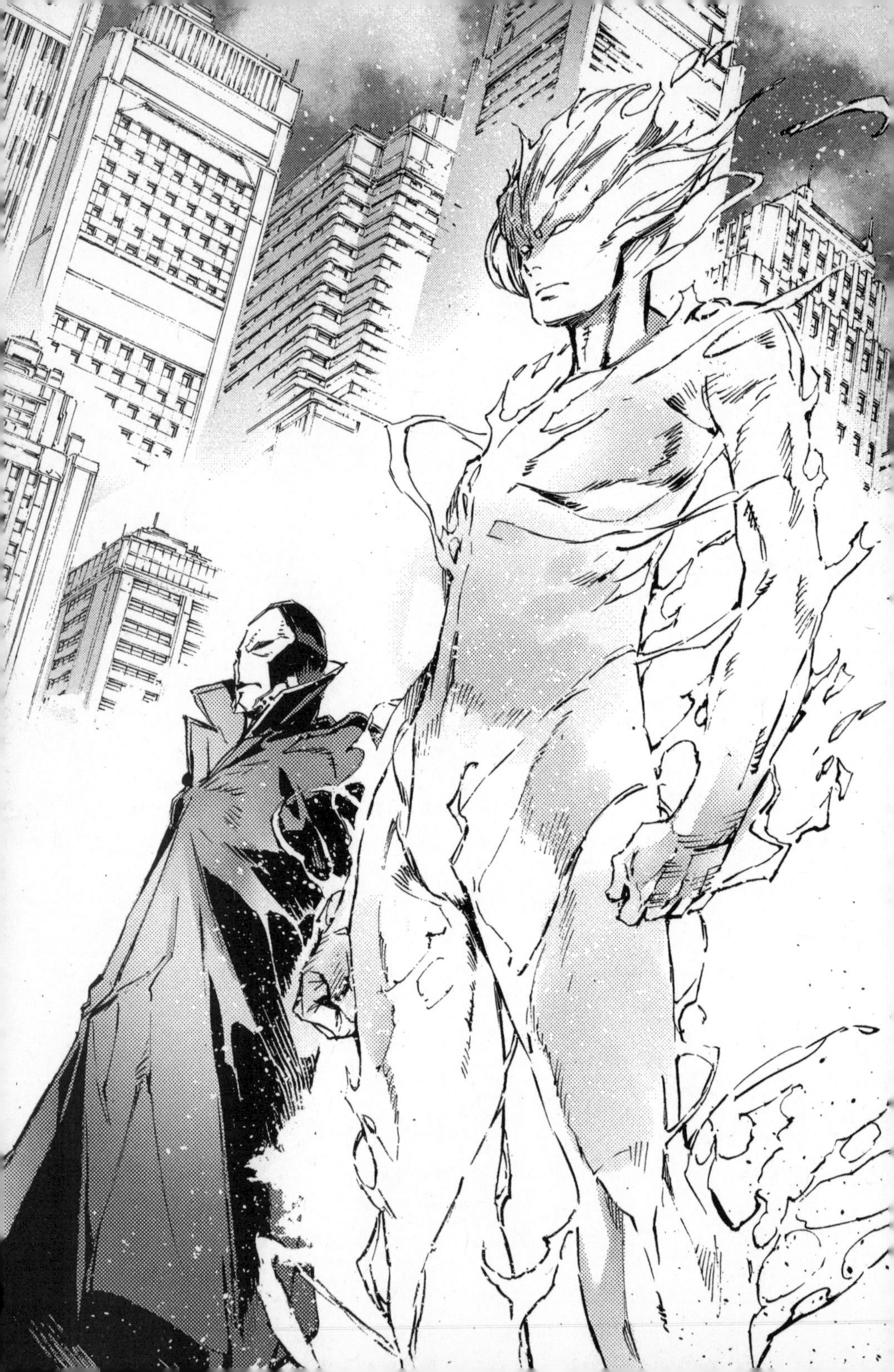

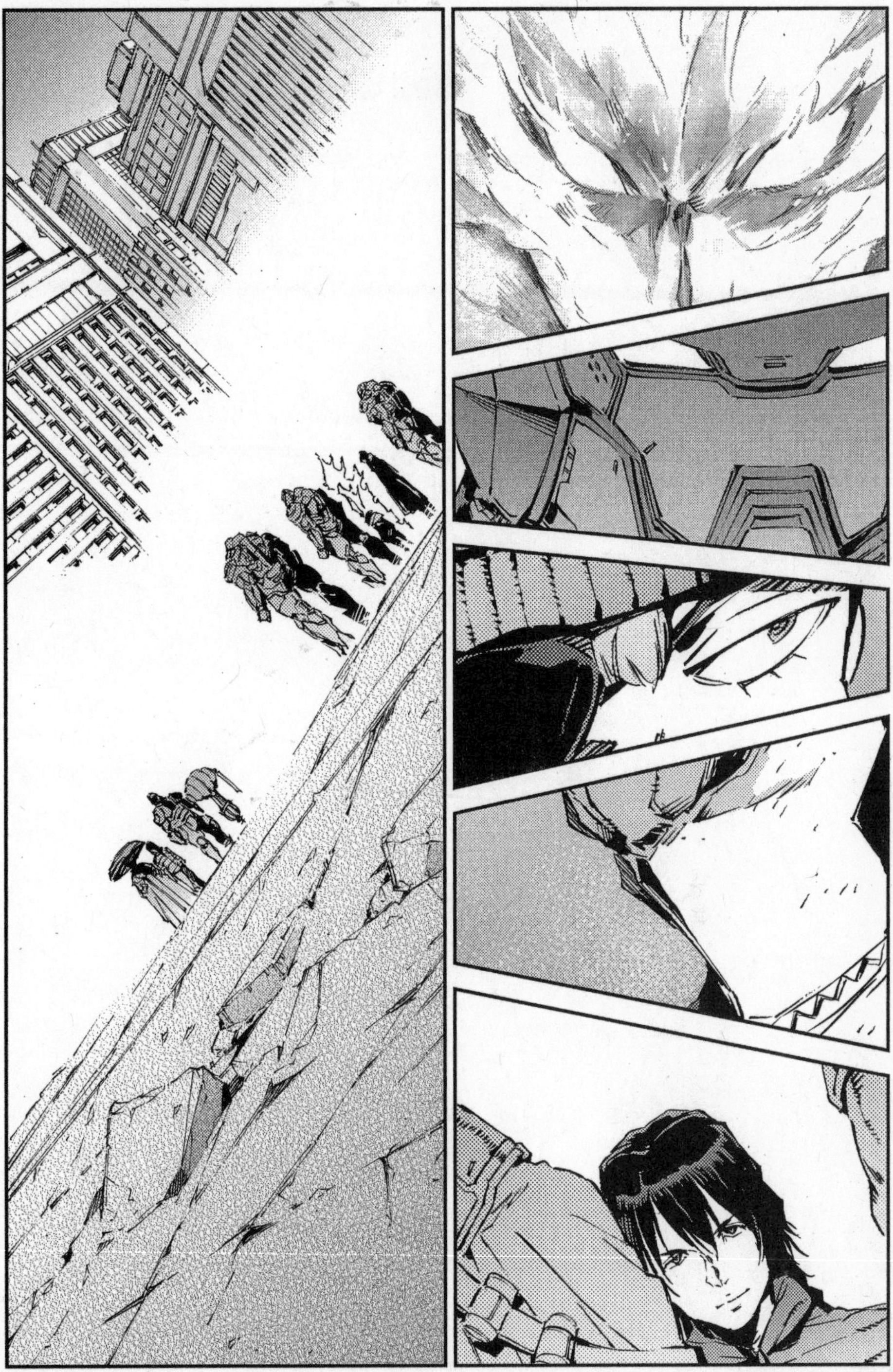

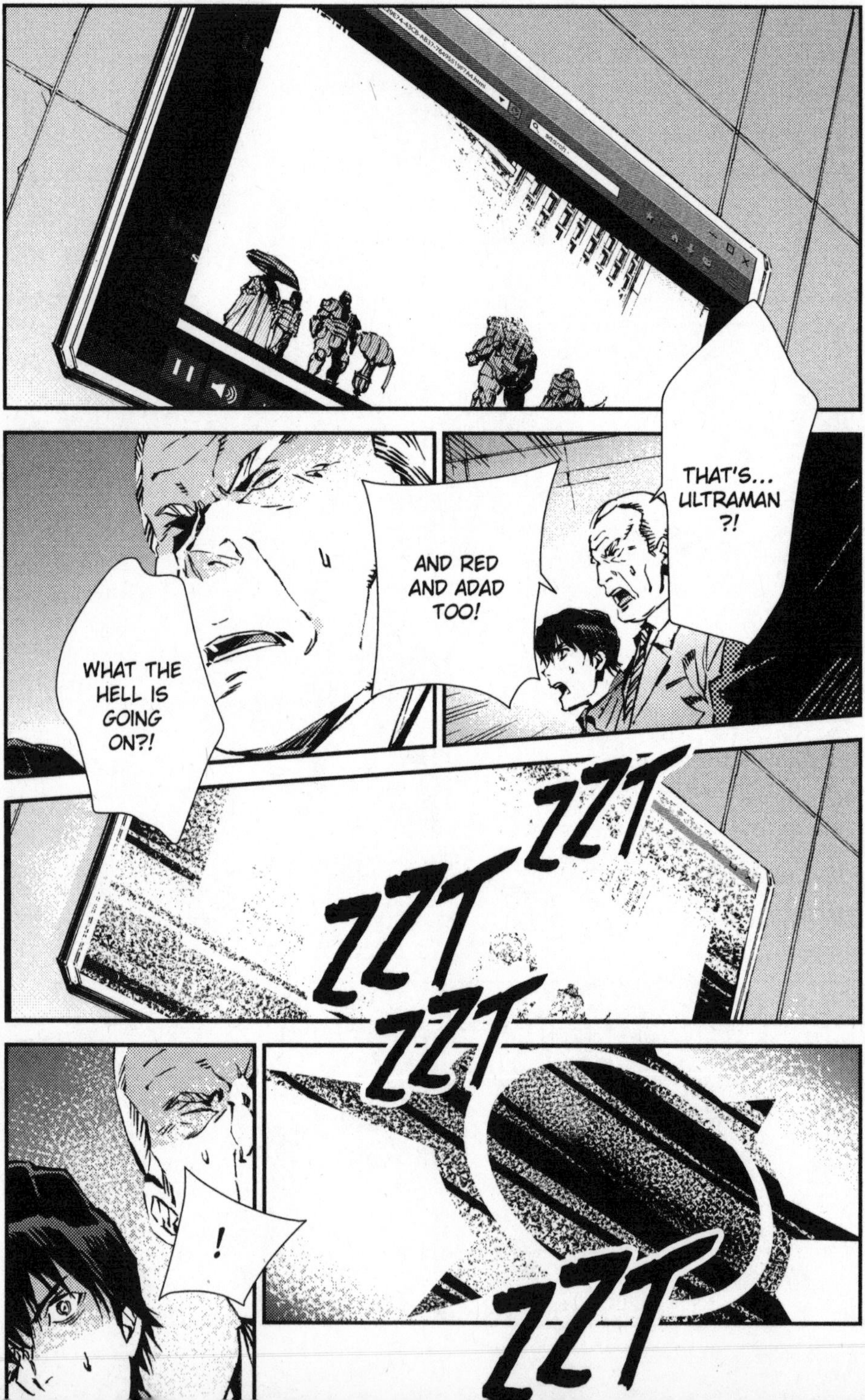
THAT'S... ULTRAMAN ?!
AND RED AND ADAD TOO!
WHAT THE HELL IS GOING ON?!
ZZT
ZZT
ZZT
ZZT
!

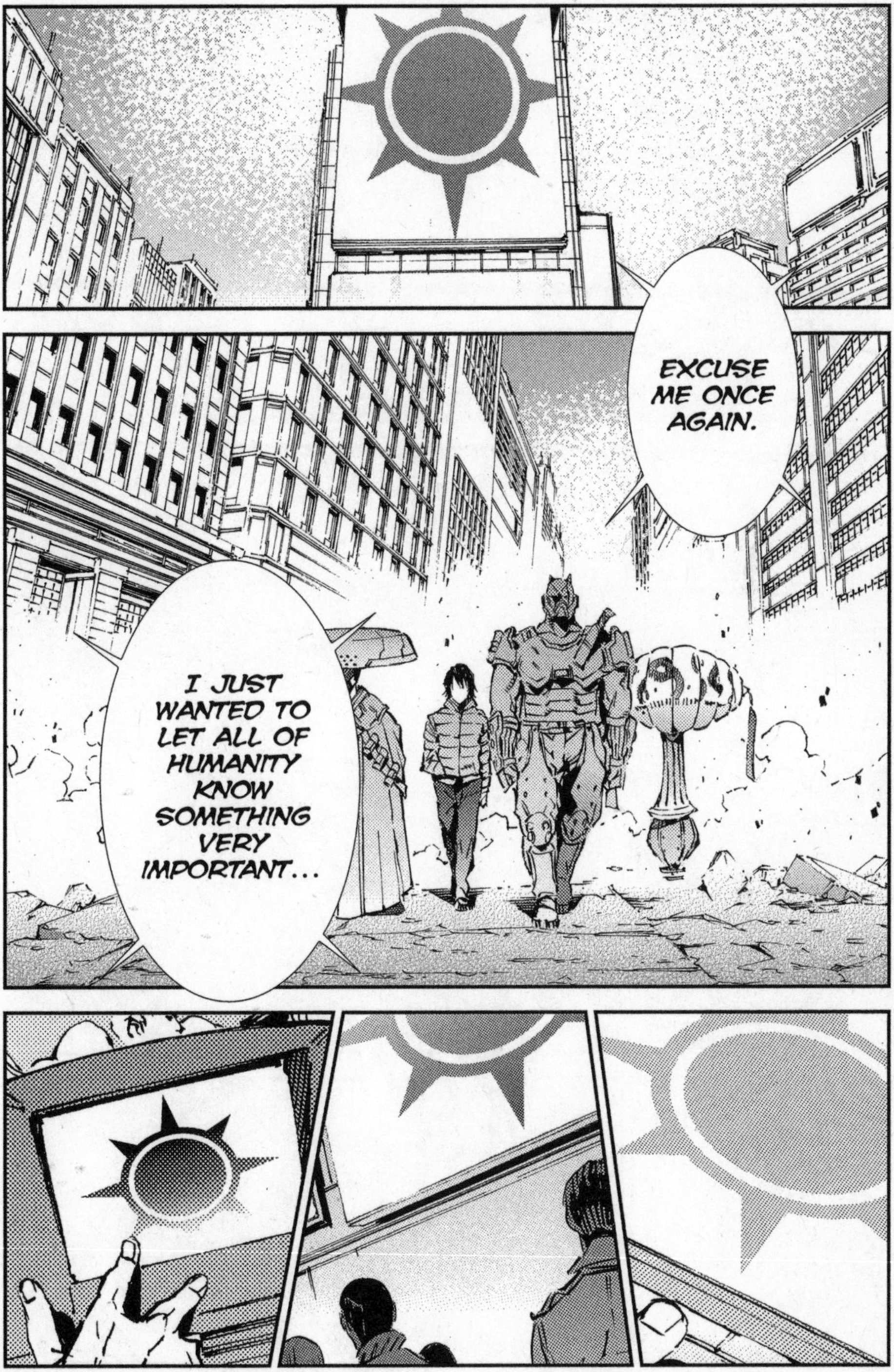
EXCUSE ME ONCE AGAIN.
I JUST WANTED TO LET ALL OF HUMANITY KNOW SOMETHING VERY IMPORTANT...

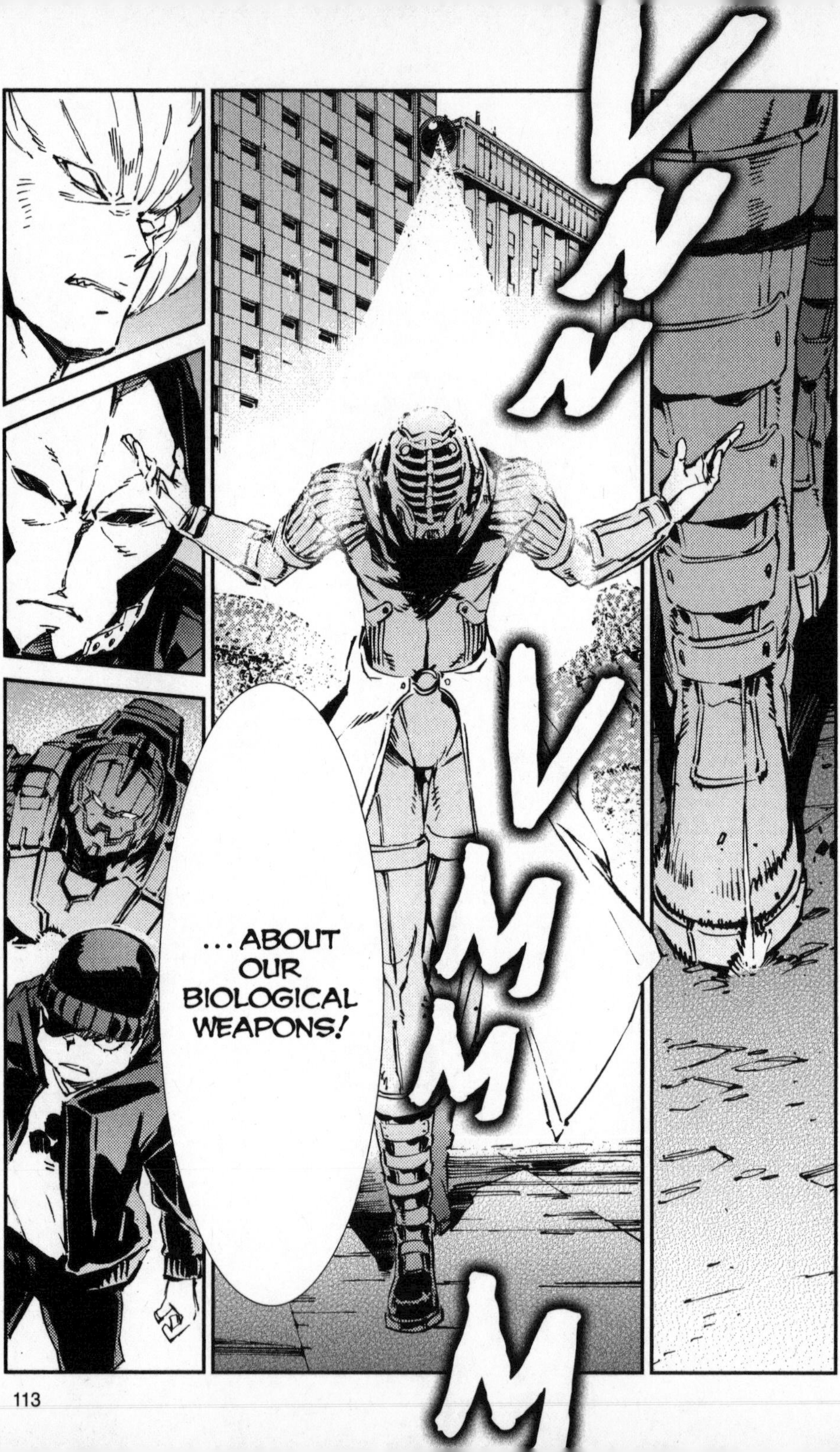
VNNN
VVMMMM
...ABOUT OUR BIOLOGICAL WEAPONS!

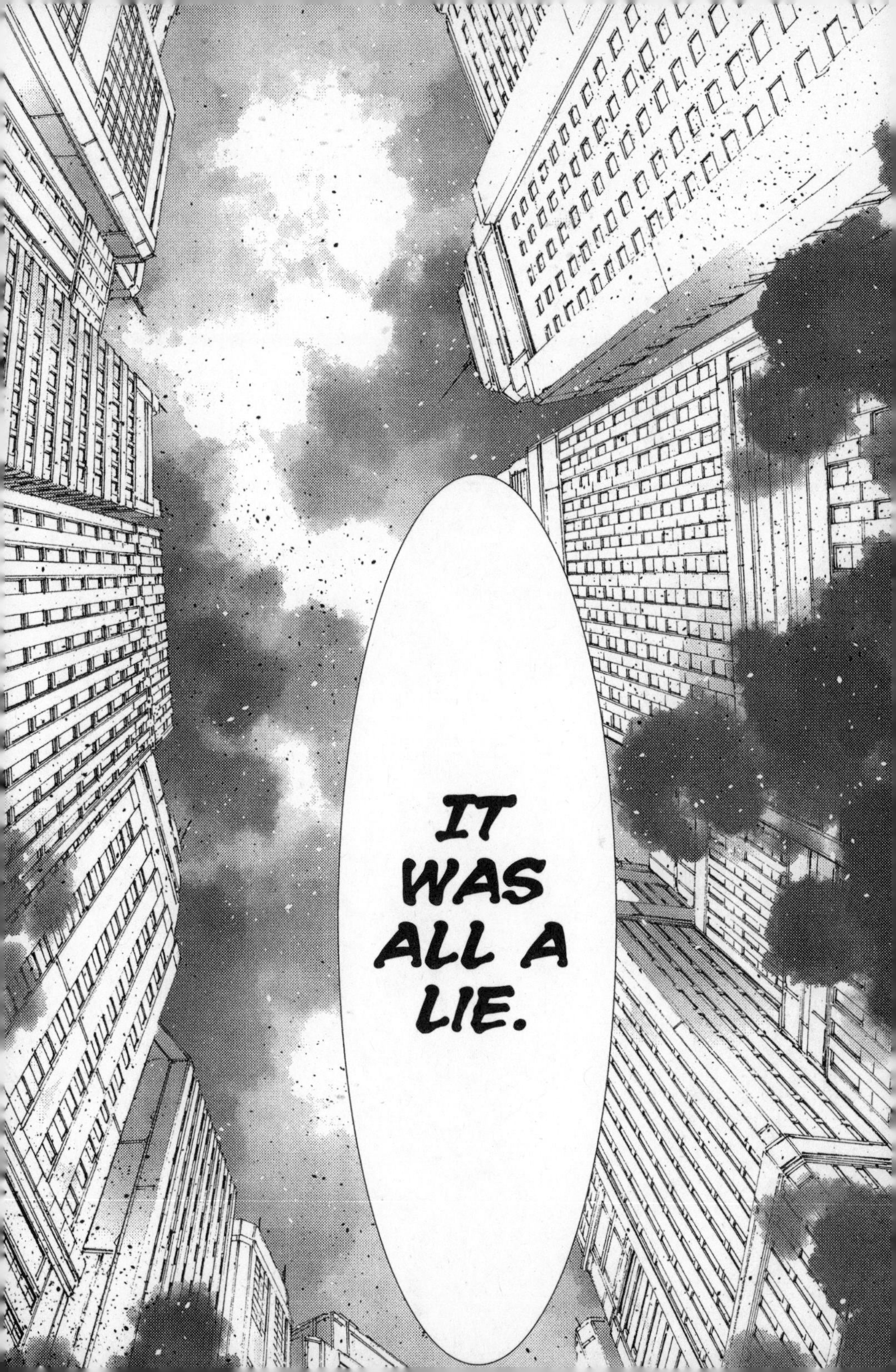
IT WAS ALL A LIE.

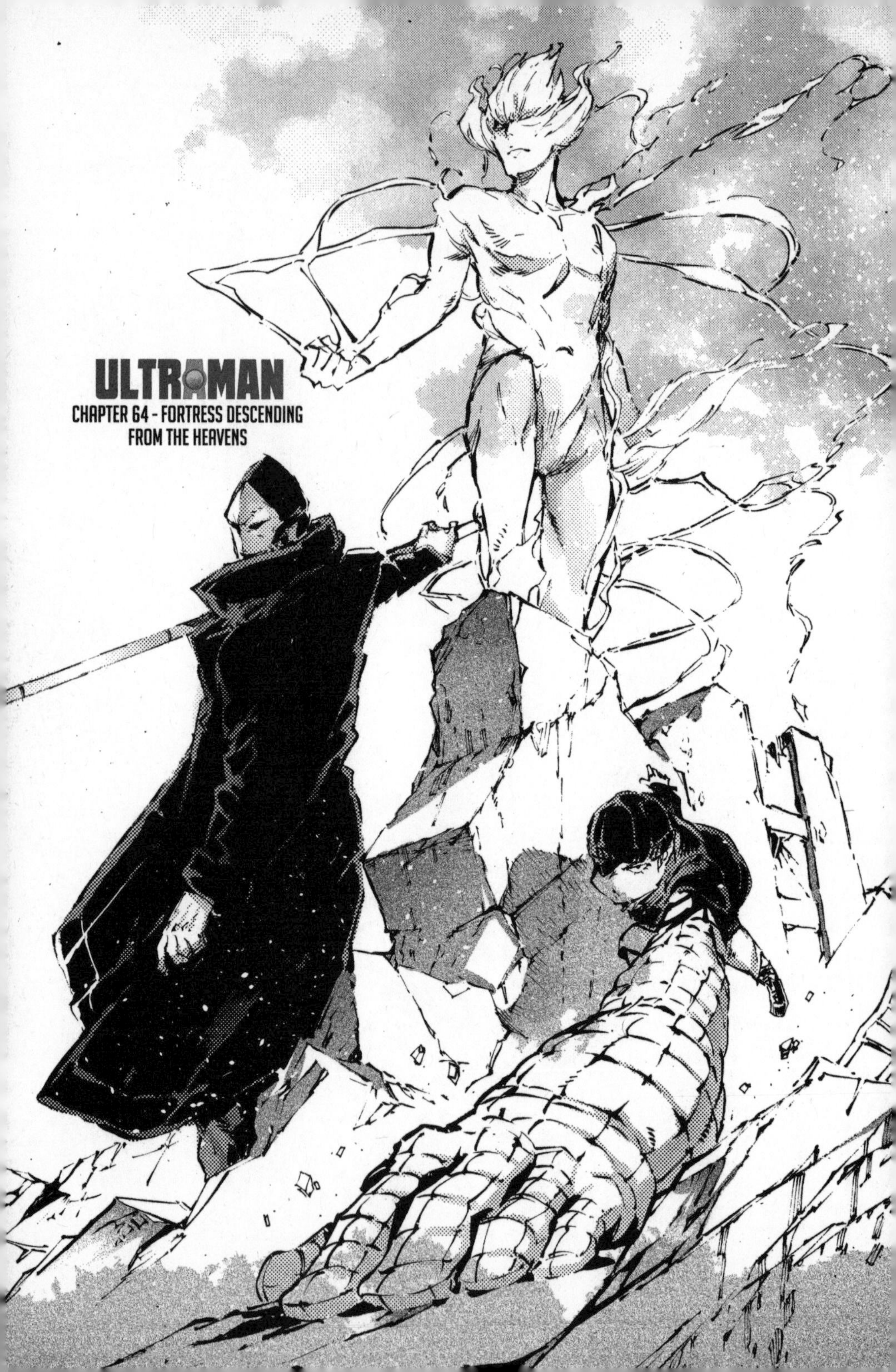
ULTRAMAN
CHAPTER 64 - FORTRESS DESCENDING
FROM THE HEAVENS

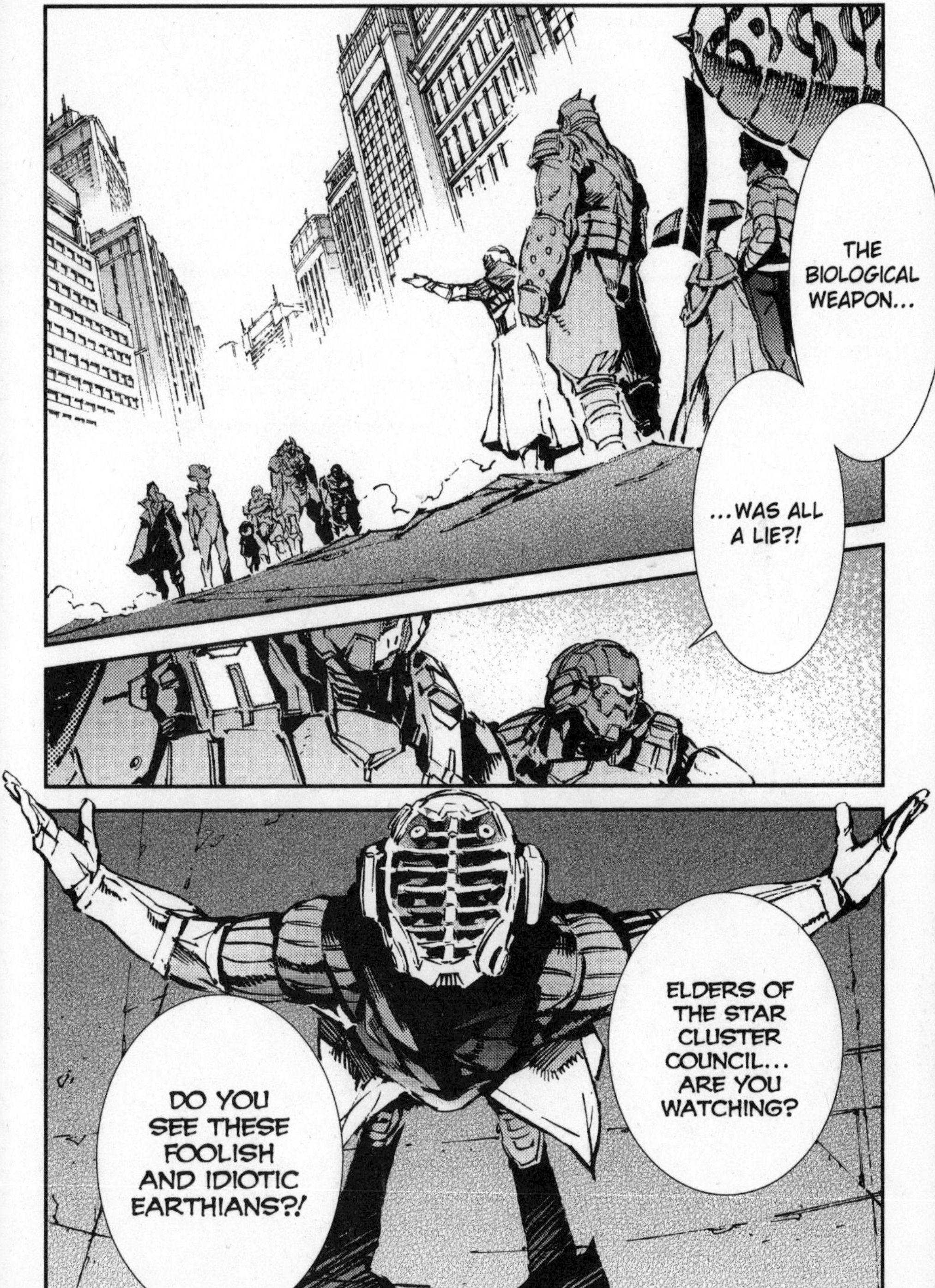
THE BIOLOGICAL WEAPON...
...WAS ALL A LIE?!
ELDERS OF THE STAR CLUSTER COUNCIL... ARE YOU WATCHING?
DO YOU SEE THESE FOOLISH AND IDIOTIC EARTHIANS?!

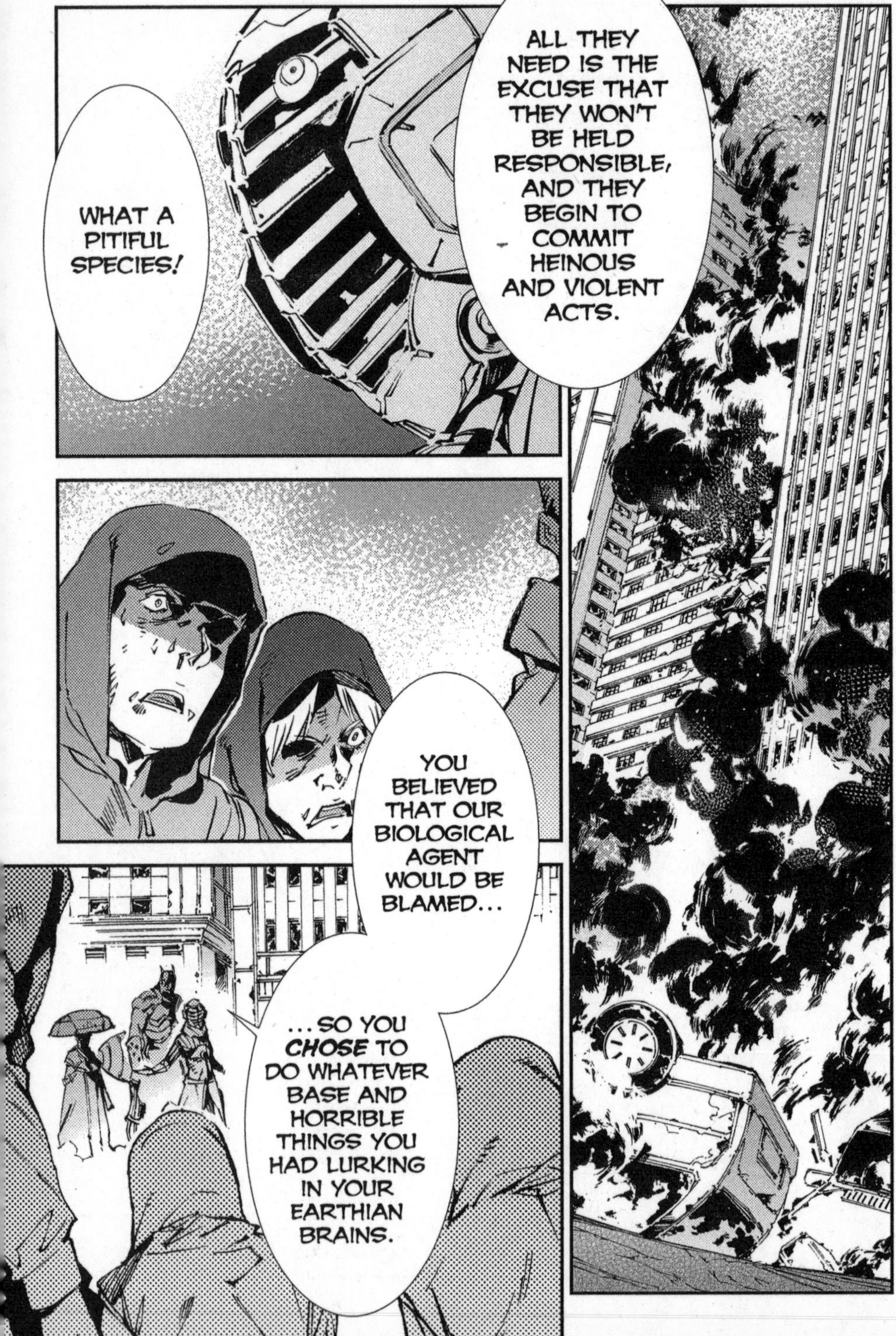
ALL THEY NEED IS THE EXCUSE THAT THEY WON'T BE HELD RESPONSIBLE, AND THEY BEGIN TO COMMIT HEINOUS AND VIOLENT ACTS.
WHAT A PITIFUL SPECIES!
YOU BELIEVED THAT OUR BIOLOGICAL AGENT WOULD BE BLAMED...
...SO YOU *CHOSE* TO DO WHATEVER BASE AND HORRIBLE THINGS YOU HAD LURKING IN YOUR EARTHIAN BRAINS.

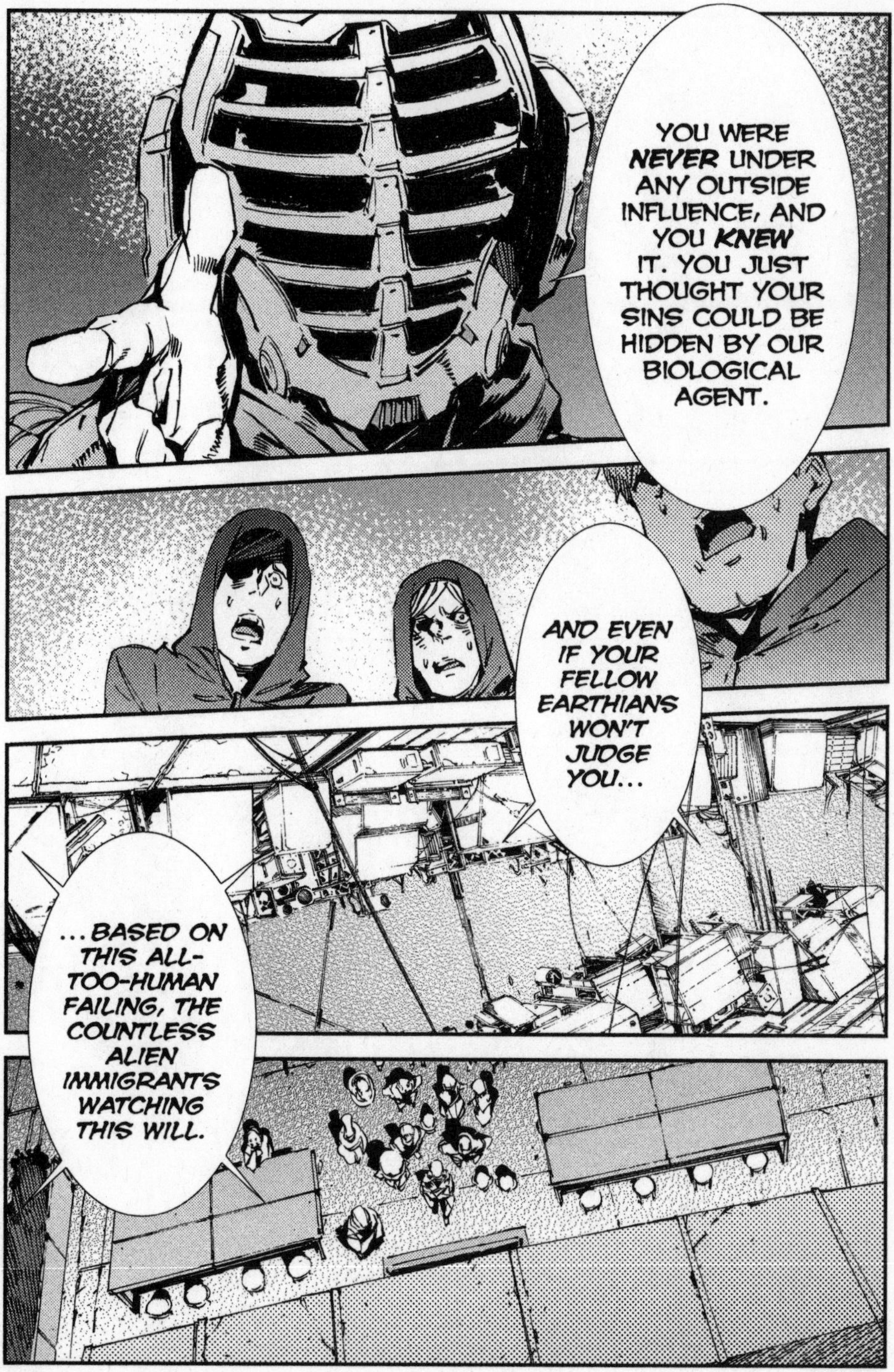
YOU WERE NEVER UNDER ANY OUTSIDE INFLUENCE, AND YOU KNEW IT. YOU JUST THOUGHT YOUR SINS COULD BE HIDDEN BY OUR BIOLOGICAL AGENT.
AND EVEN IF YOUR FELLOW EARTHIANS WON'T JUDGE YOU...
...BASED ON THIS ALL-TOO-HUMAN FAILING, THE COUNTLESS ALIEN IMMIGRANTS WATCHING THIS WILL.

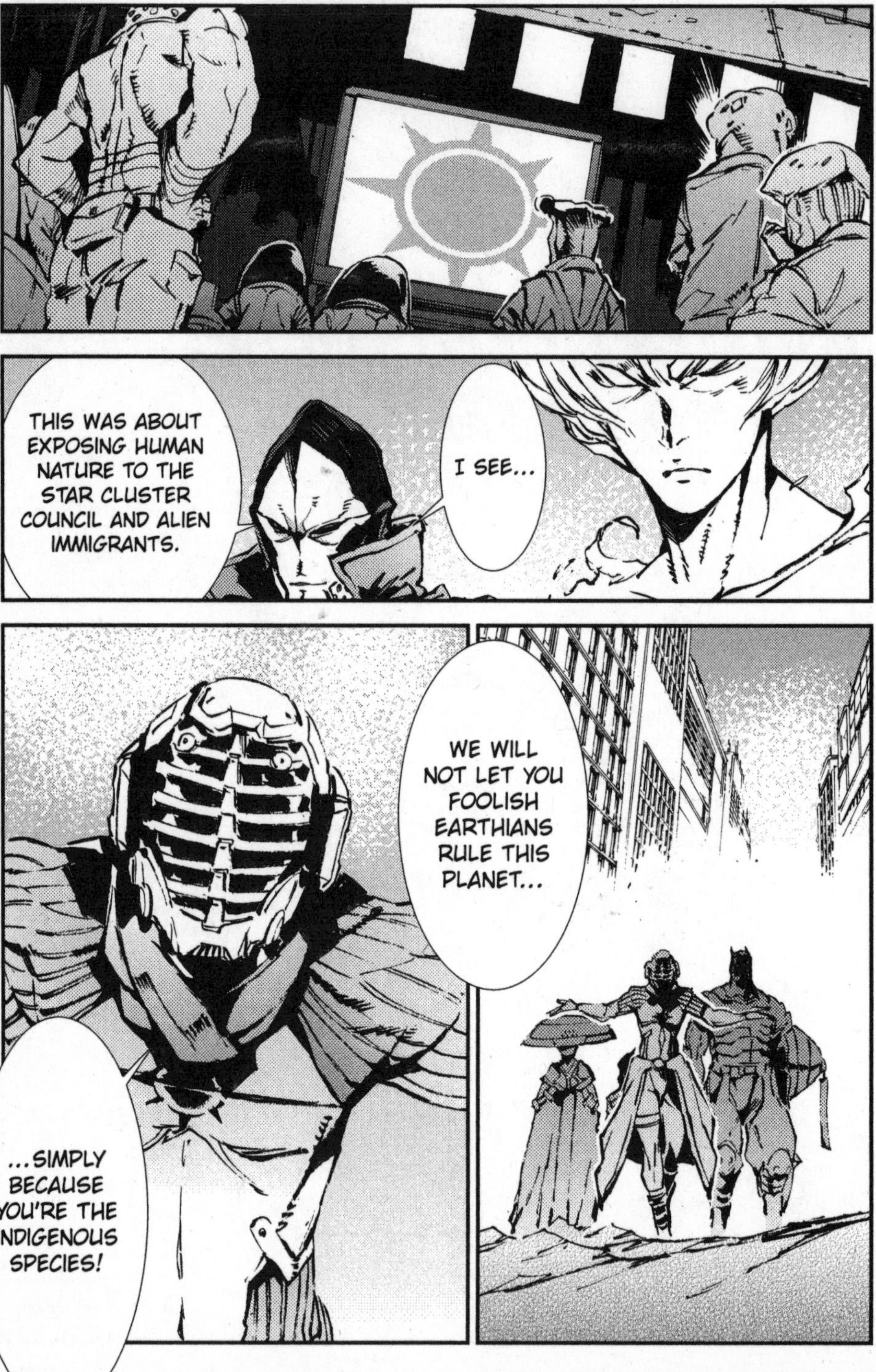
I SEE...
THIS WAS ABOUT EXPOSING HUMAN NATURE TO THE STAR CLUSTER COUNCIL AND ALIEN IMMIGRANTS.
WE WILL NOT LET YOU FOOLISH EARTHIANS RULE THIS PLANET...
...SIMPLY BECAUSE YOU'RE THE INDIGENOUS SPECIES!

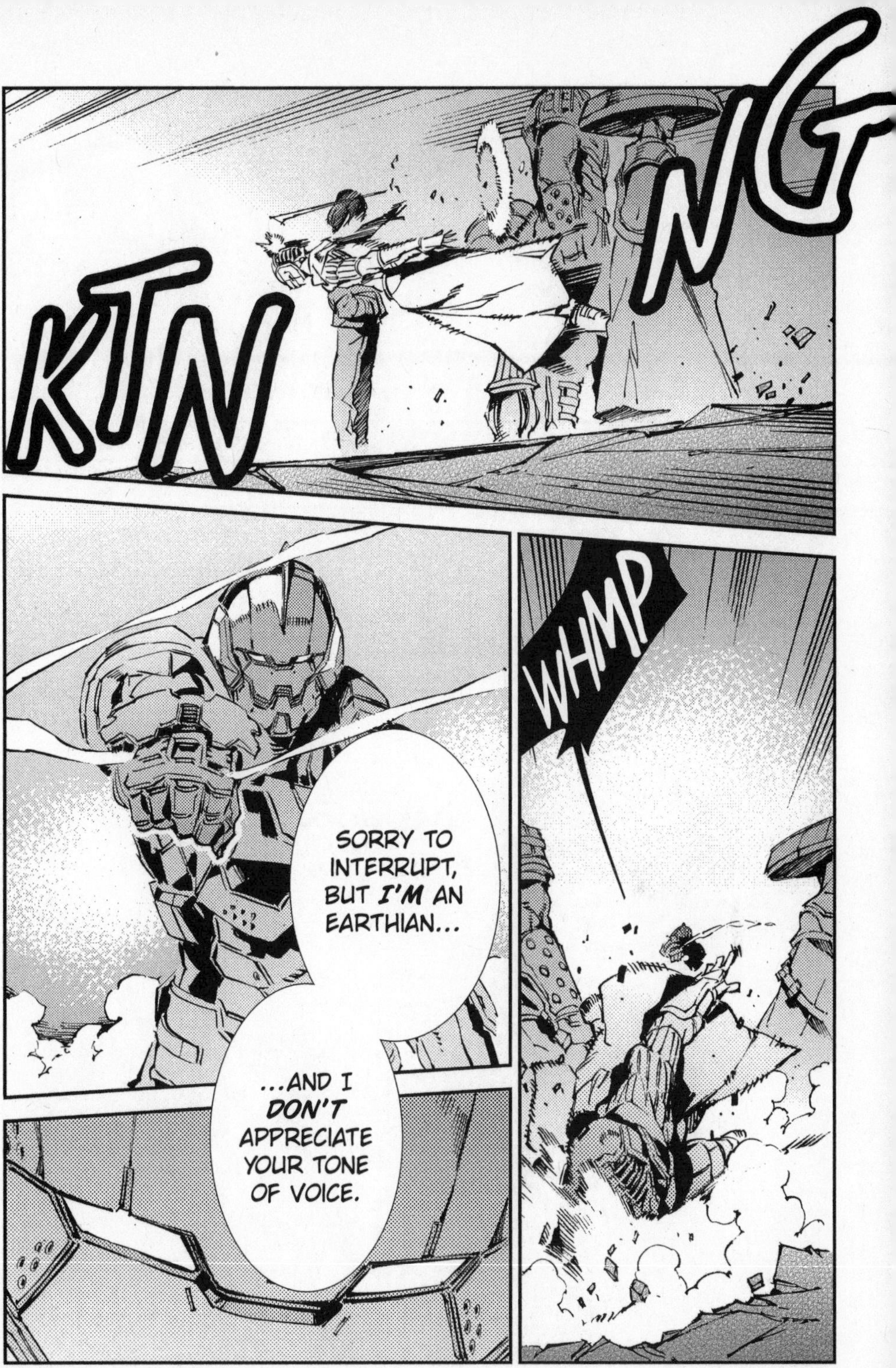
KTNNG
WHMP
SORRY TO INTERRUPT, BUT *I'M* AN EARTHIAN...
...AND I **DON'T** APPRECIATE YOUR TONE OF VOICE.

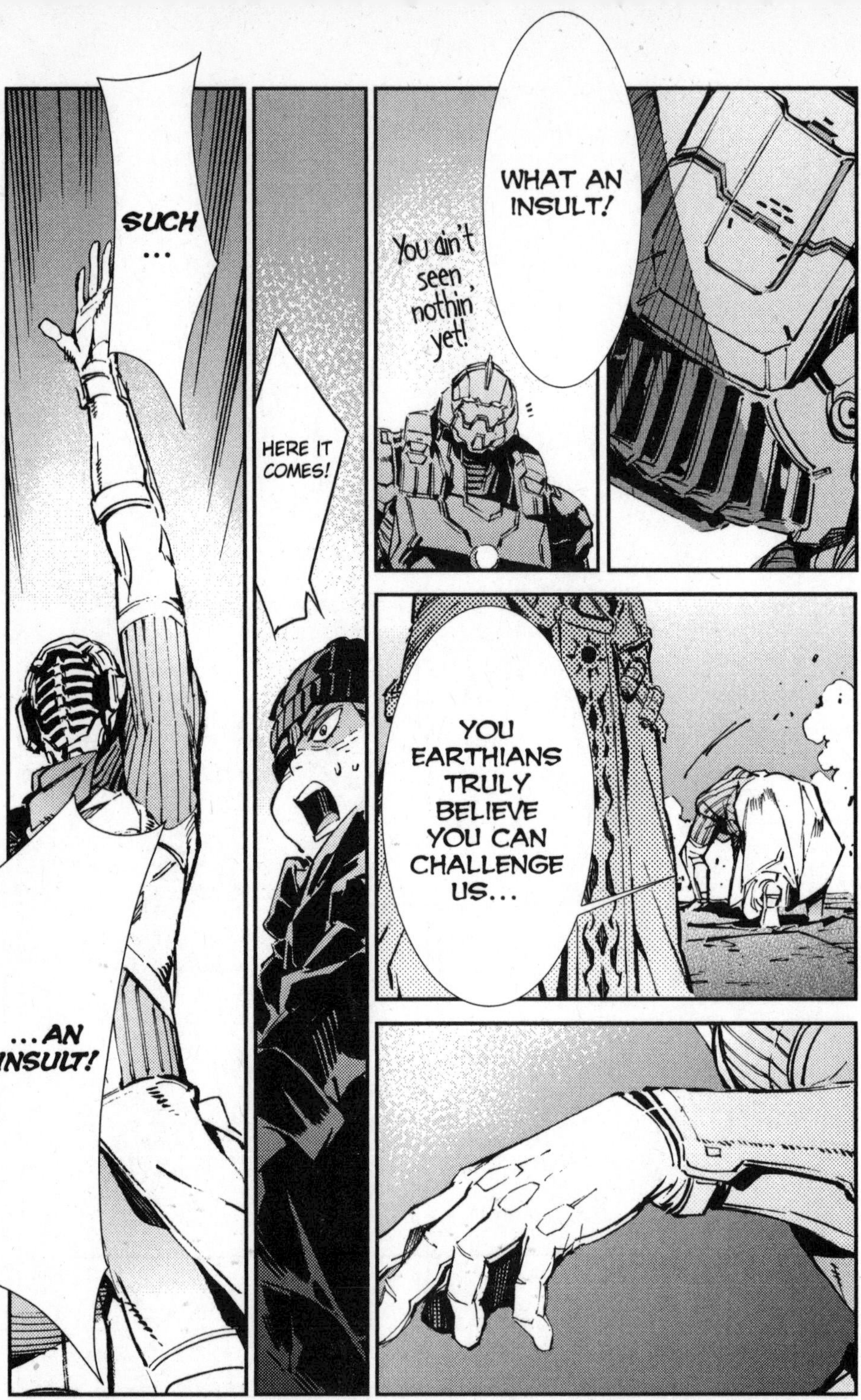
WHAT AN INSULT!
You ain't seen nothin yet!
YOU EARTHIANS TRULY BELIEVE YOU CAN CHALLENGE US...
HERE IT COMES!
SUCH...
...AN INSULT!

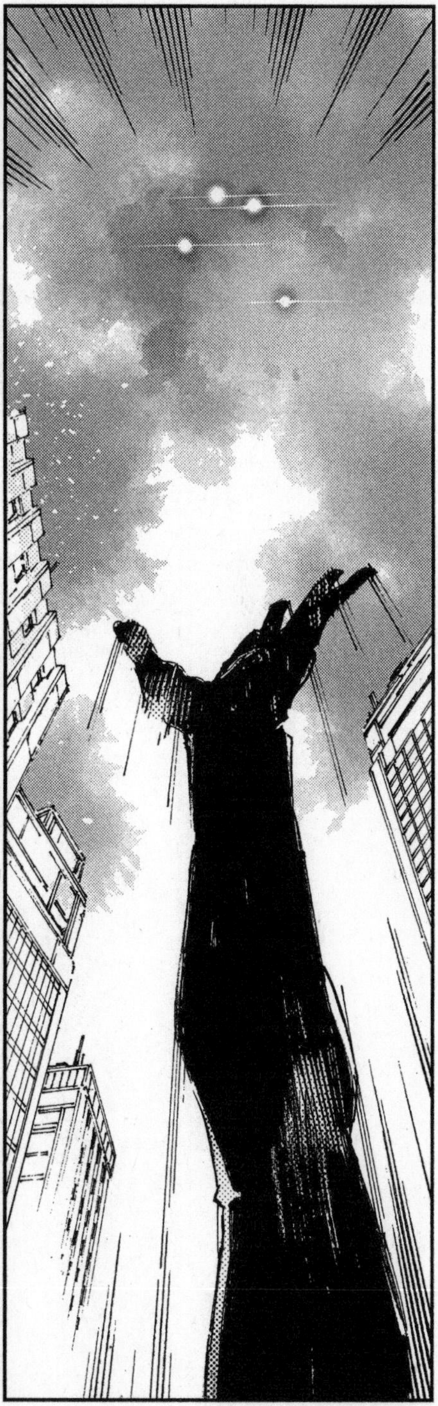
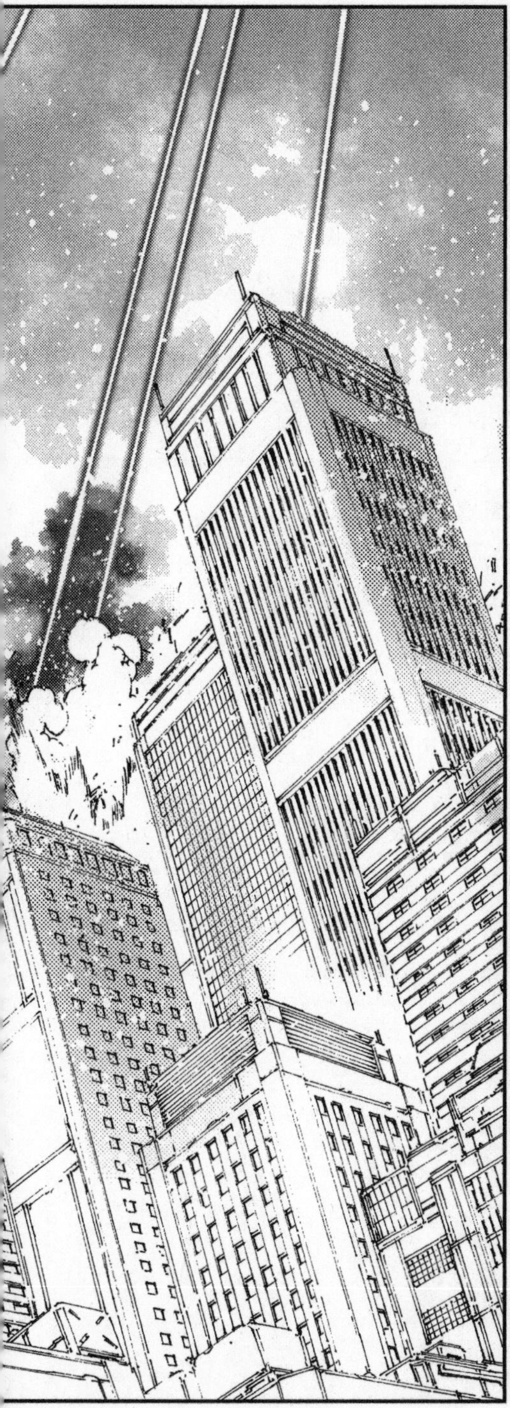

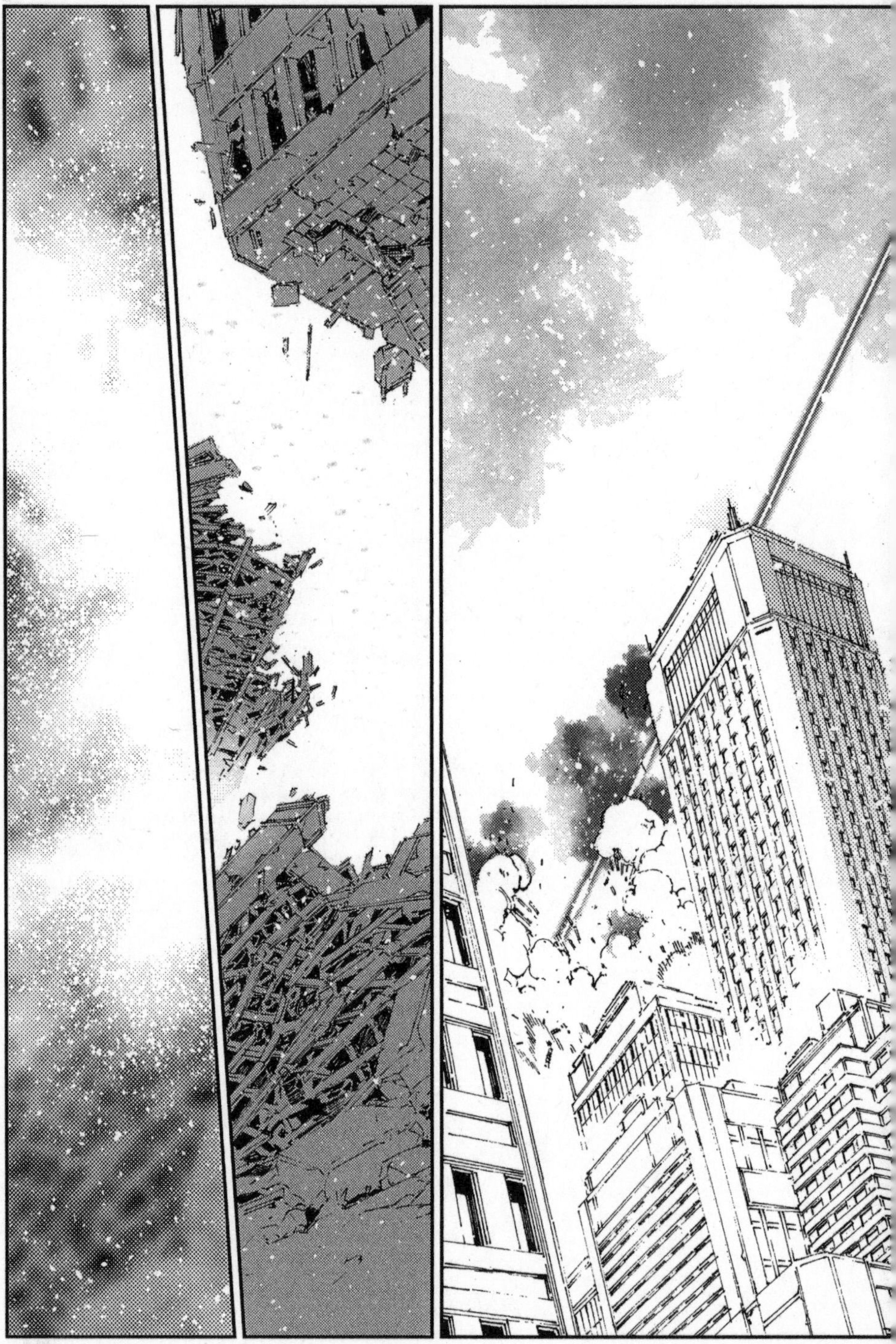

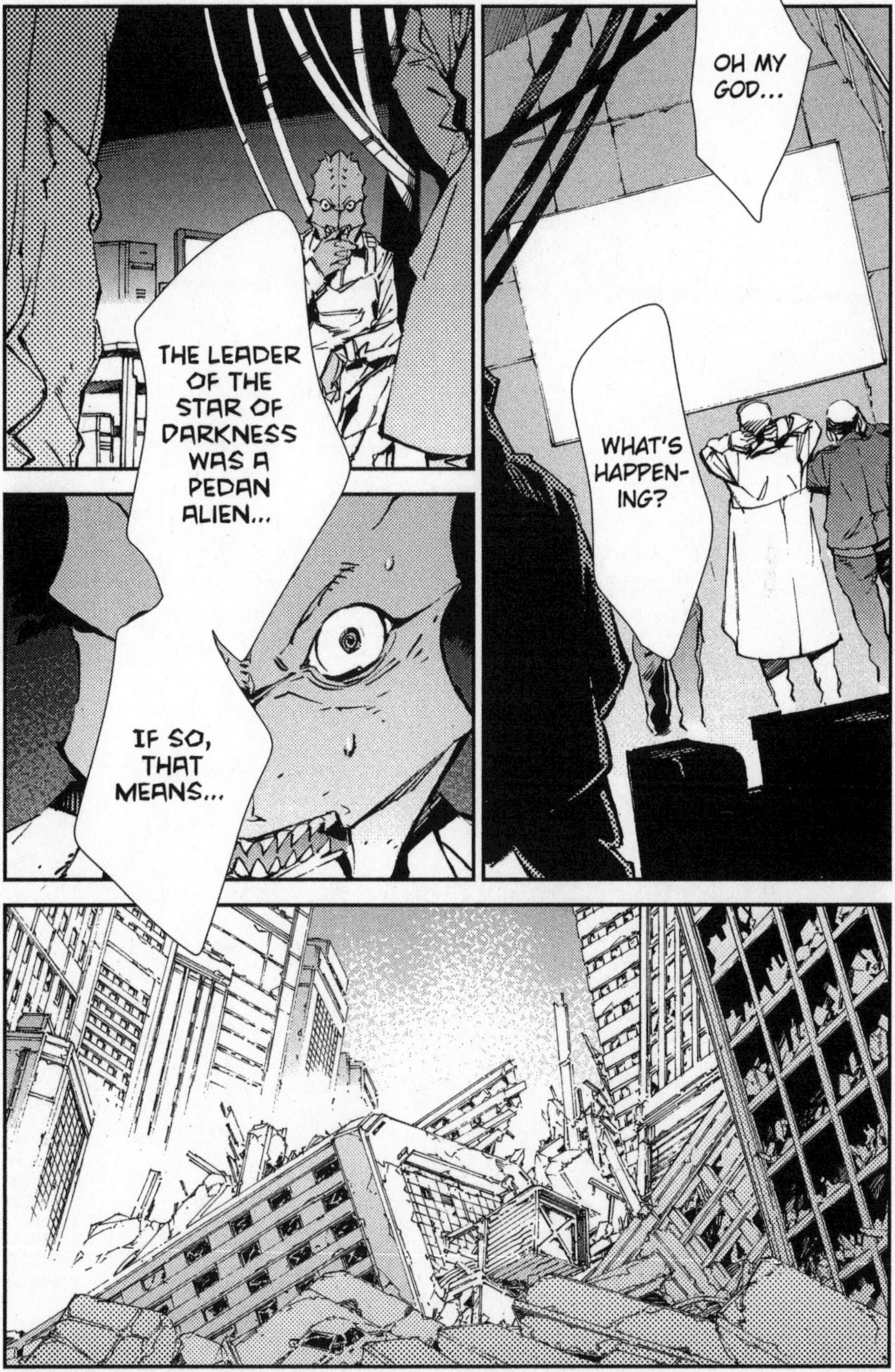
OH MY GOD...
WHAT'S HAPPEN-ING?
THE LEADER OF THE STAR OF DARKNESS WAS A PEDAN ALIEN...
IF SO, THAT MEANS...

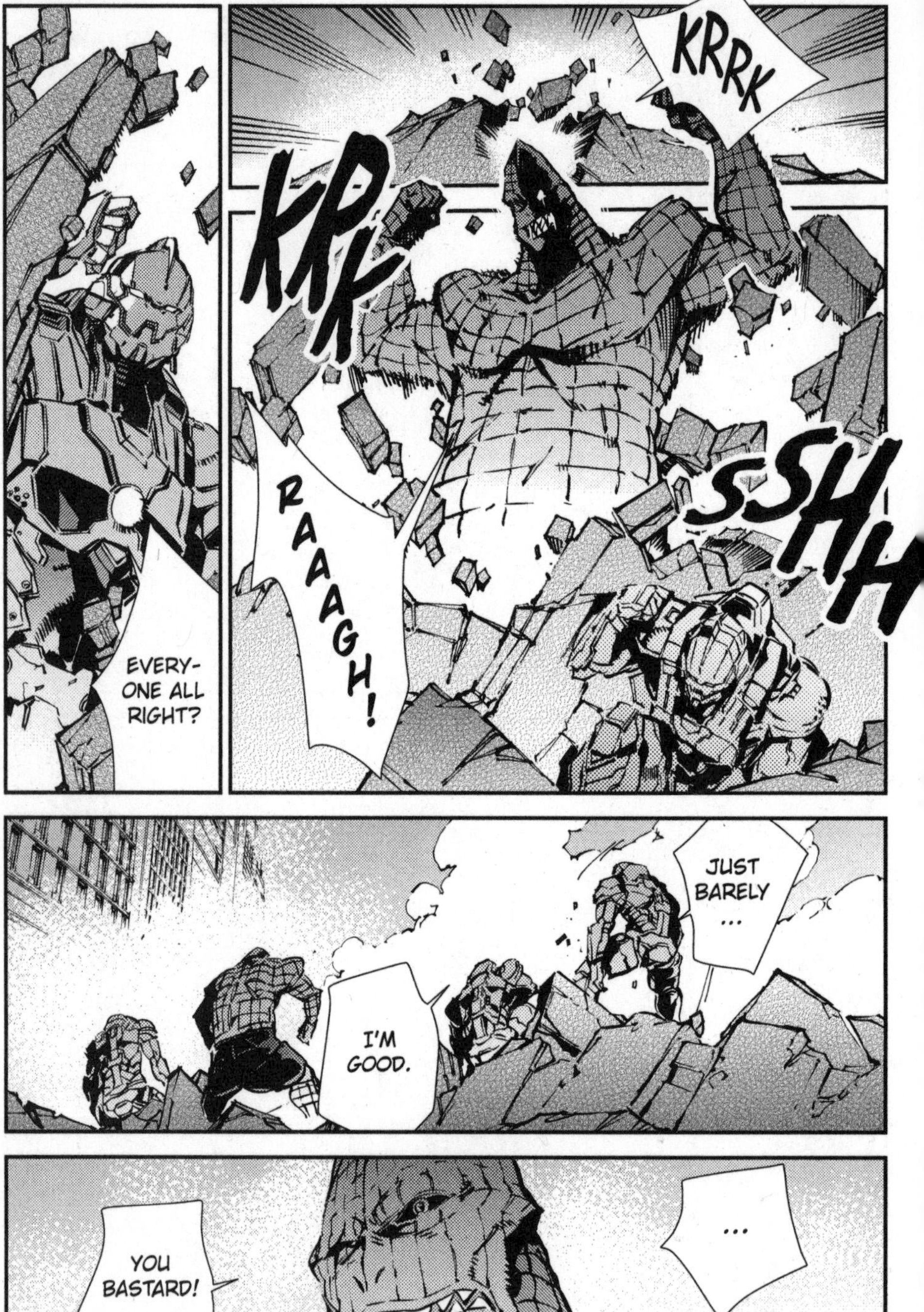
KRRK
KRK
SSHH
RAAAGH!
EVERY-ONE ALL RIGHT?
JUST BARELY ...
I'M GOOD.
...
YOU BASTARD!

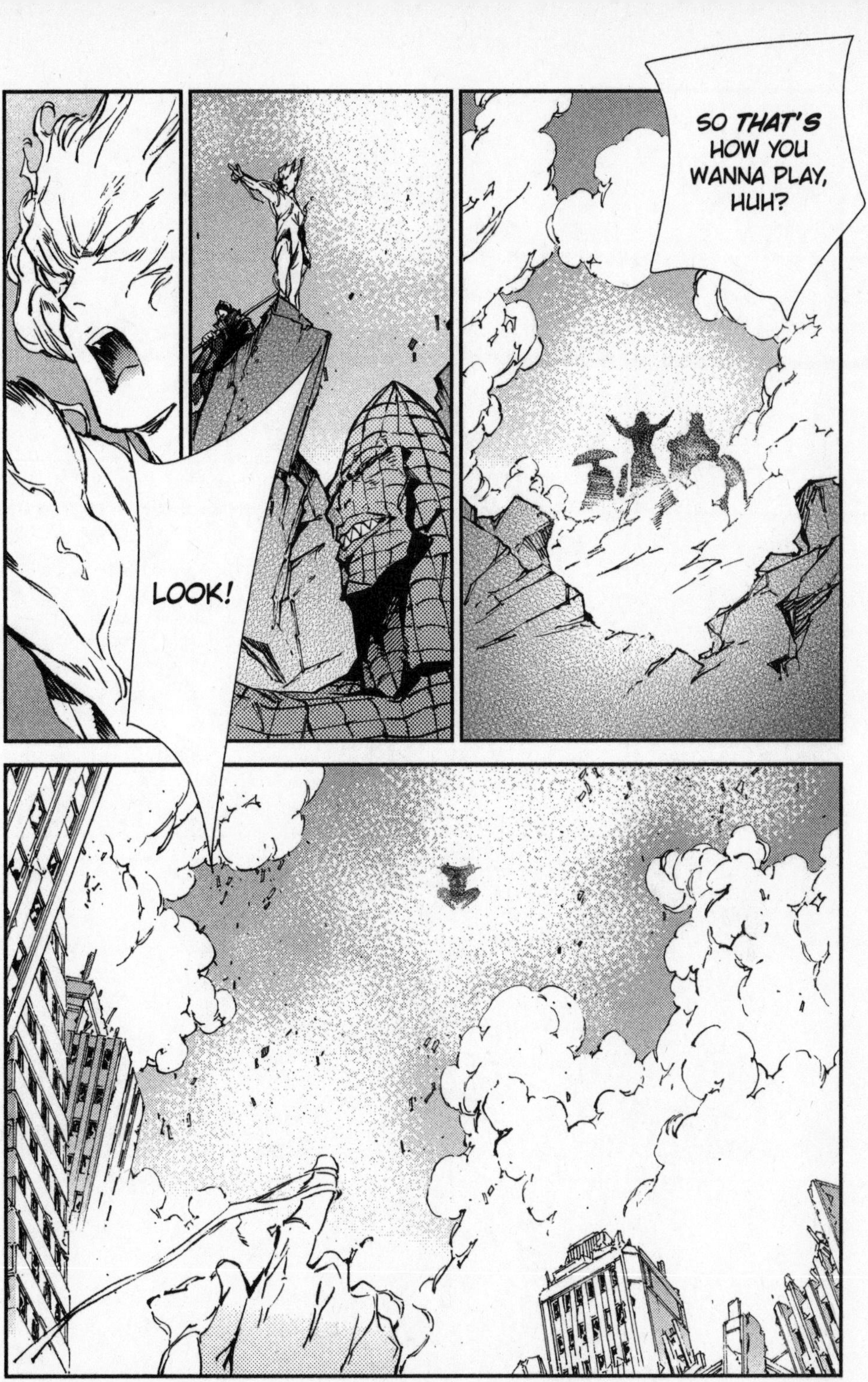
SO *THAT'S* HOW YOU WANNA PLAY, HUH?
LOOK!

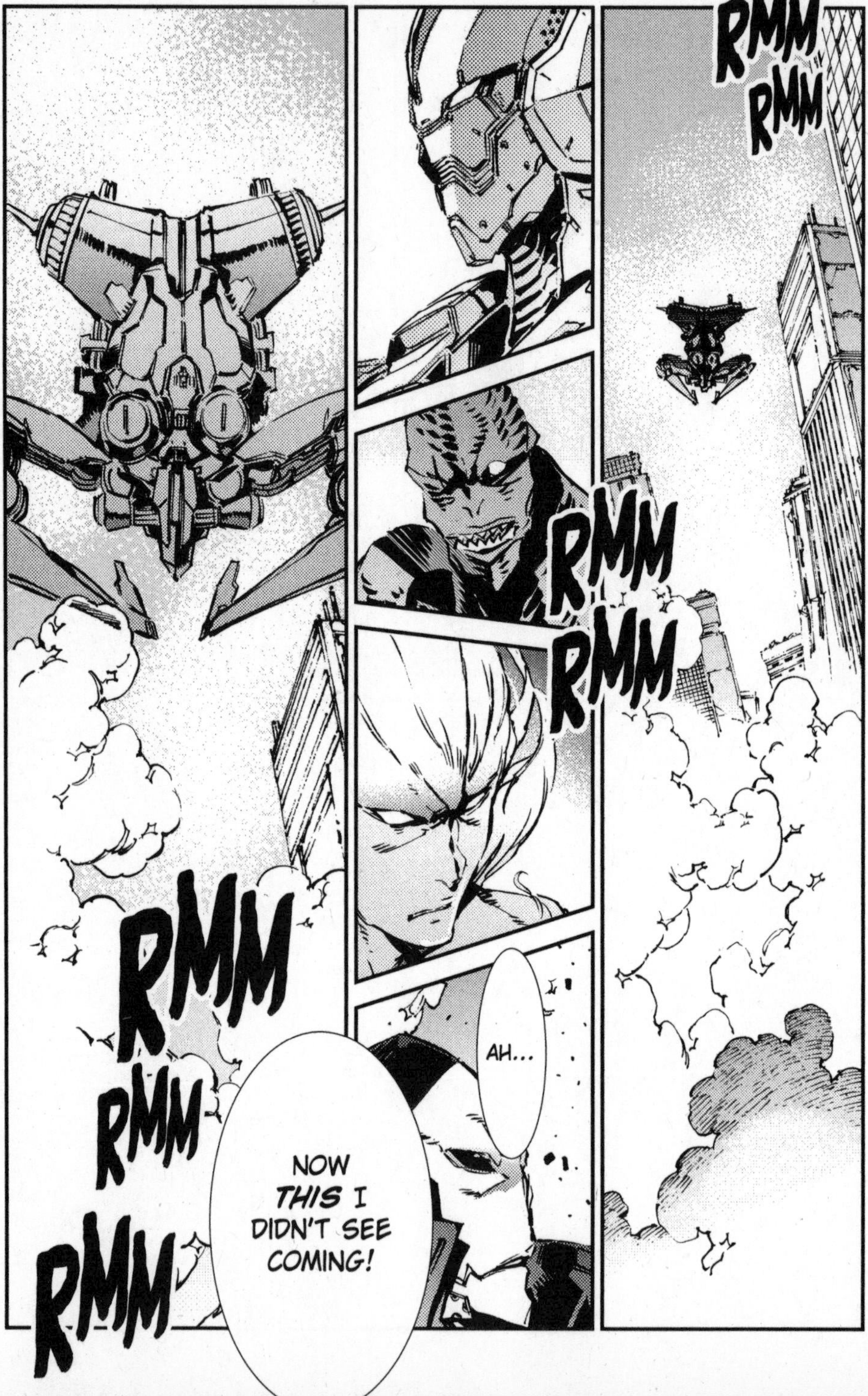
RMM RMM
RMM RMM
AH...
RMM RMM RMM
NOW *THIS* I DIDN'T SEE COMING!

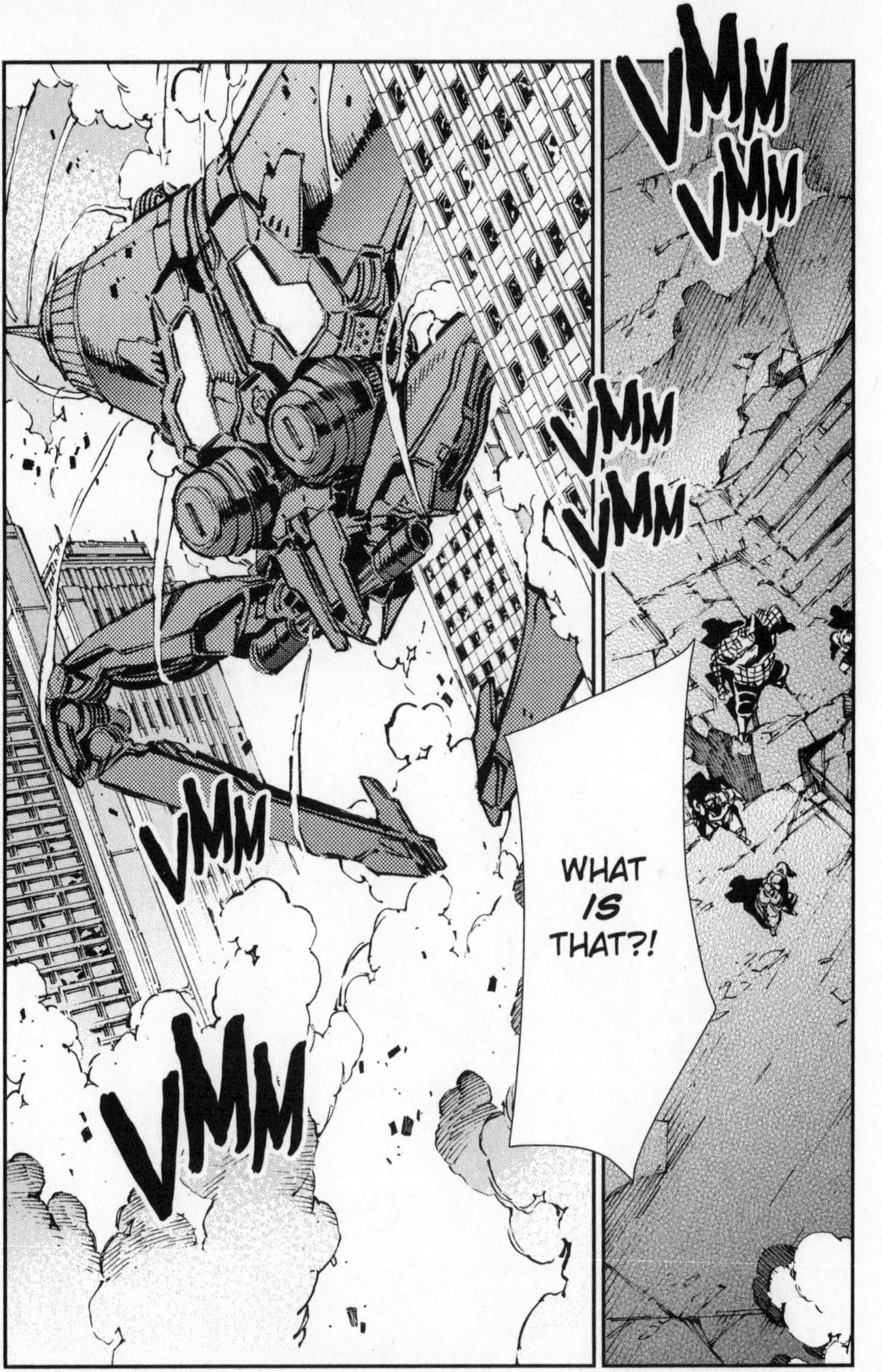
VMM VMM
WHAT IS THAT?!
VMM VMM
VMM
VMM

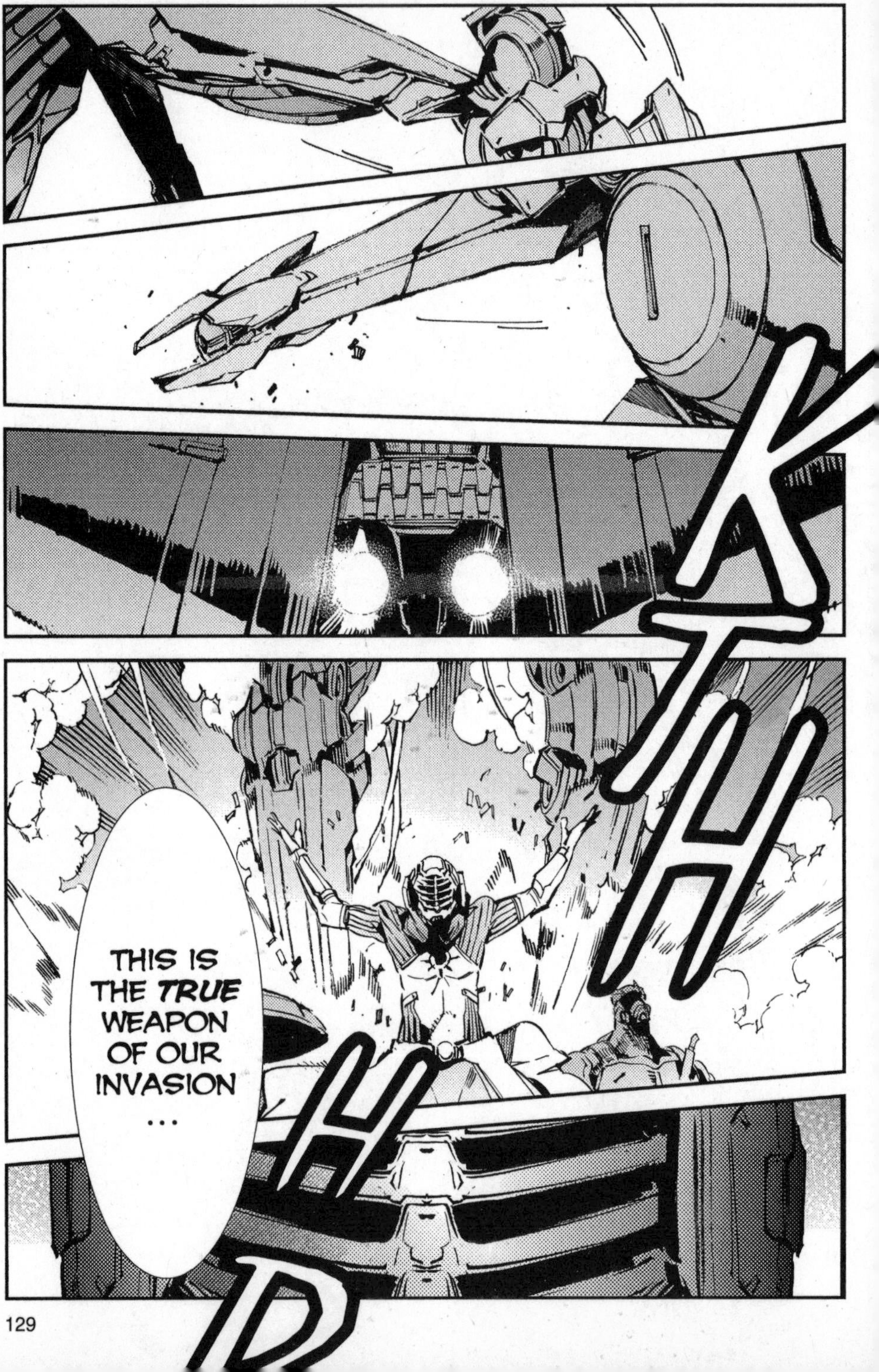
KATHHHD
THIS IS THE TRUE WEAPON OF OUR INVASION ...

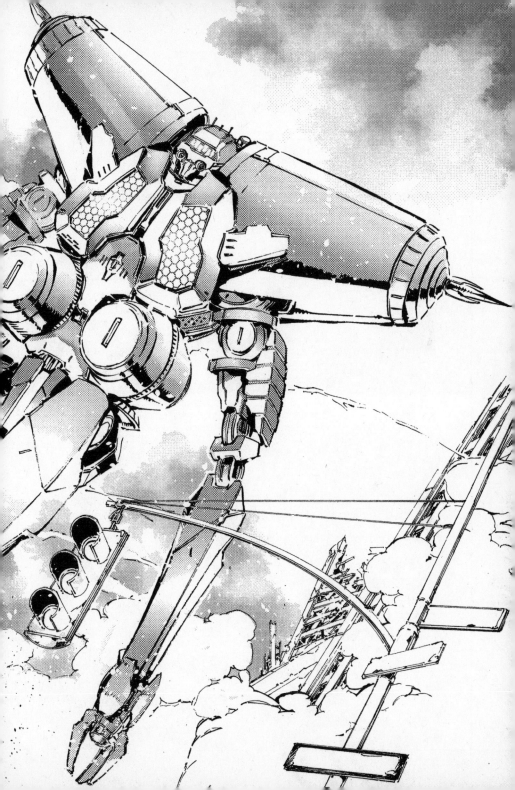

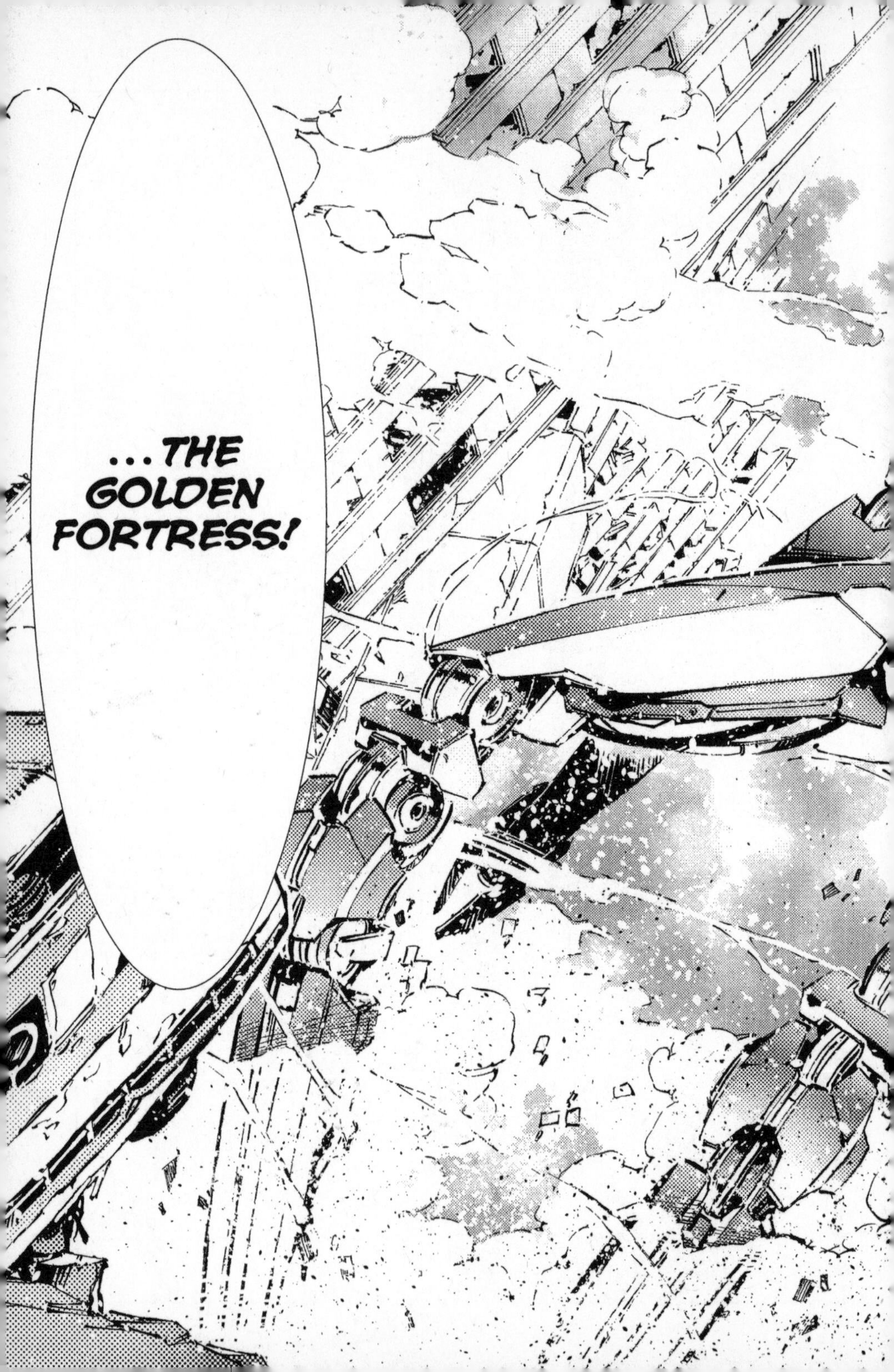
...THE GOLDEN FORTRESS!

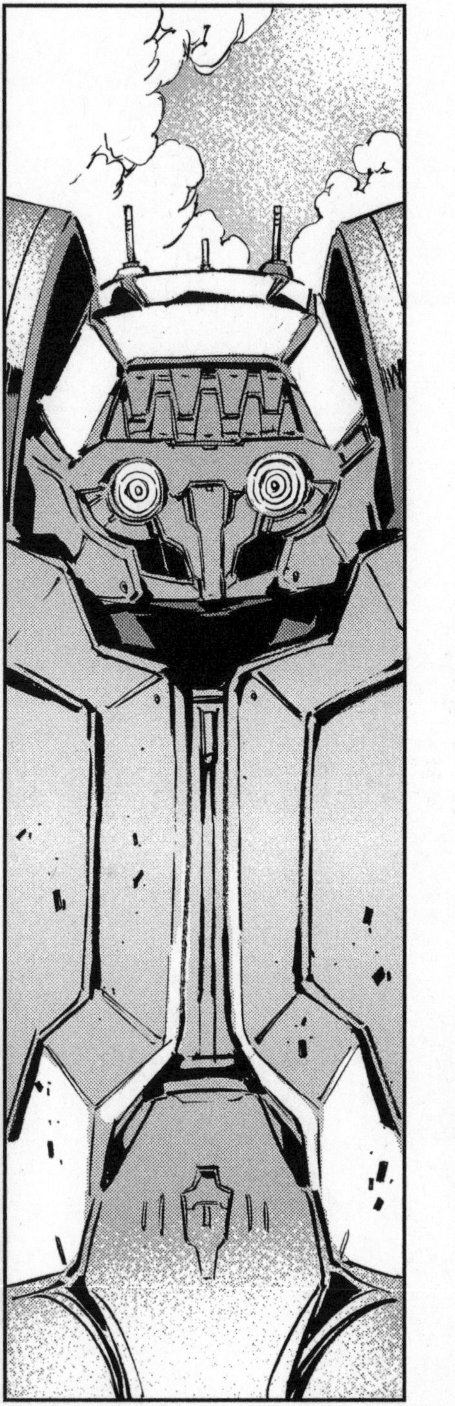
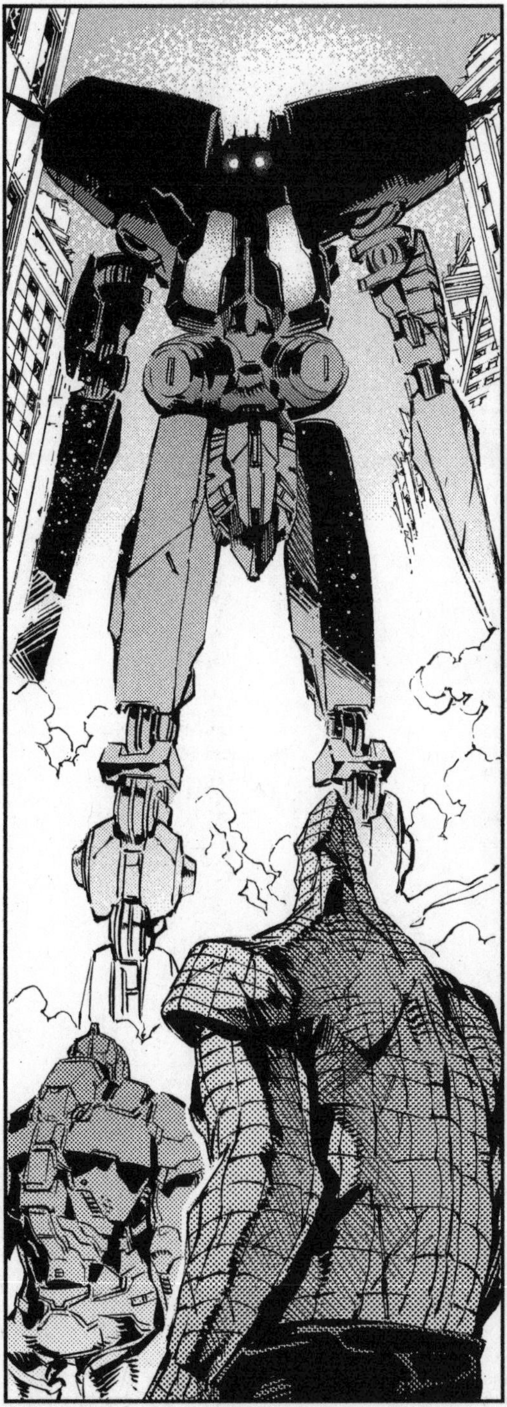

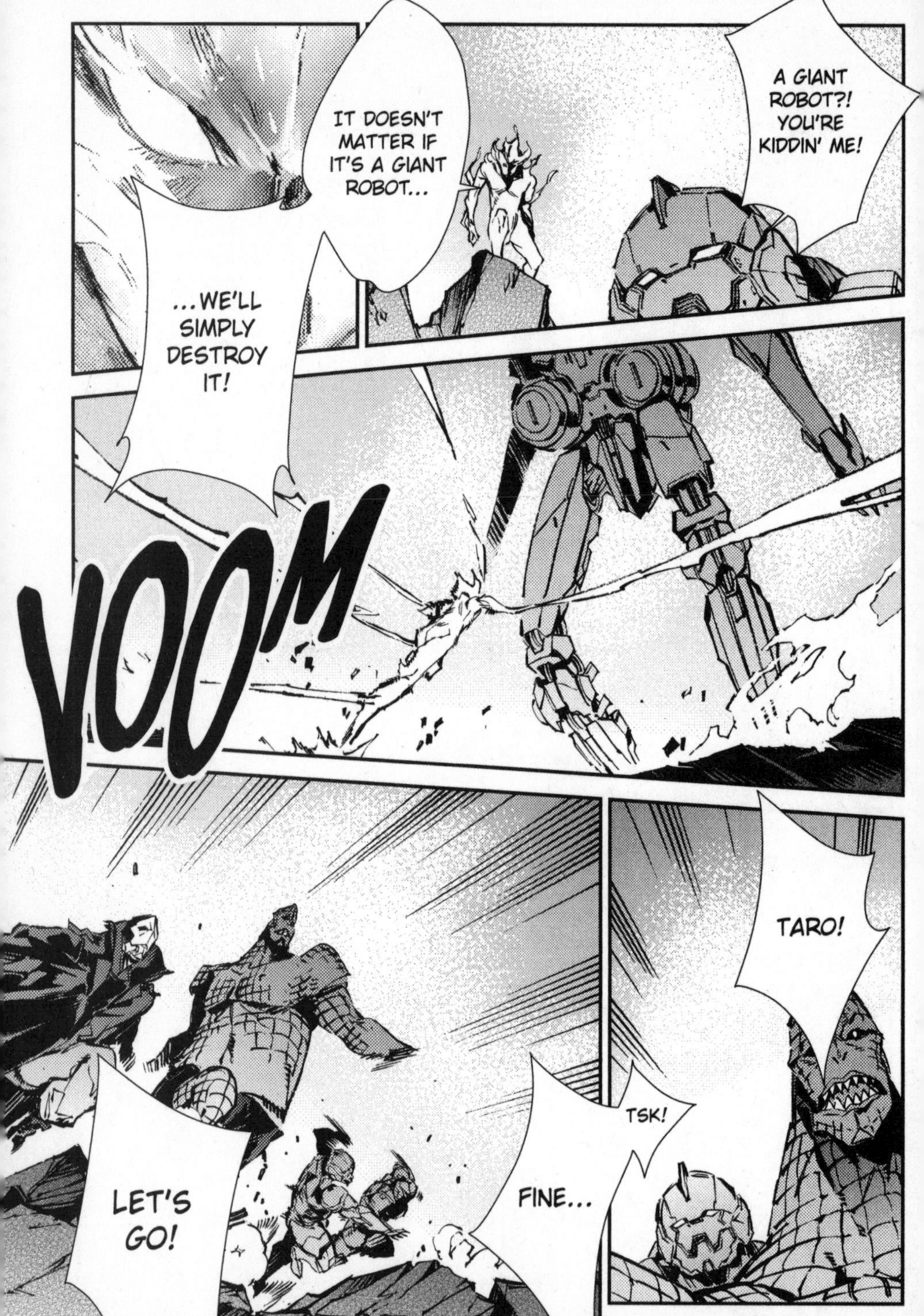
A GIANT ROBOT?! YOU'RE KIDDIN' ME!
IT DOESN'T MATTER IF IT'S A GIANT ROBOT...
...WE'LL SIMPLY DESTROY IT!
VOOM
TARO!
TSK!
FINE...
LET'S GO!

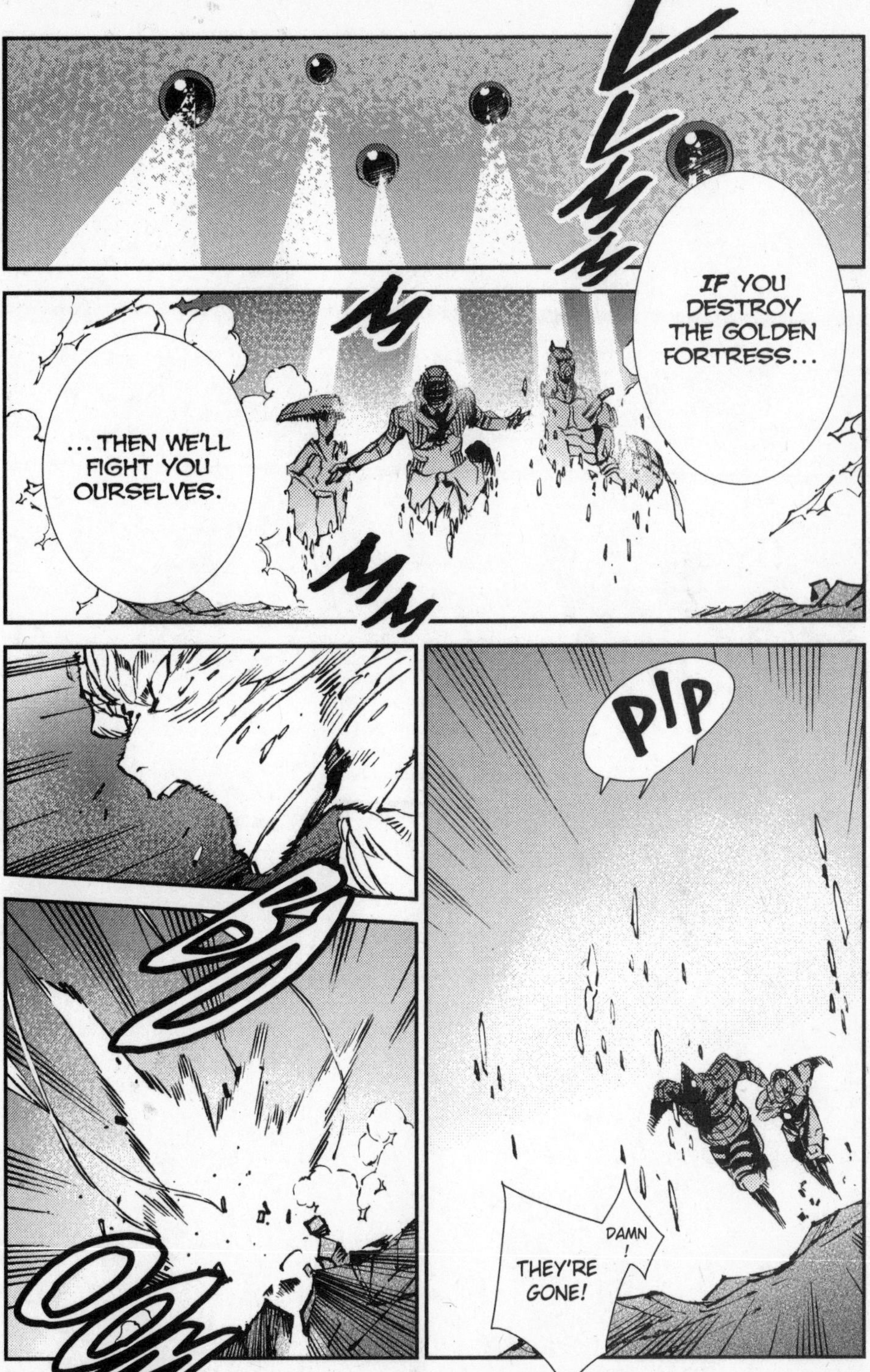
VVMMMMMM
IF YOU DESTROY THE GOLDEN FORTRESS...
...THEN WE'LL FIGHT YOU OURSELVES.
PIP
DAMN!
THEY'RE GONE!
BOOM

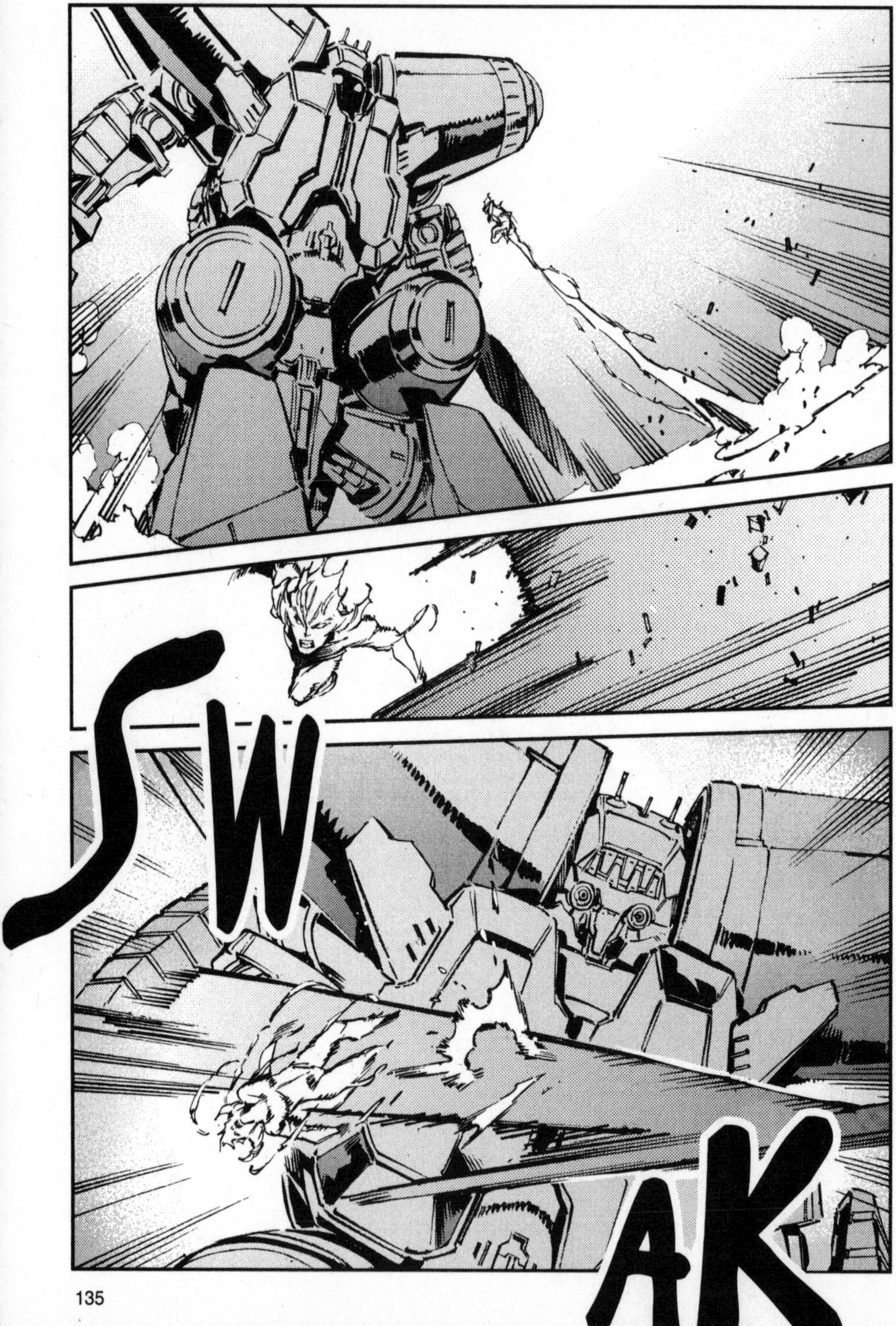
SWAK

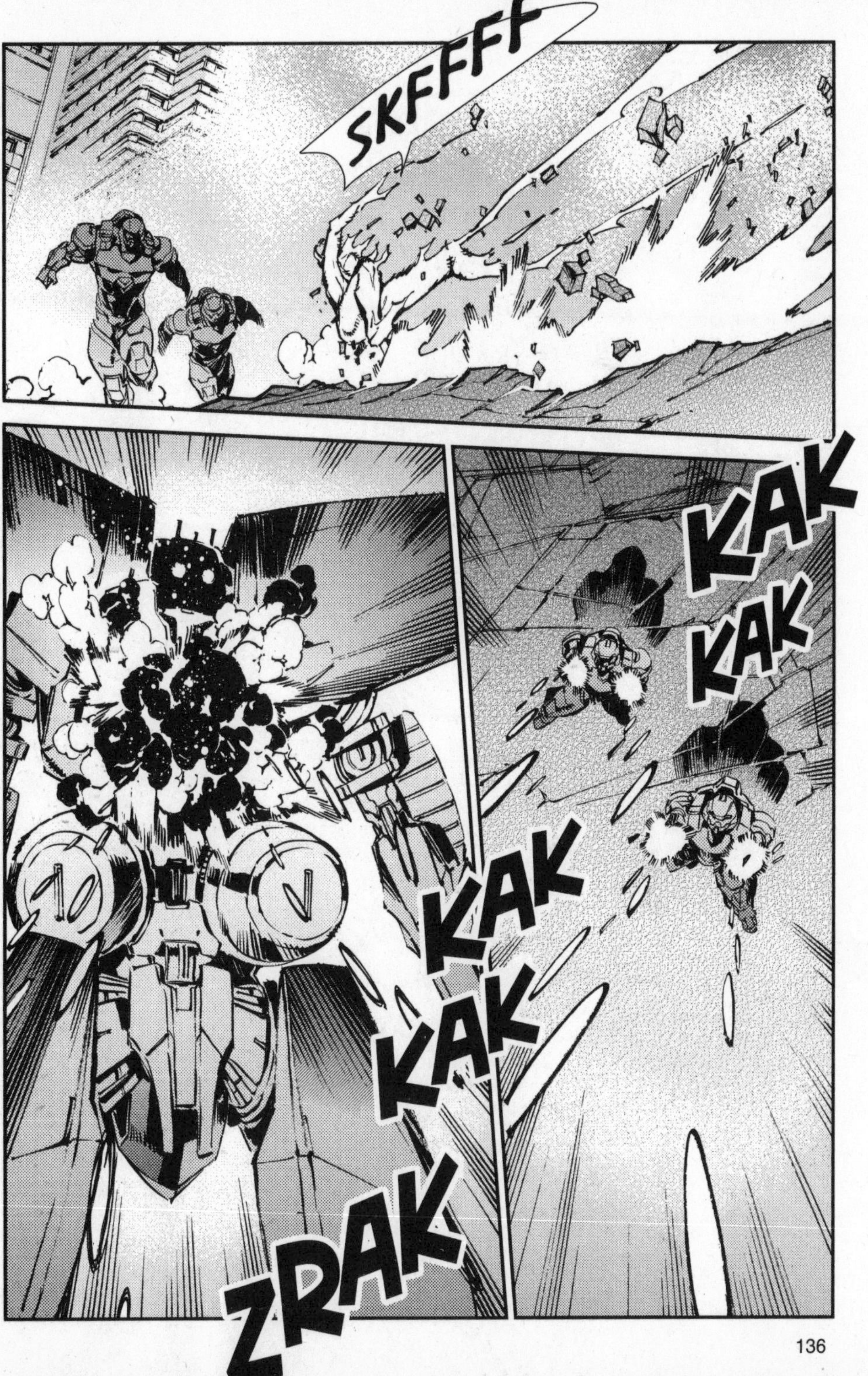
SKFFFF
KAK
KAK
KAK
KAK
ZRAK

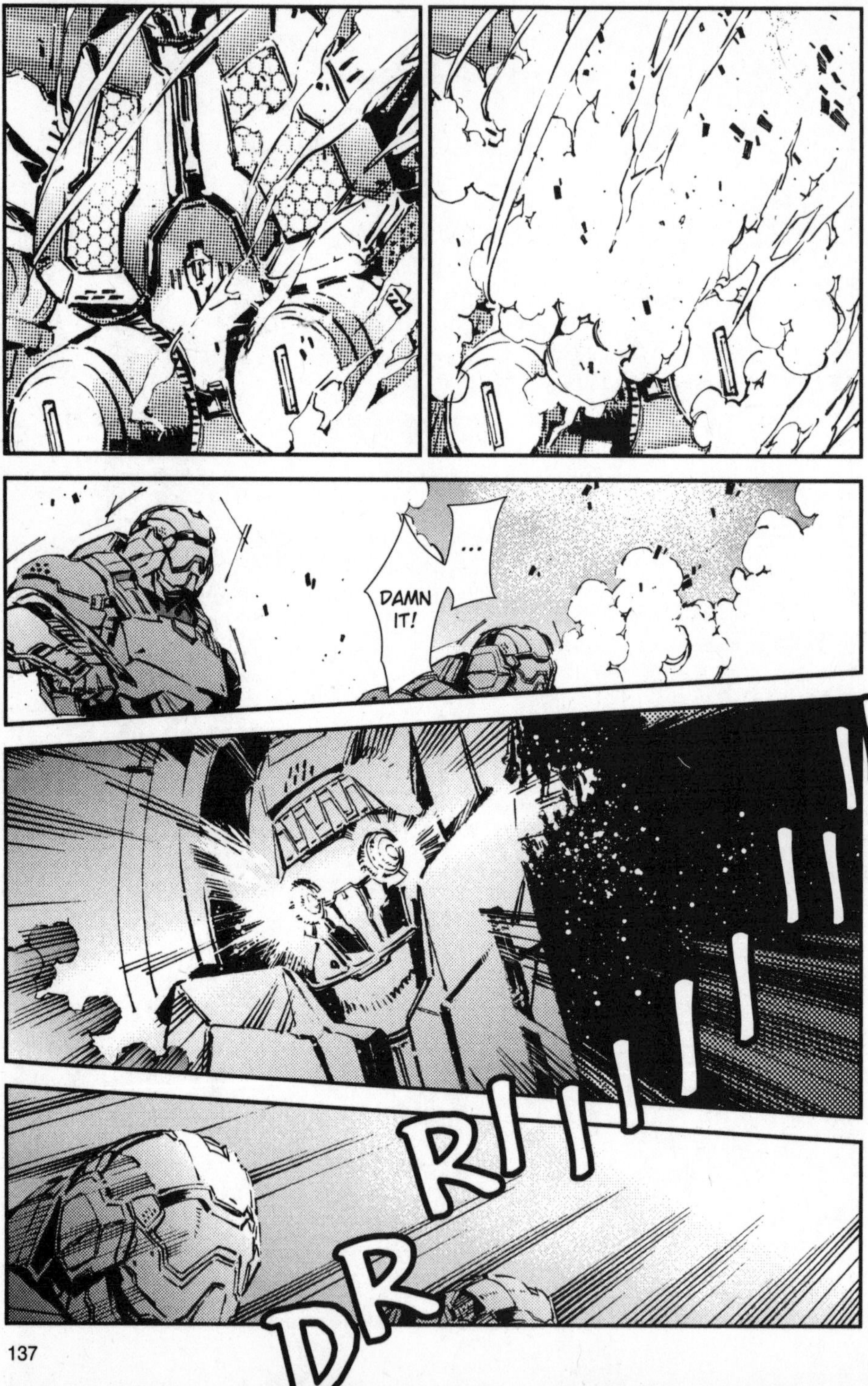
...
DAMN IT!
DRRIIIIIIIII

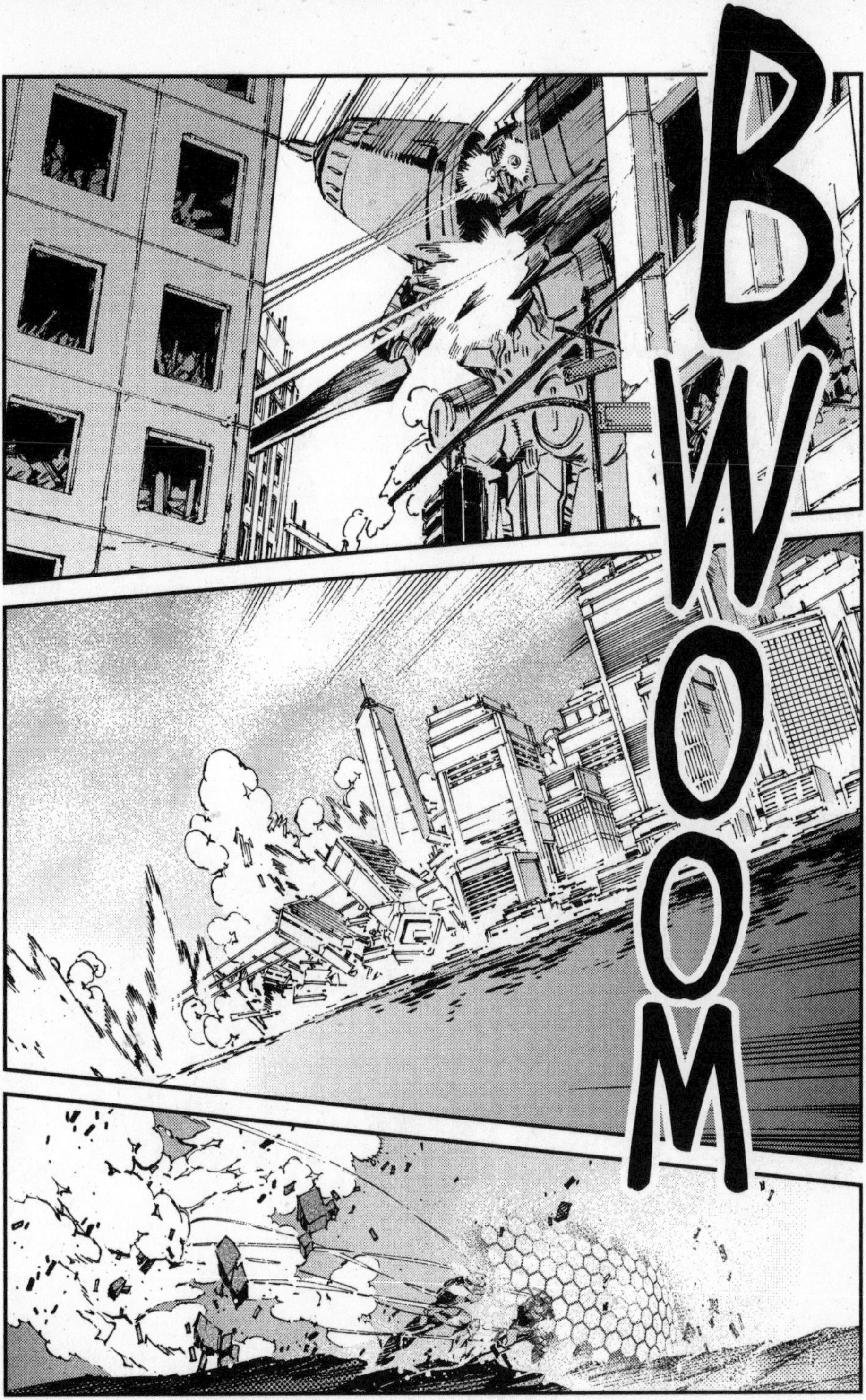
BWOOOM

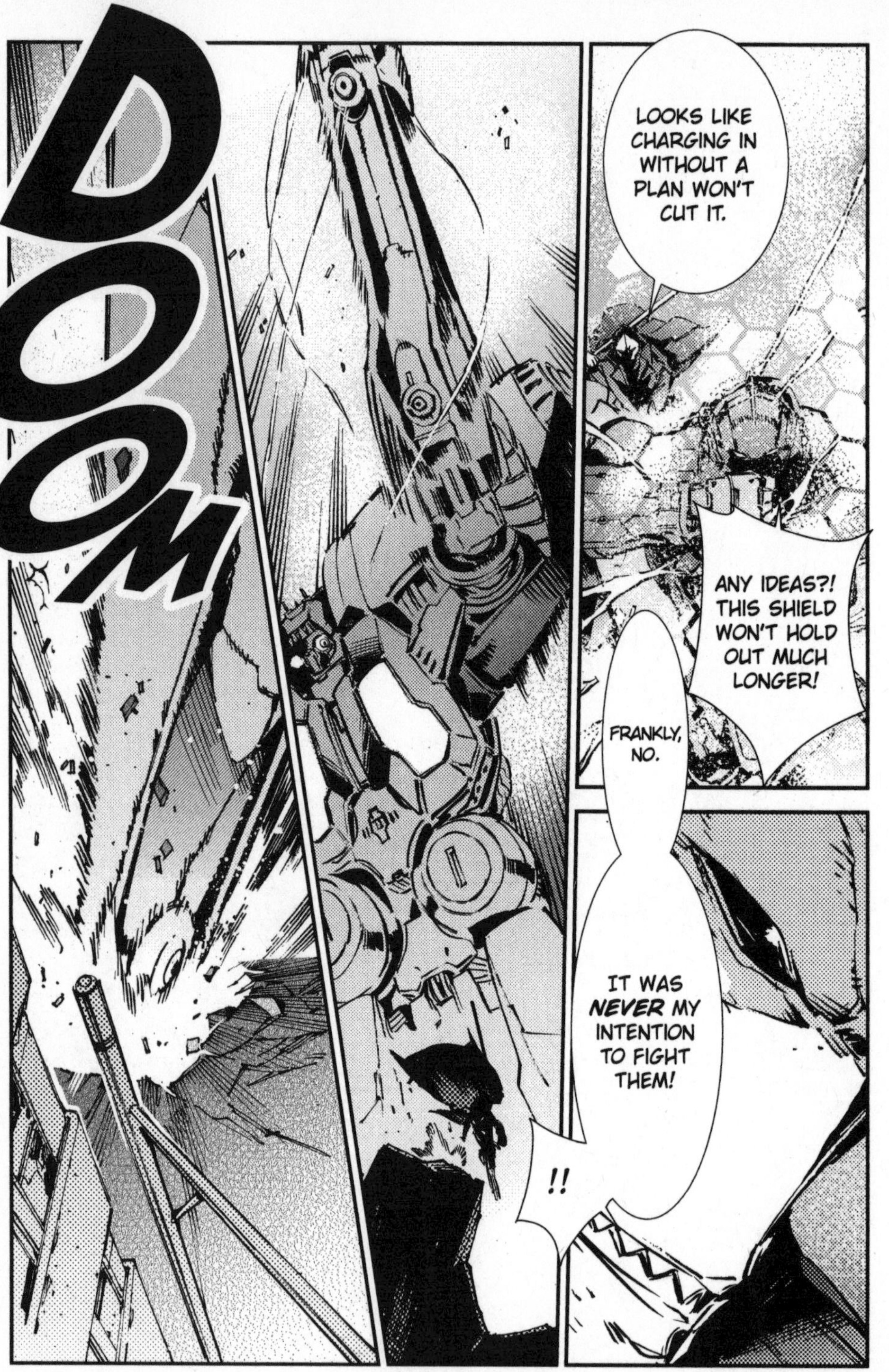
LOOKS LIKE CHARGING IN WITHOUT A PLAN WON'T CUT IT.
ANY IDEAS?! THIS SHIELD WON'T HOLD OUT MUCH LONGER!
FRANKLY, NO.
IT WAS **NEVER** MY INTENTION TO FIGHT THEM!
!!
DOOM

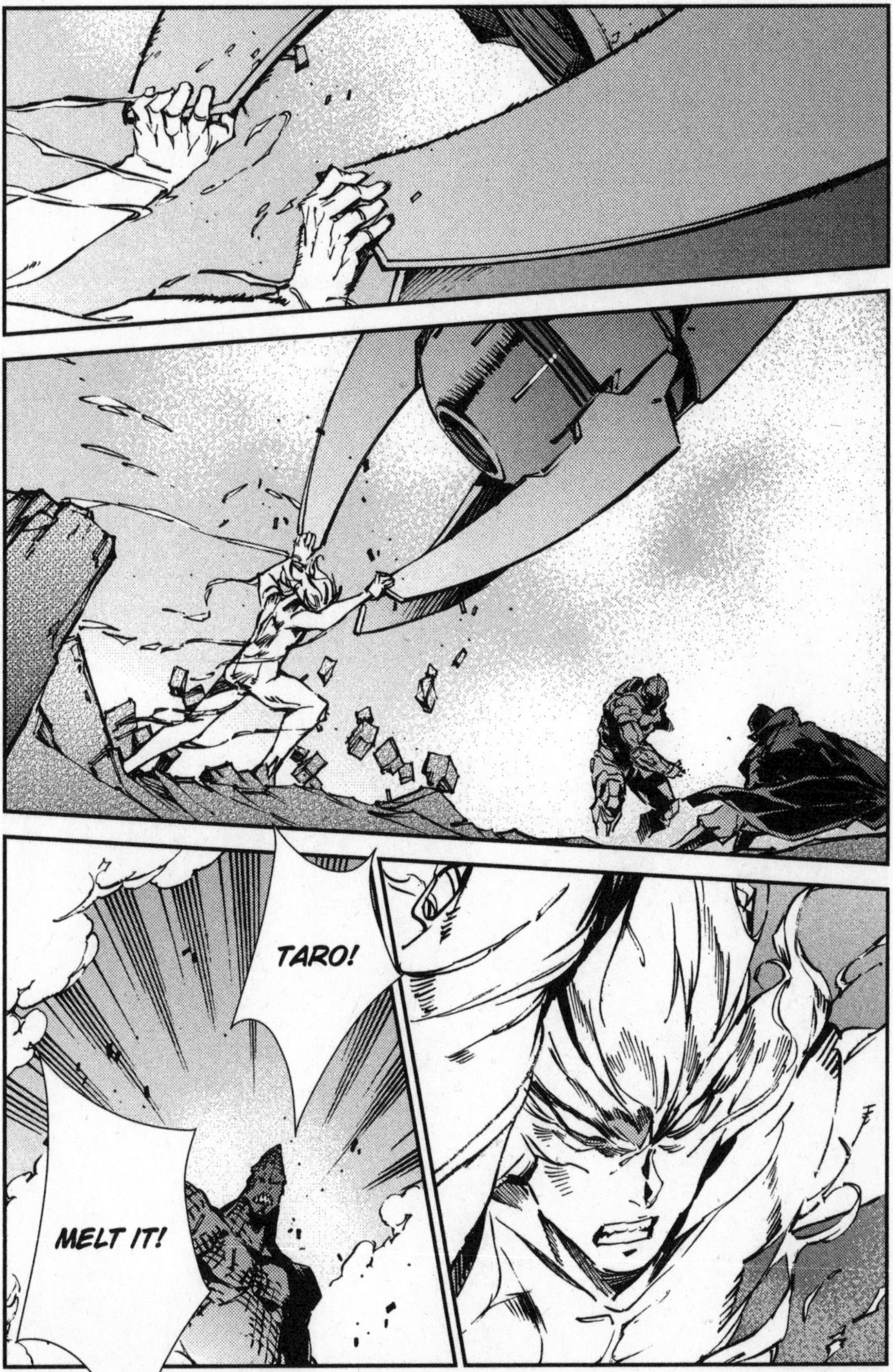
TARO!
MELT IT!

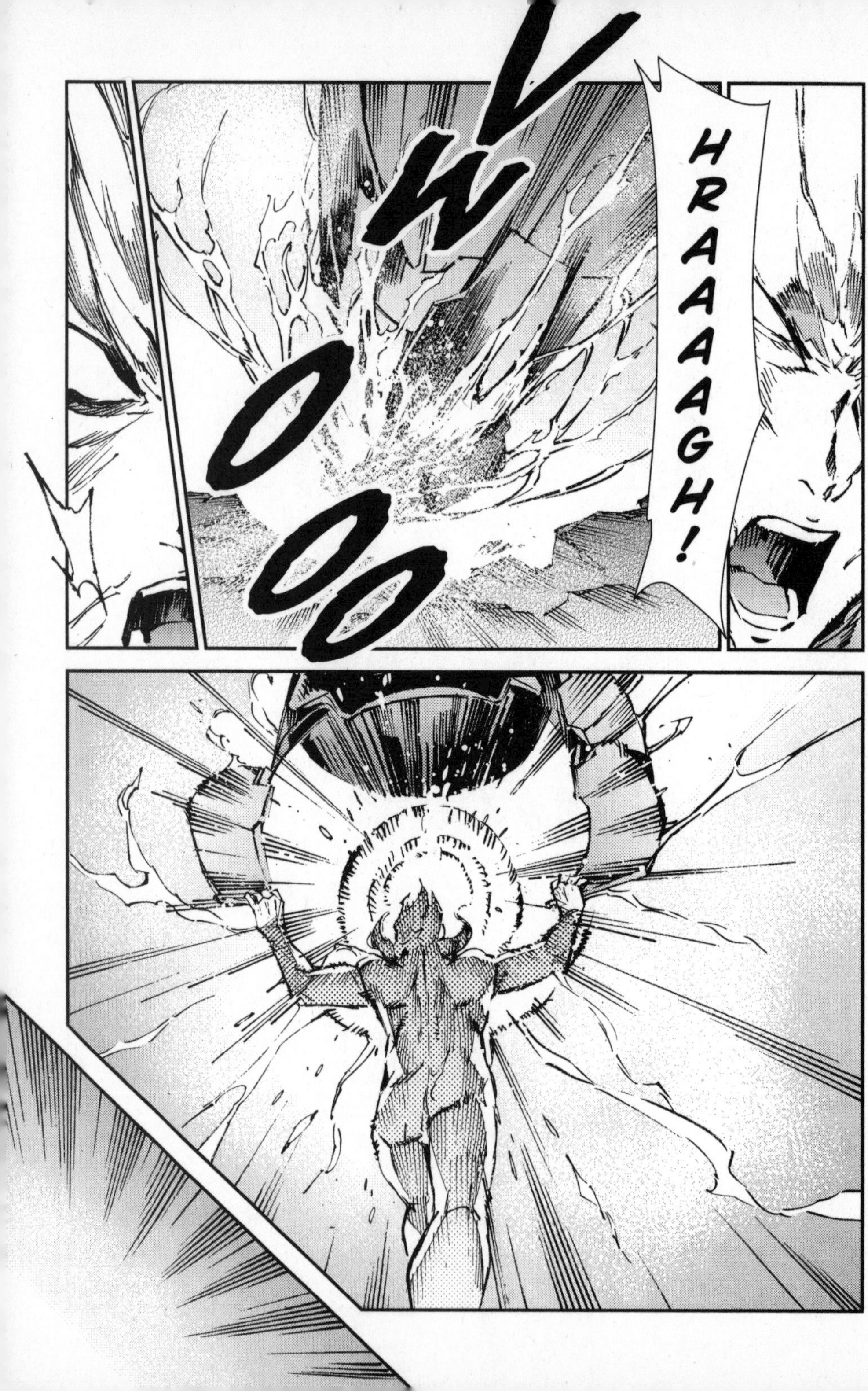
HRAAAAAGH!
VWOOOO

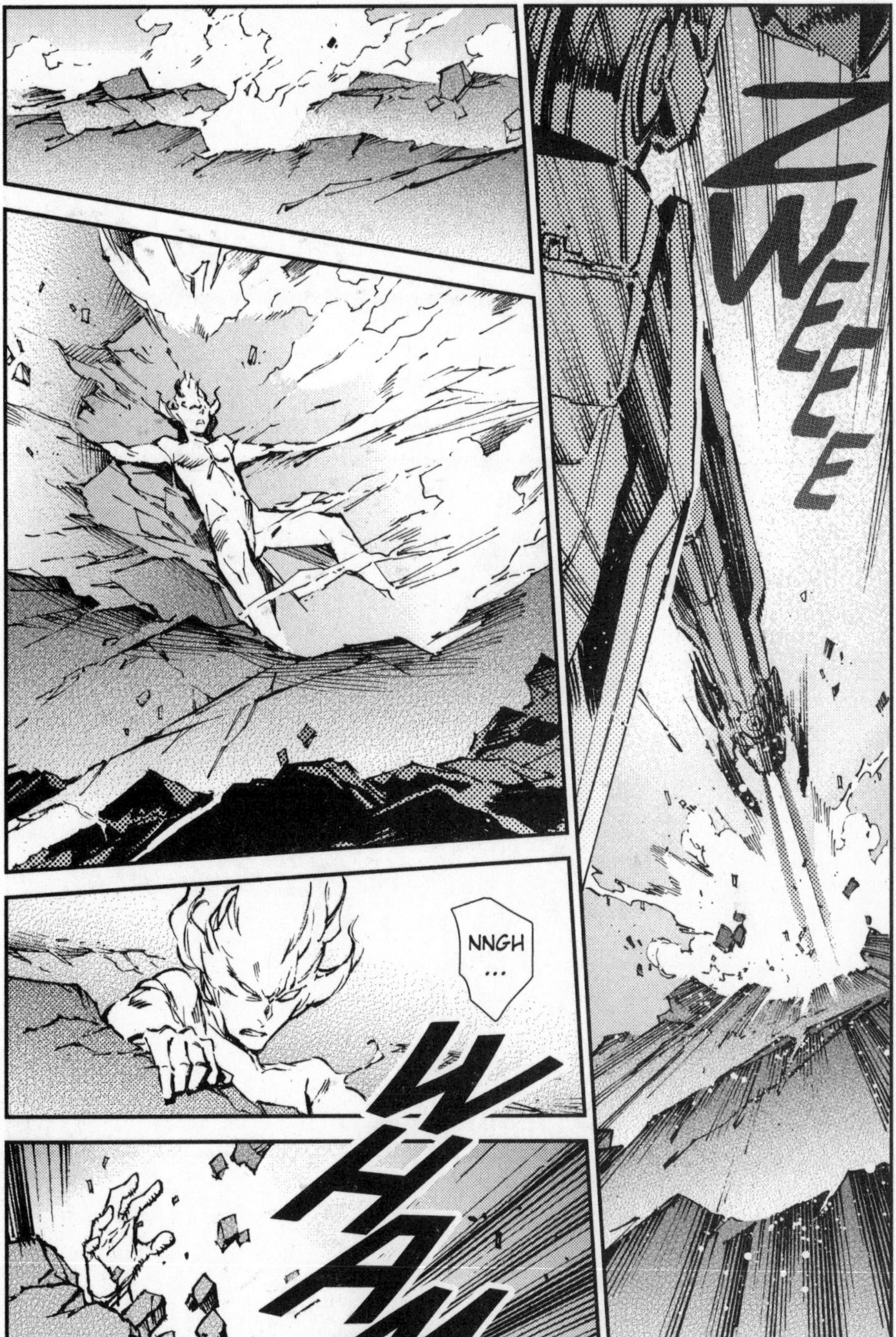
ZWEEE
NNGH ...
WHAM

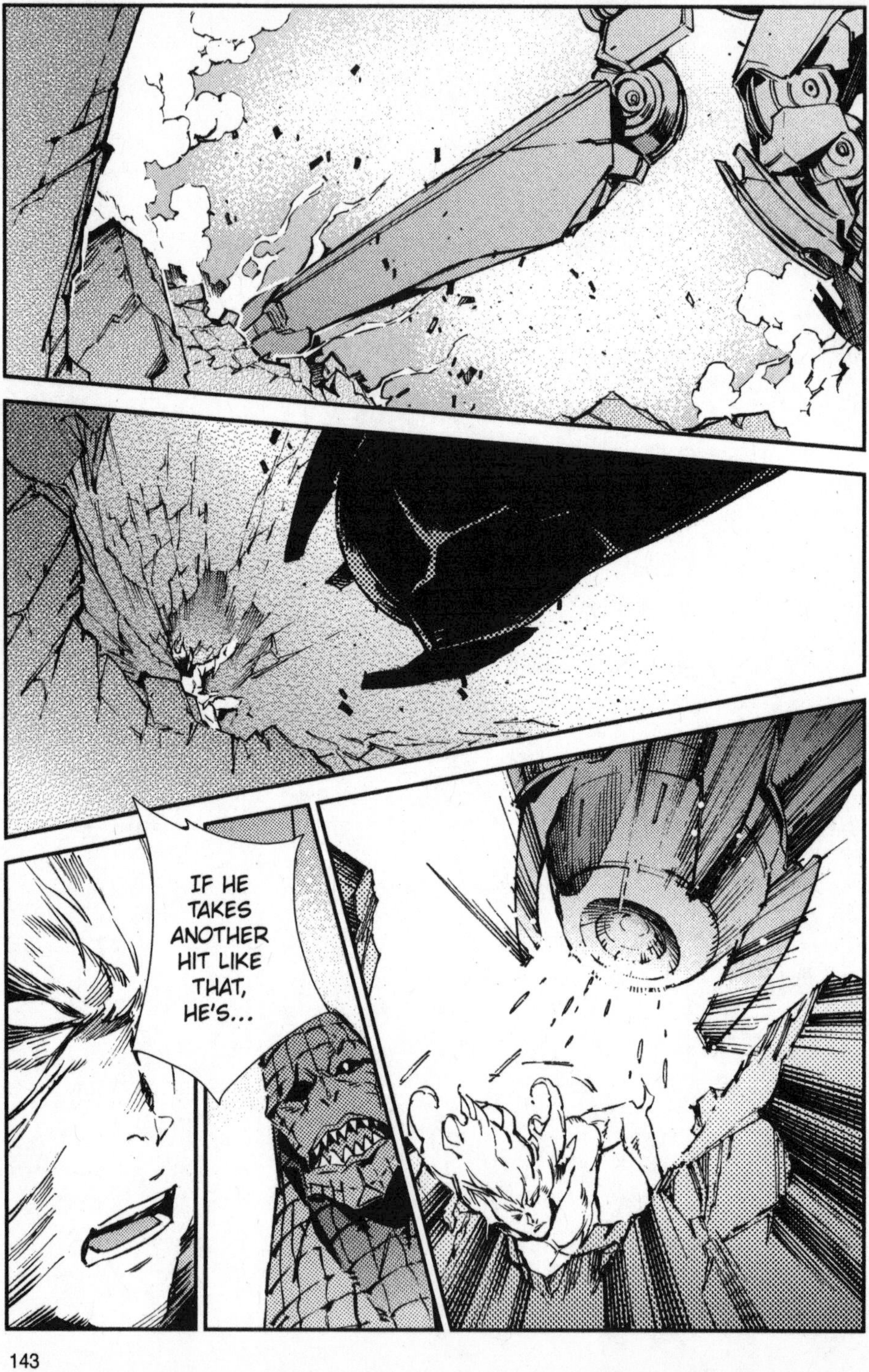
IF HE TAKES ANOTHER HIT LIKE THAT, HE'S...

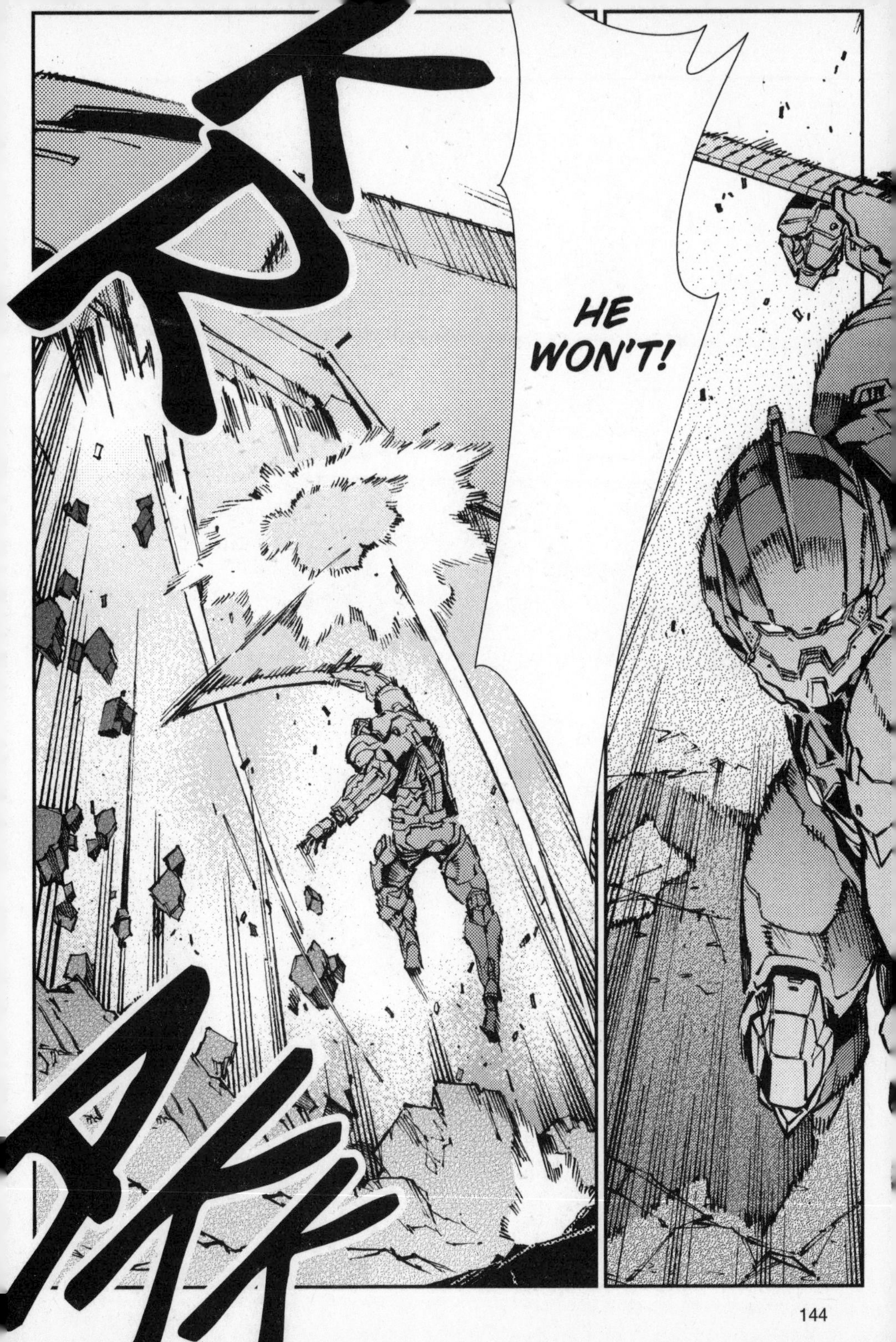
HE WON'T!

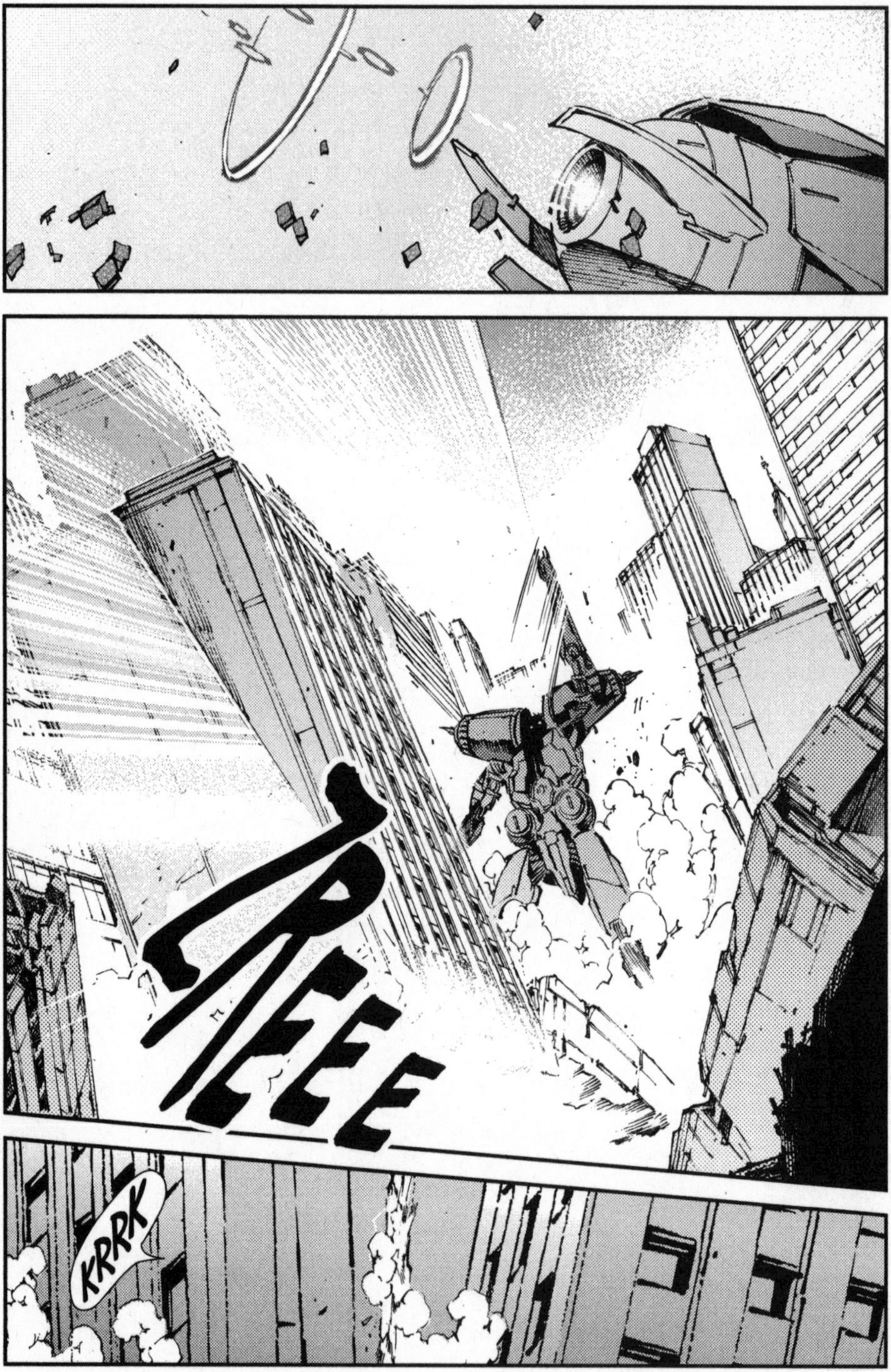
CREEE
KRRK

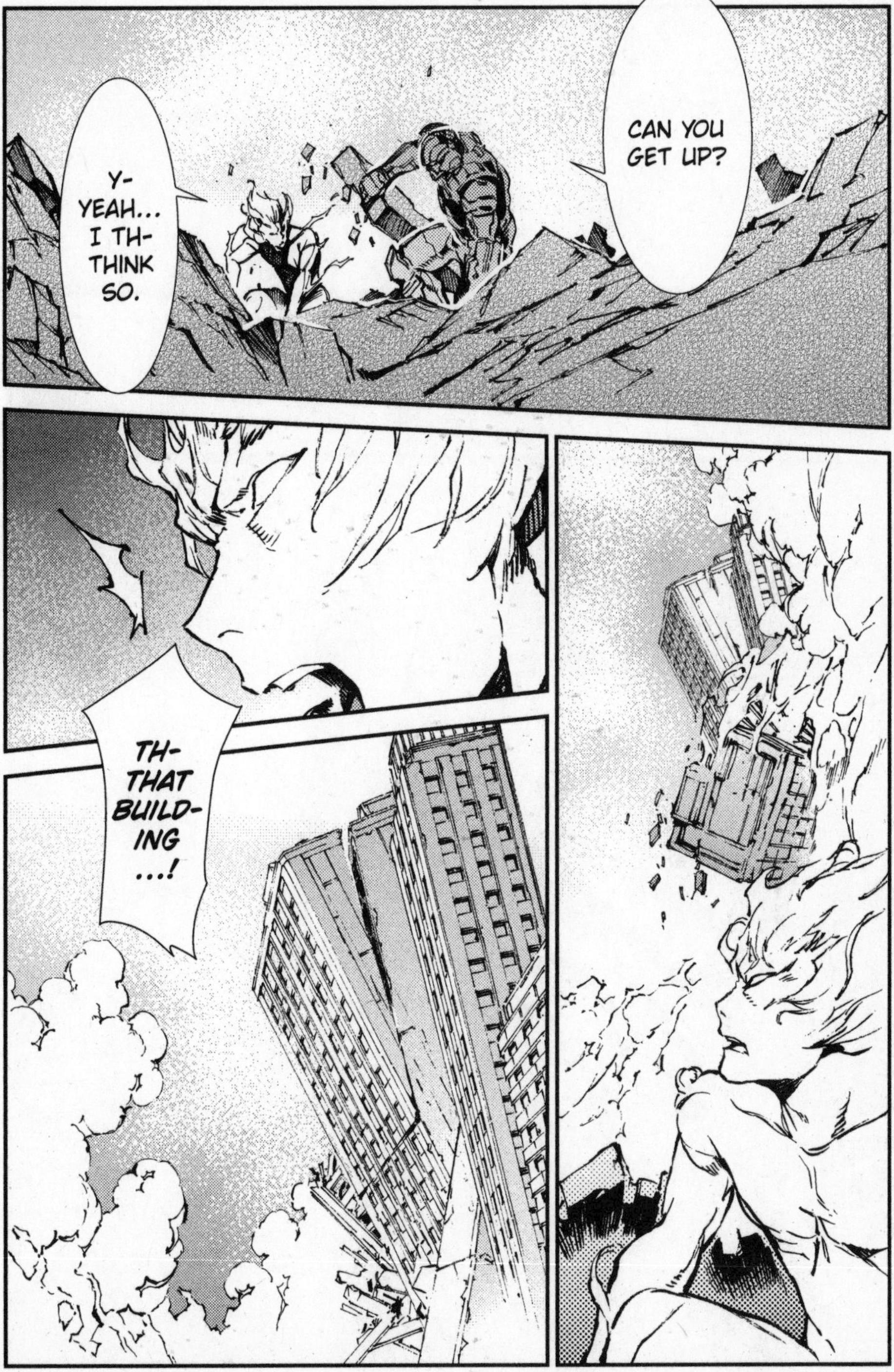
CAN YOU GET UP?
Y-YEAH... I TH-THINK SO.
TH-THAT BUILD-ING ...!

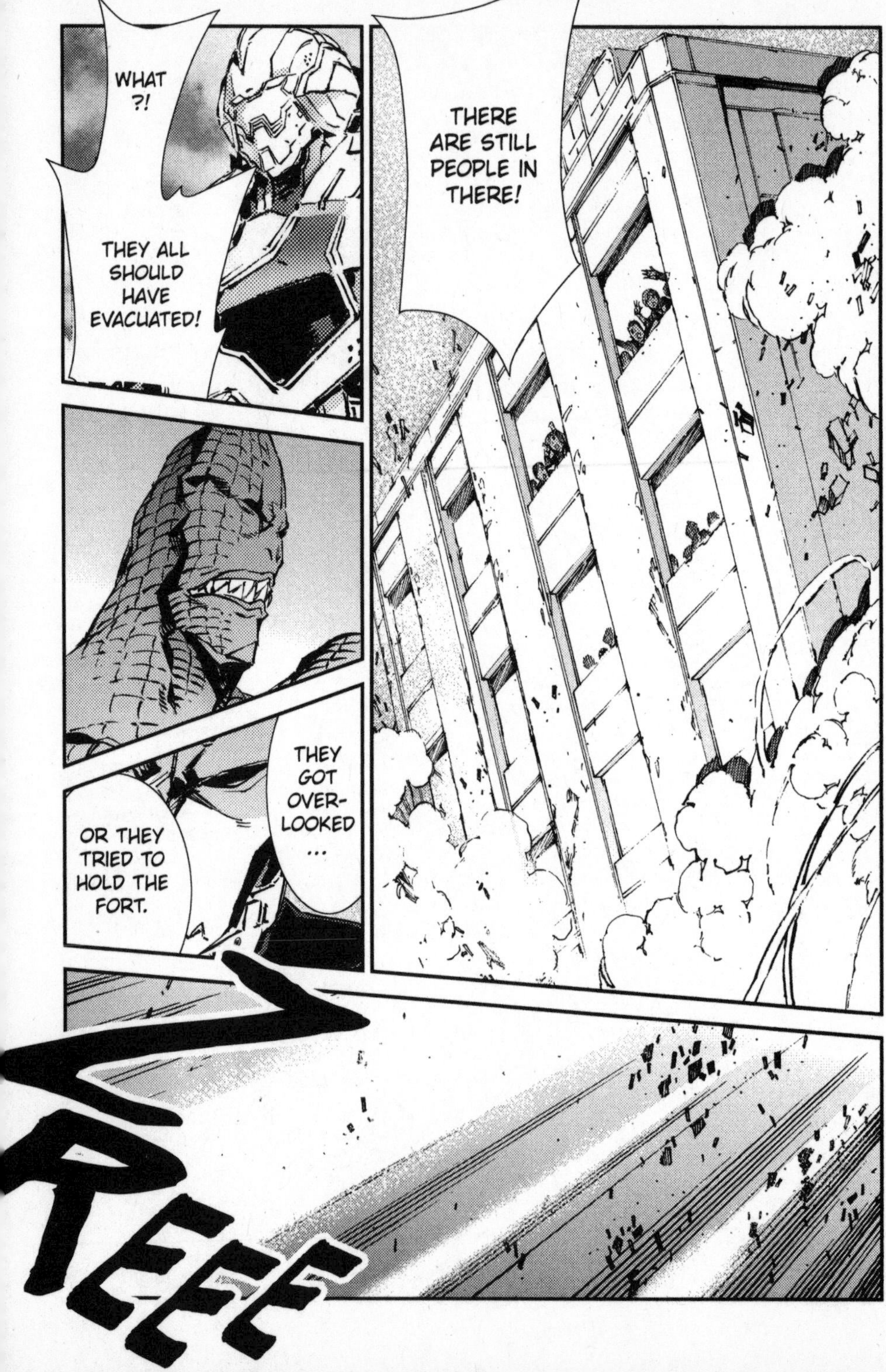
THERE ARE STILL PEOPLE IN THERE!
WHAT ?!
THEY ALL SHOULD HAVE EVACUATED!
THEY GOT OVER-LOOKED ...
OR THEY TRIED TO HOLD THE FORT.
REEE

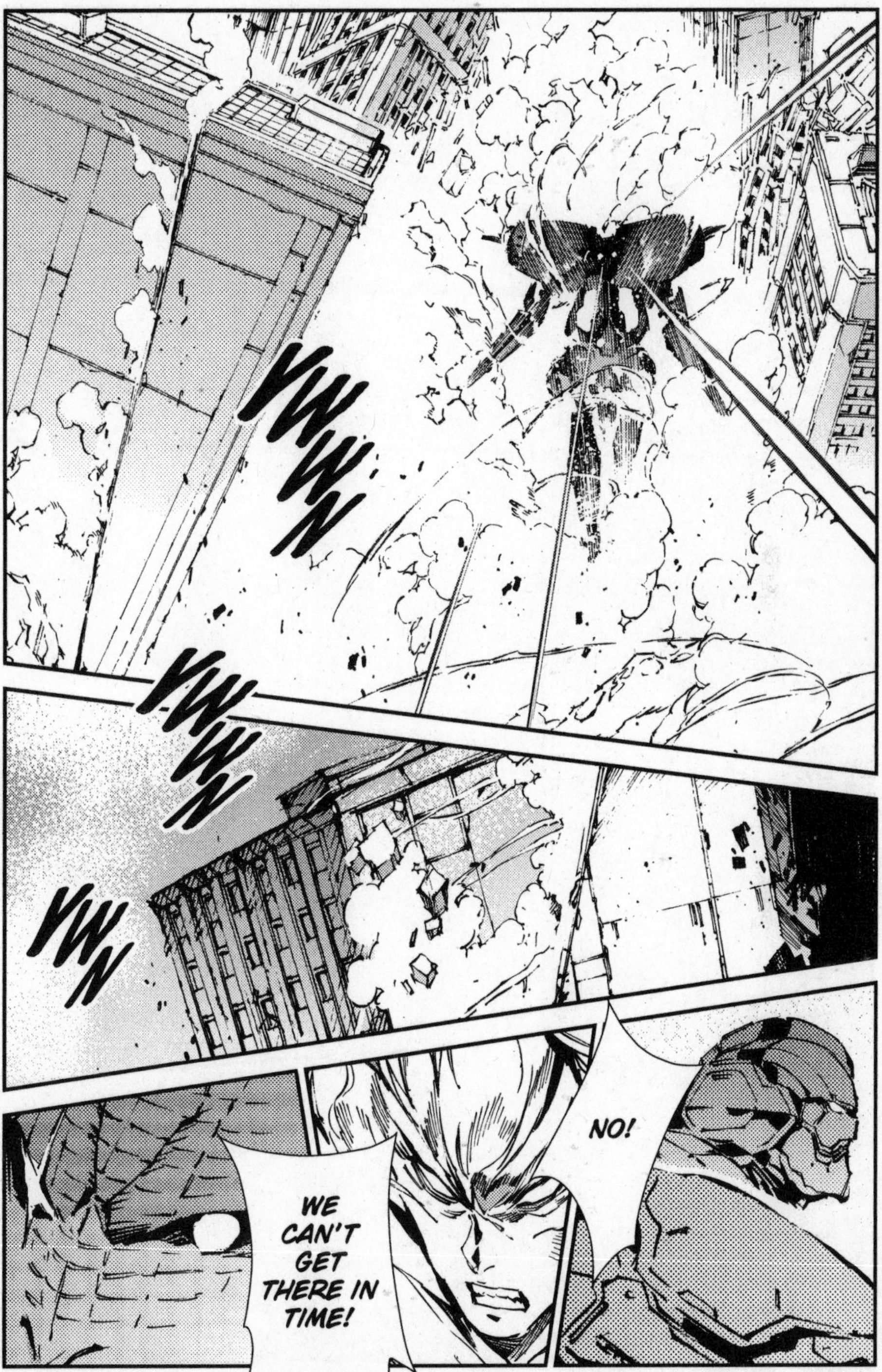
YWWWN
YWWWN
YWN
NO!
WE CAN'T GET THERE IN TIME!

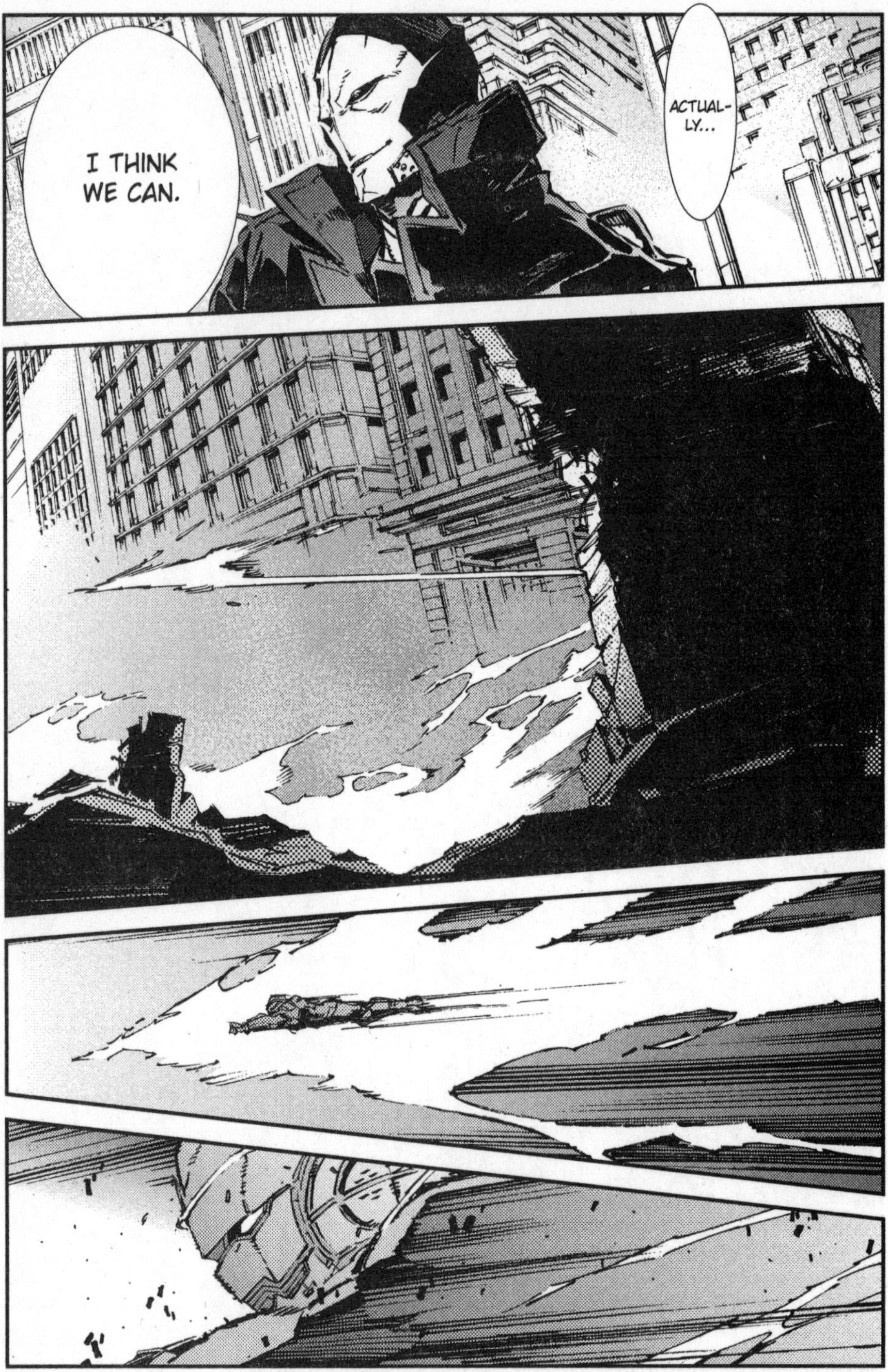
ACTUAL-
LY...
I THINK
WE CAN.

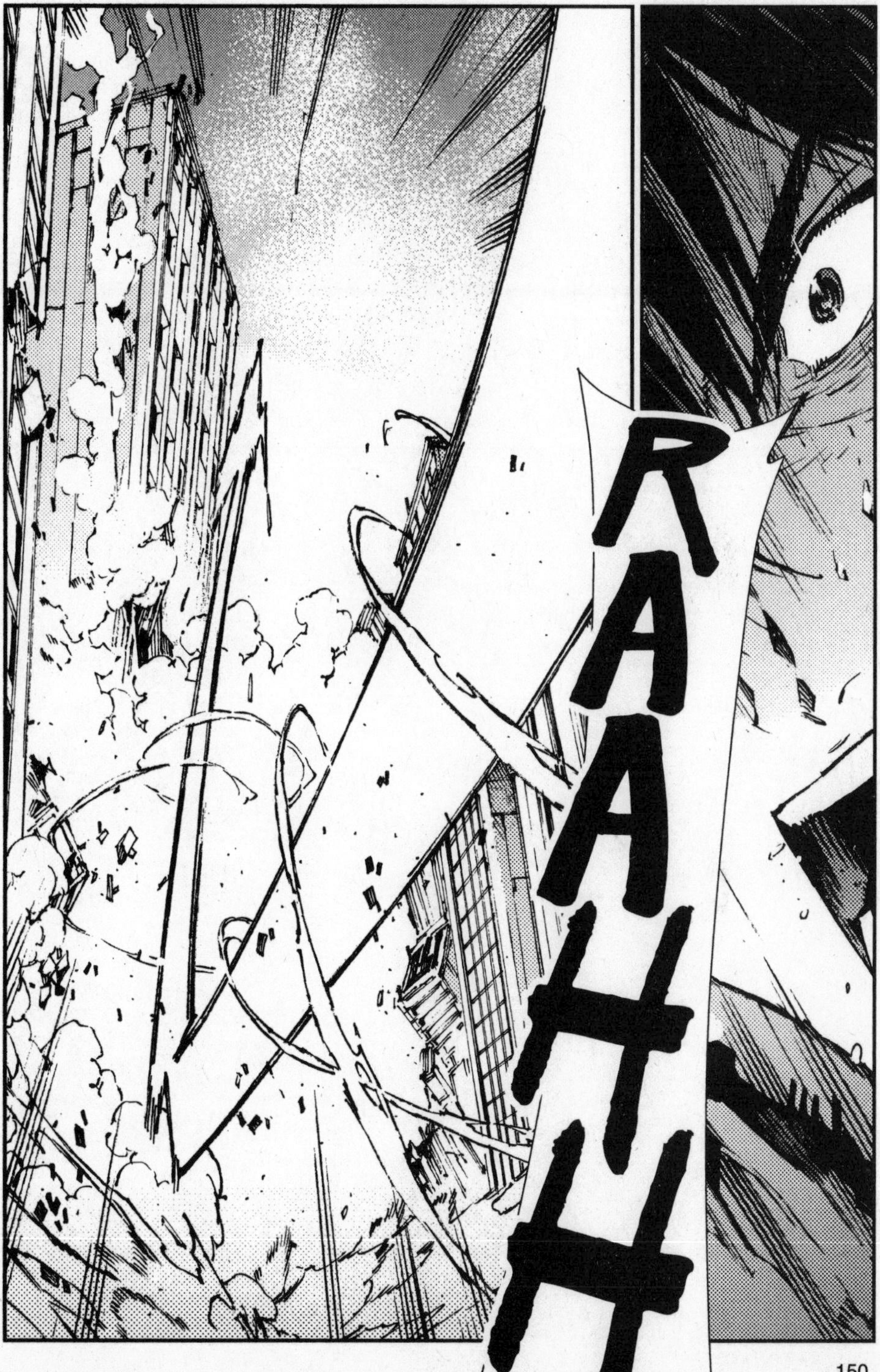
RAAHHH

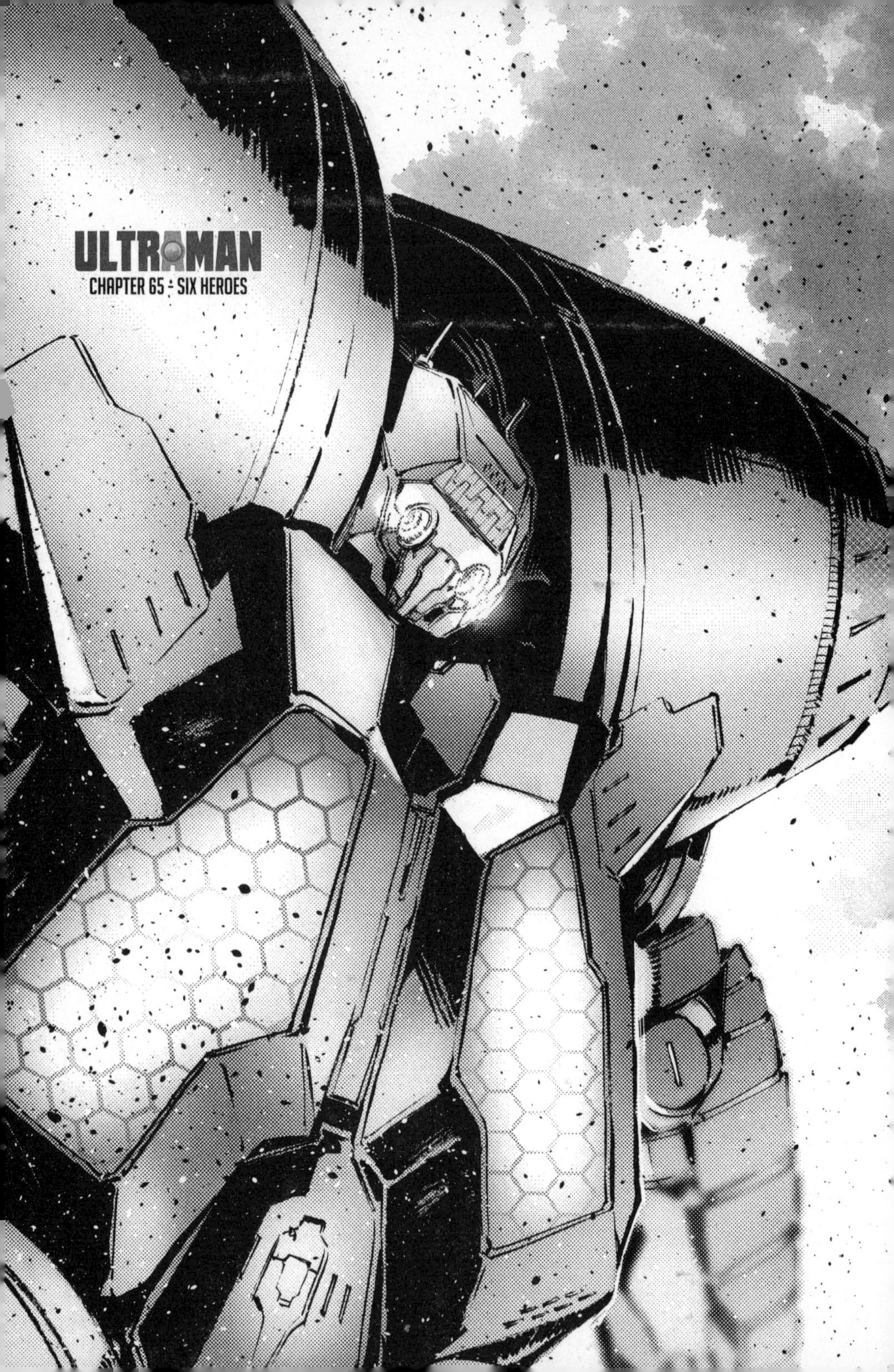
ULTRAMAN
CHAPTER 65 : SIX HEROES

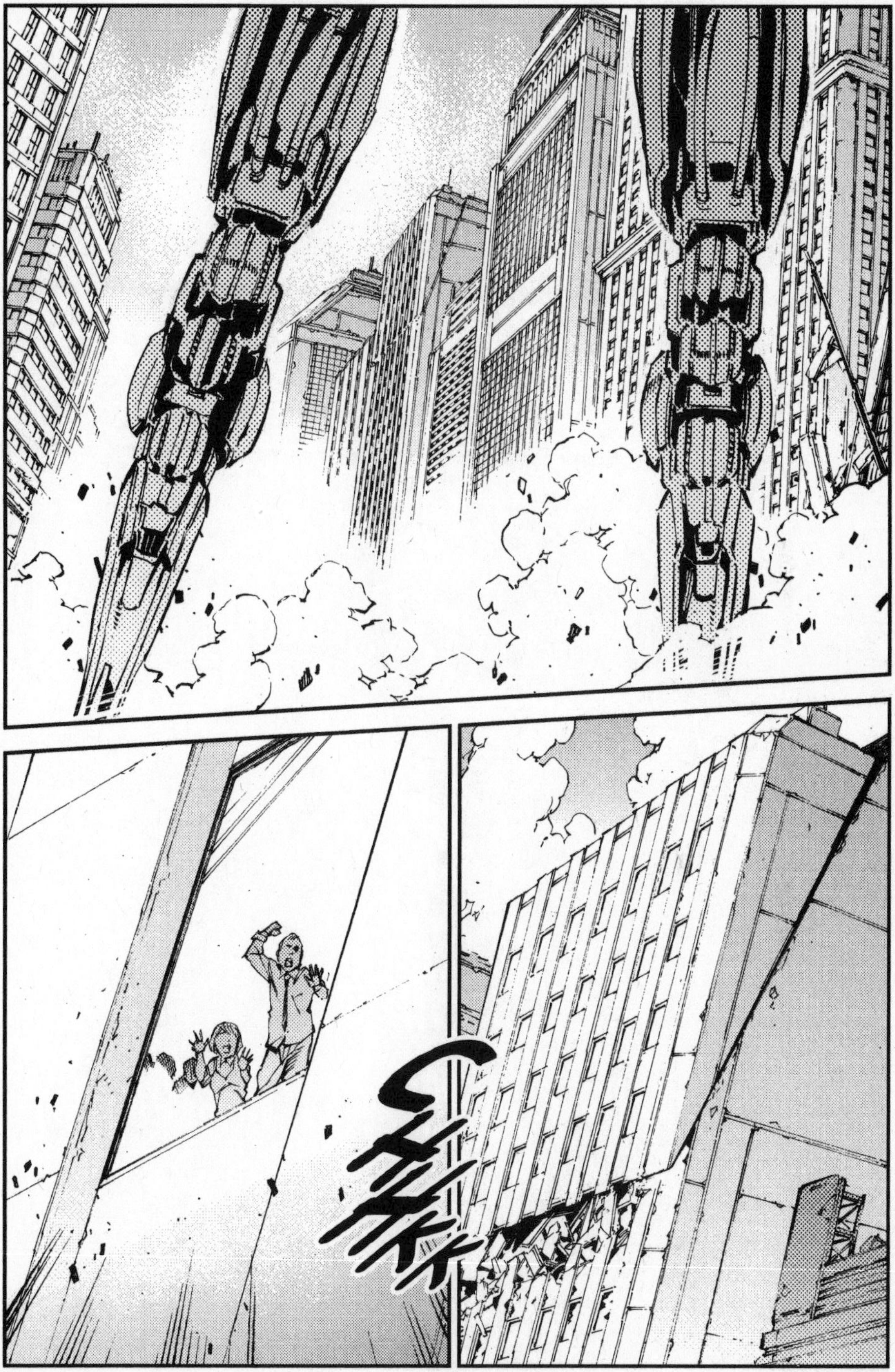
CHHHKK

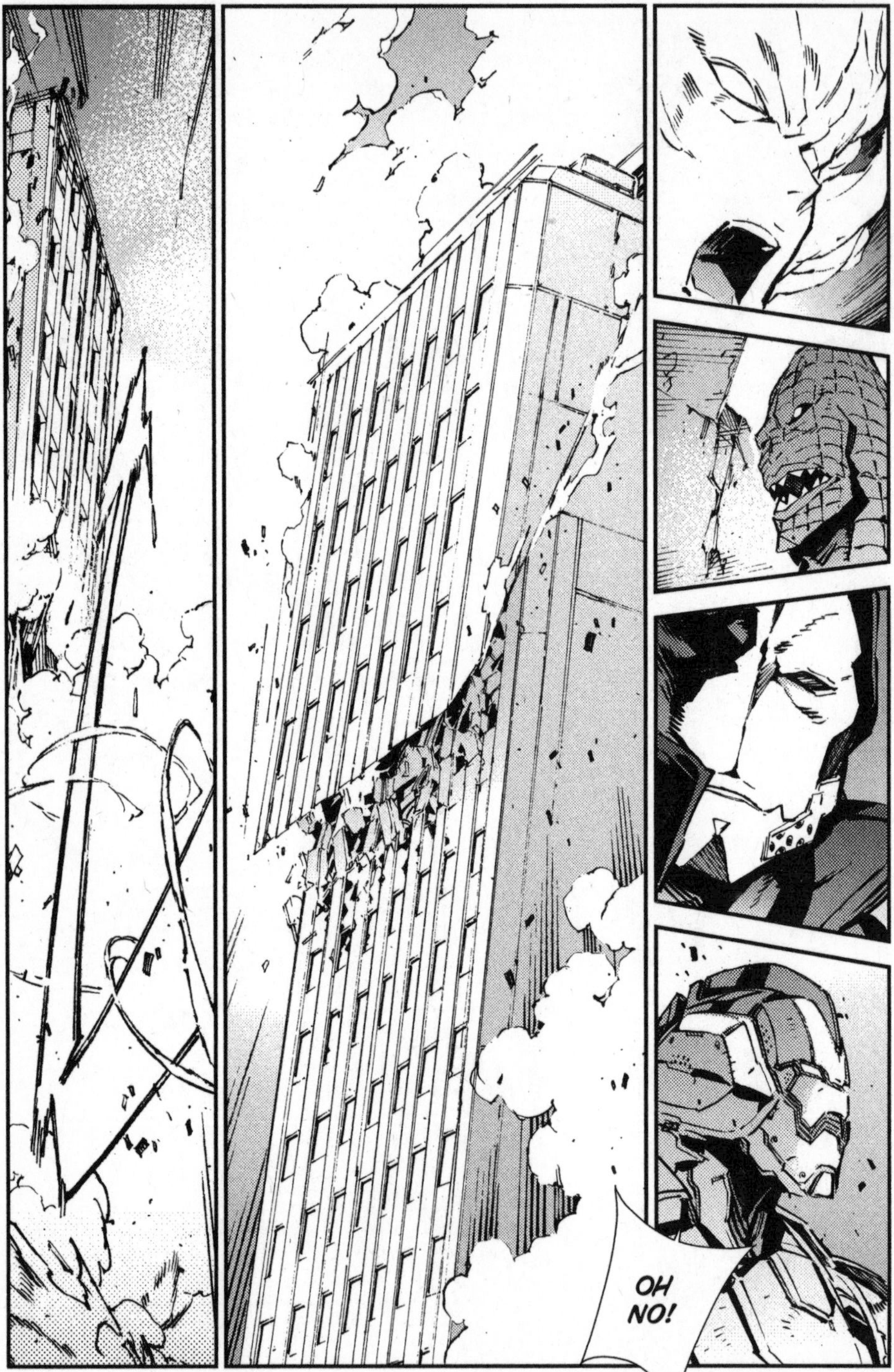
OH NO!

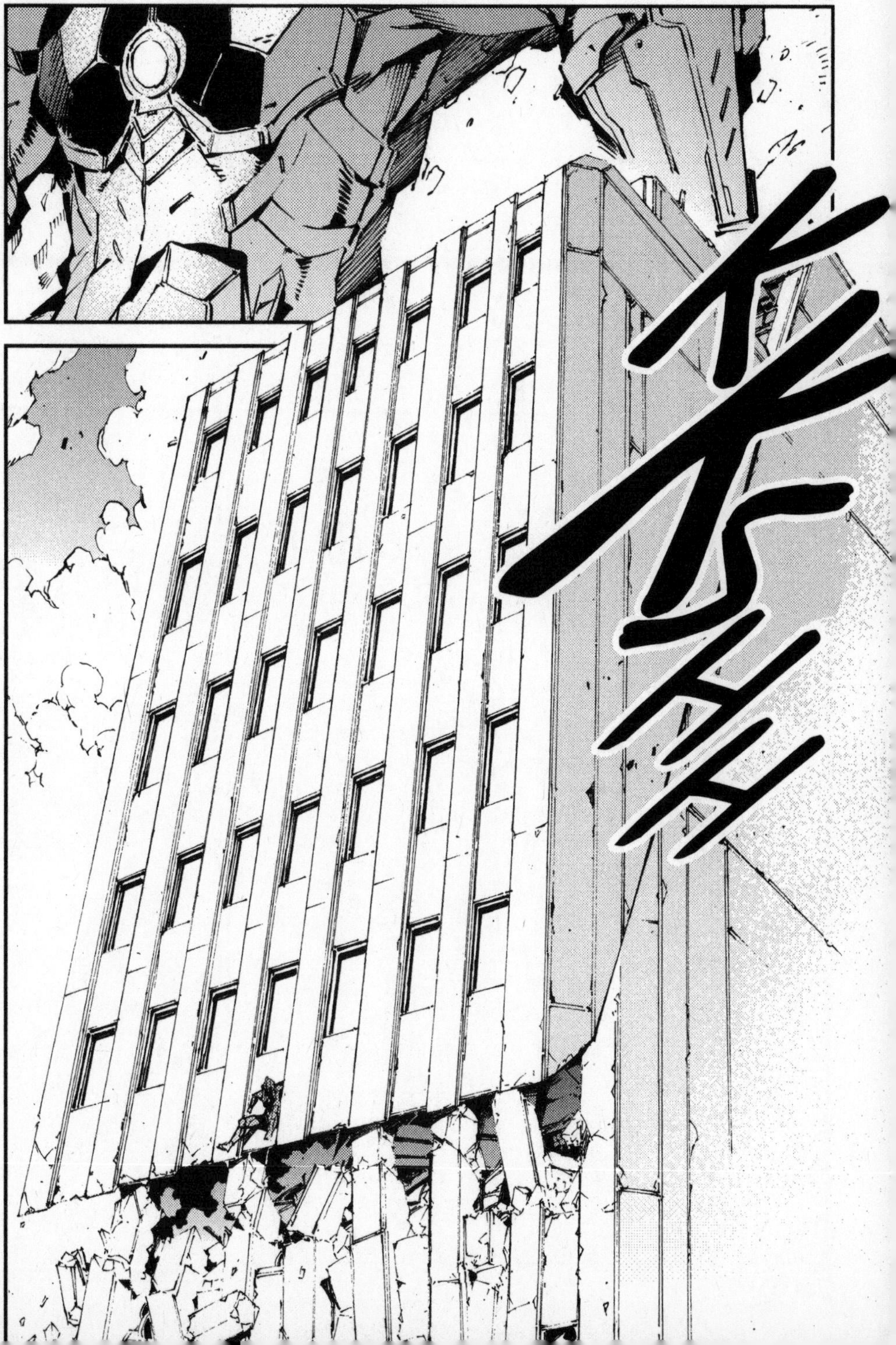
KRASHH

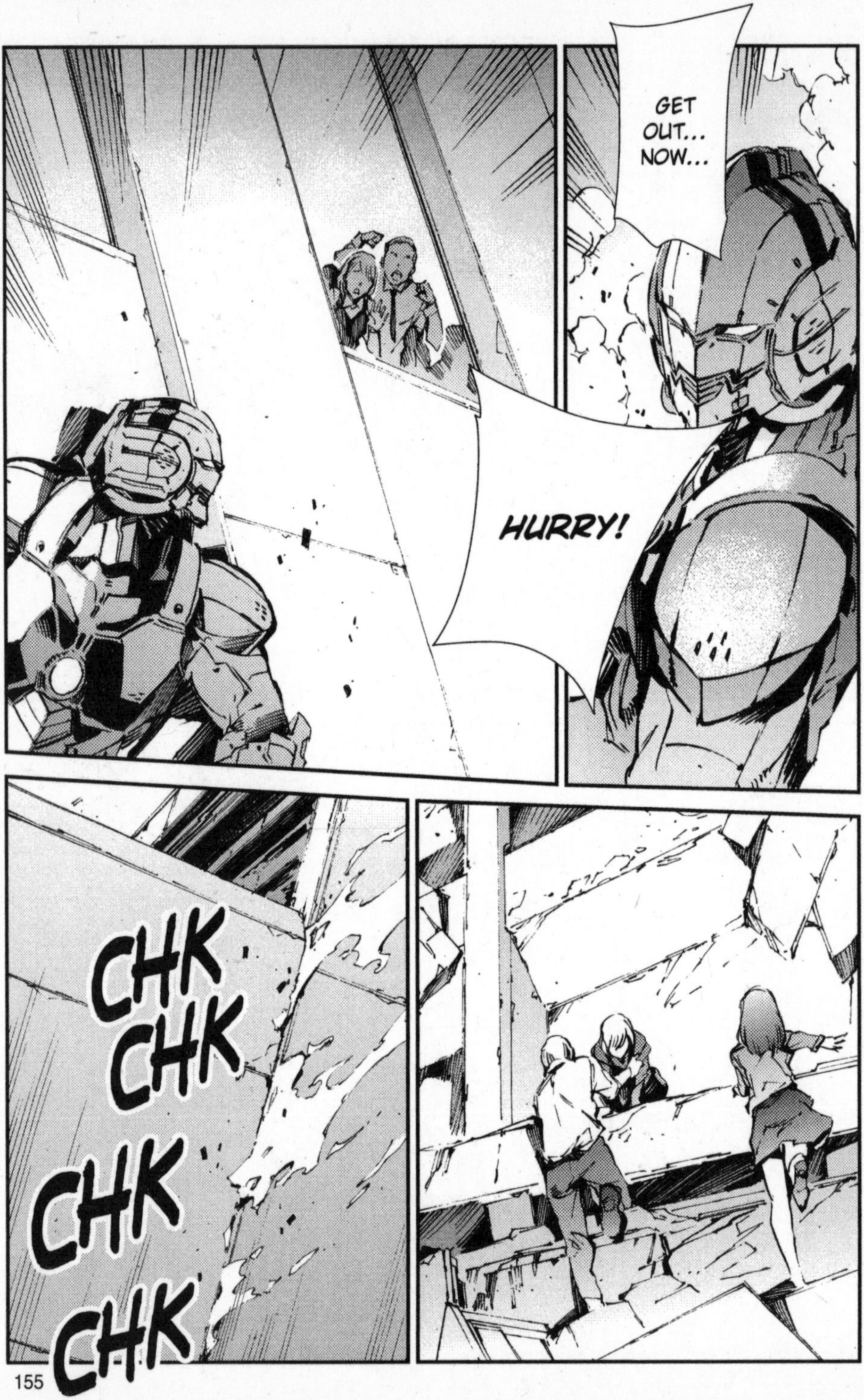
GET OUT... NOW...
HURRY!
CHK CHK CHK CHK

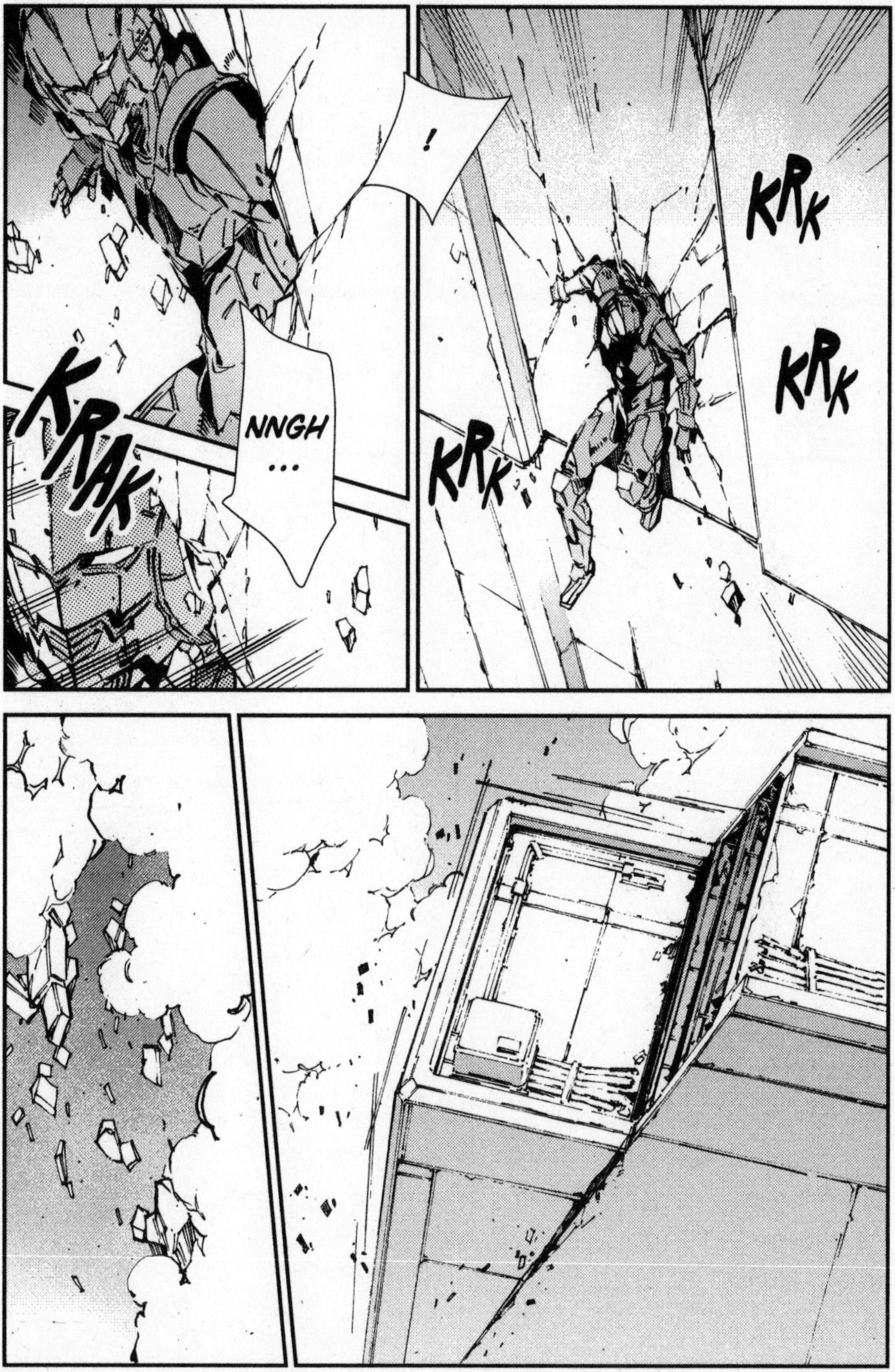
KRK
KRK
KRK
!
NNGH ...
KRAK

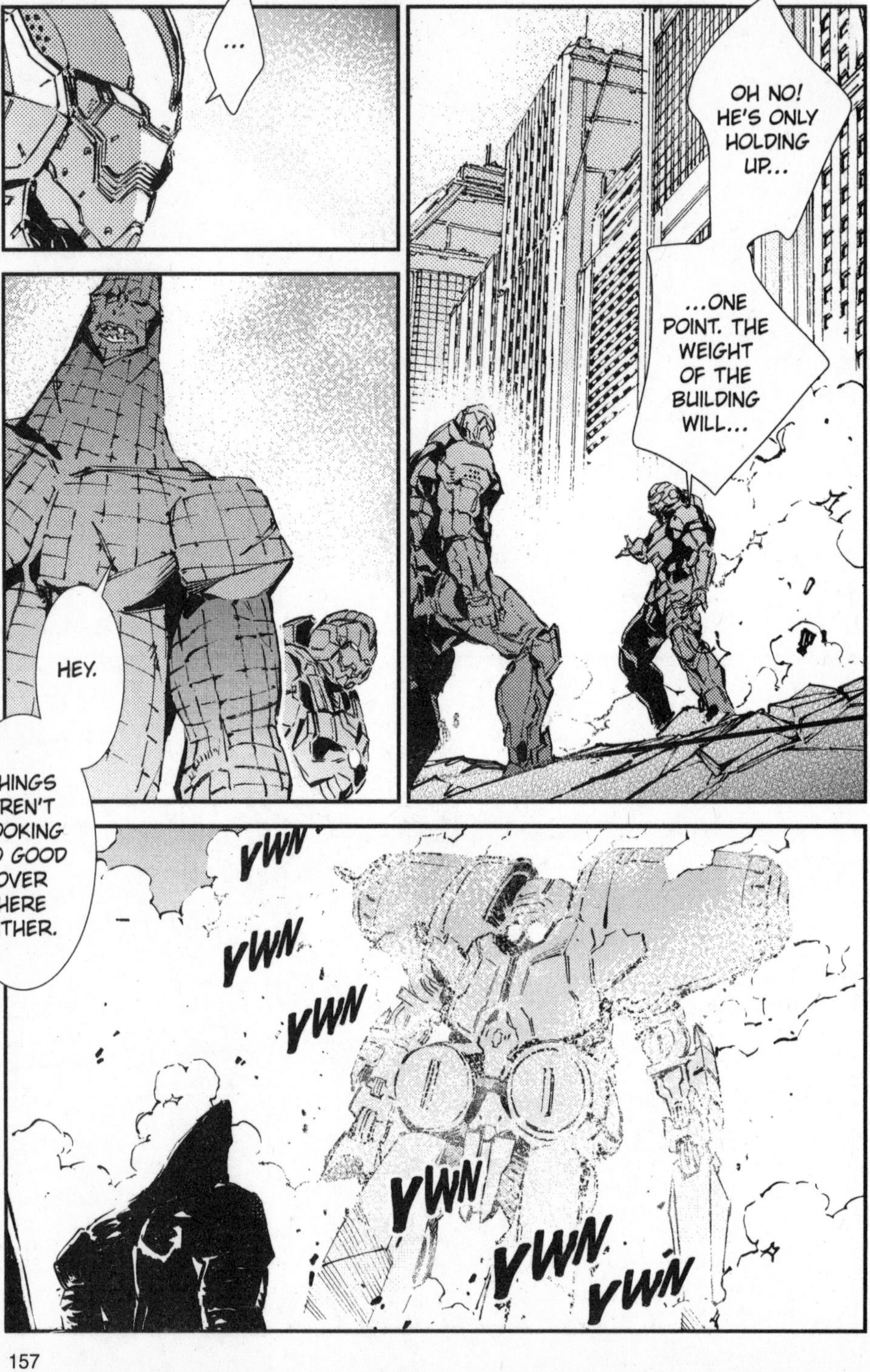
OH NO! HE'S ONLY HOLDING UP...
...ONE POINT. THE WEIGHT OF THE BUILDING WILL...
...
HEY.
THINGS AREN'T LOOKING SO GOOD OVER HERE EITHER.
YWN
YWN
YWN
YWN
YWN
YWN

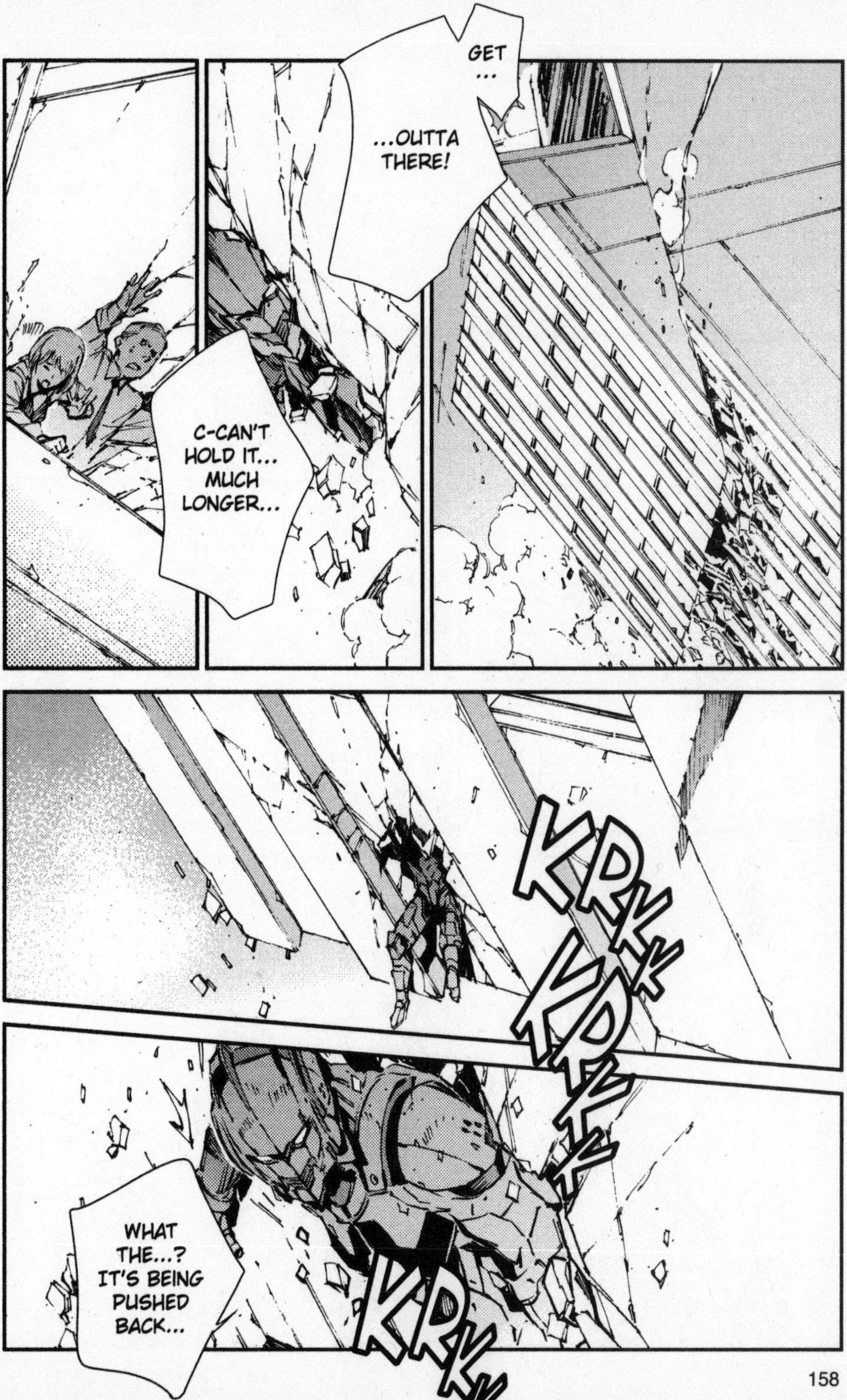
GET ...
...OUTTA THERE!
C-CAN'T HOLD IT... MUCH LONGER...
WHAT THE...? IT'S BEING PUSHED BACK...

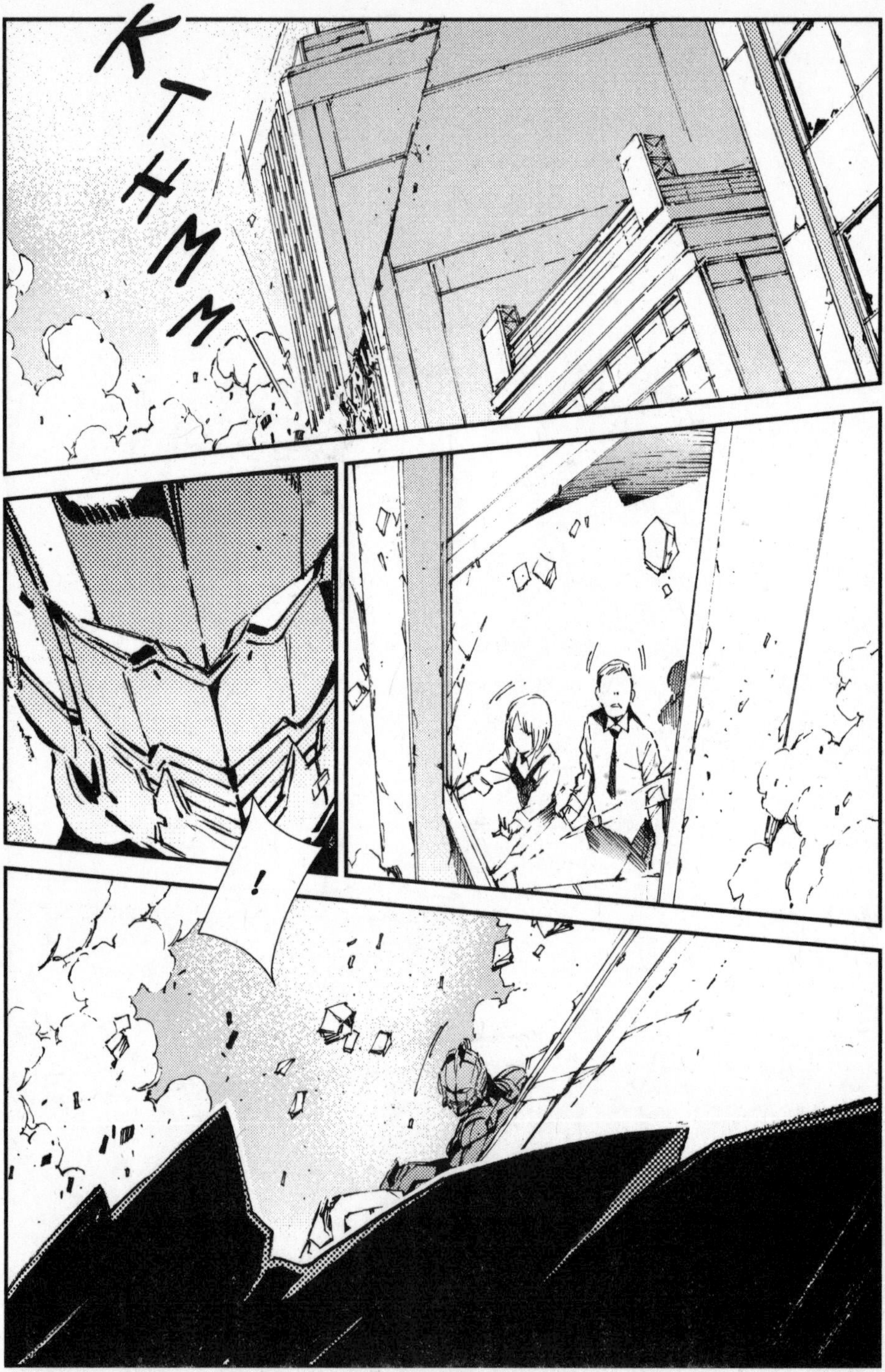
KTHMM
!

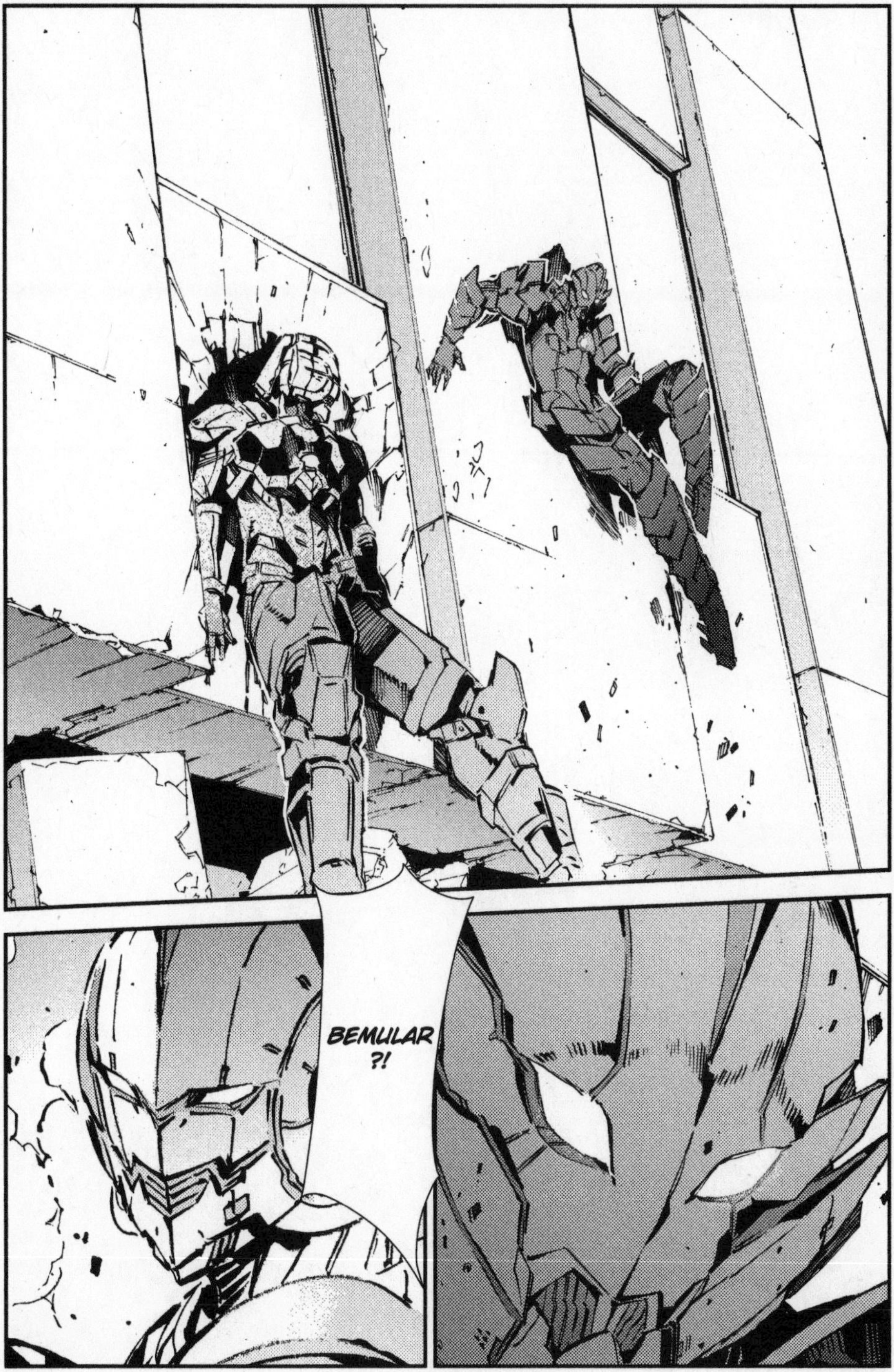
BEMULAR ?!

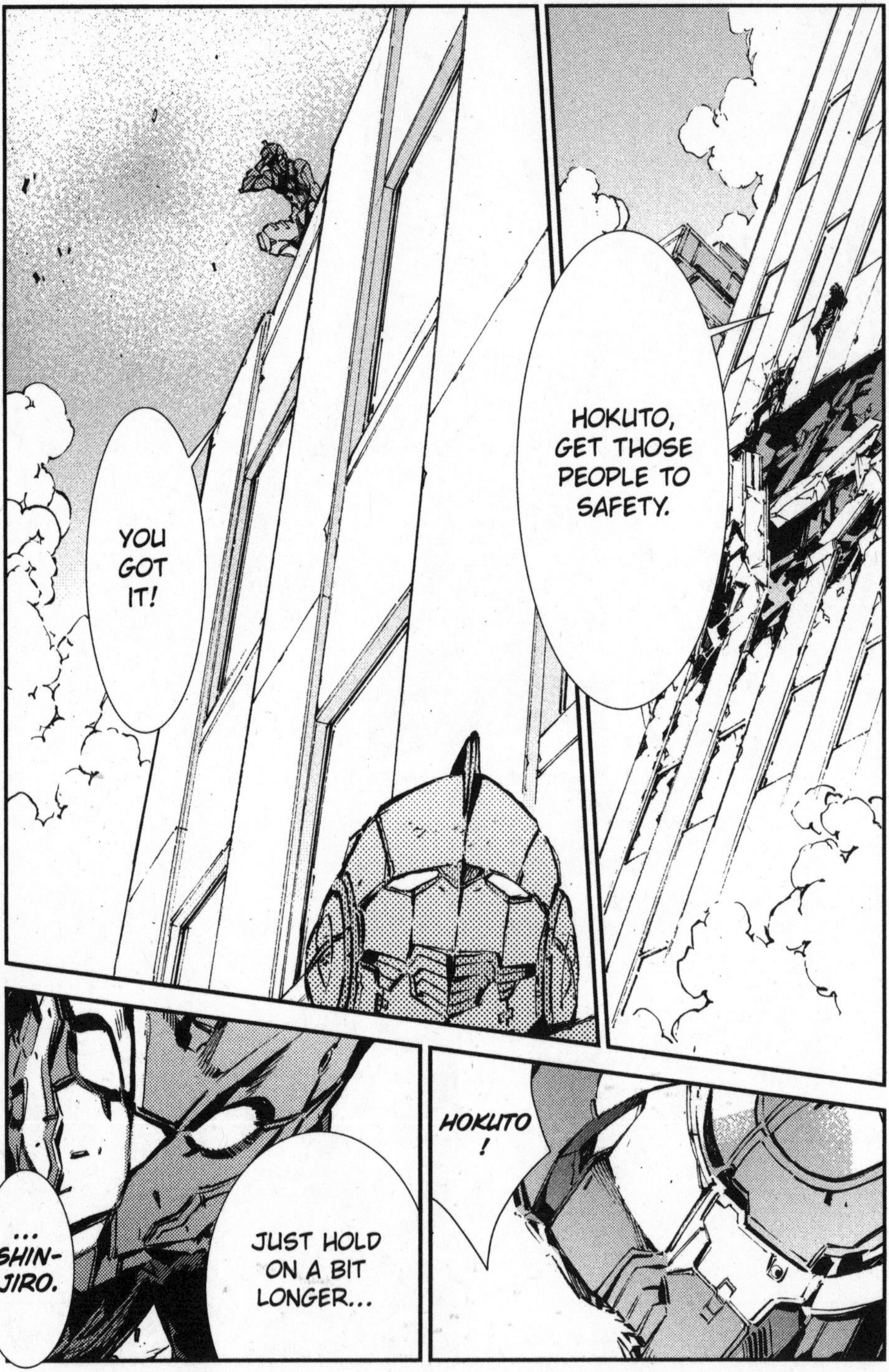
HOKUTO, GET THOSE PEOPLE TO SAFETY.
YOU GOT IT!
HOKUTO!
JUST HOLD ON A BIT LONGER...
...SHIN-JIRO.

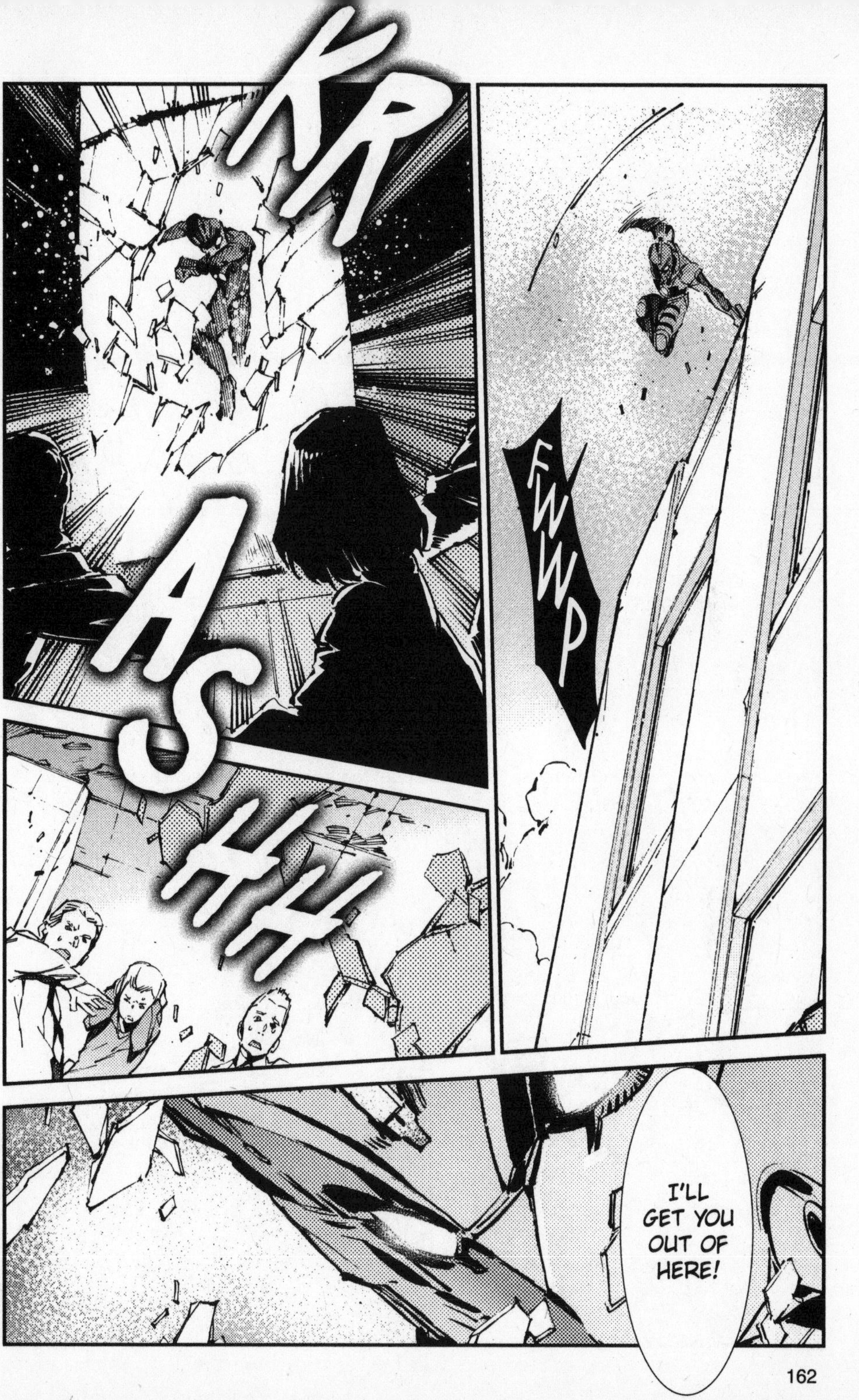
FWWP
KRASHH
I'LL GET YOU OUT OF HERE!

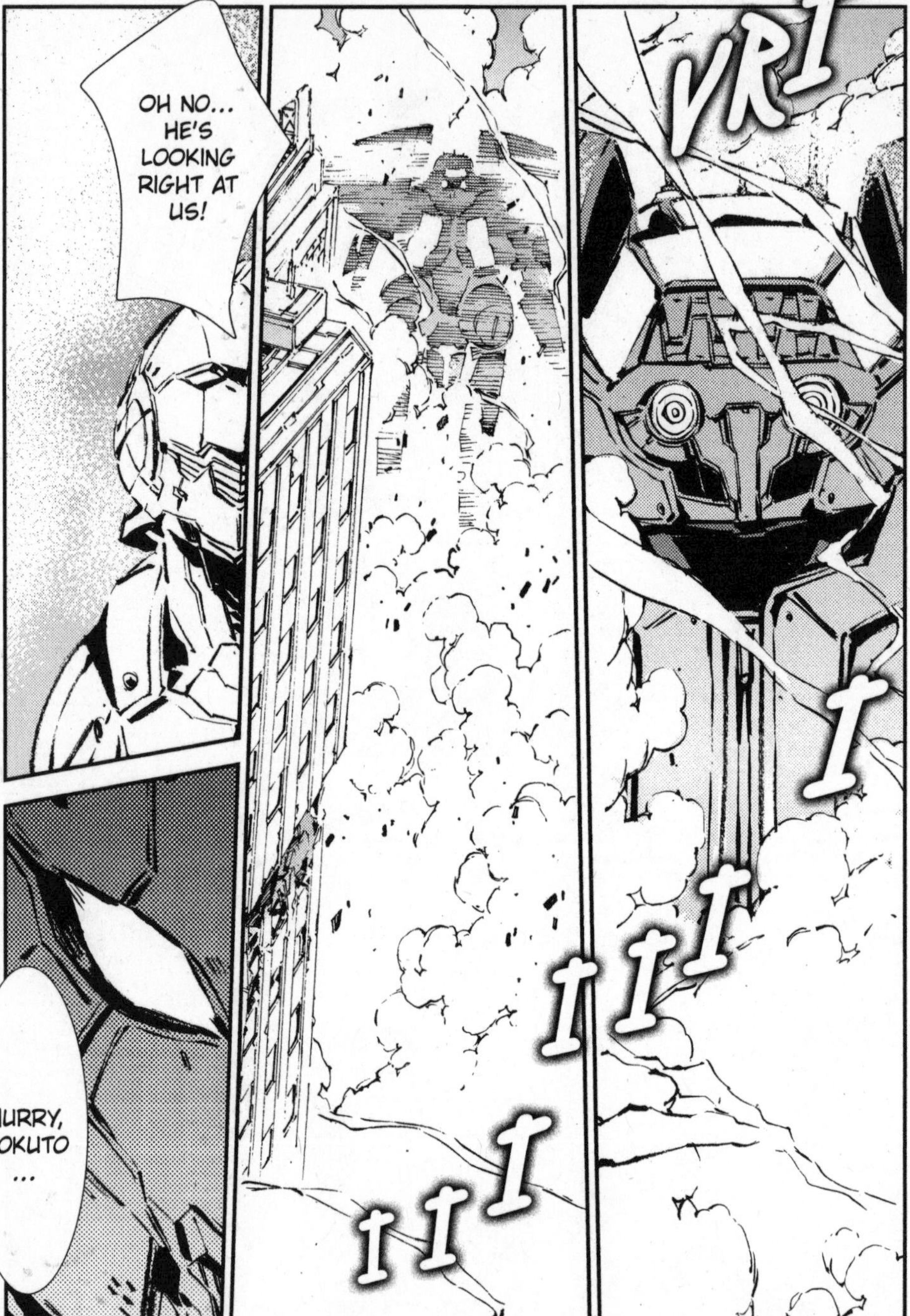
VRIIIIIIIII
OH NO... HE'S LOOKING RIGHT AT US!
HURRY, HOKUTO ...

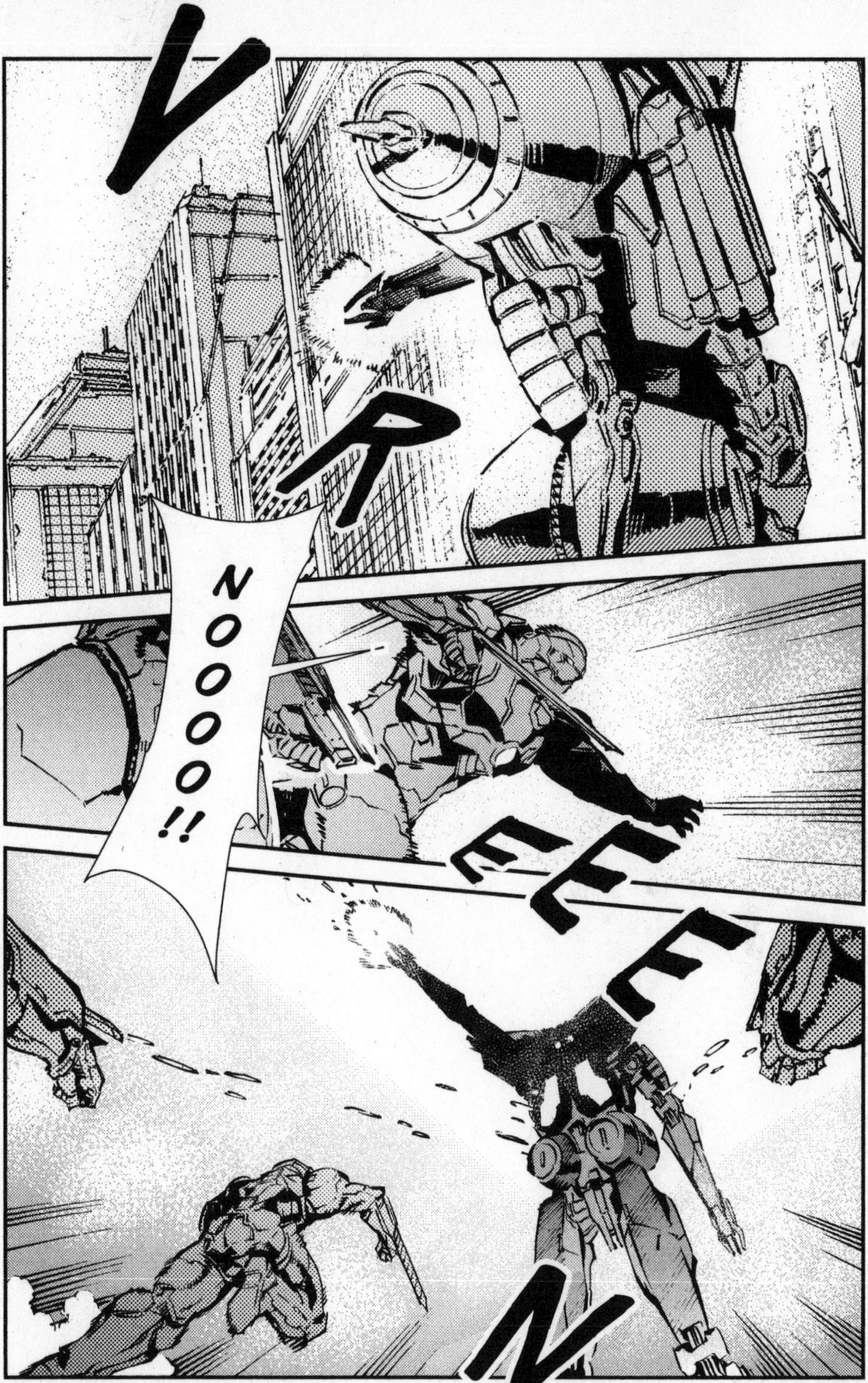
VRRREEEEN
NOOOOO!!

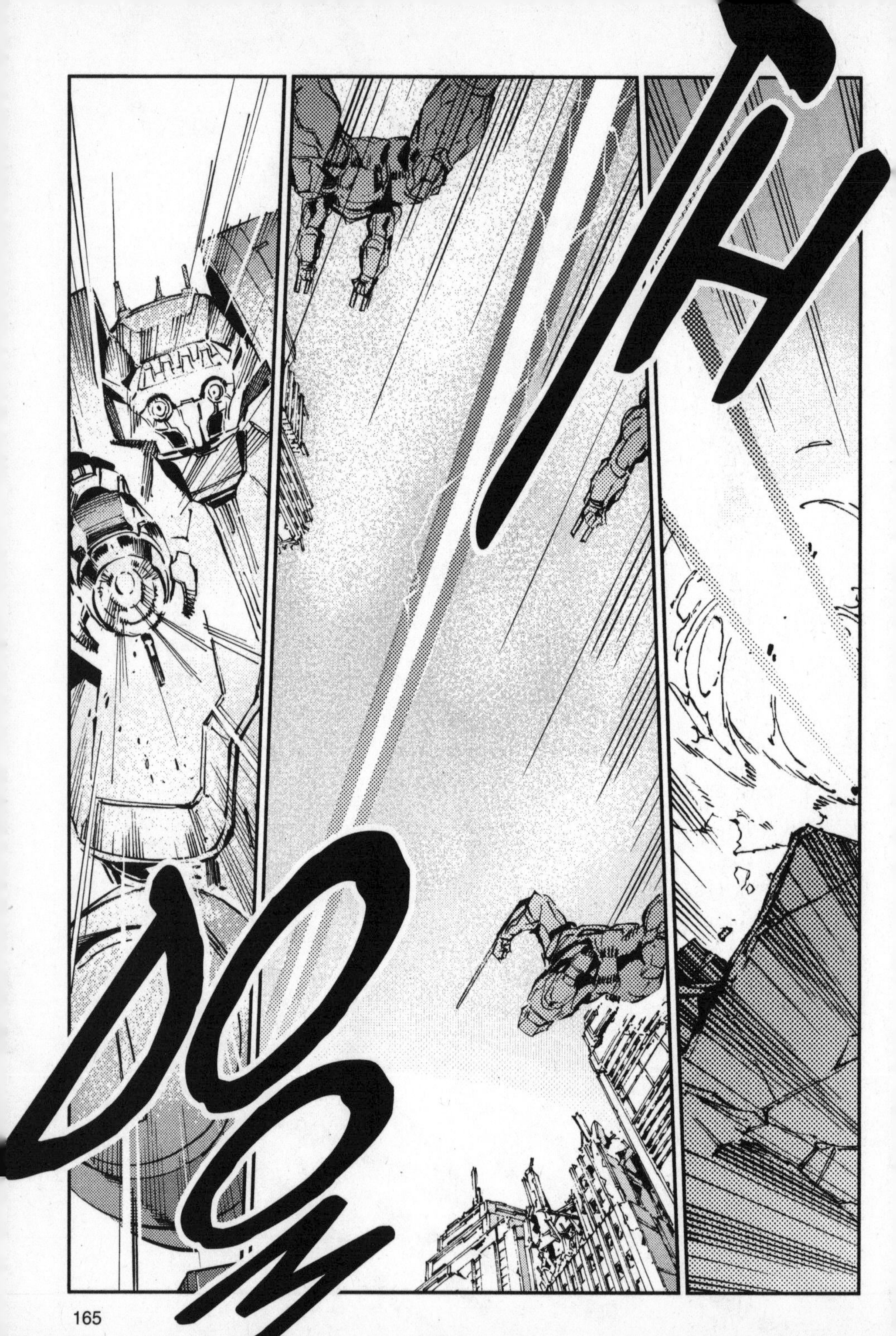

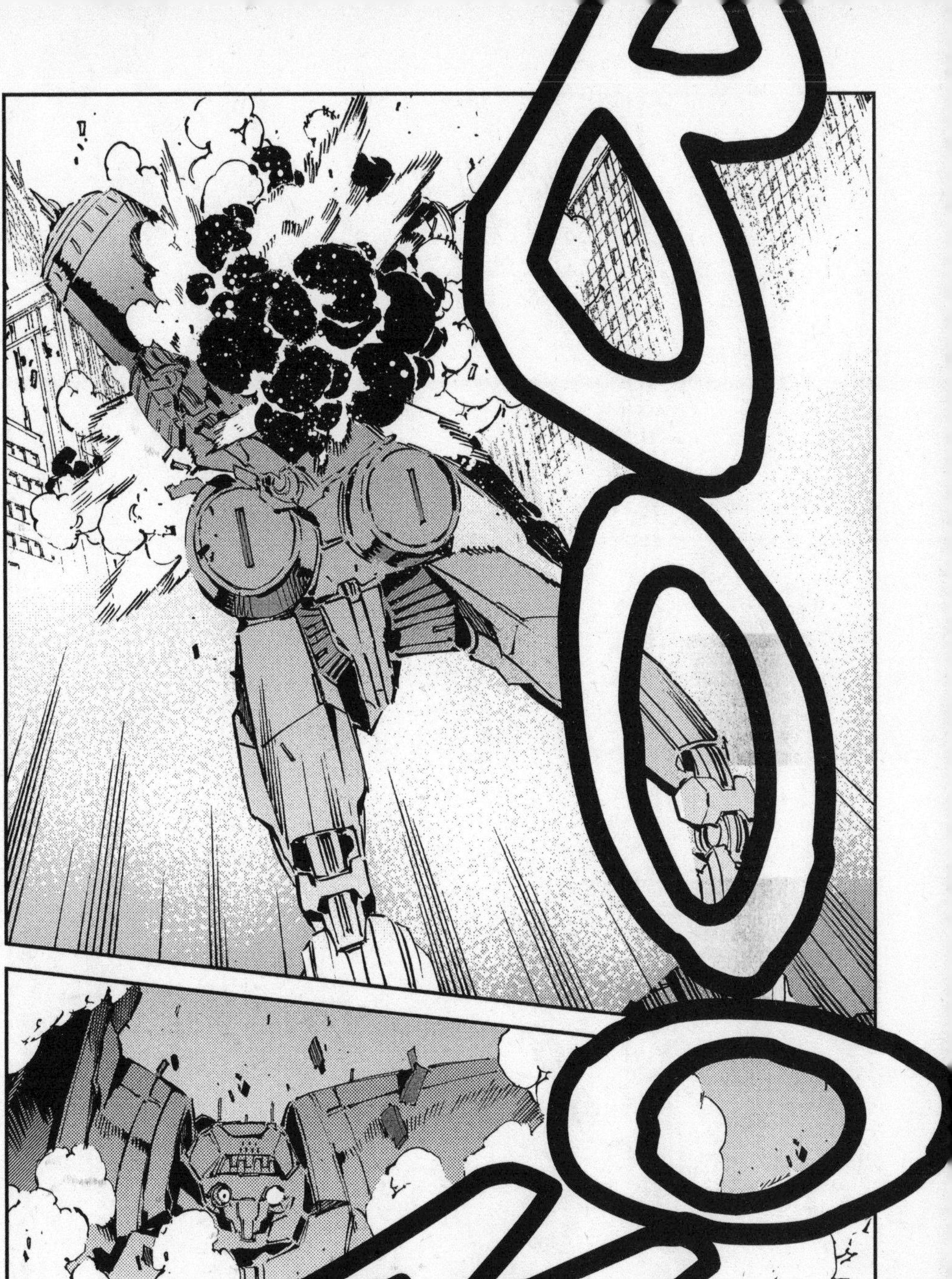
BOOM

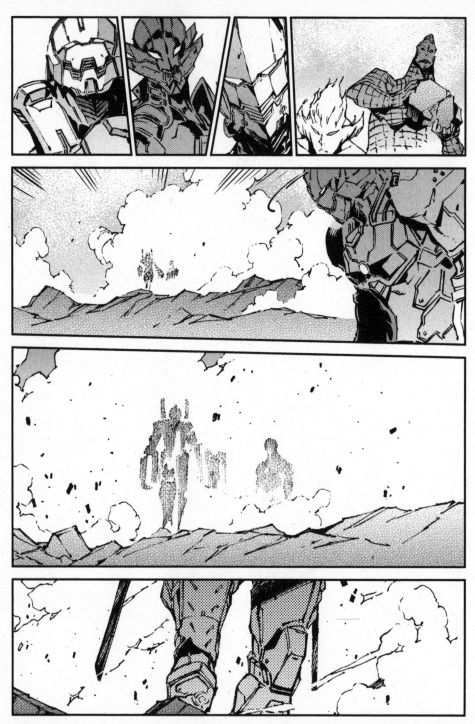

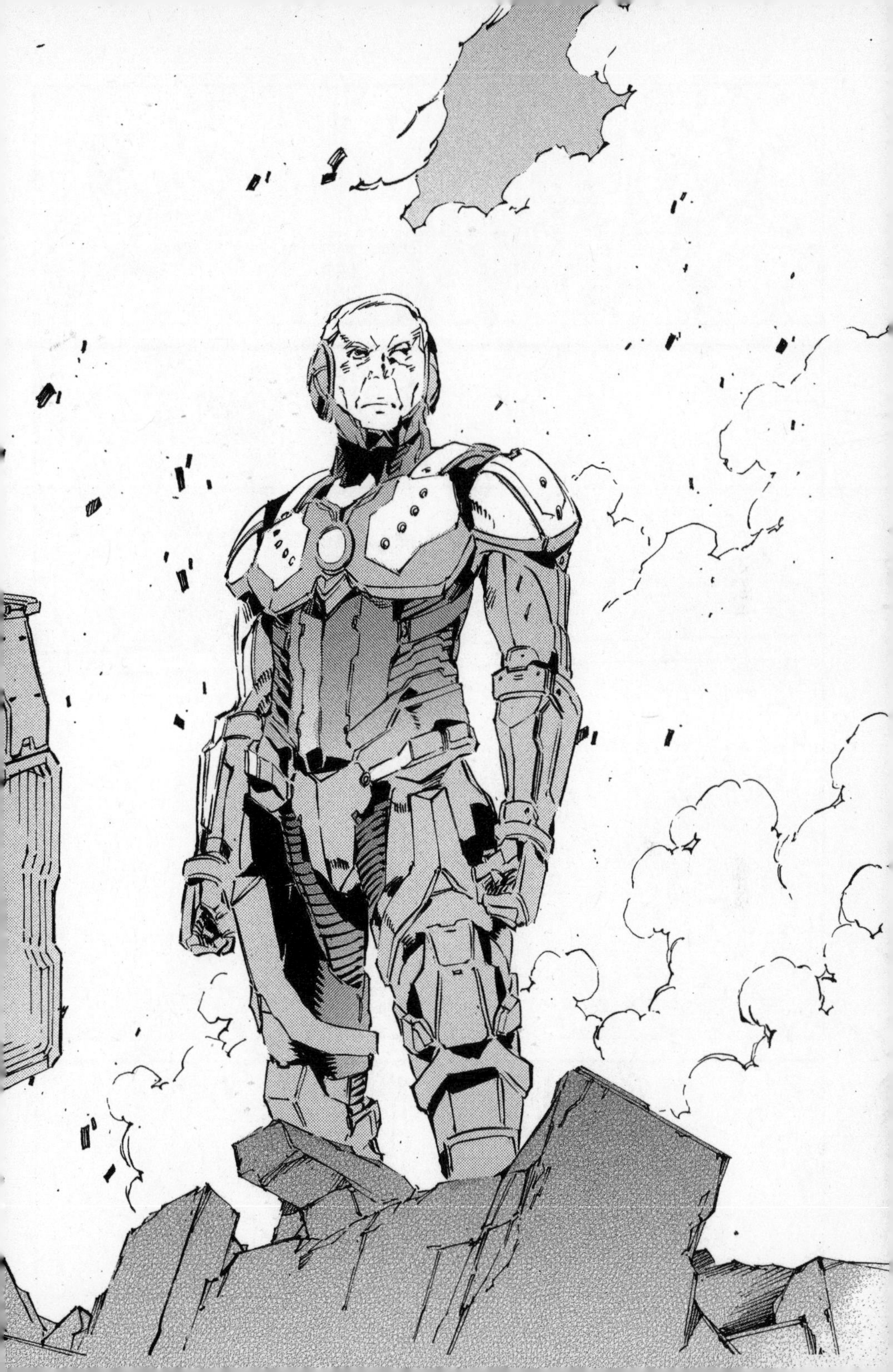

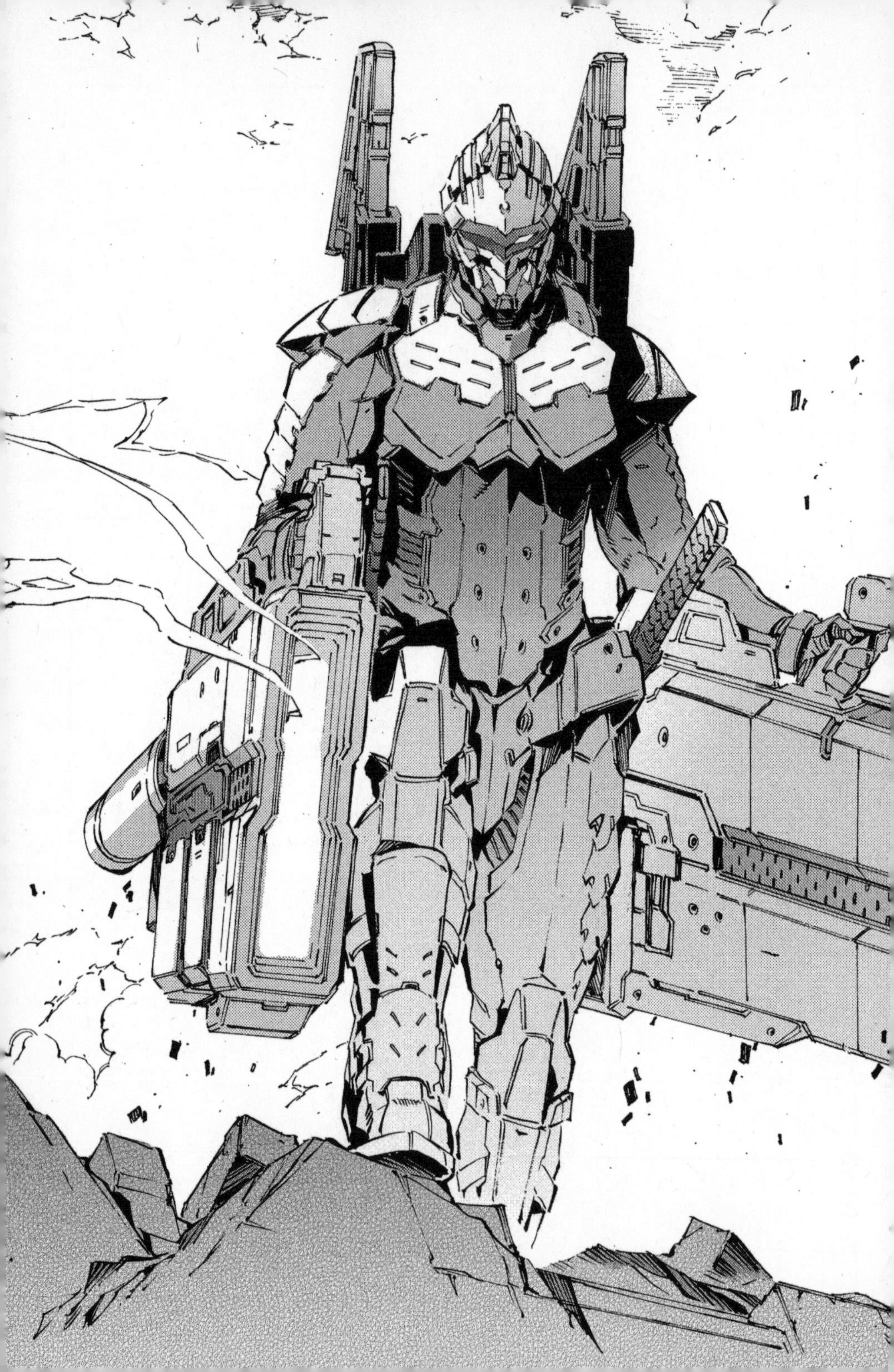

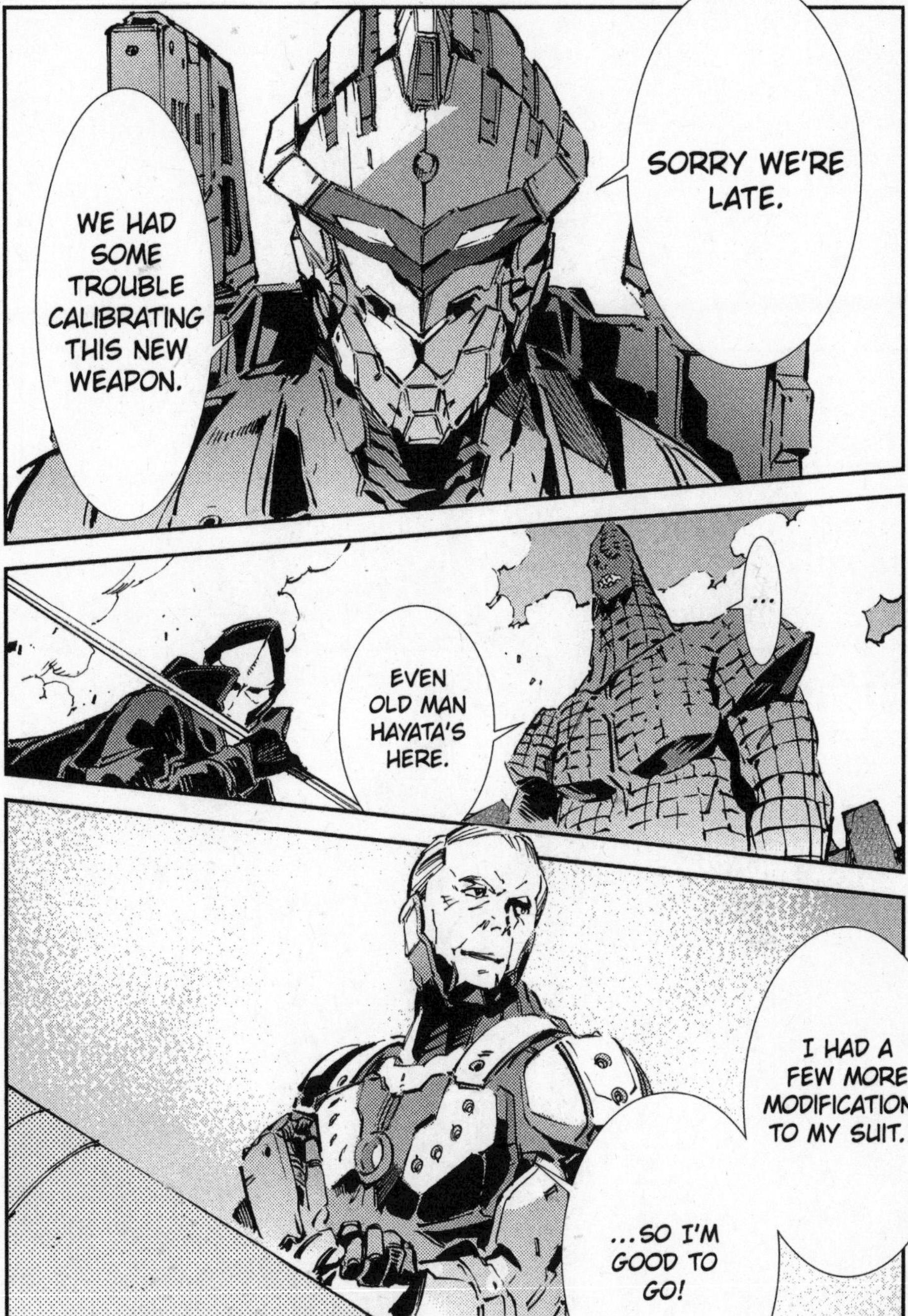
SORRY WE'RE LATE.
WE HAD SOME TROUBLE CALIBRATING THIS NEW WEAPON.
...
EVEN OLD MAN HAYATA'S HERE.
I HAD A FEW MORE MODIFICATIONS TO MY SUIT...
...SO I'M GOOD TO GO!

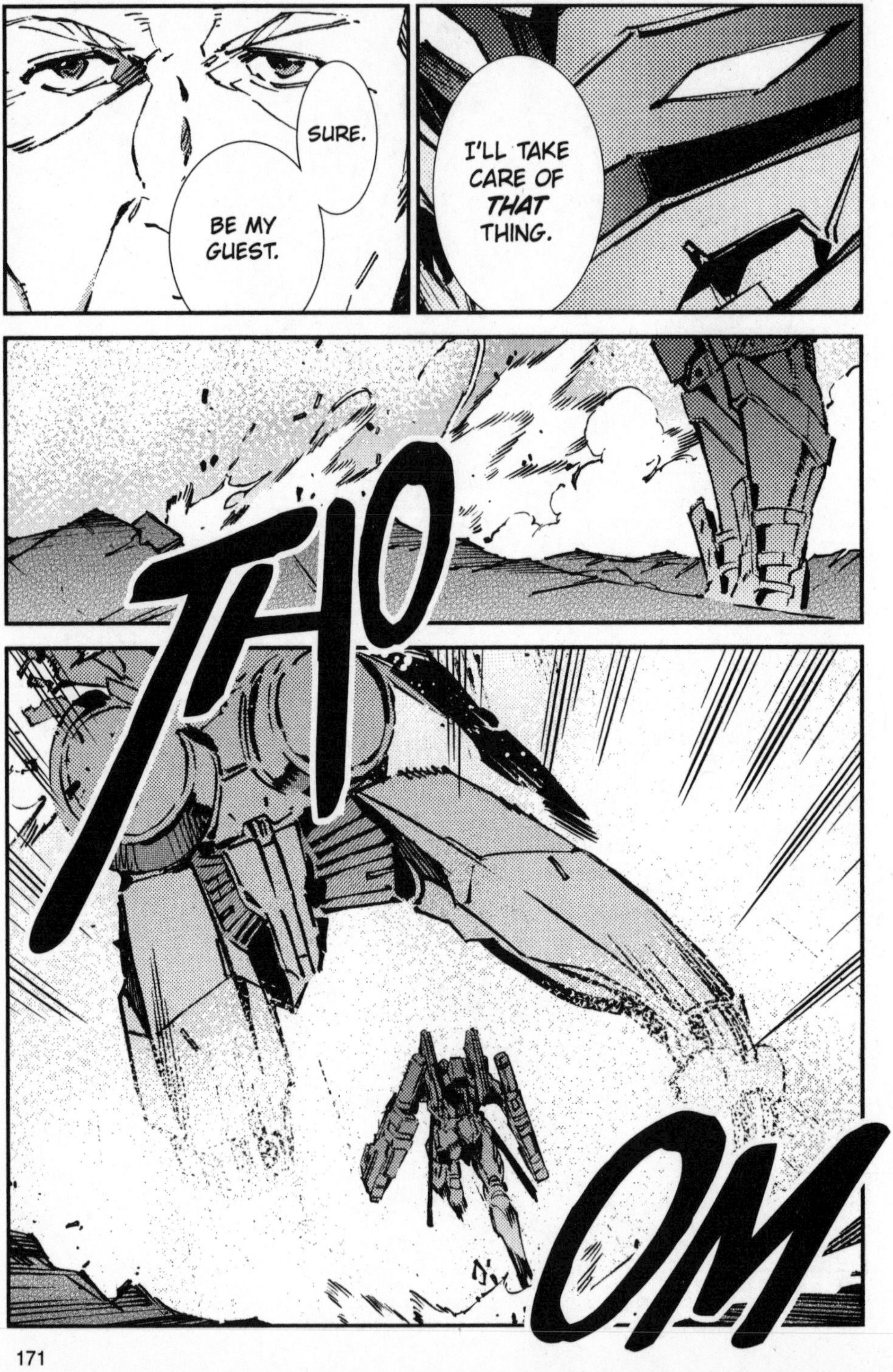
I'LL TAKE CARE OF *THAT* THING.
SURE.
BE MY GUEST.
THO
OM

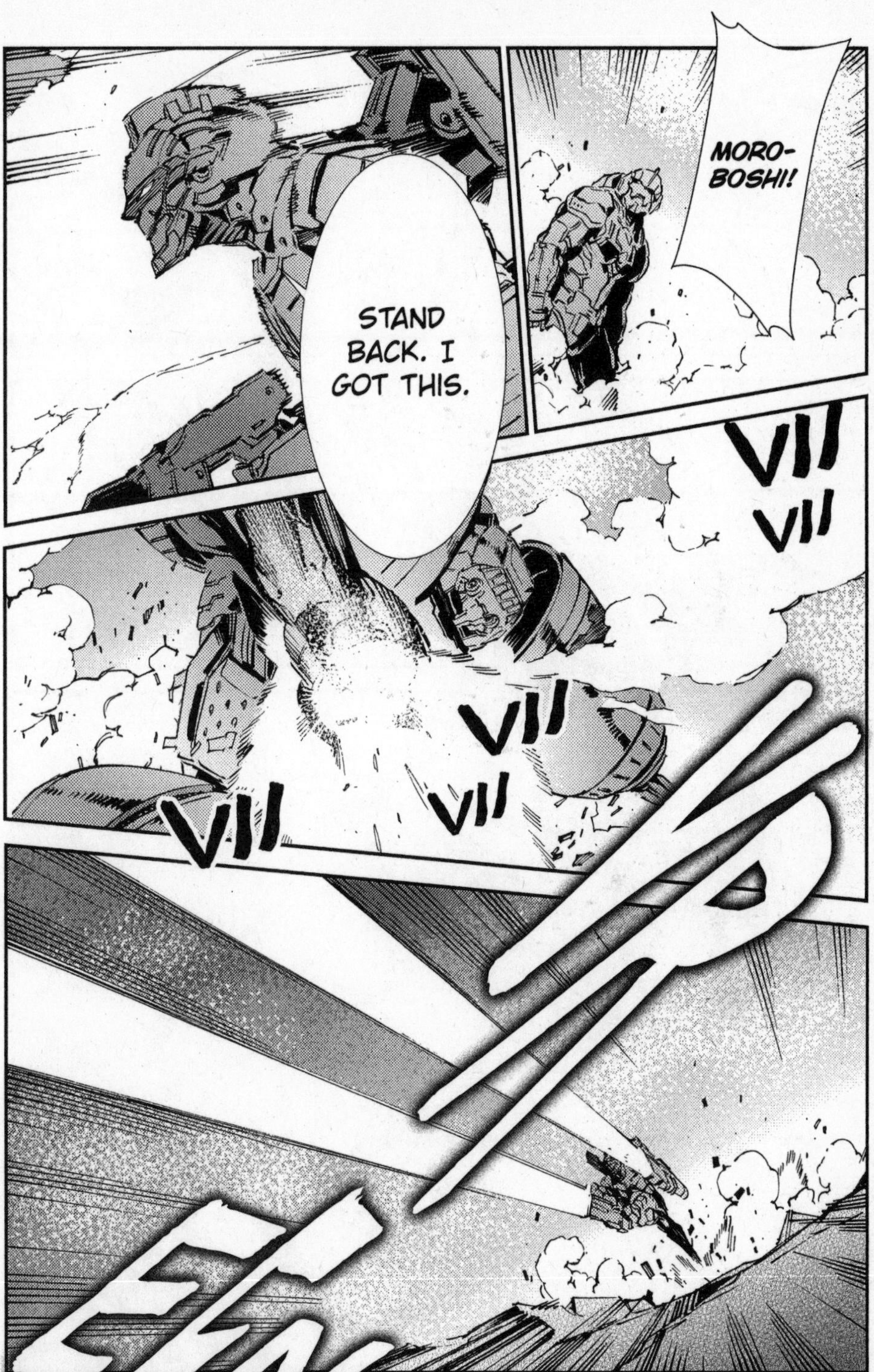
MORO-BOSHI!
STAND BACK. I GOT THIS.
VII VII
VII
VII
VII

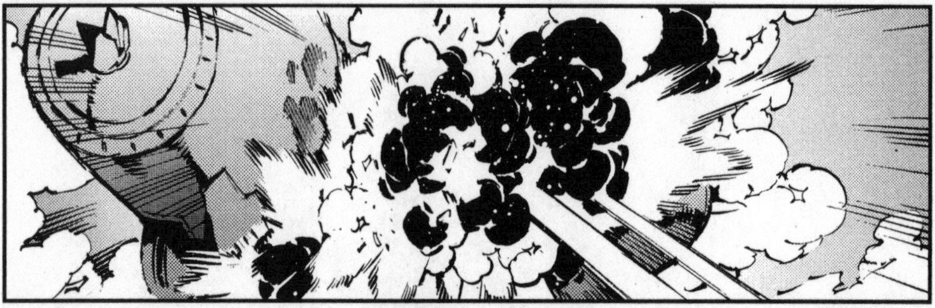
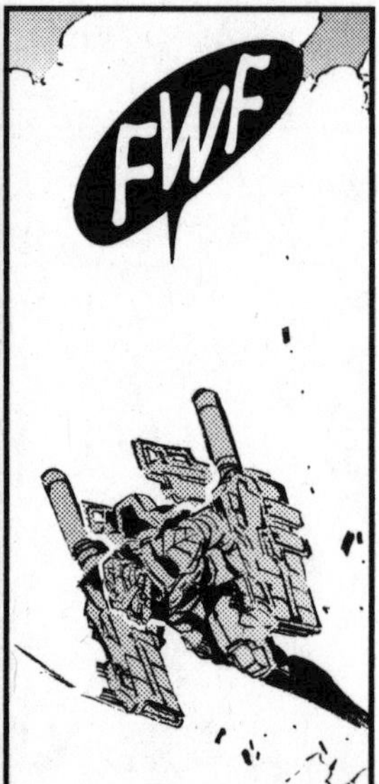
FWF
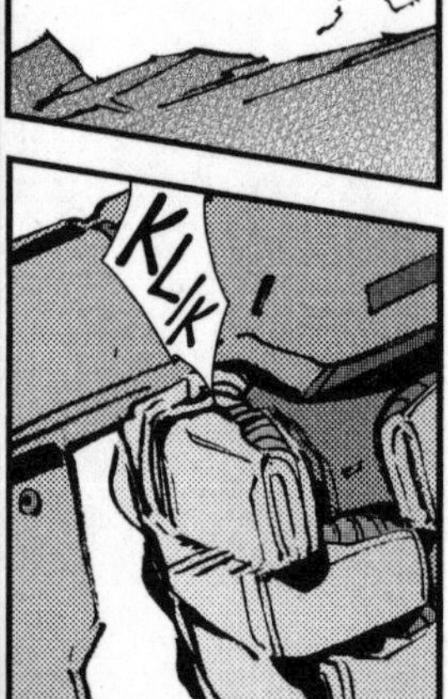
KLIK
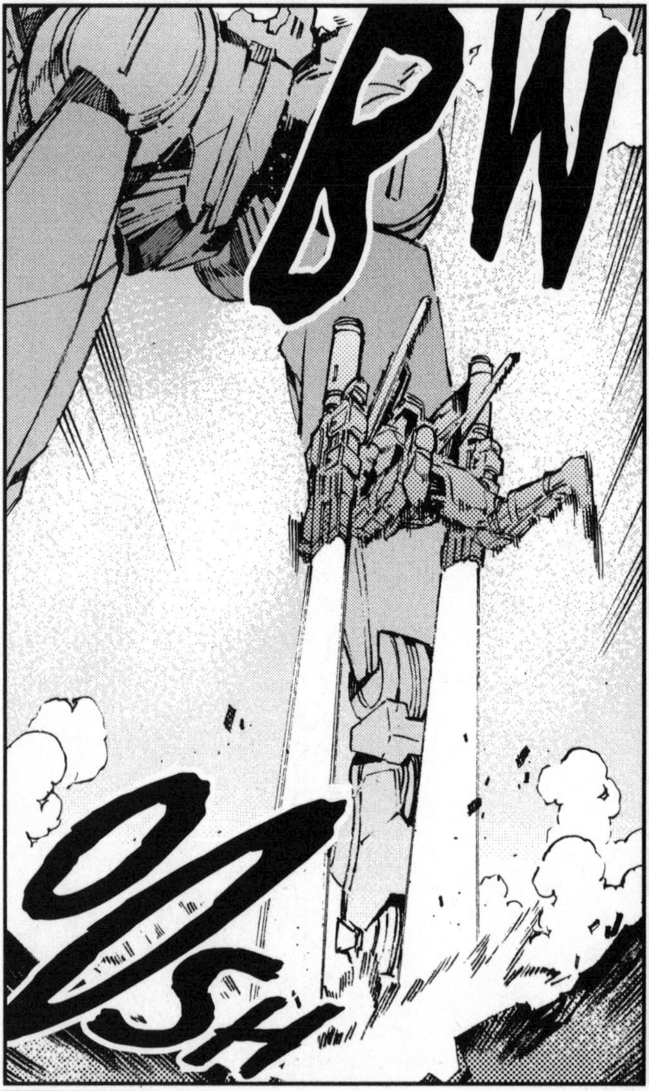
BW
OOSH

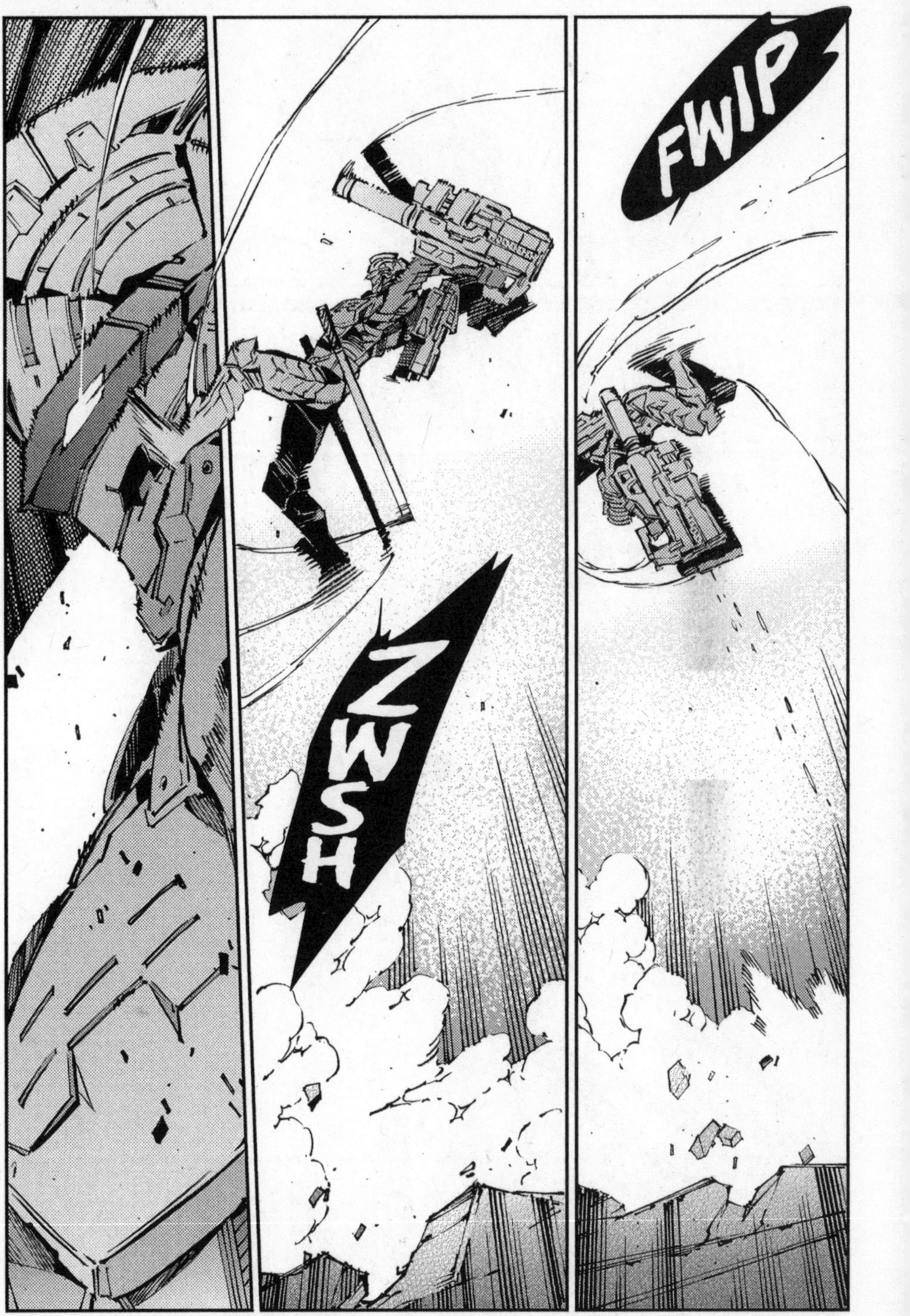
FWIP
ZWSH

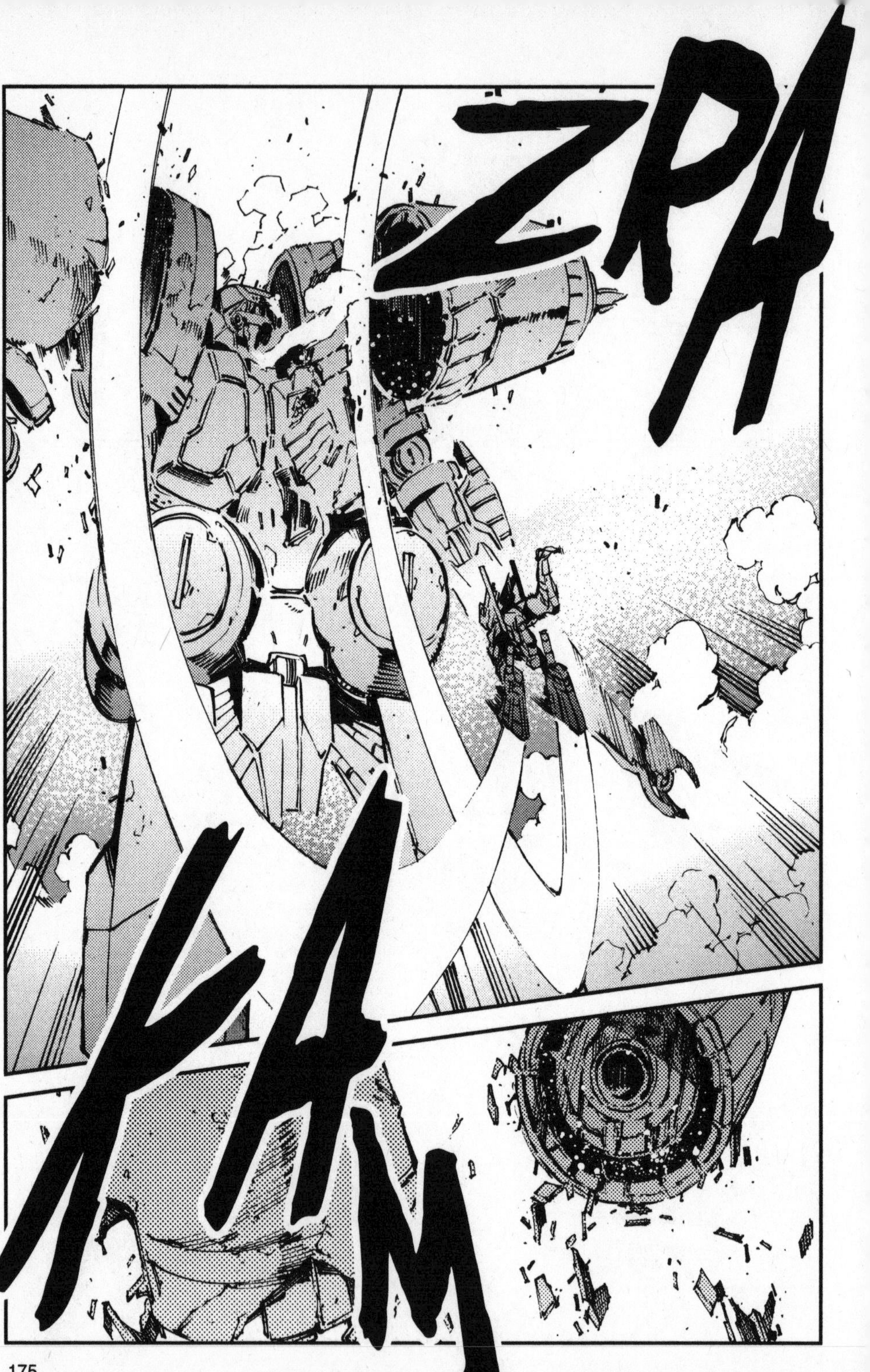
ZPA
KAM

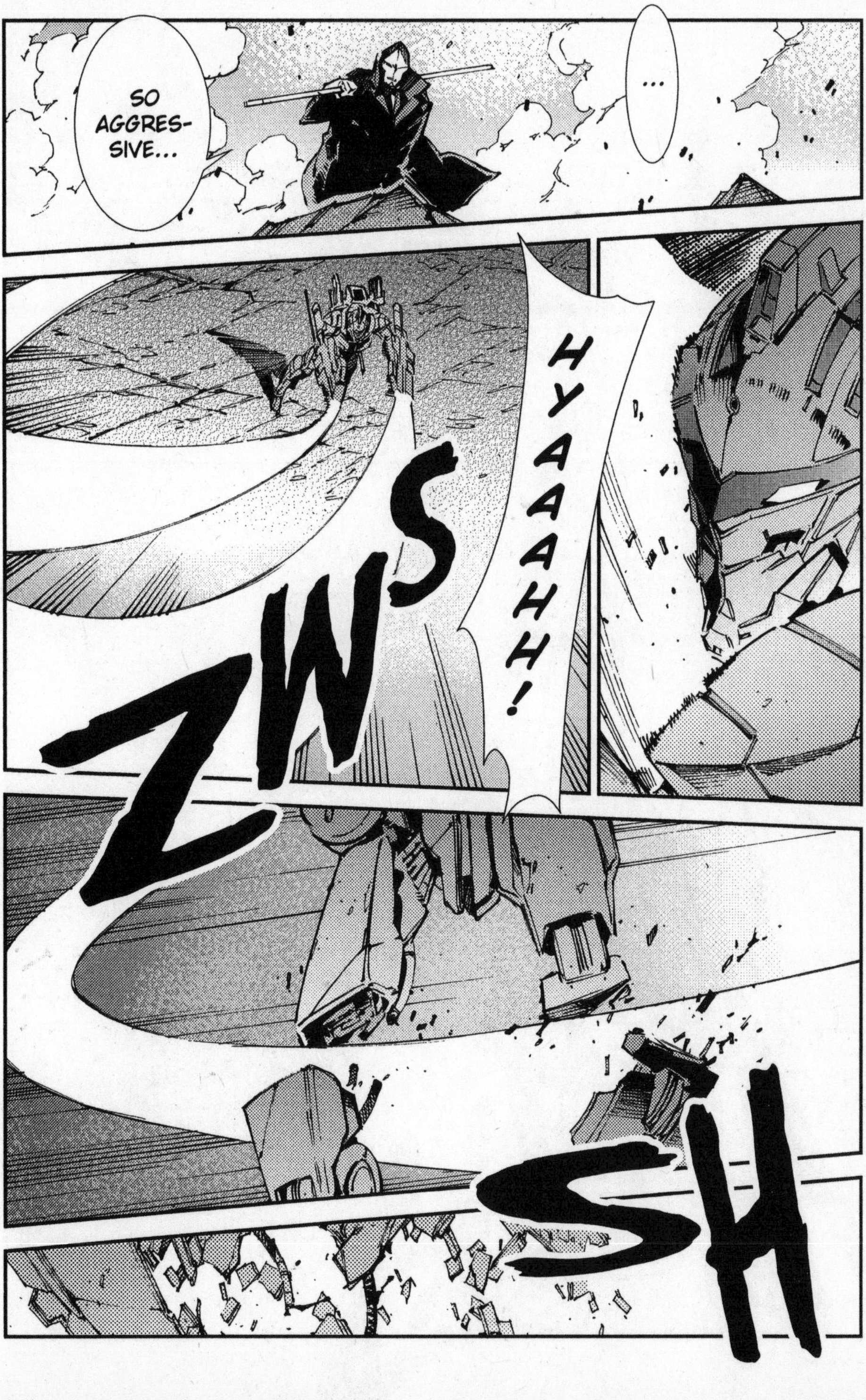
...
SO AGGRES-SIVE...
HYAAAAHH!
ZWSSH

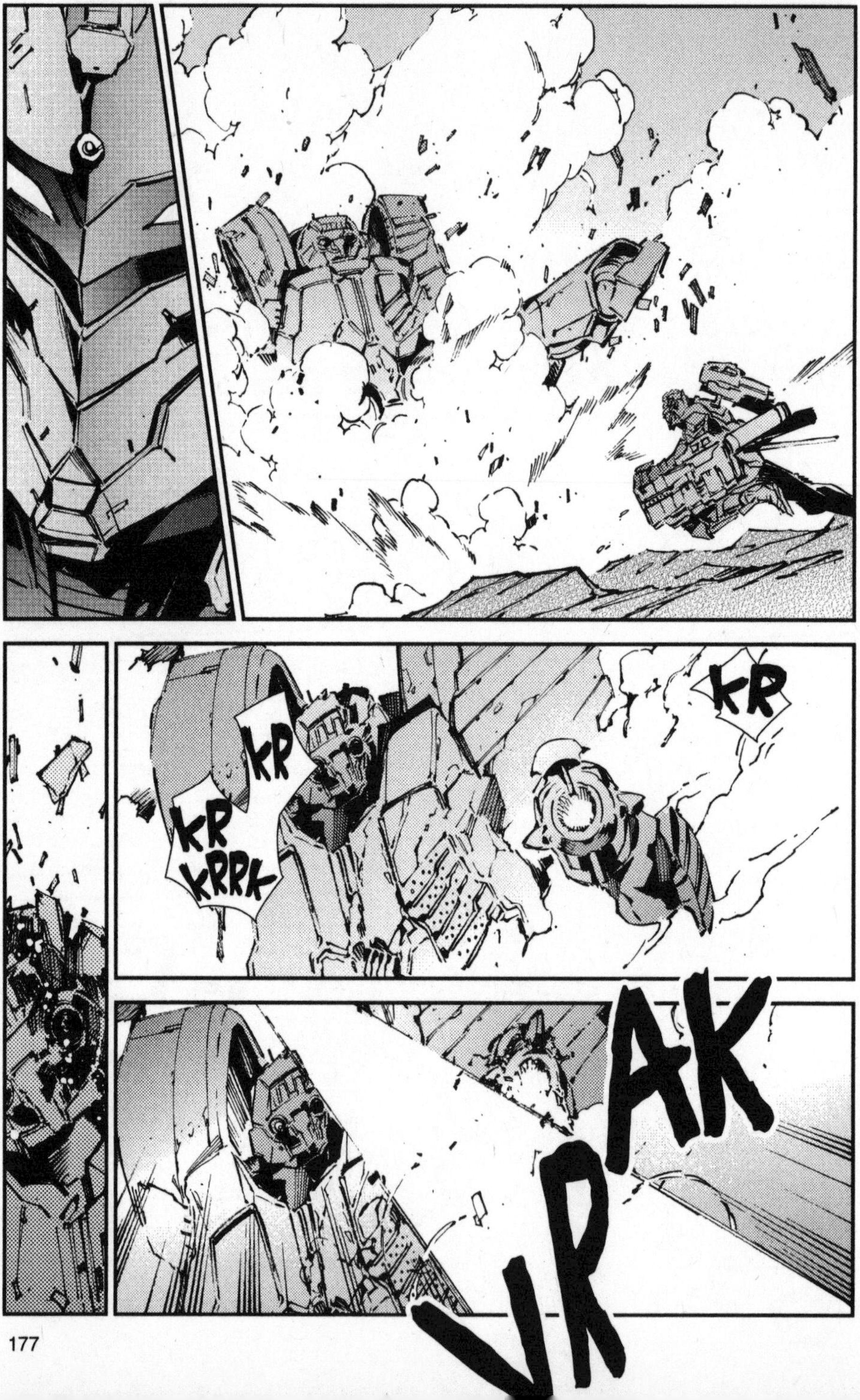
KR
KR
KR
KRRK
VRAK

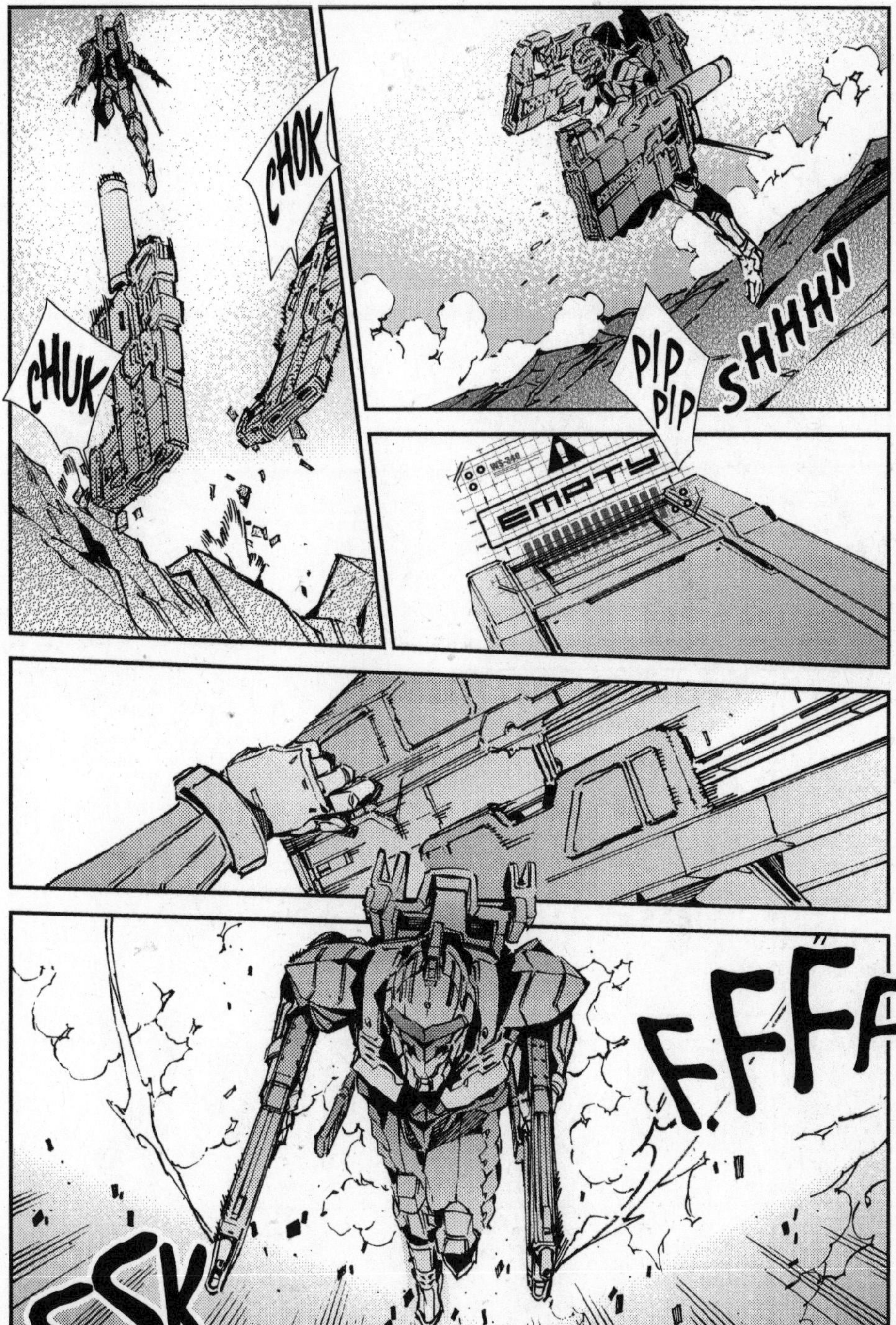
SHHHN
PIP PIP
EMPTY
CHOK
CHUK
FFFF
SSK

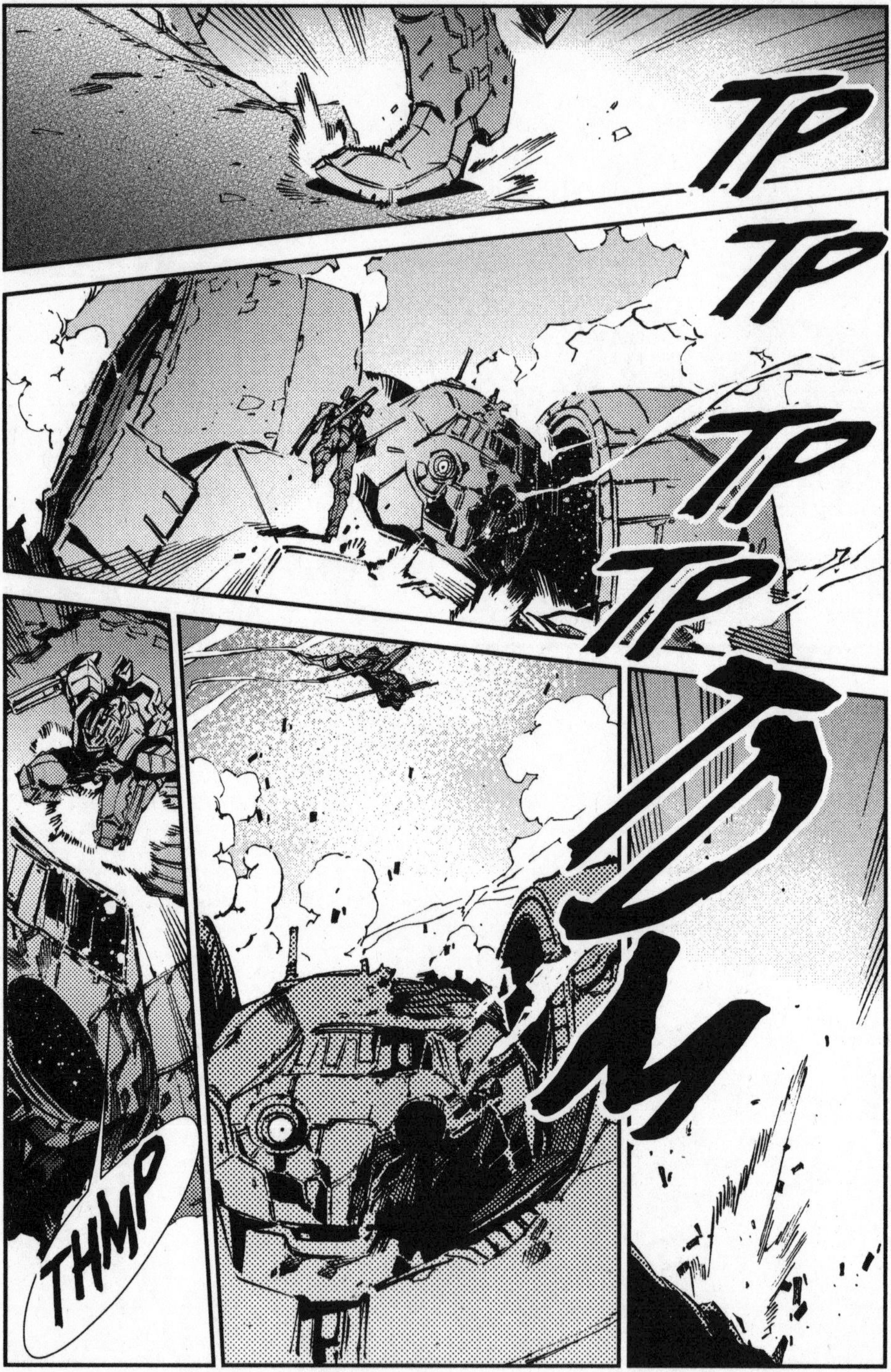
TP
TP
TP
TP
THMP

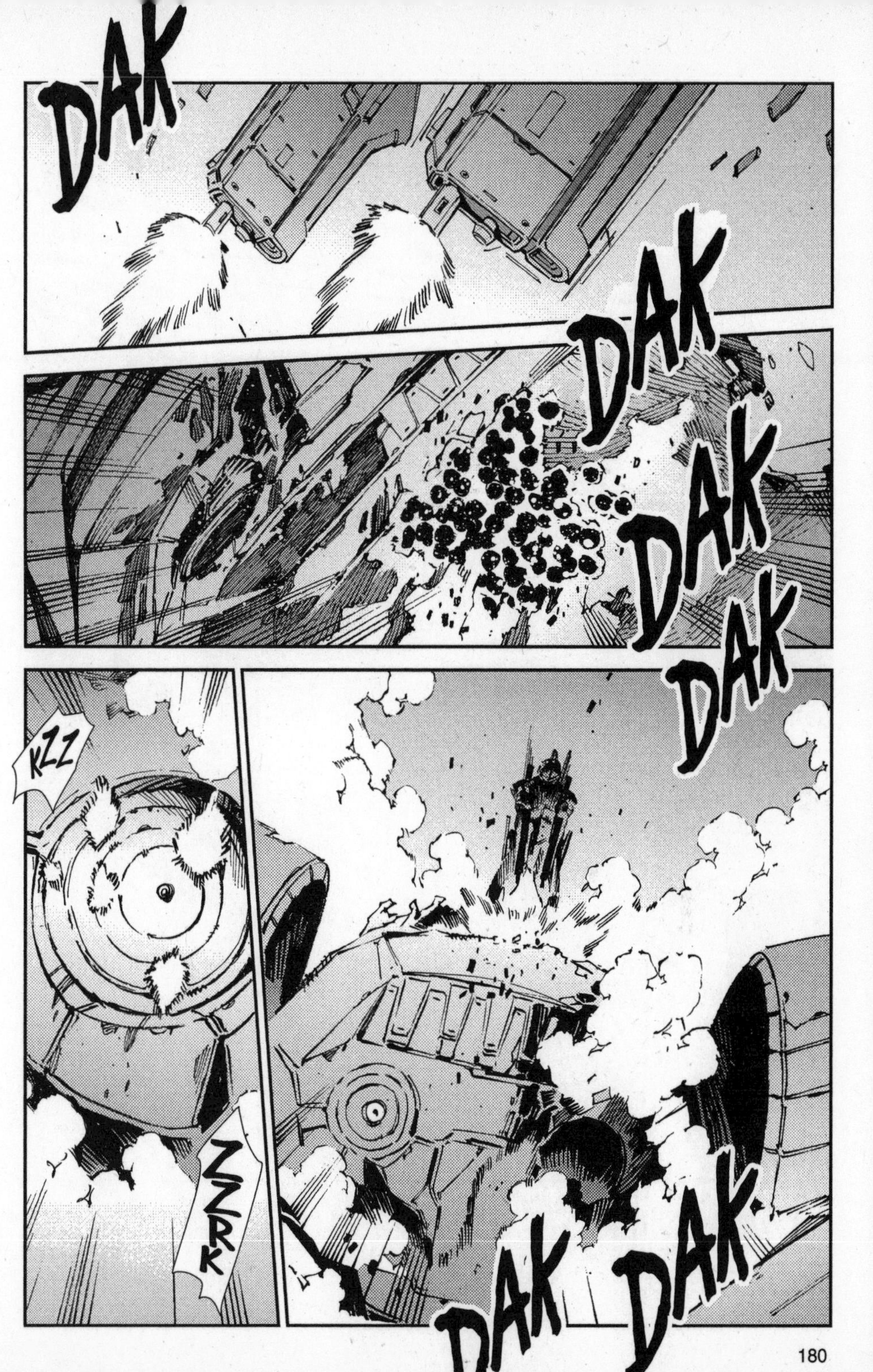
DAK
DAK
DAK
DAK
KZZ
ZZRK
DAK DAK

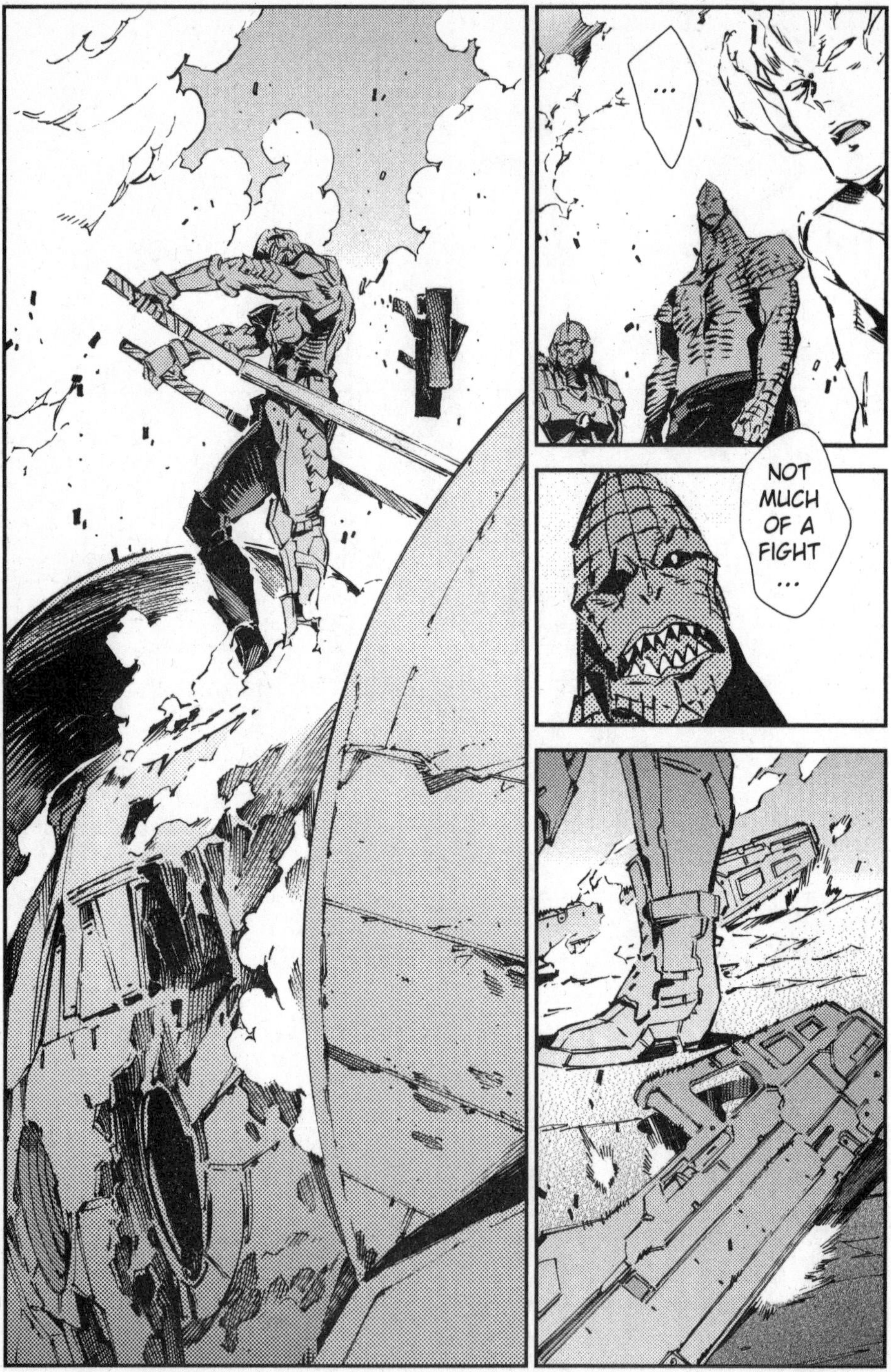
...
NOT MUCH OF A FIGHT ...

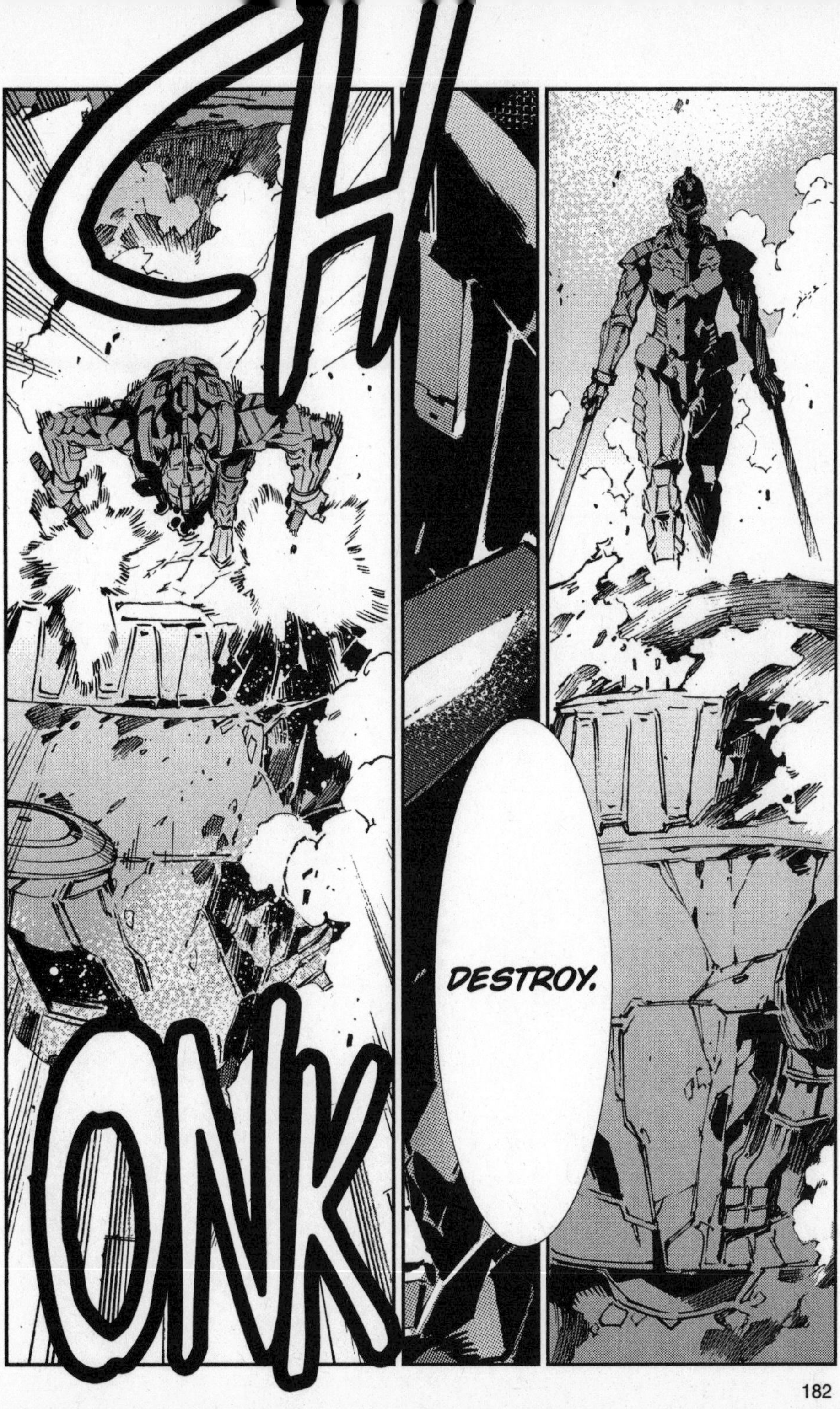
DESTROY.
CH
ONK

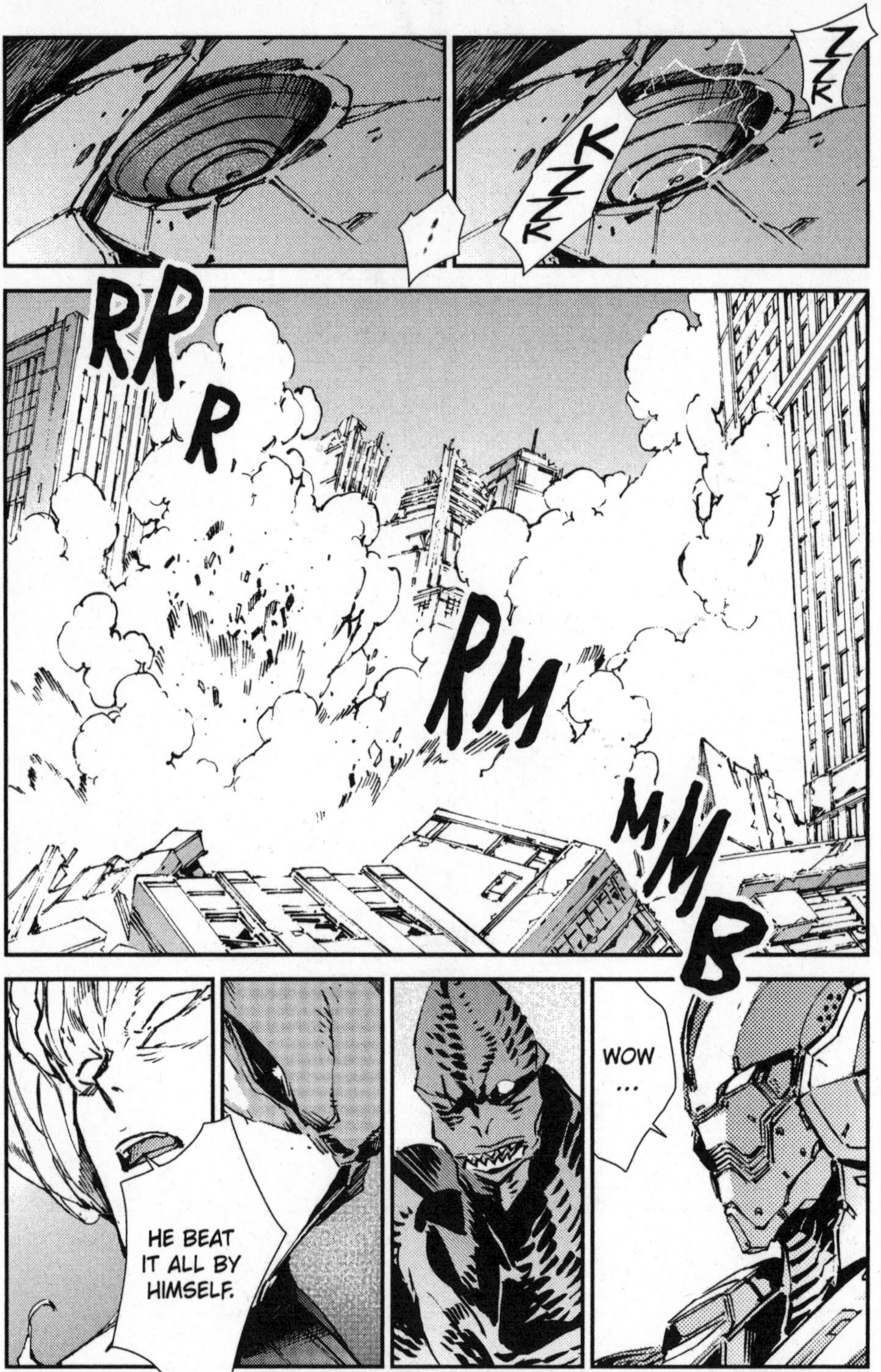

ZZK
KZZZK
...
RRR
RMMMB
WOW ...
HE BEAT IT ALL BY HIMSELF.

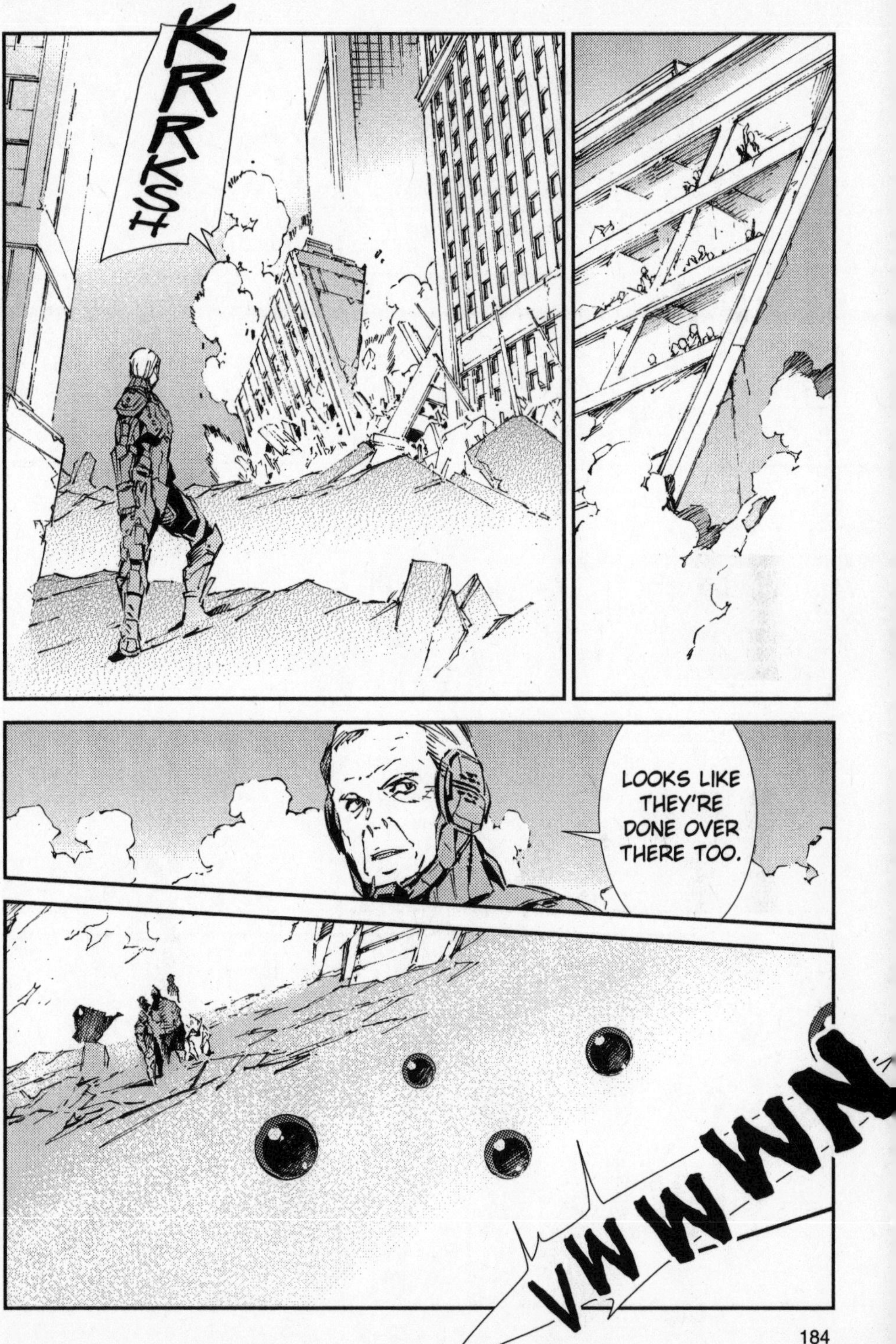
KRRKSH
LOOKS LIKE THEY'RE DONE OVER THERE TOO.
VWWWN

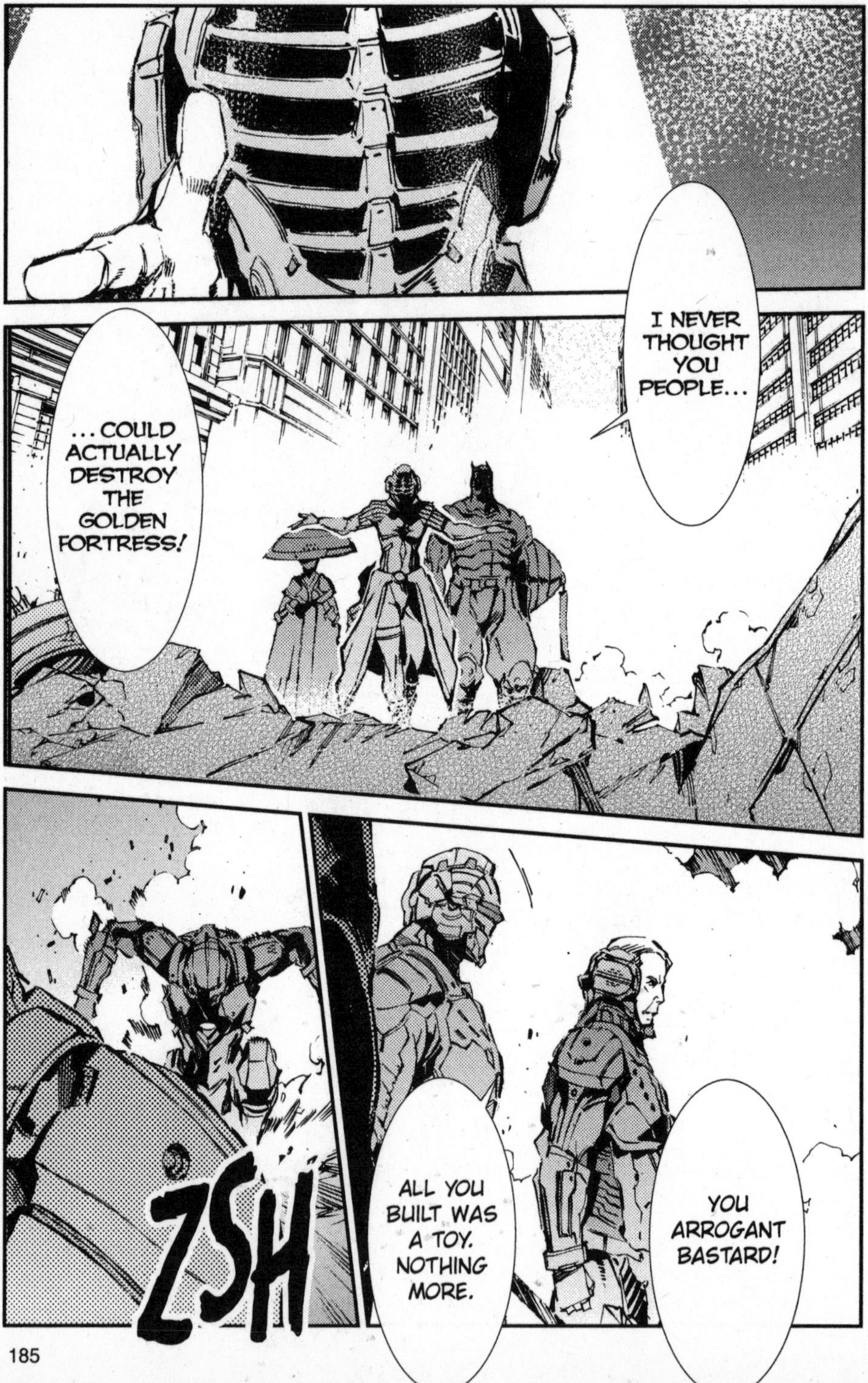
I NEVER THOUGHT YOU PEOPLE...
...COULD ACTUALLY DESTROY THE GOLDEN FORTRESS!
YOU ARROGANT BASTARD!
ALL YOU BUILT WAS A TOY. NOTHING MORE.
ZSH

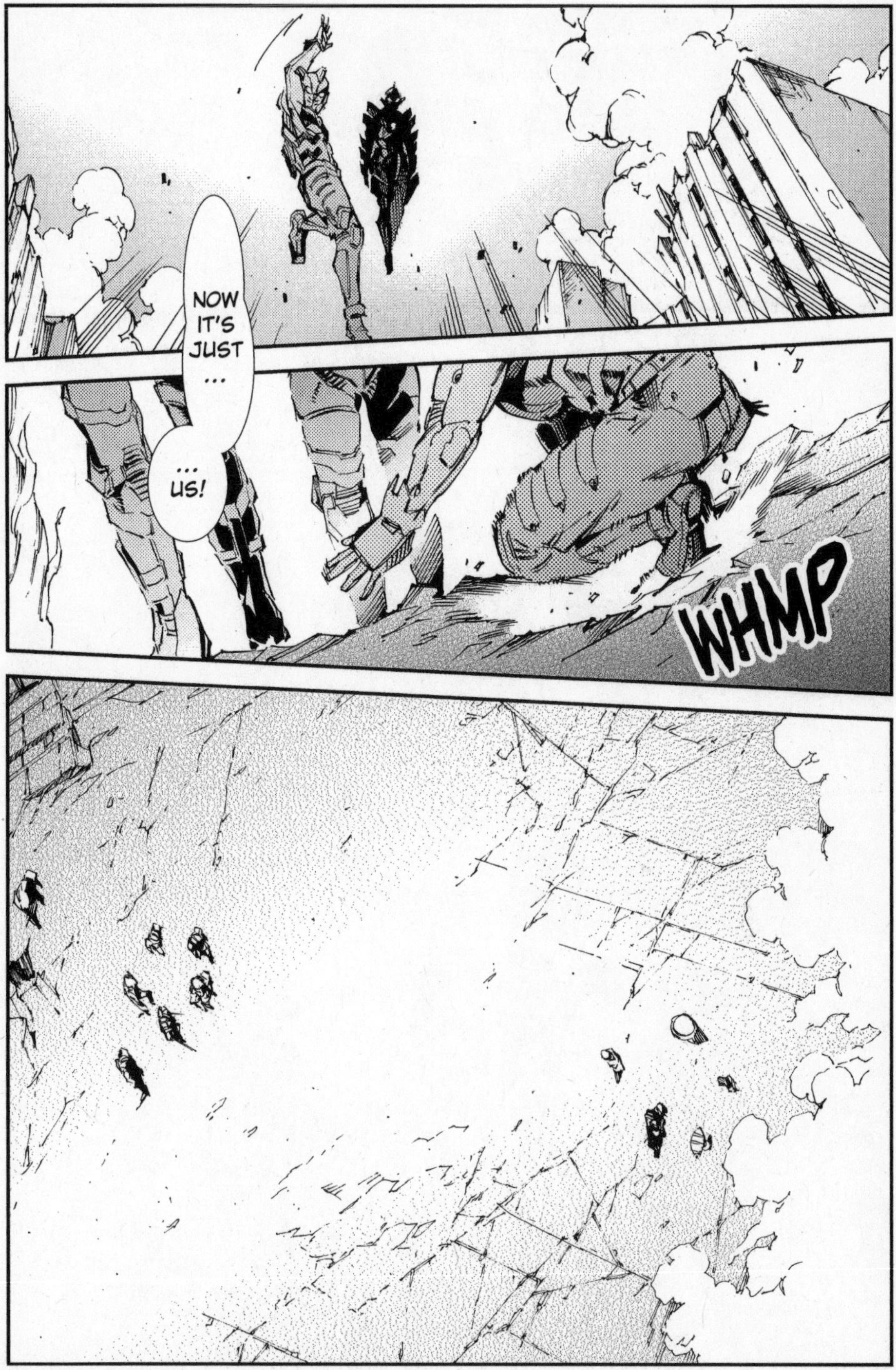
NOW IT'S JUST ...
... US!
WHMP

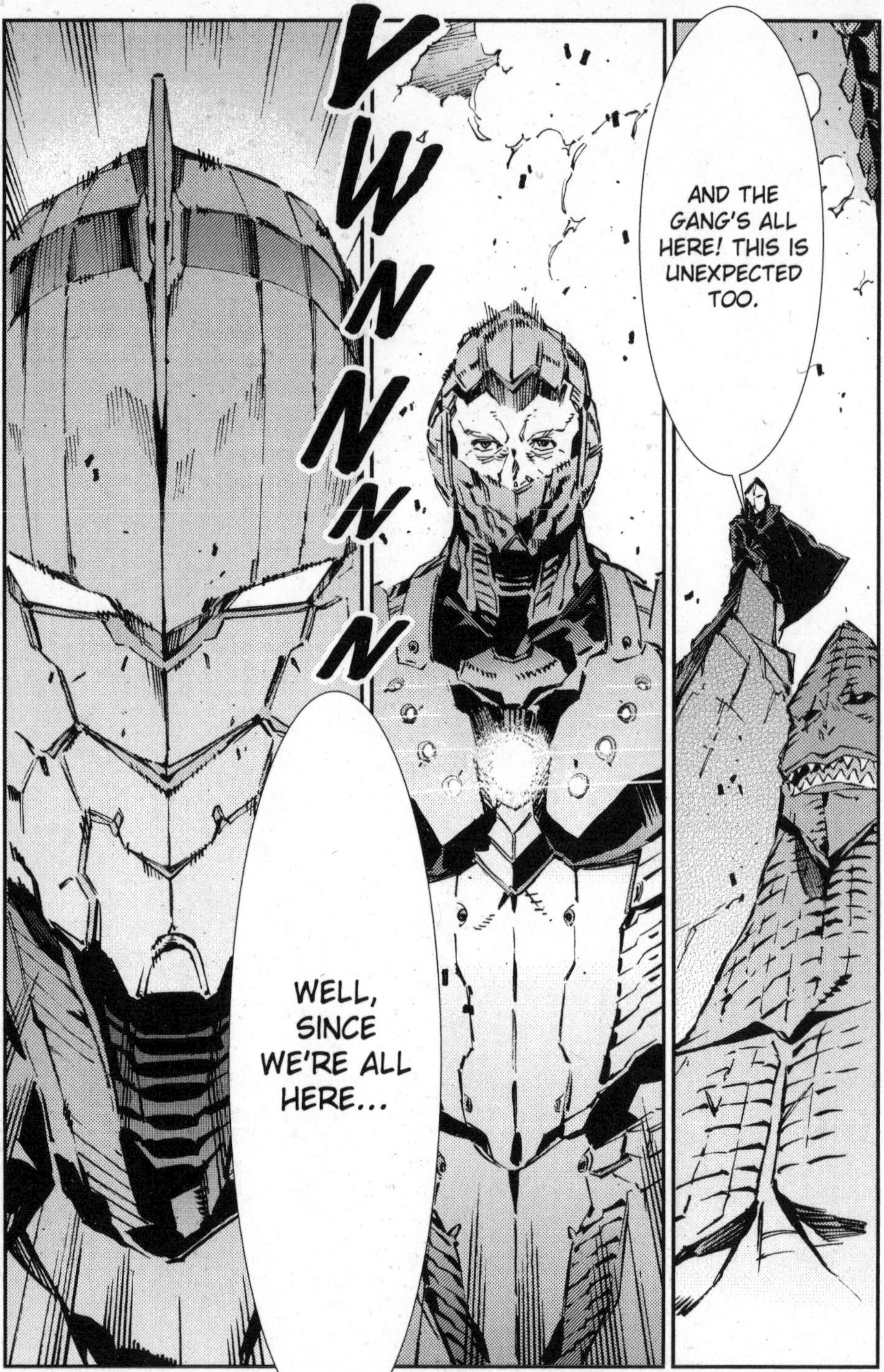
AND THE GANG'S ALL HERE! THIS IS UNEXPECTED TOO.
VWNNNNN
WELL, SINCE WE'RE ALL HERE...

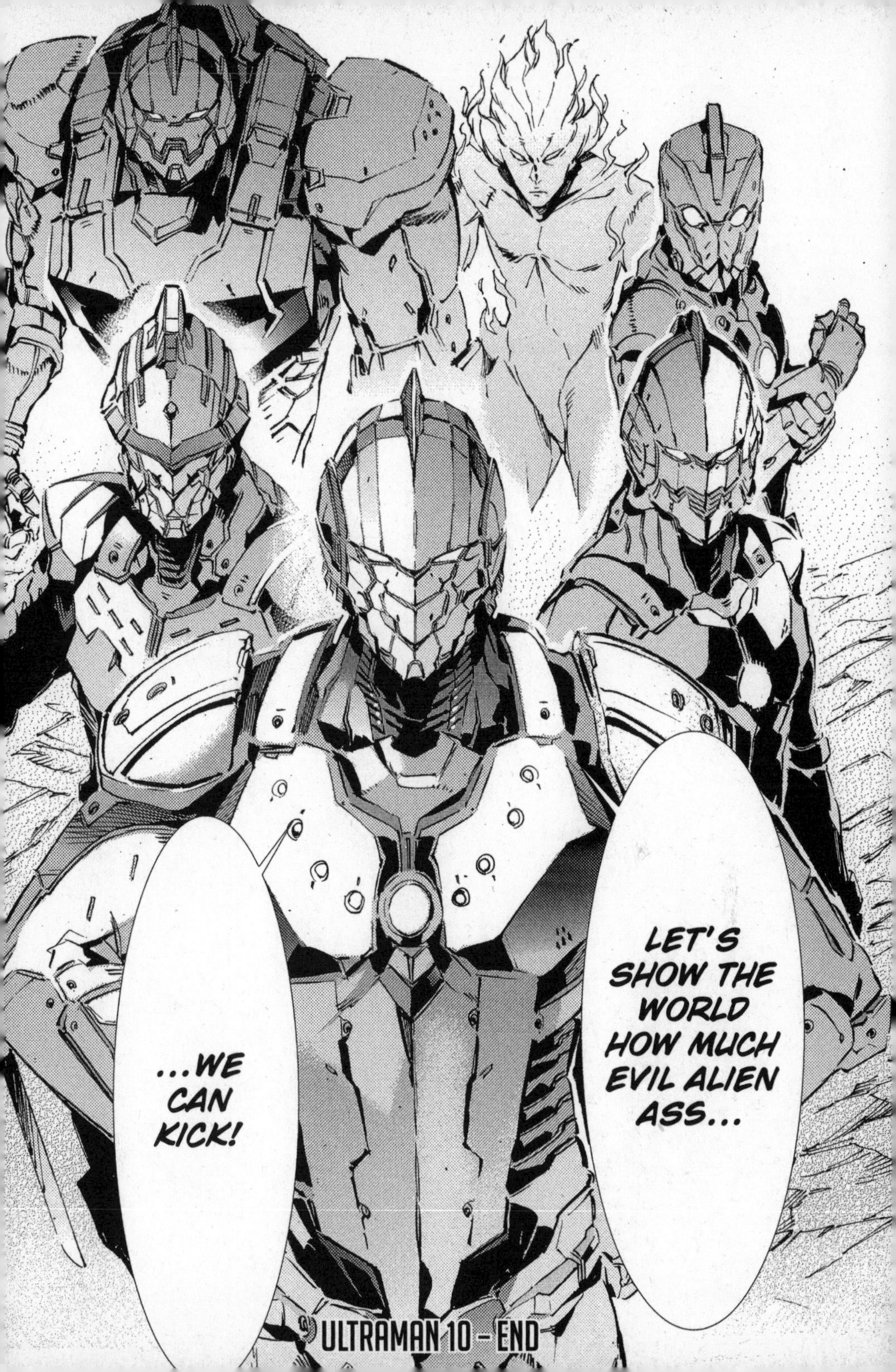
LET'S SHOW THE WORLD HOW MUCH EVIL ALIEN ASS...
...WE CAN KICK!
ULTRAMAN 10 - END

THIS IS THE BEGINNING OF A NEW AGE

ULTRAMAN SUIT Ver7.3 [FULLY ARMED]

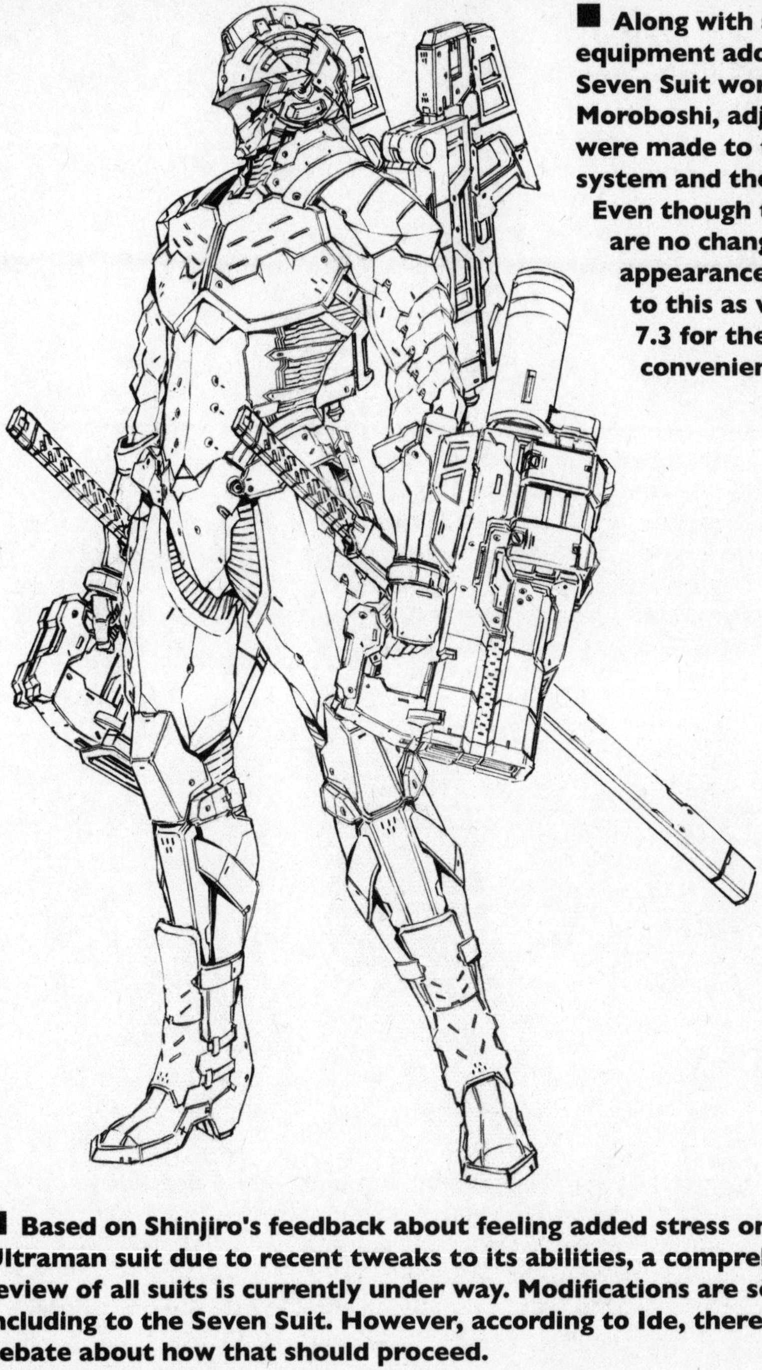

■ Along with additional equipment added to the Seven Suit worn by Dan Moroboshi, adjustments were made to the control system and the suit itself. Even though there are no changes to its appearance, we refer to this as version 7.3 for the sake of convenience.

■ Based on Shinjiro's feedback about feeling added stress on his Ultraman suit due to recent tweaks to its abilities, a comprehensive review of all suits is currently under way. Modifications are scheduled, including to the Seven Suit. However, according to Ide, there is internal debate about how that should proceed.

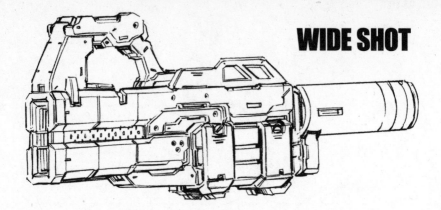

WIDE SHOT

■ A heavy Spacium weapon developed for Moroboshi, who does not have the Ultraman Factor. Although it is not the same as the Spacium Ray that Shinjiro uses, its power is nearly identical. It can be used as a beam blade by continuously discharging Spacium Energy, but power consumption in this mode is exceptionally high. Due to its large size, an operational system is currently under development, including a method to make it easier to transport.

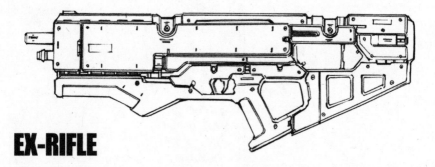

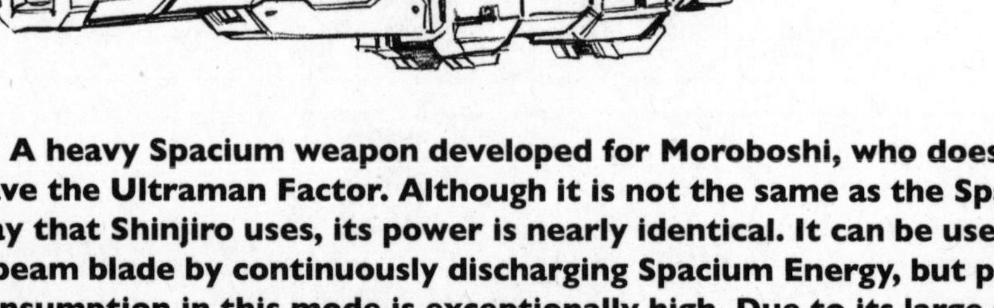

EX-RIFLE

■ A multipurpose rifle mounted on the back when the suit is fully armed. It is basically the same rifle issued to the agents in Moroboshi's unit, but the Seven Suit version can fire larger-caliber rounds. (An experimental Emerium Round tipped with crystallized extraterrestrial energy was used during the Golden Fortress battle.)

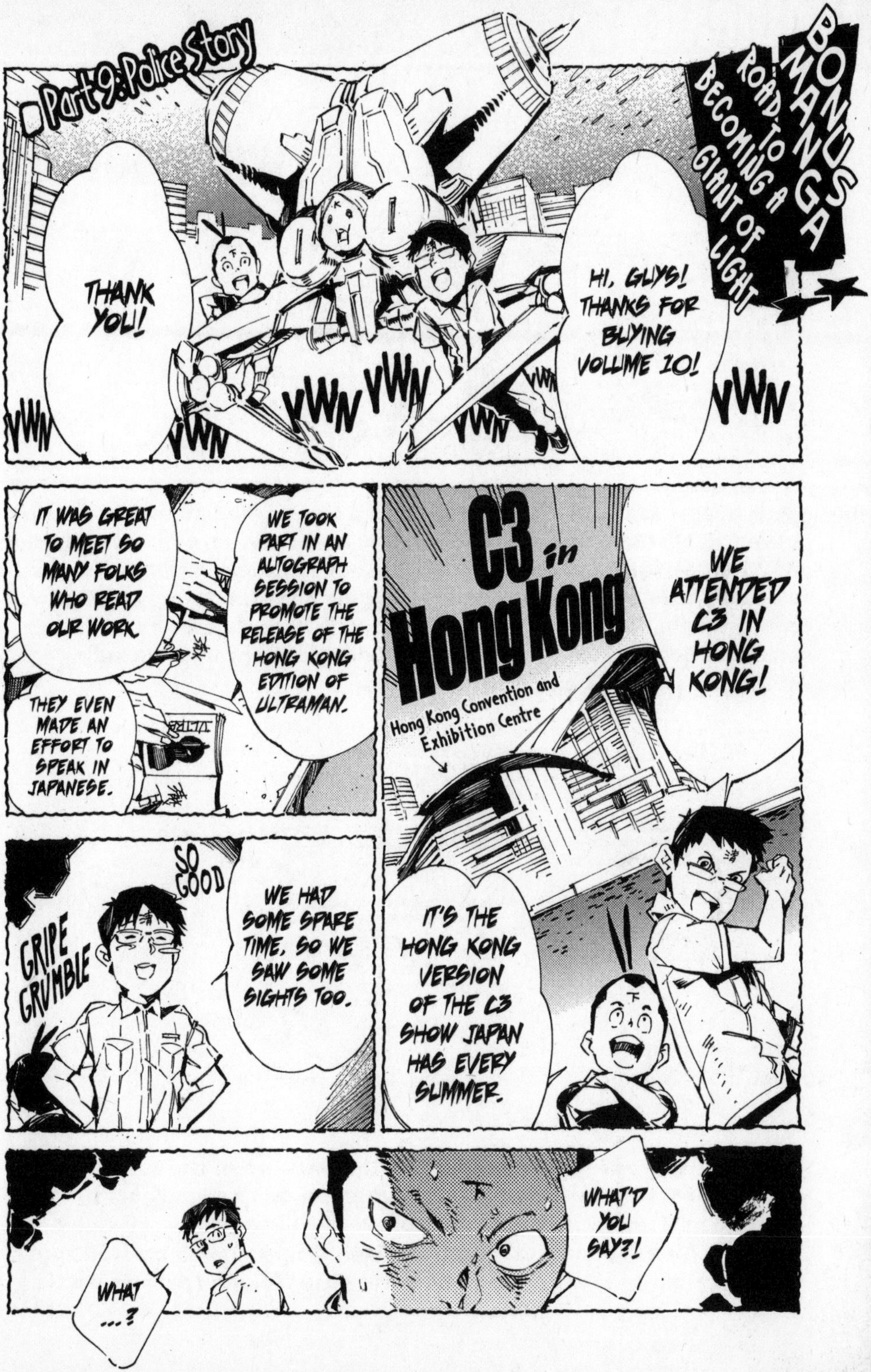
BONUS MANGA ★ ROAD TO BECOMING A GIANT OF LIGHT
Part 9: Police Story
HI, GUYS! THANKS FOR BUYING VOLUME 10!
THANK YOU!
VWN VWN VWN VWN VWN VWN VWN
WE ATTENDED C3 IN HONG KONG!
C3 in Hong Kong
Hong Kong Convention and Exhibition Centre
IT'S THE HONG KONG VERSION OF THE C3 SHOW JAPAN HAS EVERY SUMMER.
WE TOOK PART IN AN AUTOGRAPH SESSION TO PROMOTE THE RELEASE OF THE HONG KONG EDITION OF ULTRAMAN.
IT WAS GREAT TO MEET SO MANY FOLKS WHO READ OUR WORK.
THEY EVEN MADE AN EFFORT TO SPEAK IN JAPANESE.
WE HAD SOME SPARE TIME, SO WE SAW SOME SIGHTS TOO.
SO GOOD
GRIPE GRUMBLE
WHAT'D YOU SAY?!
WHAT ...?

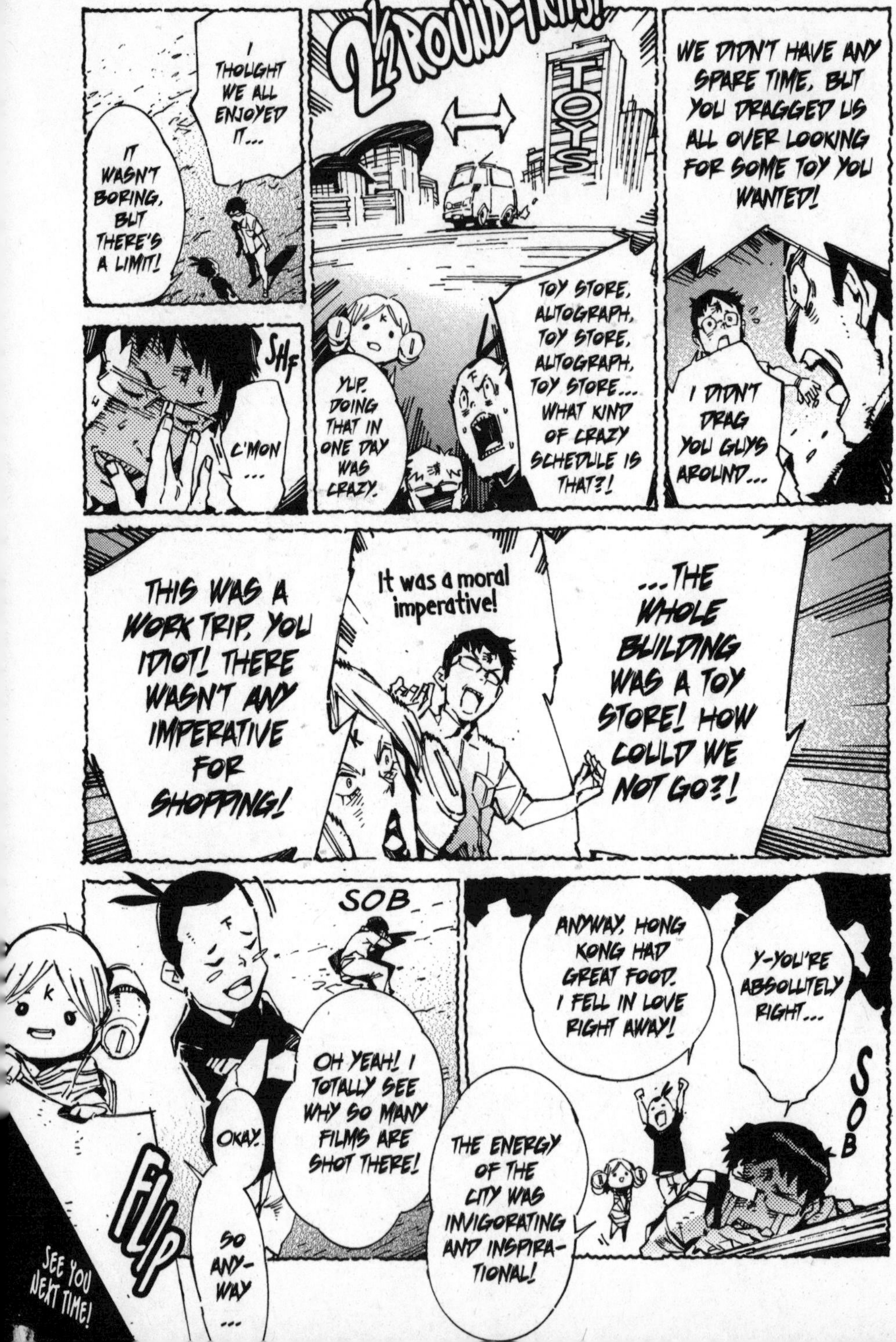
WE DIDN'T HAVE ANY SPARE TIME, BUT YOU DRAGGED US ALL OVER LOOKING FOR SOME TOY YOU WANTED!
I DIDN'T DRAG YOU GUYS AROUND...
2½ ROUND-TRIPS!
TOYS
TOY STORE, AUTOGRAPH, TOY STORE, AUTOGRAPH, TOY STORE... WHAT KIND OF CRAZY SCHEDULE IS THAT?!
YUP. DOING THAT IN ONE DAY WAS CRAZY.
I THOUGHT WE ALL ENJOYED IT...
IT WASN'T BORING, BUT THERE'S A LIMIT!
SHF
C'MON ...
...THE WHOLE BUILDING WAS A TOY STORE! HOW COULD WE NOT GO?!
It was a moral imperative!
THIS WAS A WORK TRIP, YOU IDIOT! THERE WASN'T ANY IMPERATIVE FOR SHOPPING!
Y-YOU'RE ABSOLUTELY RIGHT...
ANYWAY, HONG KONG HAD GREAT FOOD. I FELL IN LOVE RIGHT AWAY!
SOB
THE ENERGY OF THE CITY WAS INVIGORATING AND INSPIRATIONAL!
SOB
OH YEAH! I TOTALLY SEE WHY SO MANY FILMS ARE SHOT THERE!
OKAY.
SO ANYWAY...
FLIP
SEE YOU NEXT TIME!

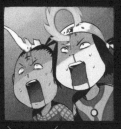

EIICHI SHIMIZU ✕ TOMOHIRO SHIMOGUCHI

Volume 10!! Entering double digits!!
Thank you!!!
To us, it feels like the series just started,
but we're already at volume 10...
We meet 12 deadlines, and a year goes by.
That's how we spend our days, according
to Shimoguchi. But anyway, we hope
you guys continue to stick with us.

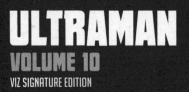

ULTRAMAN
VOLUME 10
VIZ SIGNATURE EDITION

STORY/ART BY **EIICHI SHIMIZU** AND **TOMOHIRO SHIMOGUCHI**

©2017 Eiichi Shimizu and Tomohiro Shimoguchi / TSUBURAYA PROD.
Originally published by HERO'S INC.

TRANSLATION **JOE YAMAZAKI**
ENGLISH ADAPTATION **STAN!**
TOUCH-UP ART & LETTERING **EVAN WALDINGER**
DESIGN **KAM LI**
EDITOR **MIKE MONTESA**

Printed in the U.S.A.

Published by VIZ Media, LLC
P.O. Box 77010
San Francisco, CA 94107

10 9 8 7 6 5 4 3 2 1
First printing, May 2018

VIZ SIGNATURE

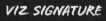

www.viz.com

HEY! YOU'RE READING IN THE WRONG DIRECTION!

This is the END of the graphic novel

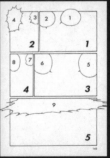

Follow the action this way.

To properly enjoy this VIZ graphic novel, please turn it around and begin reading from RIGHT TO LEFT. Unlike English, Japanese is read right to left, so Japanese comics are read in reverse order from the way English comics are typically read.

This book has been printed in the original Japanese format in order to preserve the orientation of the original artwork.

HAVE FUN WITH IT!